Lines of Flight, Assemblages of Home

Gender, Culture, and Politics in the Middle East
miriam cooke, Simona Sharoni, and Suad Joseph, *Series Editors*

Select Titles in Gender, Culture, and Politics in the Middle East

The Best of Hard Times: Palestinian Refugee Masculinities in Lebanon
Gustavo Barbosa

Fatema Mernissi for Our Times
Minoo Moallem and Paola Bacchetta, eds.

The Funambulists: Women Poets of the Arab Diaspora
Lisa Marchi

The Hammam through Time and Space
Julie Peteet

Istanbul Appearances: Beauty and the Making of Middle-Class Femininities in Urban Turkey
Claudia Liebelt

Quest for Love in Central Morocco: Young Women and the Dynamics of Intimate Lives
Laura Menin

Sexuality in the Middle East and North Africa: Contemporary Issues and Challenges
J. Michael Ryan and Helen Rizzo, eds.

Sumud: Birth, Oral History, and Persisting in Palestine
Livia Wick

For a full list of titles in this series, visit https://press.syr.edu/supressbook-series/gender-culture-and-politics-in-the-middle-east/.

Lines of Flight, Assemblages of Home

Syrian Women Displaced

Leila Hudson

Syracuse University Press

This book will be made open access within three years of publication
thanks to Path to Open, a program developed in partnership between JSTOR,
the American Council of Learned Societies (ACLS), University of Michigan Press,
and The University of North Carolina Press to bring about equitable access and impact
for the entire scholarly community, including authors, researchers, libraries, and university
presses around the world. Learn more at https://about.jstor.org/path-to-open/.

First Edition 2025

25 26 27 28 29 30   6 5 4 3 2 1

For a listing of books published and distributed by Syracuse University Press,
visit https://press.syr.edu.

ISBN: 9780815611950 (hardcover)
9780815657545 (e-book)

Library of Congress Cataloging-in-Publication Data

Names: Hudson, Leila, author.
Title: Lines of flight, assemblages of home : Syrian women displaced / Leila Hudson.
Description: Syracuse, New York : Syracuse University Press, 2025. | Series: Gender, culture, and politics in the Middle East | Includes bibliographical references and index.
Identifiers: LCCN 2025014573 (print) | LCCN 2025014574 (ebook) | ISBN 9780815611950 (hardback) | ISBN 9780815657545 (ebook)
Subjects: LCSH: Women refugees—Syria—Biography. | Syria—History—Civil War, 2011—Refugees. | LCGFT: Biographies.
Classification: LCC HV640.5.S97 H84 2025 (print) | LCC HV640.5.S97 (ebook)
LC record available at https://lccn.loc.gov/2025014573
LC ebook record available at https://lccn.loc.gov/2025014574

The authorized representative in the EU for product
safety and compliance is Mare Nostrum Group B.V.
Mauritskade 21D, 1091 GC Amsterdam, The Netherlands
gpsr@mare-nostrum.co.uk

Contents

Illustrations

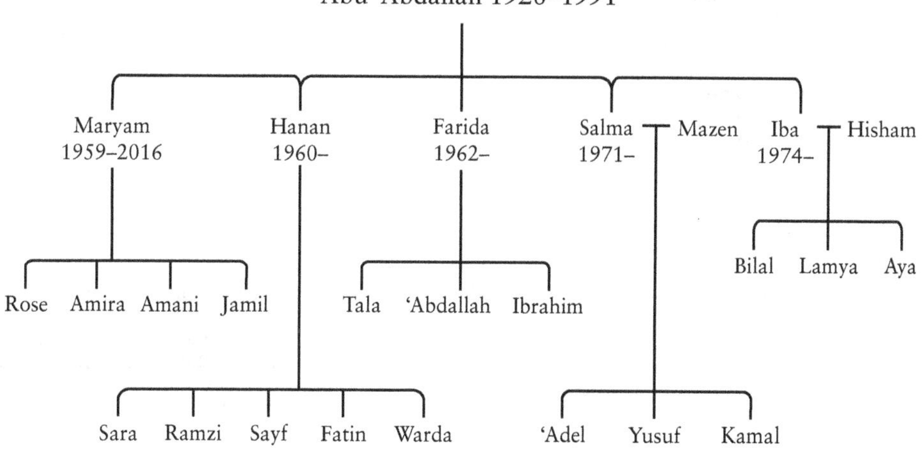

1. Araj family tree.

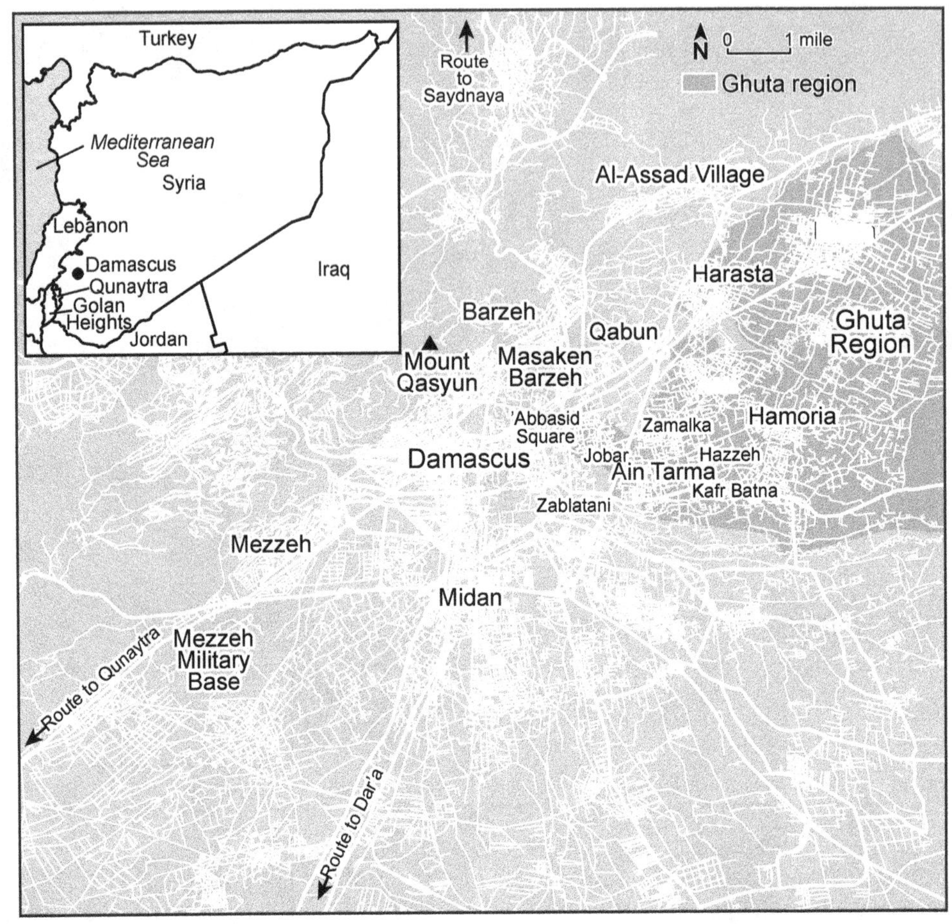

2. Map of Damascus and its suburbs. Created by Joseph Stoll, Syracuse University Cartographic Lab.

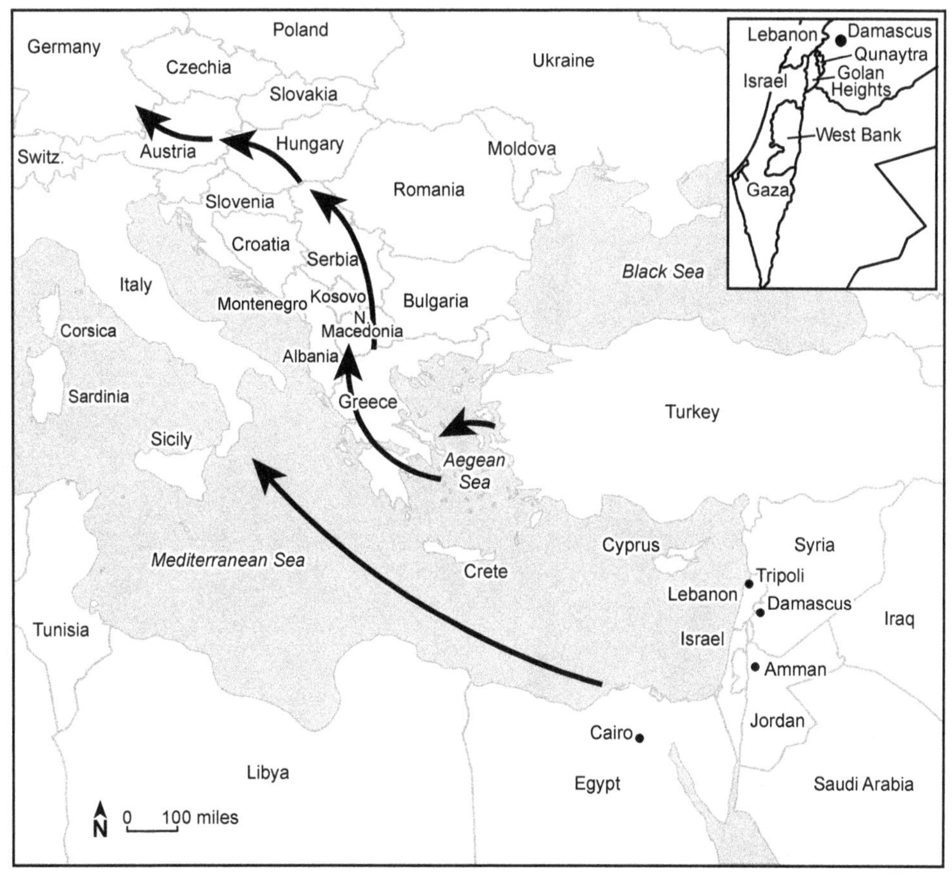

3. Map of Syrian refugees' routes to Europe, 2012–17. Created by Joseph Stoll, Syracuse University Cartographic Lab.

Preface

December 2024

As this book was going to press, the moment the Araj sisters—whose stories are told here—and most Syrians had been praying for arrived. On December 8, 2024, after a ten-day offensive out of the rebel-held city of Idlib, Damascus was liberated from the Assad dictatorship by the forces of Hay'at Tahrir al-Sham (HTS, the Entity for the Liberation of Syria), an offshoot of al-Qaeda affiliate Jabhat al-Nusra (Nusra/ Victory Front), which had held and governed the Syrian city of Idlib for years. Nearly fourteen years after the popular uprising that triggered civil war, displacement, and the flight of millions of Syrians like the Araj sisters, the revolution begun in 2011 and held at bay by the regime's ruthless slaughter of hundreds of thousands and by the backing of Iran, Russia, and Hezbollah succeeded in toppling the regime of Bashar al-Assad. The millions of Syrians in diasporic exile shared the sentiment of one who proclaimed exuberantly on social media, "I am no longer a Syrian refugee! I am just a Syrian citizen again!"

After regime forces retreated before the HTS advance, which turned its sights on the liberation of Syria rather than on the transnational caliphate that had focused extremist Islamist energies throughout the previous decade, Bashar al-Assad fled ignominiously to Moscow, where his family awaited him.[1] Disbelieving citizens of Syria and Damascus had spent the previous week watching the

1. Hamidi, "Revealed."

advance with bated breath—not daring to hope, exchanging limited information, terrified of the prospect of violence in the streets—and then watched the arrival of the HTS under the leadership of Abu Muhammad al-Jolani (later revealed as Ahmed al-Shara') and of the forces that had governed and developed the last rebel stronghold in the northwestern province of Idlib.

Syrians in country and in diaspora spent the next days exploring in person and through social media accounts both the dungeons of Assad's prison at Saydnaya and the fortified underground tunnels that joined the palaces of Bashar and his relatives through impenetrable state-of-the-art security protections. Coming hard on the heels of the liberation of city after city, it was a time of intense emotion as Syrians frantically searched for their hundreds of thousands of disappeared relatives and friends through unknown layers and corners of the "human slaughterhouse" and the growing horror of the torture chambers, the babies born to raped women political prisoners, the deaths of hundreds of thousands, the mass graves uncovered all over the region. The habitual fear of chaos and revenge tinged the joy and the grief, but the anxiety receded throughout December 2024 in Syria's biggest cities as the caretaker government demonstrated openness and successful stabilization.[2]

The rebel forces moving down from Idlib to Aleppo to Hama and Homs had intentionally broadcast a message of respect and tolerance for minorities, Christians in particular, and of clemency for regime conscripts and functionaries who renounced the old regime. Anxious Christians, Kurds, Shi'ites, and especially Alawites, whose community had been identified with the Ba'ath Party, the military, and the government, were slowly reassured that the former al-Qaeda Islamists would not immediately slaughter them as they had come to expect in a world in which Da'esh/ISIS (Islamic State of Iraq and Syria) had flourished during the decade of war. As the main HTS rebel forces moved from Aleppo to Hama south to Homs, the patterns of

2. Salhani, "The End of Fear in Syria."

the manifold challenges facing the rebels and the population would reveal themselves. The Syrian National Army (SNA), which, like the HTS, was backed by Recep Tayyip Erdoğan's Turkey, lacked the coherence and discipline of the HTS and began harassing the Kurdish Syrian Democratic Forces (SDF) in Syria's Northeast and applying heavy hands in their dealings with all minorities. The semiautonomy of the Kurdish region under the SDF forces, the oil and gas resources in the region, the residual ISIS remnants and prison camps around Raqqa, and the contingent of US military troops on the Iraqi border presented a messy counterpart to the smooth unrolling of the HTS offensive down Syria's center.

On the other complicated front, observers gauging the HTS's progress expected Damascus to take longer to fall and certainly not to fall simultaneously with the central city of Homs on December 7 and 8. Anticipating more regime resistance around Hama early in December, then realizing that Homs's capture would paralyze the Iran-Iraqi-Hezbollah supply lines across the east–west axis of Syria, people were surprised and delighted to see the southern rebel militias in the area between Damascus and the Jordanian border but not associated with the HTS securing their area and moving north from the "cradle of the revolution" in Dar'a and the Druze stronghold of Suwayda. It was those rebels of the southern front who pushed out regime forces in the South and circled Damascus's eastern flank in the Ghuta agricultural region in advance of the HTS's arrival on the morning of December 8.

Deceiving even his closest advisers and extended family members, Bashar al-Assad fled by air. His plane circled low over Homs, appearing to those watching on flight radar to have crashed but then heading east after avoiding the radar, with no closer asylum to be found than in Moscow. His former prime minister, Mohammad Ghazi al-Jalali, held power for the day while awaiting the HTS leadership's arrival. When Ahmed al-Shara' arrived on the morning of December 8, Damascus was full of the sound of celebratory gunfire, something he had personally worked hard to suppress ever since taking Aleppo. It was later learned that the Druze and other southern rebels who encircled and first entered the capital had been approached by the United Arab Emirates and Jordanian diplomats to independently declare victory in Damascus and install their own internationally vetted caretaker government. Foiled by the outgoing prime minister's refusal and his urgent phone call with Ahmed al-Shara', this failed likely Israeli-backed plot to split Syria into pieces—a southern and coastal zone friendly to Israel and the United Arab Emirates, a Sunni central core, and a Kurdish autonomous region—triggered an Israeli attack on the occupied Golan Heights as the new caretaker government attended to urban security and service restoration.[3] Israel quickly claimed a buffer zone to its occupied buffer zone in the Golan Heights and executed a series of targeted strikes on military, munitions, scientific, and archival stockpile sites in the capital and on the coast; its original plan may have even included a possible tactical nuclear strike on a weapons depot near Tartus. This preemptive attack effectively demilitarized Syria, just as HTS amnesty programs effectively de-Ba'athified the population following a very different model from the grossly ineffective US de-Ba'athification of Iraq in 2003.

In the early days after the fall of Bashar, nervous Syrians and outside observers marveled at the calm statesmanship of the former al-Qaeda terrorist turned leader of the caretaker Syrian salvation government, but many die-hard defenders of the so-called axis of resistance—the Assad regime joined by Iran, Shi'ite Iraq-based militias, and Hezbollah, mobilized by Israel's annihilation of Gaza—darkly insinuated an American or Israeli hand in the matter. In fact, the HTS rebel offensive appears to be a bold gambit supported by Turkish president Erdoğan with help from Qatar.

After Bashar's fall, the role of Turkey in backing the fourteen-year rebellion came into focus. Erdoğan's policies of strategic patience and bold expansion of Ankara's influence into the new Syria, in place of US influence, took Syrians and the world by surprise. It

3. Hearst, "Revealed."

felt like one of Lenin's weeks in which a decade happened. Leftist supporters of the so-called axis of resistance loudly bemoaned the fate of the Assad regime, which they mistakenly viewed as a pillar of the fight against Zionist settler colonialism; Syrians reminded them that Hafez al-Assad, Bashar's father, had maintained Israeli's most peaceful border since 1967 after having secretly yielded the Golan Heights to the enemy in return for his stable dictatorship and fifty-four-year dynasty.[4] Documents recovered from various intelligence buildings confirmed that Bashar al-Assad had been in contact with the Israeli Mossad since 2019.[5]

The road to Damascus went through Gaza and through the tens and possibly hundreds of thousands of dead Palestinians killed by the Israeli genocide.[6] Israel's annihilating rampage in Gaza following the Hamas attacks of October 7, 2023, shook and destabilized the entire region. Syrian observers of the massacres of Palestinian civilians, the torture camps, the wholesale destruction of the healthcare system in Gaza,[7] and the flattening of the entire built environment of the Gaza Strip pointed out that this level of unfettered Israeli destruction would not have been carried out with impunity if the pariah Assad regime had not enjoyed a large degree of immunity from meaningful international intervention for its similar acts in the preceding thirteen years. Although Hamas (Islamic Resistance Movement) and the Houthi Ansar Allah (Helpers of God) remain strong and defiant into the new year, the Israeli decimation of Hezbollah's operatives by means of the pager terror attack and decapitation of its leadership in September 2024 as well as the checkmate of the Iranian Khamenei regime that propped up Bashar

4. See Khalil, *Suquṭ al-Julan*, the memoir of a Syrian military officer that documents Hafez al-Assad's surrender of the Golan Heights.

5. "Israel Warned Assad."

6. Segal, "A Textbook Case of Genocide"; "Public Statement"; "Gaza Is 'Running out of Time'"; "Gaza: UN Experts."

7. Goodman and Abu Sitta, "Systematic Destruction of the Healthcare System in Gaza."

al-Assad were correctly identified by Erdoğan and the HTS as the circumstances permitting his trifecta. First, investing in an Islamist Syrian future with HTS, which he had supported in Turkey and in Idlib, fulfilled his neo-Ottoman aspirations of previous decades. A Turkish-dominated Syria would provide infrastructure investment opportunities galore, not to mention the support of nearly 4 million Syrians who had spent the past decade learning Turkish and working in Turkey. Second, replacing Iran and perhaps even the US hegemony in Syria would allow Erdoğan to confront his perennial enemies, the Kurdish parties, and even to dominate eastern Syria, where the oil and gas resources are located. Finally, creating the conditions for a partial return of the nearly 4 million Syrian refugees in Turkey as well as those Syrians who had moved on from Turkey to Europe would highlight and enhance Erdoğan's domestic political position and show him as a regional powerbroker who had also negotiated an African peace deal just the week before the HTS offensive and the fall of the Assad regime.

As late as 2017, two of the Araj sisters, Hanan and Farida, who stayed in Turkey, had been fans of Erdoğan and the Adalet ve Kalkınma Partisi (AKP, Justice and Development Party). But by 2024 the erosive effects of Turkish anti-Syrian racism had worn them down, and they had little good to say about the Turkish leader they once idolized. Mobility restrictions on Syrians' movement within Turkey as well as the effects of xenophobia and of skyrocketing prices and rents, especially in Turkey's rural areas, had made their lives in Turkey, although comparatively comfortable because they were supported by remittances from other parts of the world, seem bleak and futile.

As the HTS offensive unfolded in December 2024, Hanan and her son, Sayf, previously a rebel fighter, were in an anxious panic watching the Saudi news channel al-Arabiya, which presented a disparaging and pessimistic view of the HTS offensive up until diplomatic and economic relations were established in the two weeks after the fall of Damascus. Isolated in Turkey, when informed of the success of the

Aleppo initiative by outsiders, they went from fear and anxiety to agitated frustration that they could not be present in Syria to witness the liberation of Damascus. When Hanan was asked if she would return to Damascus, she didn't hesitate for a second. Although her home in the Ghuta region had been destroyed in the fighting, she would return with her son, her daughter-in-law, and the three new granddaughters born in Turkey, who spoke fluent Turkish. Her only regret, she said, laughing, was the two new sewing machines that she had acquired in Turkey. "Don't worry," she was assured by her children, "we'll buy you new ones in Damascus just like them or better."

Farida's access to news in her tiny seaside town an hour from Yalova was patchy at best. She was in the habit of turning off her phone for days on end to save money and "save Wi-Fi." Farida and her children kept strictly to themselves, avoiding contact with her sisters and their children. They had all but given up hope of returning to their home in Damascus. When she learned in the early days of December what was happening, her heart filled with joy as she listened to patriotic old songs on Facebook. She began to plan for her return, especially relieved that her youngest son would not be conscripted into Assad's army because the new Syrian government had abolished mandatory service among its first acts. Many challenges remained, not least the fact that her home, the apartment that she had left in 2013, was probably unfit for habitation after the area where it sat at the front lines between the regime and the Free Syrian Army (FSA, al-Jaysh as-Suri al-Hur) rebels was pounded by artillery.

The eldest sister Maryam's children and grandchildren, who had migrated to Germany and had received asylum and citizenship in the United States after leaving Egypt, were able to recongregate in northern Germany and envision a future return to Syria.

Middle sister Salma, along with two of her sons, had received her German citizenship in the summer of 2024. Settled in a small but cozy apartment with her husband and sons in the downtown area of a southern German city, she looked forward to becoming a mother-in-law to a Syrian young woman of Kurdish origin who did not observe hijab and whom Yusuf had met as he completed his degree in *Electrotechnik*, electrical engineering. Salma and her husband, Mazen, had received many guests in the summer of 2024—their nieces living in northern Germany accompanied by husbands and children, and others from as far away as the United States—before taking a vacation to Italy by car with their three sons. She was completing the vocational training to become an architectural draftsperson, a skill that would come in handy not only in the German job market but now also in the new Syria. Most importantly, with the fall of the Assad dictatorship she was no longer a wanted person listed for detention at every border crossing into Syria. Of all the sisters, she had been the one for whom even European citizenship provided no protection upon return to Assad's Syria. Wanted at the borders, her name on a published list of political dissidents, she could have ended up in the dungeons of any one of the secret prisons—all for the crime of not forcing her students into a pro-government rally back in 2011 and then fleeing her job without official permission.

The youngest sister Iba and her youngest daughter, Aya, had received their German citizenship only days before the fall of the Assad regime. After working as a basketball coach, a restaurant cook, and then a lab technician, Iba was now responsible for the doctoral research facilities of a German research university and had overcome her colleagues' fear of her hijab and her Syrian origins. Upon learning of the liberation of Damascus, she went from office door to door sharing sweets and chocolate with her German colleagues, explaining to them the Syrian custom of sharing her joy not only at receiving her German citizenship but also, much more importantly, at the fall of the Assad dictatorship and the completion of the revolution, which, begun in 2011, had gone on for a decade and a half. Her colleagues immediately grew concerned that she might leave Germany and the job she did so well in their office. She reassured them that her first trip back to Syria would be for vacation only. She and her husband, Hisham, who by now had spent nearly ten years learning and practicing the art of orthopedic shoemaking, were busy saving and planning for a business enterprise in Syria that would provide state-of-the-art orthotics for a regional market. What the coming weeks and months of 2025 hold in store for liberated Syria remains to be seen; for the moment, however, the joy and determination of the Araj family and their fellow citizens appear to be a powerful element of that future.

Timeline

1946	Syrian independence from the French Mandate
1948	Palestinian Nakba (Catastrophe) and Israeli War of Independence
May 30–June 5, 1967	Six-Day War, Syrian loss of Golan Heights to Israeli occupation
1971	Hafez al-Assad becomes president of Syria
October 1973	Arab-Israeli October War
May 31, 1974	Syrian-Israeli Agreement on Disengagement in Golan Heights
1979–1982	Islamist insurgency and government massacre of the Ikhwan (Muslim Brotherhood) at Hama
2000	Death of Hafez al-Assad and ascension of Bashar al-Assad to the presidency
2001	Crackdown on the "Damascus Spring" reform movement, US CIA collaboration with the regime in the global war on terror
2005	Assassination of Rafic Hariri of Lebanon by Syrian intelligence
January 26, 2011	Arab Spring protests for political reform
March 6, 2011	Arrest and torture of Dar'a schoolboys
March 18–19, 2011	Largest protests in decades in Syria
March 30, 2011	Assad blames conspiracies, commences crackdown

May 2011	Thousands of Syrians begin fleeing to neighboring countries
Summer 2011	Obama administration sanctions Syria with travel and export bans, asset freeze
July 29, 2011	Free Syrian Army founded by defectors from Syrian army
September 2011	Armed insurgency
October 2011	Assad regime's release of Islamist militants from its prisons
November–December 2011	War spreads to Homs and Damascus
January 2012	Estimated 5,000 Syrians killed by large-scale military force
July 15, 2012	Regime declares Operation Damascus Volcano, and Red Cross declares Syria in civil war, with death toll of 20,000
December 2012	US government designates Nusra/Victory Front (Jabhat al-Nusra) a foreign terror organization
May 25, 2013	Hezbollah formally supports Assad regime
August 21, 2013	Sarin gas attacks by regime on rebel stronghold in the Eastern Ghuta
2014	Rise of Da'esh, the "Islamic State" (ISIS)
August 2015	Chancellor Angela Merkel of Germany authorizes unrestricted Syrian immigration to Germany
September 30, 2015	Russian military intervention
March 2016	Turkish–European Union refugee deal negotiations
December 2016	Government retakes Aleppo
2017–2023	Normalization of relations with Assad's Syria by many states

June 17, 2020	US Caesar Syria Civilian Protection Act sanctions Assad regime for war crimes
December 2022	Estimated 580,000 dead and 13 million displaced in conflict
2023	Normalization of Syria's relations with the Arab League and Persian/Arab Gulf states
October 7, 2023	Hamas attacks on Israel
October 9, 2023	Israeli genocide in Gaza begins
September 17–18, 2024	Israeli electronic-device attacks in Lebanon
September 27, 2024	Israeli assassination of Secretary-General Hassan Nasrallah of Hezbollah
October 1, 2024	Sixth Israeli invasion of Lebanon
November 27, 2024	Rebel offensive by Hay'at Tahrir al-Sham in Idlib begins
December 2, 2024	Rebels capture Aleppo, Hama
December 6, 2024	Southern front of Free Syrian Army begins an offensive against Damascus
December 7, 2024	Rebels capture Homs
December 8, 2024	Rebels capture Damascus, Bashar al-Assad flees to Moscow
December 9, 2024	Liberation of prisoners from Saydnaya Prison
December 2024	Formation of Syrian Salvation Government by Hay'at Tahrir al-Sham

Lines of Flight, Assemblages of Home

Introduction

Seeking refuge from the chaos of the Syrian state's reprisals against the popular uprising that began in 2011, the five Araj sisters of Damascus traced a series of unfolding paths as they made their ways with their families to Lebanon, Jordan, Egypt, and Turkey in 2012 and 2013. Between 2014 and 2017, some settled in exile in Turkey, and some went on to cross the Aegean Sea to asylum in Europe. The creative and desperate decisions and routes, the physical, cultural, and emotional baggage each carried, the work they did to sustain their households and loved ones, and their interlinked but different trajectories hint at the complexity of the phenomenon of displacement, even at the level of a single extended family's experiences. When, why, and how did each person or nuclear family make the difficult decision to leave Syria? Where did they go, and why? What happened to their bodies, minds, souls, and relationships in Egypt, Jordan, Lebanon, Turkey, Greece, and Germany? These details are important in grounding the conceptual abstraction of "refugee ethnography" in real women's lives. How did their predicament change the places they came from, moved through, and settled into? What became of them, and who did they become?

As the Araj sisters—Maryam, Hanan, Farida, Salma, and Iba—left Syria in 2012 and moved from place to place, they joined hundreds of thousands, then later millions, of Syrian citizens who fled their country after the popular uprising against the regime of Bashar al-Assad in 2011 escalated into brutal reprisals, civil war, and regional conflict.[1]

1. These personal and family names are pseudonyms, most of them chosen by the author, but some suggested by the women themselves. Salma chose her

The "Arab Spring" uprisings in Tunisia and Egypt in 2011 inspired Syrians such as the sisters to imagine a future without authoritarian dictatorship. Syrians, like citizens of all Middle Eastern countries, watched the Tunisian and Egyptian popular revolts on social media and satellite news channels and were enthralled by the prospect of overturning long-term dictators—Tunisia's Zine El Abidine Ben Ali and Egypt's Hosni Mubarak.[2] Activists organizing transnationally on social media, especially Facebook and Twitter, prompted Syrians to dare to hope for an end to the permanent emergency rule and pervasive corruption in their own country that had kept them silent and repressed for decades. They began to turn out for small, peaceful rallies in early 2011. But Syrian leader Bashar al-Assad, who had inherited the nominal republic's presidency after the death of his father in 2000, chose neither to embrace change nor to leave power and instead mercilessly cracked down on reformers. His regime unleashed the full force of the fearsome one-party police state on the protesters, starting with the shocking arrest, torture, and murder of schoolboys who had dared to scrawl antiregime graffiti in the southern Syrian town of Dar'a.[3]

The sisters and their families were among many Syrians who had bridled silently under decades of repression and who now in 2011 hoped for a better future that reflected their Islamic morality and modesty; they knew to maintain a healthy distance from and to

---

pseudonym to symbolize her commitment to peace (*salam*), and Iba chose hers to reflect what she saw as her dominant characteristic, determination (*iba*). Personal details about the sisters and their families have also been changed.

2. The Arab Spring was a wave of pro-democracy protests and uprisings that took place in the Middle East and North Africa beginning in 2010 and 2011. It challenged the region's authoritarian regimes. The wave began when protests in Tunisia and Egypt toppled their regimes in quick succession, inspiring similar attempts in other Arab countries. See Masoud et al., *The Arab Spring*; Stepan and Linz, "Democratization Theory"; Bayat, *Revolution Without Revolutionaries*; Hass and Lesch, *The Arab Spring*.

3. See Bakkour, "Daraa and the Altered Trajectory of the Syrian Crisis"; Leenders, "Collective Action and Mobilization in Dar'a"; Kahf, "The Syrian Revolution."

criticize the strictly outlawed Muslim Brotherhood, which had historically challenged the regime and had been decimated by Bashar's father's murder of an estimated 40,000 people in Hama in 1982,[4] but their intense faith and increasing exposure to the world beyond Syria primed them for resistance to tyranny and hypocrisy and toward optimism. Hope for a different future, calls for reform, street demonstrations, and vicious state crackdowns hardened into civil war between religiously motivated rebel militias and the state. But what prompted the sisters, ordinary citizens and mothers, to flee was fear for their children's safety and future.[5]

The Syrian war and massive migration are often seen through orientalist and humanitarian lenses as either a set of particularly grim statistics or the cause of a European crisis.[6] The path of least resistance is to reify "refugees" under an essentializing and stigmatized identity, a natural and permanent quality of victimhood perpetuated through media representations and xenophobic politics. But "refugee" is not an ontological essence. The first modern theorist of refugee subjectivity, Hannah Arendt, wrote in 1943 in reference to those fleeing the Holocaust, "In the first place, we don't like to be called 'refugees.' We call ourselves, call each other 'newcomers' or 'immigrants'" to remake themselves as anything but pitiable victims as they strove to fit into various new homes.[7] Indeed, as the

4. The Hama Massacre happened during the first week of February 1982 as serious fighting broke out in Syria between residents of the city of Hama and government forces. A Syrian army raid on several buildings suspected of being hideouts for local Muslim Brotherhood cells precipitated the fighting. See Conduit, "The Syrian Muslim Brotherhood"; Amnesty International, *Amnesty International Annual Report 1982*, 345–48; Rabil, "The Syrian Muslim Brotherhood"; Ramírez Díaz, *The Muslim Brotherhood in Syria*.

5. Wedeen, *Ambiguities of Domination*.

6. Cabot, "The Business of Anthropology"; Crawley and Skleparis, "Refugees, Migrants, Neither, Both"; Holmes and Castañeda, "Representing the 'European Refugee Crisis'"; Yaylacı and Karakuş, "Perceptions and Newspaper Coverage of Syrian Refugees in Turkey."

7. Arendt, "We Refugees," 69.

sisters sought to protect their families from the violence that beset their neighborhoods from 2011 onward, they first became *nazihun*, or internally displaced people, then *laji'un*, seekers of international asylum or refugees—categories of vulnerable people all too easy to label, objectify, pity, and even build academic disciplines around.

But the Syrian women whose stories are recounted here do not think of themselves as refugees. Although their flight and the trauma of it have marked them in indelible ways, these events have not defined who they are. Their individual identities—rich, complex, flawed, resilient, and evolving—were never congealed into refugeehood, although at certain interludes their energies were momentarily focused on claiming refugee status to gain life-sustaining material assistance or the legal protections of the Geneva Conventions.[8] However, their journeys of displacement provide extended examples of how people and places change under the pressures of forced displacement.[9] Like the forcibly displaced who came before them, the sisters changed themselves to fit into their new circumstances with dignity and in doing so changed the world around them.[10] One stroke of good fortune was that they, unlike those of most previous mass displacements, had cell phones and social media with them to document and reconnect in diaspora.[11]

8. Pictet, "The Geneva Conventions of 12 August 1949 Commentary."

9. Peteet, *Landscape of Hope and Despair*; Allan, *Refugees of the Revolution*; al-Dewachi, *Ungovernable Life;* Z. Saleh, *Return to Ruin;* Gualtieri, *Arab Routes*; Fabos, *"Brothers" or Others?*

10. Chatty, *Displacement and Dispossession in the Modern Middle East.*

11. Building on the foundation of scholarship on Palestinian refugees, current scholarship on displacement has made important empirical and theoretical contributions. Some scholars focus on the camp as a site of survival. See, e.g., Gatter, *Time and Power in Azraq Refugee Camp*; and Totah, "Palestinian Refugees Between the City and the Camp." Others focus on the effects of displacement on labor in global and regional economies. See, e.g., Zuntz, "Refugees' Transnational Livelihoods and Remittances"; Zuntz, Klema, et al., "Syrian Refugee Labour and Food Insecurity"; and Lenner and Turner, "The Jordan Compact." Yet others contribute to a more nuanced understanding of gender norms. See, e.g., Zuntz, Palattiyil, et

The five daughters of Um and Abu 'Abdallah Araj who would become refugees after 2011 were born over the course of two decades. The eldest was born in the late 1950s, and the youngest two in the early 1970s. On any given day from the 1990s through the first decade of the twenty-first century, they could be found visiting with each other and numerous aunts, uncles, cousins, neighbors, and in-laws in the house their parents had built north of Damascus after they were displaced from the Israeli-occupied Golan Heights in 1967.

Maryam, the eldest daughter since the death of her older sister from cancer in the 1990s, married a neighbor and had several daughters before the arrival of the son that her in-laws pressured her for. Sweet, calm, and mild-tempered, she was a tall, girlish grandmother by the time of the Syrian popular uprising. Having lived abroad with her husband in Saudi Arabia as a young bride, she had made the hajj pilgrimage to Mecca and was respectfully but also humorously called "hajjeh" (pilgrim) by her family and friends. She loved to cook and experiment with new flavors as she struggled to gain weight and become plumper and more robust, and all her daughters were tall and rangy like her. She developed an expertise in herbal medicine and was the go-to sister for both home remedies for common ailments as well as creative takes on European classic recipes. Her husband traveled outside of Syria for work for long periods and was able to commit only partially to his family responsibilities.

Her sister Hanan, just a year younger, had been her inseparable childhood companion. As they grew up, teachers and friends knew them as a pair of smart, beautiful, cheerful girls close in age. Together they completed a couple of years of college and did a stint on a production line in a factory making laundry detergent before they each married in the 1980s. Hanan, with lighter hair than her sister and a broad, open, smiling face, seemed always to be laughing and

---

al., "Early Marriage and Displacement"; and Turner, "Syrian Refugee Men." Some critically illuminate the mechanics of both humanitarian aid and the norms and ethics of hospitality. See, e.g., Carpi, "Towards a Neo-Cosmetic Humanitarianism"; and Carpi and Şenoğuz, "Refugee Hospitality in Lebanon and Turkey."

was a little bolder than Maryam, blurting out jokes and convulsing in laughter more regularly and loudly. The mother of two boys and three girls, she was an accomplished seamstress and sewed clothes, especially gowns for brides' trousseaus. Her husband went abroad for work for more than a decade, leaving her to fend for herself.

Middle sister Farida, in contrast to her wispy older sisters, was strong and stout and extremely outspoken and eloquent. She was a fierce debater, a connoisseur of Arabic poetry, gregarious and outgoing, the boldest and intellectually brightest of her sisters. Hoping to distinguish herself in business or scholarship, she had strong opinions about everything she was knowledgeable about and was curious and inquisitive about what she did not know. She postponed marriage to begin a college degree, although she did not finish it and worked in various shops to support her family. She cultivated an interest in politics, religion, and psychology. She was the most tomboyish sister as a child, and her trademark feistiness made her stubborn and defiant. Her marriage was stormy and ended in a bitter divorce, leaving her a single mother to raise a girl and two boys.

Salma was the first of the sisters to be born after the family fled the Golan Heights and settled in Damascus in 1967. Blond and blue-eyed, slender and graceful, she was considered the most beautiful of all the beautiful sisters and attracted numerous suitors during her teenage years. Deflecting the delegations of mothers, sisters, and aunts of young men who hoped to win her hand was routine through her teenage years, and she became the first of her sisters to graduate from college, earning a degree in French language and literature. She then worked as a teacher and eventually married an aspiring writer who also owned a small store. She and her husband, Mazen, separated when their first two sons were young, spending several years apart. They eventually reunited and had a third son.

Iba was the last and youngest of the sisters. Her dark hair contrasted with Salma's fairness, and she, like Salma, grew up with an emphasis on education over marriage. She earned a degree in laboratory science from a vocational institute so that she would always have a skill if she ended up, as each of her sisters had, having to fend for herself. She married in the mid-1990s and had a boy and two girls. Her husband, Hisham, came from a lower socioeconomic status than hers, which was initially a source of concern for the family, but he was hardworking and intelligent, was completely devoted to his wife, and never left her alone until their forced displacement pushed him on to Europe ahead of her.

When the sisters' father, Abu 'Abdallah, died in the early 1990s, his family thought that the trauma of the US invasion of Iraq had added to the stress caused by his life of hard work and his smoking habit. Um 'Abdallah's house was from then on a distinctly women's space in comparison to similar households. Maryam and Hanan had married before their father's death in the early 1990s, while Farida, Salma, and Iba remained unmarried at home, but the married sisters visited their mother and sisters on a nearly daily basis. When husbands left the scene, the visits were more frequent; both Farida and Salma brought their small children to live in their own childhood home after separations and divorces.

In the big house in the northern Damascus suburb of Masaken Barzeh, Um 'Abdallah cooked the daily afternoon meal (*ghada)*, heaping platters of rice, piles of fresh bread from the local bakery, and vegetable stews flavored with small amounts of halal lamb meat prepared in a large pot about a meter in diameter. It was a rare day when fewer than ten or twelve of her family—daughters, grandchildren, and eventually great-grandchildren—gathered there for the midday meal. The main sitting room of her house was ringed with a set of formal upholstered chairs and couches ready for visitors to sit in, babies to nap on, and children to climb on. For meals, a vinyl tablecloth would be spread on the floor for all the women and children to sit on, picnic style, to eat. There were always leftovers for late arrivals and many hands for doing dishes, making tea and coffee, sweeping and mopping the floor before and after every meal.

One or more of the sisters would drop by their mother's house every day as they went about their business. Criss-crossing the city's neighborhoods in a privately owned minivan or by microbus (*mikro*), following regular routes used by ordinary Syrians, they would be deposited in front of the house. Leaving their dusty pumps and flats in the hallway near the front door, the visiting sisters would burst happily into the main room with relief, calling, "As-salamu 'aleikum," quickly shedding their outside dress—hijab headscarves and manteau trench coats—and sitting to roll down and take off their opaque nylon stockings. They might quickly perform their ablutions (*wudu*) in the little sink in the hallway, put on one of the prayer garments always at the ready, roll out a prayer rug, and start to pray or join a group prayer already in progress. Then there would be tea, coffee, fruit as the little cousins ran in and out of the house, and the women chatted and gossiped. They would inquire about and inspect Um 'Abdallah's plants, begging her to make a graft of one or the other for them to take to their husbands' homes.

Um 'Abdallah knew that every one of her daughters needed money and a secure home of her own, independent of the fathers of their children, who had proved all too often unreliable. So a few years before the war, she sold the house that had been built after 1967 and distributed her husband's delayed inheritance to her children, thereafter going to live with each one of them in turn. Each of their houses had a graft of the jasmine tree from the small yard of the family house that had been sold.

Juxtaposing the sisters' various displacement stories rather than focusing on just one elicits contrast and subtlety. Acknowledging the "danger of a single story" standing in for a complex reality helps dismantle the one-dimensional stereotype of the refugee.[12] Slightly different positionalities among the sisters (in terms of age, class, lifestyle, and character) produce a plane of intersections rather than just a biographical line across a static backdrop. Sharing a family

12. Adichie, "The Danger of a Single Story"; see also Deleuze and Guattari, *A Thousand Plateaus*, 4, on multiplicity, a key component of their presentation of poststructuralism.

of origin, they are not as vastly different in experience as a collection of randomly selected interlocuters might be, though.[13] In seeking to highlight women's experiences of becoming refugees, this work was driven by the sisters' inescapable family relationality but also acknowledges and examines how they differ in subtle ways.[14]

Five journeys—sometimes parallel, sometimes intersecting, sometimes diverging—give a broader sense of the ways in which these women experienced displacement. Their children and partners also contribute to the narratives, diversifying the age and gender profiles of the stories. Because all the sisters had their own families, their stories are connected through the bonds and tensions of kinship, so the journeys and narratives shed light on the changing nature of the relationships between the sisters themselves and between each of them and their respective maturing children or aging husbands.[15] What may be lost in terms of breadth of sample by focusing on a single family's members is made up in the depth of the connections, contrasts, and frictions among them. A retracing of the multiple vectors of the sisters' disrupted lives (numerous and variable in direction, momentum, reach, purpose) can be an antidote to the simple linearity of the historical narrative, the essentialism of simple cause and effect, and the stereotype of "the refugee." The intertwining of siblings' and cousins' relationships and narratives presented here can help illuminate the contours of a landscape of change. Furthermore, becoming refugees involves changing relationships with a number of different environments. Fleeing homes transformed by war, gaining footholds in temporary refuges, and traversing borders and dangerous unknown land—as well as seascapes, as the Araj sisters did—challenged their resilience and adaptability. Their challenges reveal

13. Pearlman, *We Crossed a Bridge*; Di Giovanni, *The Morning They Came for Us*.

14. On family relationality and personal experiences, see Freedman, "Women's Experience of Forced Migration," 125.

15. Juhasz and Lebow, "Beyond Story."

the contours of those places and environments both eroded and shaped by war and migration.

The idea of a landscape of change seen from the perspective of those moving through it puts an emphasis on place. The narratives highlight the transformations triggered by the upheaval of the Syrian war and migration—the transformations not just of the protagonists themselves but also of their neighborhoods; the borders they crossed; the new labor and housing markets, schools, and streets that they navigated; and their constellations of family relationships. Their narratives open the door—abruptly in the middle of things—to changing sites of various shapes, scales, and intimacies: cities, countries, borderlands but also apartments, tents, camps, checkpoints, even vehicles. Some of these sites are densely textured by history and physical structures that the newcomers struggled to enter and fit into, and find their roles. Other sites are in-between places etched in memories by fear—open, empty, and dangerous in other ways—where traditional protections were far beyond the horizon.[16] The landscape of migration is a meshwork of intersecting paths and relationships. As the anthropologist Tim Ingold has written,

> Human existence is not fundamentally placebound . . . but place-binding. It unfolds not in places but along paths. Proceeding along a path, every inhabitant lays a trail. Where inhabitants meet, trails are entwined, as the life of each becomes bound up with the other. Every entwining is a knot, and the more that lifelines are entwined, the greater the density of the knot. Places, then, are like knots, and the threads from which they are tied are lines of wayfaring. A house, for example, is a place where the lines of its residents are tightly knotted together. But these lines are no more contained within the house than are threads contained within a knot. Rather, they trail beyond it, only to become caught up with other lines in other places, as are threads in other knots. Together they make up what I have called the meshwork.

16. Anzaldúa, *Borderlands/La frontera*. See also Lysen and Pisters, "Introduction," 1–5.

> Places, in short, are delineated by movement, not by the outer limits to movement.[17]

Considering the refugee experience through the lens of an extended family network, with multiple households at various points in the domestic cycle, moving around the regional landscape, this book follows what might naively be called "lines of flight" in the sense of trajectories of escape.[18] In doing so, it also surveys the topography of localities, economies, and states that the family members pass through. The process of becoming refugees is not a simple one of pure movement. It involves being pushed or breaking out of, through, and into sedimented systems whose dividing lines made up of borders, markets, institutions, hierarchies are—for all intents and purposes—hardened, durable structures.

This family story complex gathers together the narratives of displacement and evokes the multiplicity, the divergence, and the trajectories and experiences of people intimately linked together by inherited kinship, geography, and culture. Displacement manifests as a series of interwoven narratives, affects, calculations, and consequences that trace the contours of the mass trauma. The book uses open-ended interviews, participant observation, and digital communications carried out between 2015 and 2017 to produce an oral history woven out of the five sisters' accounts of their diaspora.[19]

17. Ingold, "Against Space," 148; on meshwork, see Ingold, "Point, Line, Counterpoint," 79–81. Both essays are from Ingold's book *Being Alive: Essays on Movement, Knowledge and Description.*

18. This naive usage flies in the face of Deleuze and Guattari's notion of the lines of flight, or *lignes de fuite*, which are understood to be transformative rather than geographic escapes. But as Deleuze and Guattari also state, "A second kind of line of flight arises when the associated milieu is rocked by blows from the exterior, forcing the animal to abandon it and strike up an association with new portions of exteriority, this time leaning on its interior milieus like fragile crutches" (*A Thousand Plateaus*, 55).

19. I undertook this work as an oral history whose particularity and nongeneralizability exempted it from protocols of the University of Arizona's Institutional Review Board for Human Subject Research. On such protocols, see Shopes, "Oral

Each sister's account begins with her memories of the looming sense that she would need to leave Damascus, relayed in the chapters of part one, "Damascus Unraveling." The chapters of part two, "Unsettled Homemaking," focus on their attempts to reconstruct their lives temporarily in the cities of Syria's neighboring countries. In part three, "Taking Flight," the focus turns to two sisters' decision to risk death and head for Europe.

Listening to the Araj sisters' accounts of displacement challenges an audience to ask at the most basic level what they would do if faced with the dilemmas of those who were forced to flee Syria. Challenging readers to think about having to undertake the same risks and choose among the same options, choices faced by the sisters, blurs the distinction between refugees and comfortably settled students of other people's misfortunes. If nothing else, contemplating a series of accounts should help produce not pity but rather empathy for all those who have to leave settled domesticity behind and reassemble their lives. In addition, it should invite critical analysis of the global and local effects of violence, war, late capitalism, authoritarianism, and even climate change that have contributed to the displacement of scores of millions of people worldwide. The personal stories of individual women illuminate conditions whose scale, complexity, and heterogeneity can be obscured by ideology and the habits of anticritical attitudes.

Refugee Assemblages—from City to Home in Limbo to Digital Diaspora

Liisa Malkki's work on refugees in the 1990s helped cultural anthropology recognize the necessity of ethnographies of the mobile and the displaced with respect to both identity formation and the illumination of the fixed territories and codes that the displaced break from and seek to re-create. She was influenced (though not enthralled) by the philosophical works of Gilles Deleuze and Félix Guattari, which,

History, Human Subjects"; and Larson, "Steering Clear of the Rocks." I followed the research parameters outlined in Clark-Kazak, "Ethical Considerations."

as Paul Patton points out, afford "a political ontology that provides tools to describe transformative, creative or deterritorializing forces and movements."[20] Malkki contrasted the ubiquitous tree and root tropes of grounded and rooted cultures that dominated the field of anthropology with the expressions of exile and uprooting that do not (and cannot) take fixed place for granted.[21] Since Malkki's pioneering work, another generation of anthropologists has been inspired by the attention to the mobile, the fluid, and the emergent. The anthropology of becoming continues the critical ethnographic tradition of attending to neglected voices and positions but resists harnessing them to specific coherent social forms such as hegemonic discourse or institutions and even to resistance.[22]

Following in those footsteps, this book flirts with Deleuzian poststructuralism as particularly suited to the exploration of displacement while resisting the urge to commit fully to the paradigm, which lures the incautious into blackholes of abstraction. Therefore, serious students of Deleuze and Guattari may be horrified at the naive application of key concepts to the sisters' trajectories recounted here. Attempts to use lines and assemblages in a narrative or descriptive way will irritate critical theorists, yet they provide an opportunity for discussion and application of these challenging concepts to lived experience. Following bell hooks, "The point is not to render ideas less complex, but to make the complex clear. The difficulty of the terrain traversed should not be evident."[23] The narratives of a family gathered here offer the chance to explore the idea of "refugee assemblages."

20. Patton, *Deleuze and the Political*, 9. See also Mueller, "Assemblages and Actor-Networks."

21. Malkki, "Refugees and Exile."

22. See, for example, J. Biehl and Locke, "Deleuze and the Anthropology of Becoming"; J. Biehl and Locke, *Unfinished*; Hamilton and Placas, "Anthropology Becoming . . . ?"

23. hooks, "Remembered Rapture," 4.

The framing concept for this work, the assemblage, foregrounds the dynamic, fluid, and heterogeneous nature of the emergent and semistable "structures," such as cities, families, and information networks, highlighted by the Araj sisters' journeys. As Manuel DeLanda observes, assemblage thinking allows the bypass of assumptions of "seamless totalities and transcendent essences" to model dynamic social entities such as interpersonal networks and institutional organizations that cannot be reduced to the persons who compose them but do not totally encompass them either.[24] We can learn so much about that which seems solid and fixed by viewing it through the experiences, voices, and longings of those who move away from, through, and around it. As Niels Albertsen and Bülent Diken put it, "Unlike conventional theory, which is a theory of solids, treating flows (fluids) as a special case, [Deleuzian poststructuralism] is characterised by a hydraulic model[,] . . . which treats flows and fluids as the reality, as consistency."[25] In Maria Tamboukou's clear description of assemblages, "Unlike institutions, structural systems, identities, and axes of difference—which are the usual terms deployed in analysing the social—assemblages do not have any fixed organization, structure or centre; they are rather networks of connections, always in flux, assembling and reassembling in different ways. Assemblages are thus emergent features of relationships and can only function as they connect with other assemblages in a constant process of becoming."[26]

Following the Araj sisters' stories of displacement leads through a series of assemblages.[27] In particular, three types of assemblage that

24. DeLanda, *Assemblage Theory*, 12–13. DeLanda points out elsewhere that Deleuze and Guattari's magnum opus, *A Thousand Plateaus*, contains no fewer than seven different and difficult definitions of assemblages. DeLanda, *A New Philosophy of Society: Assemblage Theory and Social Complexities*, 3–5.

25. Albertsen and Diken, "Society With/out Organs," 235.

26. Tamboukou, "Mobility Assemblages," 236.

27. For an account of the archaeological approach that seeks to "uncover the succession of historical assemblages of one, rather small," group, see Sissons, "Reterritorializing Kinship," 374.

the sisters experience in sequence invite exploration. The first is the enveloping assemblage of their city of origin, which they are induced to leave as it transforms into a site of overt conflict. The home city is the most solid, permanent, and grounded of the assemblages, embedded in the landscape not only through infrastructure and history but also through the naturalized familiarity of rhythms that shape its inhabitants. Yet the city is nevertheless kinetic and changes through actions large and small beginning in 2011. The second type of assemblage consists of the fragile arrangements of family and other resources that the sisters must take into unfamiliar new environments in exile in Lebanon, Egypt, Jordan, and Turkey. Assemblage here is not so much a structure as a practice of agency and composition that the sisters enact as they cobble together households and livelihoods in their position as newcomers in systems where they have no established place. The third type of assemblage, emerging most clearly with the two youngest sisters' flight to Europe, is a diasporic configuration of mediated exchanges connecting over new spaces, places, and codes that form an ethereal and digital network of information and affect delivered over technological devices and through social media. The phase changes highlighted—from the rigid solidities of urban life to the liquid negotiation of household formation to the perilous and nebulous escape of asylum seeking—show life connections between people and places forming, breaking, and reforming in various processes of assemblage.

Part one sees the sisters dislodging and dislodged from the city of their birth, Damascus—an historically stable, millennia-old urban assemblage fracturing under the pressures of war. The narratives of leaving the city are classic deterritorializations that "destabilize spatial boundaries" and "create earthquakes in the grounds of the assemblage."[28] This urban brick-and-mortar environment, the most durable, structurelike, and all-encompassing of the assemblages

28. Tamboukou, "Mobility Assemblages," 237, citing DeLanda, *Assemblage Theory*, 13.

featured in these biographical accounts, had already incubated, sculpted, and impressed the women with their culture and reference points. Although a clear point of origin for them and a durable template of their habits, the city was, of course, always changing, and in the years after 2011 it changed swiftly and dramatically in ways that made their old lives unlivable.

Parts two and three present processes of rearrangement and reterritorialization of life, livelihood, and relationships unsettled by the escape from war. Like the vibrant urban configuration of a city, these processes are also assemblages. In fact, the original French word translated as "assemblage" is *agencement*. Assemblage, in this light, is as much or more agency, process, and practice than enduring system. The sisters' flight from the urban assemblage of the home they were born into forced them to reassemble their lives in neighboring countries as they created households in limbo. In part two, as they struggled to fit into new milieus as strangers, the more trenchant deployment of the concept of assemblage is not so much as a social system that predates and dwarfs them, which they are born into and inhabit unselfconsciously, but rather as the intense activity that they undertook as they attempted to rebuild their lives and households according to the past template forged in Damascus, depending heavily on sometimes elusive family collaboration to scratch sustainable lives from unhospitable new grounds. Finally, in part three, as two sisters made their desperate escapes to Europe, while others stayed closer to home, they collectively initiated a diasporic assemblage of digital communications spread over seas, over new languages, and over new European landscapes of borders and rules. The sisters—scattered, held together more loosely than ever before in their lives—reassembled their relationships to some extent by the affordance of cell phones and the internet—developing the infrastructure of digital communications, social media, and electronically mediated contact and memories that they had had for years into a newly critical format and site of family relations. Processed as immigrants in Europe, the two youngest sisters navigated a world bereft of the physical proximity of their former lives and were disabused of the idea that extended family connectivity would be their reliable fallback. Distance and European bureaucratic categories of individuality and family formalized the five sisters' separation from one another, while exchanges of information, emotion, and nostalgia via technology reassembled them in exile.

Conceptually, these forms and stages of assemblage are meshes of evolving relationships among people and between people and places. Different types of assemblage are highlighted by the phases of displacement: urban structural familiar life, household making in exile, and diasporic digital reconnections. The progression of the sisters' most defining new assembled lifestyles—from apparently inevitable, structural, and formative to fragile, practical, and under active construction, then to ephemeral, distant, and digital—corresponds to a progression set in motion by the awful momentum of displacement. Those assemblages are milestones along the journeys that constitute lines of flight, transformations that "escape" from the circumstances of their generation. Again, in Tamboukou's concise presentation of Deleuzian concepts, "society is not so much defined by its macro structures and their dialectic oppositions, but rather by what has escaped them, its 'lines of flight.'"[29] "Lines of flight" in a much more intuitive sense can refer to the trajectories of the sisters' literal flight from the dangers of their home.

In *The Mushroom at the End of the World* (2015), Anna Lowenhaupt Tsing follows the matsutake mushroom, which thrives in human-disturbed landscapes and helps trees regrow. This mushroom's sprawling and subtle trajectory "guides us to possibilities of coexistence within environmental disturbance[,] . . . [s]how[s] one kind of collaborative survival . . . and illuminate[s] the cracks in the global political economy."[30] In Tsing's classic work, the mushroom is the theme running through a "riot of short chapters"; in this book, the sisters also move through environments, and their accounts similarly

29. Tamboukou, "Mobility Assemblages," 237, quoting "lines of flight" from Deleuze and Guattari, *A Thousand Plateaus*, 216.

30. Tsing, *The Mushroom at the End of the World*, 4.

illuminate the cracks in the global political economy as well as the challenges of collaborative survival and coexistence. This book, too, with chapters framed by more traditional narrative conventions, is an assemblage of multiple perspectives, phases, and events that, with reluctance, capitalizes on the trauma of forced displacements to catch glimpses of worlds always in formation.

PART ONE

Damascus Unraveling

The courtyard houses of Damascus
Defy the rules of architecture
The structure of our houses
They stand up on foundations of emotion
And each house supports the next at its waist
Each balcony
Reaches out toward its neighbor
The Damascus houses are houses in love
They greet each other in the mornings
And exchange visits
Secretly, at night

—Nizar Qabbani, "Ablutions in the Water of Love and Jasmine," translated by Leila Hudson

The Araj sisters grew up in Damascus, taking for granted a right to the city and its sensorial cacophony, the most emblematic and romanticized of which was the sight and smell of jasmine. Works of literature from and about Damascus routinely call it the "city of jasmine."[1] The fragrant blossom exerts a palpable nostalgia on the city that the Araj sisters fled from. The vines and trees on which the flower grows form an architectural element in the city's domestic and

1. Grjasnowa, *City of Jasmine*. Also see Tergeman, *Daughter of Damascus*, for numerous references to jasmine. The ubiquity of this floral metaphor in poetry and prose makes it difficult to escape the status of a worn-out cliche. The metaphor is used, for example, to name the Tunisian Revolution and is applied simply to political moments, as in Ismat, "Nizar Qabbani."

public areas. Another Damascene exile described this sensory pervasiveness as not only visual but also olfactory: "Everyone describes Damascus as the *city of jasmine*, but I never understood why. Now, after my displacement, I pass by a certain spot on the way to where I now live, and a flashback strikes me. . . . That spot takes me back every time to my Damascus. I never understood why. Until one day, when I looked up to see a jasmine bush filling the street with its fragrance. Perhaps this jasmine grows to remind me—to never allow me to forget—the smell of Damascus."[2]

That city of their childhood, with its organic and urban landscapes, provided the sisters with most necessary affordances, and as they matured, they came to know (theoretically) how to achieve anything they needed through money, connections, and hard work.[3] The sisters were born into a tightly structured world of social cohesion. Their natal city, their state, and their family were comparatively rigid assemblages, old and encompassing, that fairly strictly defined people's roles and positions.[4] There was always room for agency, maneuver, and creativity, but only within the firm lines and rules of a well-structured game that dwarfed most individual agents and favored initiatives that fit within the established order. Indeed, success and advancement depended on knowing what the rules are and how

2. Quisetna: Talking Syria, "Seeking the Jasmine Breeze," video.

3. On affordances, see Ingold, "Back to the Future with the Theory of Affordances."

4. The assemblage concept provides "a structure-like surrogate" that "is a sort of anti-structural concept that permits the researcher to speak of emergence, heterogeneity, the decentered and the ephemeral in a nonetheless ordered social world." Marcus and Saka, "Assemblage," 101. Assemblage thinking "focuses on process and on the dynamic character of the inter-relationships between the heterogeneous elements of the phenomenon. It recognizes both structurizing and indeterminate effects: that is, both flow and turbulence, produced in the interaction of open systems. It points to complex becoming and multiple determinations. It is sensitive to time and temporality in the emergence and mutation of the phenomenon; it thus directs attention to the longue durée." Couze Venn, "A Note on Assemblage," 107.

to bend and break them, but all the while staying within the grid of respectability. Although the sisters often needed to negotiate with the city of Damascus, they knew how to navigate it—not only its infrastructure and institutions but also its culture and status hierarchies.

In the world the Damascene sisters inhabited for most of their lives, for example, children internalize their place in a kin-based universe with nearly every encounter. The reciprocal form of address by which an adult and a child refer to each other makes children's lives a constant drill in comparative kinship relations. Their mother calls the child "mama," and their father calls them "baba." Every new adult man who enters their world is an uncle, *'ammo*, and every woman an aunt, *khala*. Every verbal encounter of childhood reinforces the grid of kin in which a child can soon automatically locate themselves. This knowing of one's place in the kinship grid is further enhanced by the use of patronymics. In daily life, adults are addressed as the father or mother of their first-born son, "Abu Mohammad" and "Um Mohammad." If there is no son, they can be addressed as the father or mother of their oldest daughter, "Abu Maryam" or "Um Maryam," or in Damascene culture as the father of their own father, presuming a future son named after their father. Little details like this emphasize a richly structured culture of kinship connections, extrapolated to the world at large. Other forms of fictive-kinship address by teachers, employers, military officers (*ya ibni*, *ya binti*), and so on expand the kinship metaphor into institutional life.[5]

The streets and places of the city are similarly a landscape into which one is born and through which one learns to navigate, radiating outward from the home to the neighborhood to the larger metropolis. One also learns the ways of the authoritarian state and its agents as one learns to respect and fear power. The fixed topography that the Araj girls grew into came from authoritarian rule as much as from tradition or history. One learns quickly who carries the public

5. For more on the language of kinship, see Davies, "Syrian Arabic Kinship Terms."

power of the state or the secret power of its informants. The place the sisters eventually left in exile was a matrix of old certainties, well-known lines of difference and obligation that they never envisioned unraveling around them. It surrounded them, and they were firmly embedded in it.

The city, as a mature, layered, stable assemblage, is composed of the molecular interactions and habits described earlier. Most of the actions, utterances, errands, decisions, interactions, and habits of its innumerable inhabitants are unremarkable and unchallenging to the encompassing system. Indeed, most of those molecular transactions reinforce and reproduce the urban cultural system. Taken together, those molecular everyday transactions collectively create and reinforce the macro or molar lines of division and distinction in space, society, and culture that separate and distinguish status, type, class, sector, and geography and define meaningful differences. Most of the time, molecular actions converge to reproduce the whole familiar assemblage. Those molar lines of difference, reproduced with evolving and gradual changes, upheld by the habits and paths of least resistance, are also, however, subject to dramatic, even seismic change when enough molecular actions depart from the circumstances of their production. A critical mass of molecular change—when enough people orient themselves to a different future, dare to speak out, begin to take risks—can indeed shake the entire formation.

That is what happened when in 2011 there came a kind of tectonic shudder with the popular protests inspired by the Arab Spring uprisings in Tunisia and Egypt and other parts of the Arab world. A city such as Ba'athist Damascus is made of people and action as much as of entrenched traditions, institutions, and interests. Triggered by the Tunisian and Egyptian revolutions, which everyone watched in real time on television, the rigid lines that defined the city and state and had seemed geological in their permanence were shaken, broken as enough people dared to depart from the habits of fear. The capital's tightly compacted layers began to shake, and its packed fabric began to unravel with the energy of a popular uprising long in the making. As the roads, buildings, roles, institutions, familiarities, and formalities buckled and crumbled in 2011, people whose agency had been constrained to the limited scope and space of authoritarian gridworks were forced out on unimagined trajectories. The government named its brutal response to the Damascus popular uprising "Operation Damascus Volcano," but the initial eruption came from the actions taken by people around Syria. The destruction of the city's properties and institutions was a violent upheaval of its people, forcing out multitudes, who then needed to use their own material and character resources to resettle sustainably. Home no longer worked the way it did, no longer provided protection. The Araj sisters were among the thousands who began longer, more open-ended journeys than they had ever taken or thought of taking before. Part one interweaves memories of what life was like up through 2011, when it still seemed stable; of the compelling force of the revolution as the sisters and their children experienced it in 2011 and early 2012; and of the division and destruction of the city from 2012 on.

1

Out of Assad Village

Salma, 2011

Salma's son Yusuf was in ninth grade and his older brother, 'Adel, was in tenth when they started to demonstrate against the Syrian government. They lived in a suburb of Damascus named after the dictator they were protesting against. There were no protests in Assad Village itself, a new planned community on the north side of the capital that was home to military officers and government workers who depended on the regime for their livelihoods. But the boys had been raised in their grandmother's house in the gritty suburb of Masaken Barzeh.

As early as April 2011, Yusuf and 'Adel joined their older cousins attending the massive funeral marches for the revolution's first *shuhada*, or martyrs, from the belt of suburbs surrounding Damascus.[1] They also took an active role in smaller demonstrations. A family video from 2011 shows the two brothers, dressed in T-shirts, jeans, and baseball caps, standing on the sidewalk carrying plastic shopping bags. One of the brothers steps out as if to cross the street, causing traffic to slow, while the other places four of the plastic bags in a line across the road. Another boy steps from the shadow of the

1. The first demonstrations in Damascus, before the Dar'a schoolboys' arrest, had taken place at the Egyptian embassy on February 3 and the Libyan embassy on February 22, 2011, in sympathy with the people of those countries, as well as in the Hariqa market district on February 17 over police harassment, but the cycle of Friday demonstrations, funeral marches, and killing would not start until late March.

trees lining the streets and pours kerosene from a one-liter soft-drink bottle on and between the bags, and somebody lights a match. As the cars brake and honk their horns, the bags flare up, and a wall of fire cuts the street in half. The boys bolt and scatter in different directions, yelling and whooping. The camera, positioned one floor up across the street, pans to show that another group of boys has done the same thing on the other side of the median strip. The waist-high wall of flames burns for a few minutes, giving off clouds of black smoke, as the youngsters sprint away and disappear between buildings.

Years later, in August 2017, Yusuf, now twenty, looked up on his laptop other videos of his demonstrations on YouTube. He was taking a break from his German-language studies in a southern German town near Stuttgart, where he lived while awaiting the outcome of his asylum application. The visit to his cousins' new homes, ten hours away by train in northern Germany, was the first reunion of many of the family members who had settled in Germany. The last time he had seen his aunt Maryam's daughters back in 2012, none of them would ever have predicted a future in Germany or anywhere but their hometown of Damascus. Yusuf and his brother had finished high school in Lebanon, then worked at various jobs to support their families before continuing on the perilous trip to Germany. Mastering the German language and gaining permanent residency would open the doors to education that had been closed to them for years.

Yusuf chuckled as he watched his younger self while his cousin Rose served tea and cookies. Waxing nostalgic about his last months in Damascus, Yusuf went on to show another video on YouTube of a planned demonstration that the boys participated in. It took place in August 2012 during the fasting month of Ramadan in the neighborhood where they had grown up. A group of young men, again dressed casually in T-shirts, polos, and baseball caps, and young women, most in white hijab headscarves over jeans and jackets, unfurls a huge Syrian revolutionary flag, chanting, "Allahu akbar" (God is great). The group stands to attention and sings the national anthem of Syria as one young man waves a big inflatable hand, the kind usually seen at sporting events, whose outstretched finger could be interpreted as pointing toward heaven in a gesture both secular and Islamic. Faces are blurred out in the video as people throw confetti inscribed with revolutionary slogans, before marching down the street, singing and chanting. The mood captured in the video is energized, expectant, even festive.

Salma watched the short clip over her son's shoulder. This was the first time his mother had seen some of these videos and pictures, and she raised her eyebrows and clucked her tongue, mildly shocked, wistful for the old familiar streets preserved on video and grudgingly proud of her two older sons. It was easy for her to be more relaxed, sitting comfortably in Germany and finally reunited with relatives. But her delicate face, framed by the headscarf she wears except when she is alone with her immediate family, was etched with the stress of the past few years, tiny creases encircling her clear blue eyes. She punched her son gently on the arm, chiding him for the risks he had taken and herself for not being able to control him and his brother. Yusuf was much taller now than he had been in the videos and sported a casually scruffy hipster beard, but he still looked like his mother, light haired enough to have almost passed for a Pole or a Belgian at times on his journey from Turkey to Germany.

Salma sat with her son in her niece's living room in Germany as he flipped through digital glimpses of his old life in Syria, his new life in Germany, and the odyssey between them. This odyssey involved two years in Lebanon and a year in Turkey, struggling to make ends meet, and a grueling journey from Turkey to Germany that involved a dangerous Aegean crossing and seemed for much of 2016 as if it would end in a miserable, muddy refugee camp in Greece. Salma herself, traveling with her husband and their youngest son, Kamal, along the same route, had arrived months before Yusuf because the family could not afford to make the journey at the same time. Yusuf's older brother, 'Adel, would arrive a few weeks after Yusuf before being detained for months in a refugee-processing camp in Germany, awaiting an asylum hearing. About two dozen aunts, uncles, and cousins had made parallel and sometimes even more harrowing trips through Lebanon, Jordan, Egypt, Turkey, Greece, Macedonia, Serbia, Hungary, Croatia, Austria, and Germany over the same period.

Salma's chronic anxiety dated back to Syria when the revolution broke out in March 2011. She had existed in a smoldering, constant state of worry about her older boys, 'Adel and Yusuf, and how to protect them from the contagious and deadly activism and unrest that swept Syria in the wake of the Arab Spring. Within weeks of the Tunisian and Egyptian dictators stepping down in January 2011, Syrians were being killed every week in demonstrations like the ones her kids were attending and planning. The entire Syrian uprising was triggered when boys just like her sons were arrested and tortured for scrawling antiregime graffiti in the southern town of Dar'a. As the Damascus demonstrations became more and more dangerous throughout that spring and summer, Salma worried about 'Adel and Yusuf getting into trouble in areas of town where they did not have friends or relatives. If they had to escape arrest by troops or paramilitary thugs, they needed safe places to hide. The group that organized the protests and made videos seemed to make a point of having demonstrations all over town in provocative locations, in front of the secret-police buildings or in the poshest neighborhoods where government officials and Damascene merchants who partnered with the regime lived. To her sisters' alarm, Salma began to drop her sons off at the demonstrations and then wait nearby in her car to pick them up. She conceded that she couldn't stop them from participating, so she might as well do what she could to bring them home safely.

When the uprising of 2011 and the government reprisal began, Salma found life in Damascus more tolerable for longer than her sisters, who lived in frontline suburbs where protesters clashed with the military. Living in a safer area of Damascus known for government support, and better off, she did not flee in fear of her life from the fighting. But Salma knew there were more scrutiny and surveillance of those like her who worked in white-collar jobs, and as a teacher in a government school she also faced other kinds of pressure. Colleagues at school had fingered her in 2011 as being lukewarm to the regime when she declined to force her high school students into an obligatory demonstration of support for Bashar al-Assad. During the early days of the revolution, schools had been ordered to bring their students to pro-government counterrallies. When asked by her adolescent students whether they needed to attend the hated forced rallies, she shrugged and told them that it was up to them to attend or not; she would not force them. This response made her popular among her students, but another teacher informed on her, with reverberations all the way up the chain of command. All in all, Salma was not suffering the effects of immediate physical danger, as her sisters were, but the pressure to prove her loyalty to the regime was unbearable.

Other disturbing events also left their mark. Salma's husband, Mazen, was summoned to the local police office in Assad Village and asked about his wife and two sons. Salma, ʻAdel, and Yusuf had been anonymously accused of being responsible for rebel graffiti. Her sons were asked if they were the sons of a teacher rumored to be a regime opponent. The family pushed back and asked defiantly on what evidence this rumor was being repeated and who had accused them, so the police backed off. The family recalled later a strange incident in which a neighbor knocked at their door and peered at them and their guests as if taking mental notes of who was present. The neighbor then excused himself, claiming he had mistaken their door for his own. In the surveillance economy of Baʻathist Syria, there had always been an incentive to snitch on one's neighbors, whether to burnish one's own utility as an informer, detract attention from oneself, or even snag a coveted property or rental unit that those accused had to abandon.

Furthermore, Salma's sons were growing up. When the war started, they were pupils just starting secondary school, but now they were focused on high school graduation and the future beyond. This juncture in a young Syrian man's life was key. Would he pass the baccalaureate exam and earn a place at university? Would he have to learn a trade? Would he need to perform his obligatory military service? All three of Salma's sons would be required to serve in the Syrian Arab Army, a horrifying moral prospect for an oppositionist and a frightening one in a civil war whose outcome was far from clear. On at least one occasion, the fact that Yusuf and ʿAdel's government ID address had the name "Assad Village" in it was instrumental in getting her sons through a government checkpoint. The approaching expiration of her sons' Syrian passports would eventually make travel outside Syria impossible, and passport renewal would put her sons in the hands of the *shaʿbet al-tajnid*, the military draft board.

Salma and her family left Syria in 2012. They were part of a migration in which at least 4 million people fled the country. The conflict that pushed them out started as a nonviolent call for democratic reform at the height of what was optimistically referred to as the "Arab Spring" but soon degenerated into a war of attrition when the Assad regime, eventually lethally propped up by Iran and Russia, pursued a scorched-earth policy against a popular rebellion whose Western allies—led by the United States and a collection of regional governments—failed to support it effectively and even propelled its dissolution into an array of competing Islamist factions. The results have been more than half a million dead, a traumatized population, an economy in ruins, and the incubation of such entities as al-Qaeda's Nusra Front and Daʿesh/ISIS, among a menagerie of other groups mixing resistance, nationalism, and Islamism in an escalation of violence.[2] With more than 4 million leaving Syria and more than 7 million internally displaced, at least half of the country's population was forced into flight, and all Syria's people have been affected by the economic disaster and the culture of fear, hatred, and corruption produced by the war.

2. Jabhat al-Nusra (al-Nusra/Victory Front) was a Syrian jihadist group that was fighting against Bashar al-Assad's regime. Its aim was to establish an Islamist state in Syria. The group had approximately 5,000 members, so it was not the largest rebel group in the conflict but was described as effective. Daʿesh, or ISIS (Islamic State of Iraq and Syria), is a group that emerged from al-Qaeda. After diminishing in 2007, the group reemerged in 2011 and took advantage of the instability in Iraq and Syria, where it bolstered its population and took over territory.

Salma and every member of her nuclear family as well as her sisters and their families pointed out repeatedly that they were among those lucky to escape and restart their (and especially their children's) lives. There were so many families worse off than theirs, they always emphasized, so many people who did not survive or who had everything they loved torn away from them. Nevertheless, over the course of three years of interviews about their lives in exile, each of the older sisters experimented melodramatically but earnestly with the idea that if they had known earlier the perils and indignities of refugee life and status, they might well have stayed to die in Syria.

The mother of three very energetic boys, Salma had always been considered the most beautiful girl in a family full of beautiful girls. Blond hair, blue eyes, and high cheekbones gave her a look that her late father, Abu 'Abdallah, had called "just like the English." When she was a little girl, he used to parade her and her black-eyed younger sister, Iba, proudly on his shoulders around the neighborhood of Masaken Barzeh. That neighborhood was full of people like them—refugees from past wars, housed in shabby prefabricated buildings and cinder-block and rebar row houses that had gone from temporary shelters to permanent multistory structures on boulevards lined with thriving businesses. Masaken Barzeh as a neighborhood represented Syria's history of hosting refugees. Originally agricultural land between the capital city and the northern mountains, it was a formal resettlement site for thousands of Arabs, Circassians, and Bedouins displaced from the Golan Heights after their occupation by Israel in the Six-Day War of 1967.[3] The area also had a large population of Palestinians and sizable populations of exiled Sudanese, Somalis,

3. The Golan region is a region in Southwest Syria that was occupied by Israel in 1967. The 140,000 Syrians living there were driven out and have not been able to return to this day. In 1981, Israel annexed the Golan Heights, but this is not internationally recognized.

and Yemenis by the 1990s. During the Iraq War of 2003, it became one of many neighborhoods hosting Iraqi refugees, with a notable spike in real estate prices and Iraqi automobile peddlers. By 2010, however, it was a solidly middle-class neighborhood of some 50,000 people that was a fifteen-minute drive from the center of Damascus and had outgrown the original village, Barzeh, in the foothills of the Qalamun mountain range.[4]

Born in that neighborhood in the early 1970s, Salma had been the first and only girl in her family to graduate from college. With her degree in French literature from the University of Damascus, she had secured a position as a high-school teacher in a government school, which had allowed her to support herself, Yusuf, and ‘Adel when she and their father were separated for several years. When they eventually remarried and had a third son, Kamal, they became a two-income family, better off than any of Salma's sisters. Her husband, Mazen, owned a small bookstore and had finally taken title to the apartment in Assad Village that he had signed up for in the 1990s and paid off in subscription over the years. Salma's salary allowed them to live comfortably, and when she received a modest inheritance from the sale of her parents' house, she was able to buy a car and a small apartment in the cheaper Eastern Ghuta suburbs of Damascus, where most of her sisters lived. She and Mazen had planned that ‘Adel or Yusuf could someday live in the apartment with a wife, decreasing the heavy burden of marrying off and buying houses for three sons.

Salma's family belong to the pious Sunni Muslim majority of Syria. She was educated in the Ba‘athist public-education system, and she and her sisters lived lifestyles ranging from working-class precarity to middle-class comfort before the war upended their lives.[5]

4. Barzeh (related to the Arabic word for "promontory") may have been named for its elevation above the Damascus Basin. It was the site of a shrine to the prophet Abraham. Grehan, *Twilight of the Saints*, 109. See also al-Mawed, *The Palestinian Refugees in Syria*.

5. On this lifestyle, see Anderson, "'Order' and 'Civility.'"

Salma embodied conservative social mores in her daily habits of piety, prayer, and conservative dress and comportment. Maintaining the zone of modesty with clothing had become natural, even instinctive, to Salma and her sisters early in their lives, requiring no thought or discussion and certainly no exception. But their family had not always worn the hijab. Like many other women in Syria, Salma's mother had had a much more relaxed attitude toward dress in her youth and even into the Ba'athist era. A favorite black-and-white family picture shows Um 'Abdallah in the 1950s hugging her new husband, coquettish in a pretty dress, his policeman's peaked cap perched jauntily on her head above her wavy, shoulder-length hair. Family portraits of the 1970s show Um 'Abdallah surrounded by a growing entourage of daughters, her head uncovered or at most covered with a small kerchief knotted under the chin, Queen Elizabeth style.

The girls' father, Abu 'Abdallah as he was known, had raised his large family with difficulty on the salary of a government employee. He had lost his property in the Golan Heights in the Six-Day War between a coalition of Arab states (Egypt, Syria, and Jordan) and Israel and had brought his young family to Damascus as refugees from that defeat. Um 'Abdallah had sold her gold bracelets to buy a small rectangle of land on what was in the late 1960s the outer edges of Damascus. Abu 'Abdallah had built a small cinder-block structure on it, and it was here that Salma and, four years later, Iba were born.

Since the disastrous 1967 war, Syrians had lived under a government-declared state of emergency. Hafez al-Assad had been the minister of defense during the war that saw the beautiful green highlands of the Golan Heights, where both Um and Abu 'Abdallah had been born and raised, lost to Israel. Al-Assad then seized the presidency in a coup, and for the next forty years the Syrian socialist economy served the needs of the government and the party that dominated it, forever in a state of ice-cold war with the enemy, Israel. But the people of Syria themselves—especially the Sunni majority, who resented the corrupt, secular, minority-dominated Ba'ath Party led by the Assad family—were the government's most feared threat.[6] They were kept in line by informers and an elaborate infrastructure of competing secret-police units—the *mukhabarat*.[7]

In 1982, when the Muslim Brotherhood began to target regime officials and institutions in assassinations and terror attacks, the government destroyed entire neighborhoods of the Brotherhood's stronghold city, Hama. Estimates of the dead ranged from 10,000 to 40,000 civilians.[8] One of Um 'Abdallah's brothers-in-law had been a driver for a secret police unit that had carried out some of the Hama massacres, and one of her future sons-in-law had been a military police officer who helped clear away the bodies afterward. Neither ever talked about their experiences in Hama. Nobody talked about it, and in the days before digital photography and the internet most people pretended it hadn't happened. The rules were clear in Ba'athist Syria: silence was a safe default mode for difficult truths.

But one day in the early 1980s, Um 'Abdallah found herself and her choice of head covering at the center of tensions between the Ba'ath Party regime and the Sunni-majority population of Syria. These same tensions would eventually manifest in the demonstrations, the war, and the refugee crisis that her children and grandchildren would flee more than two decades later. Um 'Abdallah was riding a bus from her home in Masaken Barzeh to the main market of the city, probably to shop for the cloth she sewed into school clothes for her daughters because they couldn't afford store-bought ones. She noticed that the normally busy streets were quite deserted that day but was still surprised when the bus was stopped by a group of uniformed young women, a squadron of female parachutists associated with the regime, a kind of hybrid Girl Scouts and paramilitary troops. The parachute girls (*madhalliyyat*), as they were commonly

6. The Ba'ath Party is a Pan-Arabist political party first founded in 1943 in Syria. The party advocated for a single Arab socialist nation and was the ruling party in Syria from 1963 to 2024 and, in a rival form, in Iraq from 1968 to 2003.

7. On the *mukhabarat*, see Van Dam, *The Struggle for Power in Syria*, 114.

8. Middle East Watch, *Syria Unmasked*, 59–60.

known and would be remembered in family tradition, stormed into the bus, yanking the headscarves off women passengers, including Um 'Abdallah, who was wearing a small square kerchief knotted under her chin. The violation of her casual head covering by these female agents of the state felt far worse than the violation of her privacy by a strange man's gaze would have been. When she somehow made her way back to her home, having covered her head with a piece of cloth offered by a sympathetic taxi driver, she was sobbing. From that point on, she wore her hijab formally, pinned tightly under her chin, determined if not defiant, asserting her culture. Her daughters and granddaughters did, too. The hijab hadn't been political until the state politicized it, but it became their identity as Muslims and as women.

Over the next decades of Assad family rule, ordinary people like Um 'Abdallah and her daughters wore and lived their identity as pious Sunni Muslims in their clothing choices as much as in their five daily prayers and Ramadan fast. They wore the hijab-style headscarves and manteaus, or loosely belted trench coats, that announced their religious affiliation even as they concealed their hair and body shape. But they lived silently in an uneasy symbiosis with the state power that could descend on them at any time, as the parachute girls had. Salma and her sisters attended government public schools and dutifully repeated and largely internalized the state's propaganda. They wore their hijabs right up to the school door, took them off as required for class, and then put them on again when they left the school premises. Their menfolk were drafted into military service in the ramshackle army unless they could exploit the many loopholes to the conscription law. The family paid bribes and fines anytime they needed a license or a service from the government. They never dared to complain about the shortages of basic food such as sugar and cooking oil or the lack of infrastructure, let alone the lack of political rights, at least not without shuttering the windows of their house and speaking in whispers among themselves. Neighbors and even relatives were encouraged to inform on anyone suspected of disloyalty to the state.

2

Trapped in the City

Maryam, 2011

Through the 1980s and 1990s, Salma's widowed mother, Um 'Abdallah, presided over a household of daughters getting married, leaving home, having babies, returning home when they fought with or separated from their husbands, making peace, making ends meet, and making more babies. All the sisters and their children could be found weekly (if not daily) in the family's cinder-block house in Masaken Barzeh, which had grown over the decades from two rooms to three floors, each with a kitchen and bathroom. An American woman who visited in the 1990s called it "the republic of beautiful women,"[1] and for the tight-knit set of sisters and their kids it was a refuge from turbulent marriages. Over tea, coffee, and fruit, they animatedly discussed their rights and responsibilities as Muslim women, religion and nationalism, fashion and popular culture.[2] During the 1990s, they were avid followers of Shaykh Ramadan al-Buti, a Sunni preacher who had once been imprisoned but was rehabilitated by the government and given a platform on state TV. His sermons, now acceptable to the regime, combined moderate Islam with state loyalism. It provided a frame that fit the family's views for most of the 1990s

1. Personal conversation.

2. On conservative Muslim women's agency, see Muhanna, *Agency and Gender in Gaza*. Conservative Muslim women's capacity for agency has been thoroughly manhandled in the theoretical scholarship. See al-Ali and Pratt, *Women and War*.

and 2000s.[3] They would come to feel bitterly and personally betrayed when al-Buti remained loyal to the regime in 2011 and 2012.

In the weeks before her death from cancer in the spring of 2011, Um ʻAbdallah was being cared for in her daughters' apartments in the suburbs, surrounded by her children and grandchildren. She had watched the Tunisian and Egyptian revolutions unfolding on Al Jazeera and other satellite stations and saw the early nonviolent demonstrations start in Syria's cities, the horror of the arrest and torture of the schoolboys in Darʻa, and even the first deaths in the suburbs around her. She had shaken her fist feebly at the dictators, cursing them mildly, and telling them to take their stolen money and leave. Unlike her grandchildren's parents, she did not dissuade them from demonstrating; if the authorities ever asked them who taught them to be dissidents, she told them, "Let them know it was your grandmother, Um ʻAbdallah." As a girl, she had protested the French colonial presence in Syria, and all her grandchildren knew the protest chant from the 1930s and 1940s that she always sang like a nursery rhyme:

> My father is a beautiful lad, don't you dare curse him
> Curse your father, you French daughter of a dog
> Bark, bark, you dog
> You have no place in my heart
> Your heart is a dagger strike
> My heart is sugar and marzipan

It was a blessing, her daughters agreed later, that she didn't live long enough to see what Bashar would do to her country and her beloved city. She could not have imagined that Syria's president, once Syrians' hope for a less authoritarian future, would join the ranks of the dictators firing on their country's people. In fact, Bashar would make Tunisia's Ben Ali, Egypt's Mubarak, and Libya's Qaddafi look

3. On al-Buti, see Christmann, "Islamic Scholar and Religious Leader"; on the relationship between religious leaders and the state, see Pierret, *Religion and State in Syria*.

comparatively benign in his ruthless response, which would kill more than half a million and displace half the country's population.

Salma's oldest sister, Maryam, was one of the most frequent visitors to her mother's house. As the senior surviving sister, she became the gentle successor to her mother. Maryam had married the boy next door when Salma was just a little girl and had raised her family in Qabun, a short walk away across a busy highway from her parents' and in-laws' houses in Masaken Barzeh. Although she was known in her family as the most gentle and delicate of her sisters, she quickly grew to resent and despise her parents-in-law, who were a constant meddling presence in her life. She couldn't escape because of their proximity. They kept watch over her comings and goings, what she wore and the money she spent, and made her feel guilty if she failed to call on them every time she visited her own family. Years into the war, Maryam avoided discussing politics with one of her husband's brothers, who was rumored to be a government informer.

Her husband, Abu Jamil, worked as a painter and plasterer all his life, but as he grew older, making a living became a true struggle, and Maryam's family expected less and less of him.[4] Maryam and her children lived in a small apartment, the same one she had married into at the beginning of the 1980s. Her married daughters lived a couple of miles away. She had wanted better for them than her own claustrophobic married life and made sure to fend off suitors who did not own homes and businesses, but even financial security couldn't ensure her daughters' happiness.

In the conservative and pious circles that the Araj family moved in, arranged marriages were the norm. A family like theirs was embedded in a rich tangle of kin and social relations. The elders of the family generally provided animated connections with their own siblings and cousins, exchanging visits on the multiple-day-long 'Id holidays every year, dropping in on one another when in the neighborhood,

4. On families' struggle to make a living in Syria, see Gallagher, *Making Do in Damascus*.

gathering for engagement and wedding parties. Gender segregation was the prevailing ethos, but mothers, aunts, and older sisters monitored growing children, girls especially, with a keen eye for optimizing future matches with prospective grooms in their circles. Third, second, even first cousins sometimes paired up for meetings or engagements, but the system generally expanded to neighbors, school friends, work acquaintances, and their bride-seeking relatives.

As beautiful, modest, smart, but unpretentious young women, the Araj sisters entertained a constant stream of matchmakers (*khattabat*) courting them for the young men in their lives. Intergenerational delegations of relatives—mother, aunts, sisters, grandmothers even—and neighborhood ladies surrounding a prospective groom would request a visit or even appear unannounced, asking to see the girls of the family. The oldest eligible sister would dutifully appear, nicely dressed, quiet and courteous, to serve the ladies the obligatory tiny cup of coffee. For the most part, the visits were pleasant social affairs to be endured. They strengthened the network of family relationships as well as the information and intelligence exchange that bound women's circles together. The girls knew that they could sabotage the event by spilling coffee or water on their guests or by being loud or uncourteous, but they instead generally discouraged overeager matchmakers by indicating that they were planning to study and go to college, a euphemism for not being available for marriage.[5]

When the two sides got along well, a second visit might be in order, followed by a request that the prospective groom be brought along to see if an engagement were possible. With all the womenfolk present, the prospective couple would make small talk and assess whether there were interest and compatibility between them. If so, then direct or mediated negotiations about the *mahr*, or bridal gifts, would ensue. The mutual agreeability and burgeoning attraction of the couple, the approval of teams of outspoken female relatives, and

5. On the social, cultural, and legal aspects of arranging marriages, see Carlisle, "From Behind the Door"; Joubin, *The Politics of Love*; and Joubin, *Mediating the Uprising Narratives*.

the negotiation of a reasonable material transaction in which the bride's family made clear their expectations for material and lifestyle support offered a pathway to marriage that was adaptable to the young women's own preferences. But the frank discussion of matters of attraction and financial prospects among extensively interested parties not distracted by emotion resulted in a system geared toward the reproduction of class and of pious communities.

A couple of Um 'Abdallah's sons-in-law had undertaken various unsuccessful ventures to export Syrian-made consumer goods to North Africa and the Persian/Arab Gulf countries in the 1980s and 1990s, but they were minnows trying to swim with sharks of globalization, and their entrepreneurial risk-taking had compromised their marriages and weakened their families. When Maryam was looking for suitable husbands for her older daughters in the 1990s, she worked hard to match them with men who had marketable trades in the Syrian economy.

One daughter's husband, Waleed, a tailor, summed up the new Syrian economy in an anecdote. After Bashar came to power, Waleed rented a cheap basement space for a small workshop to sew men's shirts and women's manteaus. The street was lined with similar workshops taking advantage of the space that was not suitable for either residences or retail purposes. But a government inspector soon came to announce a newly imposed and prohibitively high tax on the rented spaces that seemed designed to clear out the small tailors from their new niche. Despairing, Maryam's son-in-law improbably found relief when one of his workers revealed that his wife had a connection to a prominent Alawite surgeon through her job as a house cleaner. After a few phone calls, the surgeon's help was enlisted for *wasta*, "connections," to exempt the workshop. The next time the tax collector came by, the surgeon's name was invoked, and the tax bill was waived. The son-in-law's relief was short-lived, however, when his new and unseen "partner" claimed a 50 percent share of the enterprise's profits. This casual rapaciousness reflected the pattern of Syria's transition into the global economy. Every business worth engaging in—especially tech and infrastructure, including the country's cell phone providers—would be dominated by members of the ruling elite partnering with the entrepreneurs running the operation, whether the entrepreneurs liked it or not.[6]

Maryam's three youngest children, especially her only son, Jamil, were determined to study their way to a better life. Education seemed a far more promising option than early marriage. Jamil and the sisters closest to him in age set about studying at some of the many private institutes that bridged the gap between high school and university. Especially since the accession to the presidency in 2000 of Bashar al-Assad, the ruling family's most educated and cosmopolitan son, the rising generation could easily imagine studying their way into professional careers—courses in English, business, technical medical training, graphic design, computers, and software were options for them. Syrian society, slowly opening from a drab socialist self-sufficiency, provided a deceptively calm and stable backdrop for the drama of the sisters' personal lives.

Jamil lived with his family in Qabun, one town to the east of Masaken Barzeh, a farming village turned suburb. He commuted every day to the town of Duma, a half-hour outside the city in the densely populated suburban band known as the Ghuta.[7] He was studying business administration at an institute there, a town that was the seat of government of the Rif Dimashq farming belt around Damascus, now turned suburb.

6. On the relationship between the ruling elite and business in Syria, see B. Haddad, *Business Networks in Syria.*

7. On the Ghuta region, see the classic work Kurd 'Ali, *Ghutat Dimashq*; see also Khayr, *Ghuṭat Dimashq*. The Ghuta region had a number of sensitive regime sites. Air Force Intelligence and the Sironix Electronics factory were located in Qabun. The Center for Scientific Research, associated with the regime's chemical weapons programs and likely destroyed by an Israeli missile strike in 2018, was in Masaken Barzeh. Military depots located in Harasta were targeted by rebels in 2012 and 2013.

Duma was renowned locally for its stubborn rural ways and its working-class piety.[8] All of Syria was rocked by the violence in Dar'a on March 6, 2011, and some of the earliest demonstrations in the next week were held in the center of the capital city, but provincial Duma was the first town around Damascus to rise up in sustained rage at the atrocities in Dar'a. It would become one of the hottest opposition quarters around the capital and one of the first places in the Damascus region where demonstrations turned into street battles with the police and paramilitaries.[9] It was the first part of the Damascus region to be formally besieged by the regime.[10] Other suburbs soon experienced the same pattern of rebellion and siege.

Traveling daily by *mikro*, shared taxi, into a town that had more in common with Dar'a than with cosmopolitan central Damascus, Jamil had a preview of the coming conflict, witnessing the brutal regime response to the demonstrations in Duma—teargas, shooting,

8. Batatu, *Syria's Peasantry.*

9. The Day of Rage emanated from Dar'a as the citizens demanded the release of their boys on March 15, and it then resonated around the country. There was a demonstration that day, organized through Facebook, at the Hamidiyya Market in the heart of Damascus. The next day, March 16, protests erupted in Marjeh Square, the heart of the downtown commercial and government district. On March 18, the protest spread to the Umayyad Mosque, the city's religious center, with calls for dignity and freedom. A heavy security presence arrested demonstrators and kept the protests in check.

10. On March 25, 2011, in the outer suburbs the first truly sizeable antigovernment demonstrations took place in Duma, Barzeh, and Qabun, the boys' home territory. Barzeh's first martyrs were shot that day outside the al-Salam Mosque. The rhythm of protest was established by the next Friday, April 1. Bashar al-Assad attempted to quell the rising anger with a damage-control speech on Thursday, March 31, but crowds mobilized around the central mosque of Duma, and government troops fired into them, killing a dozen protesters and injuring many more, Duma's first martyrs. Duma was besieged by the regime on April 25. The hometown of Army of Islam leader Zahran Alloush, who had been jailed by the regime for Islamist activity in 2009 and released in June 2011, would become a stronghold for that Saudi-supported faction in the next years.

roadblocks.[11] In the early demonstrations—completely peaceful with no weapons at all, he emphasized—Jamil noticed that there would be three times as many police and paramilitary troops as there were demonstrators. Even at that time, in the very first days of what people called "the revolution," he was seeing snipers on the rooftops in the opposition stronghold of Duma. It made him nervous that even at Friday prayers in Duma, secret-police officers would check the congregants' government-issued or university IDs going into mosques.[12]

On April 3, a mass funeral for those killed two days earlier was attended by more than 100,000 mourners and accompanied by a general strike, so Jamil could not get to his business school in Duma from Qabun. This rupture of his daily commute was the beginning of the disruption of his education. He and his cousins in Masaken Barzeh instead attended a sympathetic demonstration in honor of the martyrs. The pattern of movement established during

11. On March 25, 2011, hastily organized loyalist counterdemonstrations, loudly proclaiming fealty to the Assad regime, dominated the main squares of Damascus, and the momentum of protest began to shift from the city center to the capital's popular peripheries. The mosques of the ancient and very traditional southern quarters Kafr Susa and Midan became the new center of urban demonstrations. Between April 3 and 7, the government tried making concessions by sending officials to pay condolences to the town officials of Duma, but it was too late for half measures. By the middle of April, people all around Damascus continued to demonstrate, security forces continued to attack them, and the government tried to manage the crisis by blaming the Muslim Brotherhood and external actors. Smaller demonstrations were taking place in many neighborhoods of central Damascus and at the University of Damascus campus. On Friday, April 15, the afternoon protests of several Ghuta suburbs, including Jobar and Zamalka, started moving toward the center of Damascus from the east. Troops fired randomly into the crowds and blocked their progress with makeshift barriers, preventing them from reaching the east-side traffic hub of 'Abbasid Square.

12. In "Syrian Protesters Clash with Security Forces," the journalists Liam Stack and J. David Goodman also noted this checking of IDs at the main Umayyad Mosque in Damascus. See also "Taqrir kamil 'an al-Qasf wal-Damar wa Harq Mashfa al-Fatih Kafr Batna," video from September 8, 2012.

those demonstrations of late March and early April would foreshadow the coming battle for Damascus: the residents of working-class and pious suburbs would boil up and move toward the city center; then the regime would use a series of escalating measures to stop them.[13]

Jamil, about twenty when the revolution broke out, was not only the youngest child but also the only son. Raised among girls and fiercely protected by them, he was a gentle and sweet-natured boy, neat and very fashion conscious, with shoulder-length hair that raised some eyebrows in the tough village of Qabun, with its reputation for rural machismo. His mother, Maryam, Salma's older sister, would have physically confined him to their small apartment if she could have, and his father sternly forbade him to attend the weekly demonstrations outside the local mosque. He was their only son, they kept reminding him. Also, Abu Jamil often remarked quietly and cautiously that the regime was far too strong to take down. "They have been preparing to repress an uprising as long as they have been in power," he warned his son. "They knew this day would come, while we are like children, naive and hopeful."

Having seen the early government response in Duma, Jamil avoided Friday prayers in his home quarter of Qabun. But like his younger cousins, 'Adel and Yusuf, he could not stay away from the impromptu protests in the streets around his home and covered his face in a scarf to hide his identity when he went out and marched. On more than one occasion, he was first embarrassed and then delighted to run into his own father at the demonstrations in spite of Abu Jamil's ban, and they marched along together. Qabun would be one of the first places to see an armed FSA presence, defectors from

13. On this pattern, see Yazigi, *The Story of a Place*, 79, 57, 33, 125, 169; Fassihi and Solomon, "Syria Regime Rocked by Protests"; Slackman, "Syria's Cabinet Resigns"; and Lesch, "Bashar's Fateful Decision," 128. See also Firas, "Awal Mudhahara fi Duma (Salat al-'Asr fi Sahat al-Baladiya)," video; and Al Jazeera English, "Violence Continues Across Syria."

the Syrian military who took their sidearms with them to protect the protestors.[14]

The demonstrations provided a thrilling sense of popular solidarity and will as the crowd offered protection and inspiration. Jamil's sisters later remembered taking their young children in strollers out in spring and summer of 2011 for some of the bigger funerary protests. The spirit of the crowd was irrepressible, and the presence of armed FSA soldiers provided a sense of security, although it turned out to be a false sense. Jamil's older sister Rose shuddered palpably over tea in her German apartment in 2017 when she recalled those protests and what could have happened to her two young toddler sons, now middle-school students in Germany.

In the beginning, there was some protection in the size of the massive crowds at protests, but the young men of the Ghuta suburbs—targeted by a sniper, pulled aside at a checkpoint, hustled into a car, or summoned by a knock on the door in the night—were exposed and vulnerable. One incident was particularly alarming for Jamil as he crossed from the safer district of Masaken Barzeh into the restive Qabun area. He had been visiting another sister's house. She had just given birth, and he had gone to meet his new nephew. In a good mood, happy for his sister, he was walking back home a couple of miles along the busy main street of the neighborhood in the rain, but when he got near the intersection that separated the two quarters, he suddenly noticed with a chill that the usually busy street was empty.

A plainclothes officer got out of a taxi parked, engine idling, at the corner. The man demanded Jamil's identity card (*hawwiya*), and Jamil felt his innards tighten. His phone, he noticed, was dead. The man invited him into the car and asked again for his ID. Thinking

14. The Free Syrian Army is a rebel group formed by army deserters in 2011. Its banner was adopted by armed groups across Syria. Based in Turkey, the FSA's leaders had decreasing operational control over what was happening on the ground in Syria as the decade of conflict dragged on.

quickly, he asked if his Ba'ath Party membership card would be acceptable, implying that he was a regime supporter. He had prepared it for just such an occasion and handed over the *hawwiya* and the party membership card at the same time. When they asked him where he lived, he did not mention the name of the rebel suburb Qabun or give his address but just said he lived near the police academy, continuing to salt his answers with references to the regime.

A driver and an officer sat in the front seat, and Jamil was squeezed between another officer and a local informer who had his face covered with a scarf. The informer was probably one of his neighbors, who was able to bolster his loyalist credentials and supplement his income by informing on people in the neighborhood. They asked Jamil pointedly if he had attended antiregime demonstrations. He denied it, claiming to be "a very respectable person" who strongly preferred law and order. He was lying, of course, because, as he put it later, "he hadn't missed a single demonstration." He asked the officers if everything was OK, and they told him that he was to be taken to the neighborhood police office just to check everything out. He feigned nonchalance, concealing his rising panic.

Halfway to the police station, they parked the car on the side of the road. Suspecting a trap, he kept up with the lie. He urged them to continue on to the police station, but they, seemingly persuaded that he had nothing to hide and would be a waste of their time (or, worse for them, was connected to a party official), told him he was free to leave. When he got out of the car, his legs were shaking so much that his knees were literally knocking against each other. He trudged home in the rain. He didn't tell his parents and sisters what had happened until much later when they were safely in Egypt. He concealed everything from his family because he had no doubt that they, his mother in particular, would never let him out of the house again.

3

A River of Hope

Hanan, Spring 2011

The other three sisters—Hanan, Farida, and Iba—living to the east and south of the capital city, experienced the erosion of normalcy more directly than their better-off family in the northern areas. They lived on the far side of the highway that bisected the core city from the outer ring of former farming villages and orchards that were now restive suburbs. Throughout the end of 2011, the easy access to the central city that the sisters had always taken for granted was slipping away. The city and its sprawling suburbs, a complex assemblage of forces, institutions, and flows, never static in the dullest of times, were changing along their lines of flight, tracing a trajectory of escape from the structures of authoritarian habit.[1] The Damascus suburbs where most of Um ʿAbdallah's daughters lived would be in open rebellion by the beginning of 2012. After the rhythmic weekly cycle of popular protest, bloody government reprisal, and mass funeral march circled in on the capital throughout 2011, the rebels of the FSA began to organize armed resistance in Duma, Qabun, and the neighboring towns.[2] These neighborhoods were some of the most dangerous to live in because they would

1. A substantial literature on the city as assemblage exists; see, for example, Farías, "The Politics of Urban Assemblages"; McFarlane, "Assemblage and Critical Urbanism"; and Mills, "Cultures of Assemblage."

2. On the early organized military resistance, see O'Bagy, *The Free Syrian Army.*

quickly go from bloody clashes to all-out urban warfare by the middle of 2012.[3]

Middle sisters Hanan and Farida were younger than Maryam and older than Salma. As partners to ambitious husbands in the 1990s, they had once lived in rented apartments in better areas in the center of Damascus proper, but now, after having been abandoned by their husbands for years, they considered themselves lucky to have shabby, tiny apartments in the Eastern Ghuta suburbs of Hamoria and ʻAyn Tarma. Their apartments were on the top floors of five-story walk-ups, unfinished buildings with dark and dingy stairwells and neighbors who rarely socialized together. These sisters' fortunes had declined, but they were cheerful and positive, thanking God constantly, and their apartments were spotless and decorated with paper flowers and other homemade ornaments. Hanan, whose husband lost his fortune and reputation in failed overseas business ventures, worked as a freelance seamstress, specializing in glamorous evening gowns that a bride could custom order for her engagement and wedding celebrations. Hanan's daughters and nieces would design fanciful confections of satin and tulle in drawings featuring huge-eyed manga cartoon princesses, and Hanan would sew them in sparkly cloth from the city's textile markets.

Hanan and her sisters had been unlucky in marriage, failing to vet their suitors effectively for financial and emotional stability and paying the price over decades (although Salma and Iba's husbands later met the challenges of exile well).[4] But Hanan's faith, family, and work anchored her, and she projected a happy resilience. In nostalgic prose, she later described her domestic life in the suburbs, connected to family and friends throughout the city in her mind and in daily and weekly visits. "We lived in a modest house, and our life was calm and quiet. In the morning on a typical day, I would

3. On the shift from clash to warfare, see Azmeh and LSE Middle East Centre, "The Uprising of the Marginalised."

4. On the outcomes of arranged marriage, see Hoodfar, *Between Marriage and the Market.*

hear the birds singing, watch the sunrise from my balcony after the morning prayer, and water my plants. I would drink my coffee and think of my mother and sisters and our neighbors, all drinking their coffee and watering their plants on their respective balconies." Hanan's morning routine was bound up with her sisters, her married daughters, and the city. As she looked out over the bleak landscape of apartments as poorly built as her own and a haze of air pollution from kerosene heaters and diesel minivans, she imagined her sisters, although all of them separated now by marriage and urban geography, moving through the same routine of prayer, coffee, gardening.

Like many traditional Syrian women, the sisters tended their houseplants with affection and enthusiasm whether they had a balcony, a courtyard, or even just a windowsill. Plant life, usually potted in cut-off multiliter tins that once held olive oil or ghee, was one of the ways a house was made a home. Sisters and friends inquired about one another's gardens with real interest and expressed their friendship by exchanging shoots and grafts of their favorite or most beautiful plants. The daily tending to the plants—watering, conversing, singing to them—was a ritual, a bit like prayer. For Hanan, the daily rituals of caffeine and sugar—tiny cups of strong sweet coffee drunk in the morning, midafternoon, and night and strong black tea brewed straight in the pot with abundant sugar until it reached the dark-orange color they called *mith 'ayn al dik*, "like the rooster's eye"—were what synchronized her with her sisters.

For Hanan—a half-hour to the east of downtown in the hamlet of Hamoria, where dozens of small workshops still lining the streets produced the elaborate carved furniture sets favored by Syria's upwardly mobile households—crossing from her embattled area of town into the government-controlled city center was in the spring of 2011 increasingly like going from one country to another. Several government checkpoints at key intersections slowed and filtered passage from the rebel suburbs to the quiet city proper. The ID checks were not particularly threatening for her as an older woman, but her son and son-in-law faced constant scrutiny, and, like all young men, they went far out of their way to avoid the checkpoints.

Hanan expressed her feelings about the beginning of the revolution. She and her sisters were respectable, pious, older women. They were not drawn to the excitement of the demonstrations as their sons were, but they felt the historic importance of the moment more acutely than their children did.[5] Hanan remembered the sense of foreboding that coincided with her mother's terminal illness and the sense of urgency that something huge was about to happen.

She took the time to express her feelings in a letter.

> It was a day that Syrians had never dared to believe would come. They never even dared to dream it when they were asleep. It was something that could happen all over the world, but never here in this country. And yet it happened. It came, like an unexpected guest, and the people welcomed it as they would someone returning from after a long, long absence, in which they didn't know if he were alive or dead. It was a day that finally arrived, and when the spark was lit, it blew up the whole sky with light. The revolution was like an earthquake, and people were watching silently, waiting and watching. This was during the time that my mother got sick. I wanted to enjoy every minute with her, and I wanted her to see that the revolution was coming. Everyone without exception was living in a state of extreme watchfulness, suspended animation, to see what would happen. We all knew, with certainty, that if the spark was lit, this would be a unique time in history. Unprecedented in hope and joy, but also in ugliness and bloodshed.

Aside from the strong sense of imminent change, Hanan's first real indication of the revolution, as for many of her sisters, had to do with access to different parts of the city. Since the economic opening up of the 1990s, a dense network of privately owned, diesel-fueled minivan *mikroyat* ran routes joining the suburbs to one another and to the city center.[6] Although the sisters' homes were scattered about the metropolitan area, they saw each other on a daily basis because

5. On women's view of the war, see Mikati, "Women and the Syrian Conflict."

6. For more on urban transportation in Syria, see Hopfinger and Khadour, "The Development of the Transportation Sector in Syria."

of the *mikroyat*, which cost a regular fare of five to fifteen Syrian lira per passenger (about ten to thirty US cents.) As Damascenes who happened to be living in the suburbs, they felt deeply and took for granted that they had the right to every part of the city—the downtown markets, the family's ancestral Midan quarter to the south, the Masaken Barzeh northern suburbs, even the cafés and institutes of the posh and largely loyalist western suburb of Mezzeh.

Hanan's first indication that the anticipated day had arrived was when she and Maryam went to a neighborhood in the south of the city to sell some of their handicrafts at a craft fair and exhibition. Her family called her on her cell phone and told her to stay where she was, take shelter with relatives who lived nearby, and not try and come back on the main street into the Eastern Ghuta. The army had blocked the road back and was firing live ammunition. The two sisters "dropped in" on a cousin for an extended visit and waited until they received notice that the street was clear again, but this experience was a warning of things to come.

On Friday, April 22, 2011, Hanan felt that the day of revolution had finally arrived as she was returning home from an adult literacy class she taught at a mosque in her suburban town, Hamoria. She was engulfed in and swept along in a demonstration that moved her profoundly. Designated "Great Friday," as the culmination of the previous weeks' Friday protests and the actual day of the Christian celebration of Good Friday, marking the crucifixion of Christ, huge demonstrations in all the towns of the Ghuta converged toward the point where the Ghuta met 'Abbasid Square in Damascus.[7] The square was the eastern main traffic circle and site of the city's soccer stadium. Young men in the neighborhood had put an amplifier on a three-wheeled vehicle (*turtaira*) and were blasting the song "Ya

7. The early uprising was distinctly secular and multifaith, and it was focused on political reform, although by 2012 the resistance would begin to take on an Islamist and sectarian tone as resistance became armed, casualties skyrocketed, and Sunni extremists released from Assad's prisons and Iraq took leadership roles. See Phillips, "Sectarianism and Conflict in Syria."

hayf" (What a Shame) by Samih Choukeir. The song's powerful lyrics shamed the government for what it was doing to the young people, and Hanan felt it permeate the city's atmosphere in those first weeks.[8]

The new feeling of hope and anticipation was in her later descriptions of that period: it was "a tiny shy green shoot that split a rock and emerged." Her memories of the time are full of plant and water metaphors. She elaborated in her letters. "The young men were like flowers, and the whole event was like a beautiful living artwork, like a river of hope. Demonstrations, demonstrations, demonstrations. Banners and singing, like a beautiful living creature, dancing through the streets." Seeing the young people out in the street gave her generation hope. She was inspired by the young men "shaking off the dust of so many years." She felt "as if her heart was being washed clean" of all the years of cynicism and resignation.[9] The young people were like "olive branches," and the hearts of their elders were restored to life by the sight. They reminded Hanan "that we deserved to live like human beings and not like stones. So many people kept that hope alive in their hearts, afraid to show it to the butcher."

But that very day at the Zablatani crossing near ʻAbbasid Square, where the demonstrators hoped to join with downtown demonstrations, the regime "drew back its lips and showed its canine teeth (*kashar ʻan anyabih*)." Those boys Hanan likened to olive branches began to fall immediately, first on the Zamalka Bridge on the way to ʻAbbasid Square. She found the predatory metaphor perfectly expressed her feelings. "The regime was like a predator that was more than ready to attack its prey. There would be butchery and revenge like we had never seen. Almost immediately the victims began to fall, young people like flowers, in the flower of their lives. Their blood was clean and pure, like a benediction for a long journey ahead."[10]

8. On music and the rebellion, see Agha, "Intonations of Grief."

9. For a classic analysis of cultural and psychological complexities of life in Baʻathist Syria, see Wedeen, *Ambiguities of Domination*.

10. On the atmospherics of protest, see Aciksoz, "Medical Humanitarianism Under Atmospheric Violence." On the Arab Spring, see Gregory, "Tahrir";

More than a hundred protesters were thought to have been killed that day. The next day, April 23, another massive funeral for the martyrs brought even more highly energized people out into the streets of the Ghuta. With this wave of massive and emotional protests two days in a row, the situation was beginning to look like an uprising, no longer a containable series of protests. On April 25, the government changed its strategy, and both Duma to the north and Dar'a to the south were blockaded and besieged for weeks. Qabun and other towns along the eastern periphery of the Ghuta would be among the places where armed rebels began to appear.[11]

One of Hanan's sons, Sayf, was at the Zablatani massacre, and he came home later that night exhausted. He had twisted his ankle running home amid gunfire and made it back to the neighborhood with difficulty. He came in breathlessly telling his mother and sisters stories that "were like horror movies." Now that he had seen these sights, it would not be long before he would take up arms with the defecting Syrian army soldiers and officers who formed the FSA.

In the meantime, daily life was becoming impossible in the suburbs. Hanan's daughter Fatin was pregnant with her second child in late 2011. Her mother made arrangements for labor and delivery at a hospital in the city center where Hanan's aunt was the head nurse. When her daughter went into labor, and Hanan called her aunt at the hospital to let her know they would be coming, her aunt sounded uncharacteristically shifty and evasive. Hanan was puzzled,

---

Kanna, "Urban Praxis and the Arab Spring"; and Ramadan, "From Tahrir to the World." See also Yazigi, *The Story of a Place*, 126; "Sham – Dimashq – al-Qabun bi Mudhaharat al-Jum'a al-'Adhima 4/22," video; Redmarch 1, "Zufaf Shuhada' al-Qabun," video; and Albayan, "Mudhaharat Jum'at Isra al-Huriyya Hay al-Qabun," video.

11. In the widespread demonstrations that took place after Friday prayers on April 22, 2011, Qabun would feature prominently. The day was dubbed "Great Friday," and after-prayer protests were scheduled in at least twenty towns across Syria. That day in Qabun, government forces killed at least a dozen people in the streets. They killed five in Barzeh. It was the deadliest day of the year so far and the first of several notable massacres in Qabun.

but, flustered as her daughter's contractions quickened, she and her daughter got into a taxi and navigated their way to the hospital. As they sat in the waiting room, the staff went about their business with hushed whispers. When soldiers ran through the halls, Hanan and her daughter realized that the hospital was being raided by government troops.

The troops suspected that a wounded rebel was being treated in the hospital and were searching for the suspect, room by room. Hanan's aunt, the head nurse, hadn't dared mention the situation on the phone, simply wanting them to stay away until the raid was over. When Hanan's son-in-law joined them, he was roughly questioned and accused of being a rebel. As Fatin's doctor decided to deliver by C-section, government troops burst into the sterilized operating room. Fatin's anesthesiologist was accused of having treated the wounded rebel. They cornered him in the operating theater and threatened to remove him from the surgery. The obstetric surgeon was able to summon enough medical authority to shame the troops out of the operating room. The baby was born, and the family traced its way back home. But Hanan's children persuaded her that she, her elderly husband, and unmarried daughter, Warda, should leave town for the safety of her married daughter Sara's household in Jordan.

4

Rebelling Suburbs

Iba, Spring 2012

The youngest of the five sisters, Iba, also co-owned a house with her husband, Hisham, in the Eastern Ghuta area that by 2012 became the frontline of the battle for Damascus. Looking back on the time when the revolution turned into an all-out war, Iba invoked a phrase that had caught her eye in her readings. "We were like frogs in a slowly boiling pot of water," she said. "Only a few were able to get out in time, while most waited until it was too late." Iba's piercing brown eyes and strong features gave her a contrasting appearance to most of her fairer sisters. Unlike her older sisters, who moved to the suburbs following declines in their marriages, she married for love directly into the scruffier working-class neighborhoods of the suburbs. In the early years of her marriage, she had for a time worn a niqab that covered her whole face—in part out of her intense piety but more as a shield against the male gazes in the rough lower-income neighborhood where she now lived. Her siblings had raised her to be strong and assertive, and she would be decisive in leaving Damascus as the war encroached on her neighborhood.

Iba and Hisham were married in the mid-1990s, and by then a working man with only basic education and limited family support, like Hisham, who had nine siblings, could not dream of buying a house with legal title. Hisham had dropped out of school and trained as a shoemaker to make the slippers and heel-less sandals that were ubiquitous indoor footwear throughout Syria. He supplemented his income by driving taxis and a minivan *mikro*. The couple had to pool all their resources, including her small inheritance and money saved from her premarriage work in a clinical laboratory, and borrow money from their relatives to afford a tiny house in the area between ʻAyn Tarma and the neighboring town of Zamalka.

But after Iba made her way from Lebanon to Turkey to Greece and eventually to southern Germany, she nostalgically described her neighborhood in the town turned suburb, ʻAyn Tarma.

> The neighborhood I used to live in was a quarter whose people were middle class and poor. This neighborhood of ʻAyn Tarma was built on agricultural land. Sadly, people had to build on agricultural lands and live in them because living in the city became extremely expensive and fantastically disproportionate to incomes. It was practically impossible when a young man wanted to get married to even think of living in the city because his income would not suffice for living, and it wasn't possible to even imagine buying our humble house in the city for a reasonable price. Even in the suburbs it was prohibitive, so, really, how would it be in the city?

The Ghuta, once an orchard hinterland for the walled city of Damascus, was an assemblage of older agricultural towns, uneven property rights, tangles of electricity distribution cables, groundwater wells and privately controlled water-distribution systems. The eastern farming villages of the Ghuta did not share in the mountain river systems of the northern suburbs, which were close to the Qalamun range dividing Syria from Lebanon. These villages drew their water from the valley aquifers, and their transformation into urban sprawl came after the more orderly settling of Barzeh and Qabun. For generations, the Ghuta had been the city's playground, a place of birch trees and irrigated orchards where families gathered for picnics and festivities. In Bashar's Syria, though, it was increasingly difficult to find a place there for a picnic.

Iba and Hisham's apartment building was illegally built, so each unit was precariously owned. The municipal infrastructure was insufficient, permits were hard to come by, and the nature of life reflected these limitations. Iba described the haphazard provision of electricity and water.

> And one of the bad things about living in places like this was the randomness and lack of any regulation. Everyone would build a building as they liked, after they paid the necessary bribes to the municipality, of course. And utilities and services were extremely weak. By this I mean water, electricity, and telephones. Every building would supply the services for itself by digging a well for water, for example, and this of course was against the rules, but the municipality didn't provide any other alternative. People would tap into electrical wires from the main cable on the nearest street, and this caused ugly and harmful scenes because the wires would hang down and be very dangerous, and sometimes they would get cut and hang down to the ground because there would be so much pressure on them, more than they could handle, and this would be even more dangerous in the winter, when there are puddles of rain on the ground.[1]

The assemblage also contained all the neighbors thrown together and the relations between them. Iba was proud of the role that her husband, Hisham, played in the quarter, mediating, solving disputes, starting the flow of money into a pool for collective services.

> And in addition, there would be fights between the neighbors because of the hanging of electrical wires, and people would accuse each other of taking too much electricity or running their space heaters constantly. And often these quarrels would take place right under my balcony, and we would hear everything because our house was on the corner, and we were living on the first floor. And my husband would go to see what the matter was and to try to resolve the matter between the neighbors. I would hear his voice, "OK, OK, hold on everybody. People, everything will be solved if

1. On housing, see Goulden, "Housing, Inequality, and Economic Change in Syria"; and the first three chapters of Ababsa et al., eds., *Popular Housing and Urban Land Tenure in the Middle East.*

> we just discuss this rationally. It's not a big deal. We will get some more wire. It's not worth fighting over a little bit of water and electricity! We are neighbors. Pray for the Prophet (sallu 'anabi)! God requires you to be nice to your seventh neighbor down the road!" And many times, he would come into the house and put his hand into the pocket of the shirt that hung behind the door to take money, and he would be the first to contribute to a pool of money to pay for the new wire for electricity even if he wasn't directly involved in the problem, just to solve the problem and sort everything out.

Despite these troubles, Iba loved her home. It was located between some old unbuilt fields but was on a corner of the main streets, so it had good access to transportation:

> Luckily the building that we lived in was on the main street and on the edge of the newly built area. Most of the buildings were crammed together, and the windows looked out on other buildings. And the buildings around it didn't differ in its structure and finishing at all from regular buildings, and it was on the main street and on the main transportation line as an added benefit. Behind the building was an old field that my son used to play in when he was little, ten or eleven years old, with his friends. And my daughters would also go down there and play in the shadow of the building with the neighbor girls. And it would make me very happy and relaxed when I used to hear the children's voices when they were playing happily there where I could keep an eye on them as I would sit on the balcony. And it would also make me happy to look out the window and see the orchards that hadn't been built over yet and the old sawmill that was across from my balcony and the sight of the wood piled up there. The smell of the wood was really nice, and it was a beautiful smell when it rained. I was so lucky and happy that I could live in a house and see from my window or my balcony the sky and green gardens and not just other buildings in my face.

Many of the people of the Eastern Ghuta were ready for a fight when the uprising began in 2011. Most of them happened to be

Sunni Muslims. There were the original villagers, pious agriculturalists whose traditional garden properties were largely cashed in to meet the city's housing needs, and the old Damascenes, who could no longer afford the inner city. The latter, mostly Sunnis, thought of themselves as the original Damascenes, pushed out by Ba'athists and the economy of corruption they associated with them. In the eastern and southern suburbs, loyalists and partisans of the regime were far outnumbered by those electrified by the popular energy of the Arab Spring and the possibilities it held.[2]

The FSA and its classically named brigades of fighters were gaining the upper hand and pushing the fight from their Ghuta stronghold into the city.[3] The barriers and checkpoints separating neighborhoods had become permanent features of the landscape as early as the fall of 2011. Rebel strongholds such as Duma, Zamalka, and 'Arbin were first besieged by the Syrian regime in August 2011. The rebels, who had local knowledge of the area and were beginning to receive aid from sponsors outside Syria, were able to establish supply lines and often to regain territory, so that areas changed hands violently throughout 2012. Regular regime shelling of FSA positions imperiled civilian populations, and although the rebels remained very popular for the first years of the war in the Ghuta, their presence was also unsettling. Just as the demonstrations had earlier circled the capital from the suburbs, the rebel brigades began to do so operationally in 2012. By January 2012, there were rebel contingents all over the Ghuta. In February 2012, a fierce battle on the highway outside Qabun killed as many as two hundred regime soldiers. Around that time, on another battle front in Homs, the regime began using aerial bombardment from helicopter gunships.

The FSA, which was increasingly composed of neighborhood-affiliated brigades with classical Islamic names, seemed to be gaining

2. On the Sunnis' political position in the suburbs, see Pierret, *Religion and State in Syria*, 226–30.

3. Spyer, "Defying a Dictator"; Baczko et al., *Civil War in Syria*.

ground. Rebel bombing campaigns hit targets in the city in December 2011 and in March and May 2012. At the outset, the demonstrations were coordinated by the Local Coordinating Committees, which were secular, political, and nonviolent in their constitution and aims.[4] Even though the vast majority of mosques were staffed by state-appointed clerics who dared not deviate from the government's line and did their best to quell protests, Friday prayers were the prelude to demonstrations, and mosques were the geographical starting points.[5] The Midan quarter, to which the sisters' family traced its origins, was an ancient and conservative part of the city proper, but it extended through the southern suburbs of the Ghuta. Its mosques and their preachers were among the most outspoken in providing advice (*nasiha*) to Bashar on how to deal with popular demands for reform. As the Friday protests of 2011 gained momentum, the Midan's key mosques were preemptively blocked off in anticipation of protest, but protests simply moved from blocked mosques to neighboring unblocked mosques. The Midan demonstrations were notable because they were also well attended by opposition-linked artists—musicians and television personalities—who were distinctly secular.[6]

But religion crept into the fabric of the protests. Anyone killed by the regime was a *shahid*, or martyr; this was the default linguistic convention nurtured by decades of journalism about resistance fighters throughout the Arab world. It was simply a respectful way of referring to those who sacrificed their lives in a struggle against tyranny. But as more and more *shuhada* fell every week, the anticipation

4. On these committees, see Abu Hamed, *Syria's Local Coordination Committees*; al Shami, "Syria"; and Syrian Local Coordinating Committees, "We Are All Syrians and Syria Is for All."

5. Yassin-Kassab and al-Shami, *Burning Country*, 121–22.

6. In the Midan, demonstrations migrated from one closed mosque to the next, and artists joined the followers of the one rebel preacher who dared to stand up to the regime, Shaykh Karim Rajeh. The ninety-year-old cleric was forced to resign in May 2011. The regime bombed the Midan mosques in January and April 2012, anyway. Yazigi, *The Story of a Place*, 230.

of death was easier with a religious worldview. References to God, the battle cry "Allahu akbar!," and the utterance of the Islamic *shahada* as last words became fortifications at the personal level. At the organizational level, bands of local youths found that using the name of a hero of classical Islamic antiquity was more effective than using the name of a local *shahid* or of a neighborhood school or street. This was especially true as funding from sponsors in the Gulf states made its way into the FSA structure as Islamists such as Zahran 'Alloush of Duma were released from Assad's prisons and moved into key roles, and as Shi'ite militias, such as the one founded by the notorious Abul Fadl 'Abbas, organized in the Shi'ite shrine village of Sayyida Zaynab in the Southern Ghuta.[7]

An uncle was killed in a street battle in the Midan district in the southern part of the city, caught while running an errand. An old family friend shocked everyone by ostentatiously declaring loyalty to the regime, including obsequious praise of the Syrian government and military, on his Facebook page, which was then regarded as toxic. Iba in particular went from wondering how she could contribute to the revolution to fighting a rising sense of vulnerability and anxiety. At the beginning of 2012, she felt that she was stable and blessed enough to contribute to the revolution. By the end of the same year, that optimism had vanished, and she knew in her bones that her children were in danger from snipers, mortar fire, even aerial attack in 'Ayn Tarma, the rebel stronghold suburb where she lived.

The first battle that Iba remembered took place in Duma, due north of 'Ayn Tarma. She and Hisham had been shopping in the city center and took the *mikro* to head home. There was more traffic than usual, so the driver could not take the usual route, and nervousness filled the van as strangers murmured to each other. As the driver inched through the traffic, he would ask the other drivers in nearby *mikroyat* what was going on. His face looked worried. Iba was sitting in the

7. On the Islamists, see Lund, *Syria's Salafi Insurgents*; on the militias, see Anzalone, "Zaynab's Guardians," 16.

back and couldn't hear because of all the car horns and traffic noise but was watching the driver's face in the rearview mirror. It was clear that something big was happening, and she felt it was in her neighborhood. She was instantly fearful for her children. As she imagined that something had happened to her children, she felt her heart racing in counterpoint to the vehicle's glacial progress. When she and Hisham finally reached their stop after a circuitous detour, they sprinted to their house to check on the children. They flung open the door to find the three children playing in the living room. The kids were alarmed at their parents' questions. Iba and Hisham went out to the balcony and saw smoke rising from the east, and they heard gunfire. This was the first time they saw what would become a very common sight over the next year. They could not decide if they should take the children and leave or stay put. The sounds and smells of war eventually faded, and they decided to stay in their apartment. Later they learned that the battle had been in Duma, the large town to the northeast of Damascus where Iba's nephew Jamil had studied. It was the first time in the months of alternating demonstrations and government crackdown that the rebels took up arms and fought the government.[8]

The fighting spread down the eastern flank of the Ghuta to Kafr Batna, and Iba heard that the injured of that town directly to her east were so numerous that they were lying on the floors of Fatih Hospital. Iba felt she had to help. With her background and certificate in medical testing from a professional institute, she could be of assistance. She asked Hisham to take her to Fatih Hospital in Kafr Batna, where she heard that injured protesters and defecting regime soldiers were stacked in the hallways and lying on floors. Hisham begged her not to go, to remember her children, and she developed a headache and fever and decided not to go. The next day they learned that the hospital had been bombed, and there were many casualties.[9] She

8. On the Duma battle, see "Through My Eyes."

9. Cumming-Bruce, "U.N. Reports Syria Uses Hospital Attacks as a 'Weapon of War'"; "Taqrir kamil 'an al-Qasf wal-Damar wa Harq Mashfa al-Fatih Kafr Batna," a video showing the destruction of Fatih Hospital.

took it as a sign of divine intervention that she had been dissuaded from going there that day.

A few weeks later, the regime—in the form of the feared Fourth Brigade—besieged Kafr Batna, the neighborhood where Fatih Hospital was located. The practice of encircling a rebellious quarter that housed FSA soldiers and their weapons with checkpoints and troops and preventing supplies from entering had started in Duma and became increasingly common by the second year of the uprising. Hisham started to hear rumors that there was no bread to be found in Kafr Batna. No heating oil, no electricity, no flour. By this time, gangs of local rebels had begun to attack government checkpoints in ʻAyn Tarma, attacking and then melting back into the civilian population. On a visit to Salma and Mazen in Assad Village, as Iba and Hisham described the situation in the Ghuta, they wondered if there was anything they could do to help the civilians trapped there. They hatched a plan. Hisham had recently sold his car, so the sisters decided that they would load up Salma's car with no more than a dozen bags of flat bread. With that amount, they might be able to claim it was for their own family use. If they were caught breaking the siege, they would instantly be arrested.

Hisham would drive the Matiz because he—unlike Salma, a novice driver—knew well the narrow lanes of the interconnected Ghuta suburbs. The presence of the two women in the car would go a long way toward diverting suspicion. Male-only expeditions were much riskier. It was a big risk either way, though. They were nervous but also excited because they were doing something. As they approached Kafr Batna, the traffic fell away, and the streets were practically empty. No cars, no pedestrians. Theirs was the only car in the street. They saw an army checkpoint in the distance and fell silent with fear. As they stopped the car at the checkpoint, the only thing Iba noticed was the badge reading "Fourth Regiment" on the officer's sleeve. Those two words were enough to reduce even the most courageous Syrian to terror. The officer leaned into the car and, with a thick coastal accent that Damascenes associate with members of the Alawite community and the regime, asked where they were going. Salma, Iba, and Hisham were too frightened to answer and sat in silence because giving the wrong answer could lead to disaster. Hisham searched for his ID and the car papers, while the sisters covered the bags of bread with their legs, and they breathed a sigh of relief when the officer looked up from the car's interior. He told them that the road was closed and that they should take another route. They took a roundabout way through the quarter's side streets until they reached Kafr Batna's main square. It was like a ghost town. By now, they simply wanted to give their bread to someone and get out, but there was no one to give it to.

Finally, they saw a man sitting outside the door of a house, looking depressed and broken. Hisham got out and greeted him and asked about the situation. The man, thanking God as pious people do, described the closing of the quarter. Hisham told him that people on the outside were thinking of them and wanted to help but didn't know what to do. He gave the man a few bags of bread and asked about his neighbors. The man told him that everyone had fled; there were no neighbors now. Hisham asked him to take the rest of the bread and distribute it as he saw fit. By this point, they were acutely aware of how dangerous getting trapped in this area after dark would be. The man thanked them and blessed them repeatedly.

As they left the man and drove away, Iba was haunted by the look in his eyes. It seemed to her that it reflected more than just physical hunger; it was a hunger for empathy and care, a need to be seen and heard by fellow human beings. She thought she saw that a need not to be invisible and forgotten was etched in the man's gaze. She doubted that she would be able to conceal her emotions should they pass any other checkpoints and was lucky that Hisham knew the back roads of the Ghuta well enough to get them back to ʻAyn Tarma without incident. For the next few weeks, she was dogged by the feeling that there were people two or three kilometers away who were suffering deprivation and that there was so little she and others could do to help. Two kilometers to her east, people were besieged and bombarded; two kilometers to her west, residents of the capital were eating out in cafés and restaurants and having parties and weddings.[10] Old custom required that if your neighbor was in mourning, you would temper your own celebrations out of consideration, she thought. This human value had died in Damascus. We got to this stage, she decided, because of a lack of humanity and caring. She could not shake the feeling that what her neighbors were suffering would come to her and her family in due time. "We began to lose when we stopped feeling empathy for our neighbors," she thought at the time. "What is happening to them, as they are forgotten, will soon be happening to us."

10. For the dynamics of a suburb coming under siege, see FreeShamSon, "Iqtiham al-Amn wal-Shabiha Hay al-Qabun fi Dimashq," video.

5

War at the Door

Maryam, Summer 2012

By June 2012, the rebels of the Ghuta were strong enough to block thirty roads into the city, and by July 6 fifty roads were blocked to the government forces. By July 18, rebel forces seemed poised to enter the capital city from the south, and on July 22 came the attack that killed members of Assad's inner circle.[1] These strategic successes of the rebellion marked a turning point in the war. Life further transformed as the regime waged an all-out urban-warfare offensive in the Ghuta: Operation Damascus Volcano.[2] The battle for Damascus introduced aerial bombardment from helicopter gunships as well. By the late summer of 2012, the regime's retribution had come to the suburbs in the form of airpower. The southern suburbs as well as Barzeh and Qabun in the North were retaken quickly once this happened.

Maryam's middle daughter, Amira, lived with her husband and two small sons in the suburb of Harasta, halfway between Qabun and Duma. Amira's husband, Mustafa, had a small apartment there and a sewing workshop in a basement four doors down, where he

1. For the early days of the conflict, see Van Dam, *Destroying a Nation.* In May and June 2011, the government's desperation manifested itself in the crippling siege of Homs, which would last for three years, from May 2011 to May 2014. A year later, in May 2012, it would be expressed in the Houla massacre of families.

2. On the regime's offensive, see Gregory, "The Everywhere War"; and "War Reaches Assad."

specialized in manufacturing dress shirts for one of Syria's new high-profile export companies. He also made elegant manteaus, the trench coats that pious *muhajjabat* coordinate with their headscarves. Like so many others, for Amira the first step toward displacement meant leaving a neighborhood that had attracted the government's wrath and seeking temporary shelter with family. Harasta was another hot spot for the demonstrations that were turning into a full-on rebellion; back in the first days of the uprising, some of its inhabitants had stormed a government checkpoint, provoking a street battle that had many casualties. By the summer of 2012, Harasta was subject to random shelling. Amira recounted events that led to leaving her husband's house. Every day there would be shelling, and they would hide in the shelters in the basement. In the morning, there were helicopters; in the evening, tanks and gunfire punctuated the day. Her two young children would hide behind the wardrobe. When the tanks fired, they all would congregate in the bathroom, the only safe place, and try to sleep.

In September 2012, Mustafa heard from the neighbors that the army was coming in on foot after that day's round of shelling. He knew that meant the family had to leave or be trapped, at best cut off from supplies for an undetermined period or at worst be sitting ducks for rampaging security forces looting, raping, and killing. Amira took the children and went to her mother's house in Qabun. Later, Mustafa called Amira and told her not to come home. He said he was hiding in a basement, and all he could see from the window were the boots of soldiers in the street. Under cover of night and keeping to backstreets, he made it out and joined his wife and children at Maryam's house. A few days later, the state news announced a cease-fire in the battle with "terrorists" in Harasta, so the residents of Harasta had an opportunity to get their belongings. The buildings on Amira's street were punctured by mortar fire; cars parked at the curb had been rolled over and crushed by tanks. Amira had never seen anything like it, not on the news, not anywhere, and she froze, paralyzed with horror. Her father yelled at her that they had only a few minutes to collect her things. The apartment building was riddled with bullet holes, every apartment door had been broken down, and each apartment looted. They had half an hour to collect whatever belongings they could carry, and as they were gathering outside to leave, they saw the soldiers on the street call in a helicopter airstrike. They just ran.

Amira's husband had a workshop full of new sewing machines that he had worked for fifteen years to fully pay off. He was a master tailor, and by the start of the war he was a business owner as well (although partnered with a regime insider). He lost everything. His entire atelier was looted and stolen after the buildings were attacked. If he could have sold his machinery, his family could have lived very well, but all of it was destroyed or stolen. By the time Amira and her family went to stay with Maryam and her unmarried children in Qabun, the campaign of door-to-door violence was spreading there as well. Like many of her neighbors and family members, Amira felt that wherever she went to escape, the war followed. In Qabun, a curfew was imposed after five o'clock, and no one dared leave the house in the evening.

The final straw for Maryam's family took place right under their window in Qabun. Amira and her family were there with Rose and her family, who had also fled Harasta. Even Iba and Hisham were there with their children for a respite from the troubles in 'Ayn Tarma. Regime soldiers and paramilitary thugs (*shabbiha*) were going from house to house, pulling out activists. It was widely rumored that even as the regime was arresting and jailing scores of peaceful activists, it had also released unknown numbers of violent offenders and extremist Islamists from its prisons, especially the sinister Saydnaya Prison outside of Damascus.[3] Even more feared than the security forces of the *mukhabarat* were the terrifying *shabbiha*.

3. In May 2011, Assad granted an amnesty to political prisoners in Syrian jails. Leaders of future Islamist factions were among them. See Abouzeid, "The Jihad Next Door"; Lister, *The Syrian Jihad*, 54; and Sands et al., "Assad Regime Abetted Extremists to Subvert Peaceful Uprising."

Their name meant "ghosts," and they appeared on the scene in mid- to late 2011, as if out of thin air.

When Rose and Amira looked from the windows, the *shabbiha* screamed for them to go back inside and fired shots in the air. The adults peeked from the window as two young men in Maryam's building were dragged into the street. The *shabbiha* had come looking for an activist who had been posting videos of the demonstrations and government reprisals on social media. When they could not find him, they dragged two of his nephews from the house, threw them to their knees, and pulled their shirts over their heads. The *shabbiha* slit the throat of the older boy, and blood, more blood than any of them had ever seen, poured out onto the street, like that of a sheep being sacrificed, and left a distinctive metallic smell. The second son was hustled into a car, and his parents were threatened that they, too, would be killed if they told anyone their older son had been killed. The mother hysterically wailed that her older son was not dead—it was a lie that he had been killed.

Amira was haunted by this scene for years. A boy had his throat cut on the sidewalk right in front of his twelve-year-old brother. "What will that poor boy remember of that day?" she asked. Amira's husband went down to the street after the killers had gone; the victim's family had taken his body away, and Mustafa hosed down the sidewalk, washing the blood away. Maryam's son, Jamil, was shaken. He had seen the effects of shooting and sniping and even the destruction of whole buildings by tanks as he made his way to the institute in Duma each day, but he had not seen people pulled out of their houses and killed in broad daylight.

What Jamil's neighbor had been doing until his brother's murder was the last link between the Arab Spring uprisings and the gathering storm in Syria. Young Syrian media activists very quickly learned to navigate the terrain of the internet. Equipped with cell phones, which had begun to proliferate in Syria in the early 2000s, and a working knowledge of the internet and of how to avoid Syrian government controls on it, young people inspired by the Tunisian and

Egyptian revolutions were quick to use cell phones to shoot and upload video to YouTube.[4] The combination of cell phone video, the internet, and new social media in the first two years of the Syrian conflict seemed like a potent weapon against the regime, but it was quickly overwhelmed by the ruthless response. The neighbor was using the technology and access pioneered in the Arab Spring uprisings to document the regime assault on the Damascus suburbs. But those armed only with mobile phones were mown down, and so serious resistors took up arms of a different kind.

Hanan's son Sayf, who had witnessed the massacre at Zablatani in April 2011, was one of those who grew cynical about nonviolent media activism and so joined the FSA. He was older than his cousins Jamil, 'Adel, and Yusuf by a few years.[5] He had completed his military service and thus had acquired basic training. Within weeks of witnessing what he and many others came to consider the futility of nonviolent resistance against the state, he took up arms, adopted a nom de guerre, and began receiving a salary paid with funds sent by Gulf state sponsors of the revolution.

Maryam was frantic for Jamil to leave Syria. The very next day she went to the local jeweler and sold her jewelry to buy him a plane ticket to Egypt, as she did later for herself and her two unmarried daughters.[6] Amira and Mustafa could not go back to their apartment

4. On the use of video and the internet, see Wall and el Zahed, "Syrian Citizen Journalism"; Harkin, "Good Media, Bad Politics?"; Smit et al., "Witnessing in the New Memory Ecology"; Brownlee, "Mediating the Syrian Revolt."

5. Sayf was the only one of Um 'Abdallah's dozen or so male grandchildren to take up arms; although wounded, he survived, and the rest of his story is briefly told in chapter 20. Among the other male grandchildren, one was killed as a noncombatant, two stayed in Syria for two years more, and the rest left Syria by themselves or with their families.

6. Three videos capture the sense of impending danger and the lives that were lost or, in the language of war, *martyred*: "Barmu wa li Shuhada' Hay al-Qabun al-Dimashqi"; Freeqabon, "Dababa tuhadim al-Mahalat fi Hay al-Qabun"; and Freeqabon, "Dimashq, haaaam al-Tahsinat hawl Fir' al-Mukhabarat al-Jawiya wa Nasb lil-Mudhadat al-Tayran 'ala Suth al-Fir'."

in Harasta. All Amira had left in the world were two gold bracelets left of her wedding finery. Within weeks, she sold them to transport her husband, her two children, and herself to Egypt as well.

In fact, by the time violent death struck Maryam's family directly, she had already joined Jamil in Egypt. Her nephew Sa'd was in his thirties. He was the son of her oldest sister, who had died when he was a small boy. Sa'd owned a thriving retail business and an apartment home and had started a family. As a property owner with a wife, small children, and a business tying him to the capital's rapidly expanding suburbs, he did not think seriously about leaving his home when the uprising started in 2011 or even when his relatives began to leave in 2012. His paternal family had already been displaced once from Palestine.

Sa'd's murder came when Syrian government troops entered Qabun on Ramadan in 2013 in one of an ongoing series of battles for the rebel town. The secondhand accounts differ as to what happened because so many of his maternal relatives received the news through a code of fearful staccato euphemisms over phone lines or WhatsApp messages in their exile in Lebanon, Jordan, Turkey, and Egypt. None of Sa'd's aunts or cousins felt comfortable asking for details on the phone. Everyone knew that communications were under government surveillance. Knowing too much, speaking too much, even while living outside Syria, could implicate one's contacts back in Damascus.

But all accounts agree that government soldiers systematically searched and looted Sa'd's apartment building. The building's residents, most of whom were fasting, were herded into the basement to wait for hours while their homes were ransacked. Locked there for hours with no food or water, they waited as the time to break their fast came and went. Sa'd needed his epilepsy medicine, and when the guards prevented him from getting it, he lost his temper and cursed them, calling them criminals. According to another account, Sa'd merely asked the soldier guarding them for permission to go up to his apartment to get milk and diapers for his children, who were crying and hungry in the dark cellar. He may have raised his voice in exasperation but not actually cursed the guards; either way, his request was a fatal mistake. Instead of letting him go upstairs to get supplies, the guards wrestled him up and out of the basement. Some residents of the street later recounted that they saw him forced into an unmarked car.

After the soldiers took Saʿd away, his wife was allowed upstairs to get food for her children, but she was advised to leave Qabun immediately, so they fled to her natal relatives in a safer part of the city as they waited for her husband's return. Saʿd's wife, father, and brothers held out hope over the next days, then weeks, that he would return after being forced to collect and bury bodies, a common excuse for government forces' rounding up of young men off the street. But he was never again seen alive. Weeks later, a neighbor told Saʿd's father he had spotted Saʿd's body in a neighborhood basement where dozens of bodies had been burned beyond recognition. Saʿd's maternal aunts and cousins clung to a rumor that seemed to circulate only among them—that he may have been shot immediately for protesting against the looting. But the horrifying detail that the only way his wife could recognize the charred corpse was by his distinctive belt buckle persisted beyond their conversation and haunted them. The sisters could not attend their nephew's funeral, unthinkable as that would once have been. Many families of the government's victims did not get even as much closure as they did. Thus, though their life in exile would be a grueling challenge, for Maryam and her children there was no question of going back to Syria until the violence ended.

6

Resisting Displacement

Farida, Summer 2012

Unlike Maryam and Iba, who were frantic to leave as the turmoil reached their doorsteps, their middle sister Farida was determined not to leave her apartment in 'Ayn Tarma. She had bought a small fifth-floor apartment a year earlier and had lived in it for only a few months. Through all the long, miserable years of her marriage and her single motherhood, she had never lived in a home of her own. When Um 'Abdallah died, Farida used her share of the inheritance to buy a tiny apartment in 'Ayn Tarma near her youngest sister, Iba, and not too far from her older sister Hanan. It was entirely consistent with her bad luck that the house she had finally bought on her own would be made uninhabitable by war. Within a year of her mother's death in 2011, the aerial war came to the Damascus suburbs, and she was forced away from her new home.[1]

Farida fell squarely in the middle of the sequence of five sisters. She was the strongest-willed and most articulate of all of them. Farida had been the tomboy and philosopher of the pack, and although she never finished college, she felt better educated than her two older sisters. She was also not shy about asserting that "as a second mother" she had raised her two younger sisters to be smart, studious, and successful. When the sisters were visited by the Qubaysiyyat Islamist women missionaries, it was Farida who would challenge and unravel

1. For theorizing verticality in aerial conflict, see Elden, "Secure the Volume."

their specious arguments about why women should not wear trousers.[2] As the sharpest and boldest of her sisters, she had dared to see a bigger future for herself when she postponed an early marriage and eventually chose her best friend's brother. There was never any question but that she had the intellectual power and energy to be not just a model Muslim wife and mother but also a teacher or even a business owner, but she put her education on hold to secure what she thought would be a good match, a husband with prospects.

Farida's marriage was stormy and financially disastrous. When she discovered that her husband had secretly taken another wife, she found the willpower to leave him. But he provided no support for his three children, let alone for her. She and her teenagers—a girl and two boys—were on their own. She kept house and took care of other people's children while her two older children worked sporadically and jumped from job to job. When she left her home, she was desperately poor and a single mother, dependent on help from her siblings. Persevering in the frontline neighborhoods of the Eastern Ghuta, she was one of the holdouts in what was becoming a ghost town. The rebels seemed to be winning, but siege, checkpoints, snipers, and shelling altered daily lives and took a toll on mental and emotional health.[3] The war, which had been closing in on Farida's family for more than a year, arrived on their street in August 2012.

On the day that Farida and her children finally left, they woke up at 11:00. They had not fallen asleep until 5:00 that morning because the gun battles were now directly under their windows. They slept on mats in the interior windowless room of the building's top-floor apartment, which was safer than the others. Only a few families were left on their street in 'Ayn Tarma because the shelling had been continuous over the past few days. All kinds of explosives—mortars, snipers, helicopter missiles—were coming in from what seemed

2. On the Qubaysiyyat movement, see Imady, "Organizationally Secular Damascene Islamist Movements."

3. On these conditions, see Thomas, "The Battle of Grozny"; and Thomas, "The Caucasus Conflict and Russian Security."

to them like every direction. The scene was hellish, impossible to bear. The active fire zone in which they now found themselves was about three hundred meters across in the heart of a civilian residential neighborhood. By 2:00 p.m., the fire increased significantly. A rocket landed every thirty seconds. The sound was terrifying. Not for the first time, Farida prayed that she and her children should be killed outright and all together, preferably by sniper fire, although that seemed increasingly unlikely in the shelling.

Later that afternoon, a young man who lived on the second floor of her building called Farida's oldest son and told him to bring his whole family down. Everyone else on the upper floors of the building had already gone down to a lower level to reduce the risk from helicopter bombardment. Farida was determined not to leave her home. She had no intention of being displaced. Her gut told her that if she left her apartment, she would never return again, and she resolved to stay until by some miracle the shooting would stop or the regime would fall. The neighbor called again, telling Farida's son that they were in real danger of dying on the top floor of the building. Never, Farida resolved. Her house, the house of her own that she had waited all her life for and had lived in for barely a year, was her dignity (*karama*). No house, no dignity.

The neighbor called a third time, threatening to come up and bring her down bodily. She finally took her keys and her three children and went down. It was about 6:00 p.m., dinnertime. The neighbor and his family received them cheerfully, relieved to have persuaded them to come down, and Farida was impressed that he was already sheltering about twenty men, women, and children in the small apartment. Farida's mood was dark, and when the shells whistled down the street and exploded, all the children huddled together would scream simultaneously. Throughout this mayhem, though, the neighbor and all the women of his family were in the kitchen busy cooking. They cooked and cooked to distract themselves and to feed all the neighbors gathered in their home. They served the meal, and everybody ate. If anyone was shy or scared, their host encouraged them to eat. Then they drank tea, the same way they would after every meal, as the building shook and the children screamed. Farida had never been in such an emotionally overwhelming situation.

As the explosions intensified, the assembled adults began to wonder if their building was being specifically targeted. The neighbor who was hosting them said that he had heard that the regime had Russian technology that located groups of people from the combined signals and radiation of their cell phones. Perhaps the assembled group looked like a communications cluster? Farida was skeptical but agreed, along with the others, to remove the battery from her phone. When the group's seven phones were disabled, the bombing lightened and then stopped, and she was convinced that the phone-signal cluster might have been the target. In those two hours, she reported later, she felt more fear, more terror, more horror than she could find words to explain. "You can't understand it until you have lived through it, and, God willing, you never will."

In the street in front of the house, one of the neighborhood stray dogs had concealed a litter of puppies that Farida's kids had heard whining and yelping at night before the bombardment had begun. During the time they spent on the second floor of the building, one of the shells exploded nearby, and Farida heard the mother dog scream "in a way I had never heard an animal do before." That mother's pain and terror touched her in a way she never would have imagined feeling for a stray dog. Then immediately there was no more screaming or whining. "That poor dog didn't need any more pain. And I'm sure the dogs never wrote antiregime graffiti on the wall." At about 9:00 p.m., the bombing stopped. Farida and her children thanked their neighbor and went back up to their apartment, carrying candles since the electricity was out.

FSA rebel soldiers spread the word by phone and by going door to door that the remaining residents should leave the area because the *shabbiha* thugs were coming to "comb" (*tamsheet*) the area the next morning. A few days earlier, the *shabbiha* had combed the neighboring town of Zamalka. Like demons, they had broken down doors and killed many of the residents, shooting them in front of their family members, and it was up to these killers who would be left alive. Farida had heard that they raped the women and many of the boys before killing them. Other people were dragged to the prisons and tortured "in ways you never see in films," said Farida later. Anyone who survived the combing of the neighborhood, house by house throughout the quarter, would end up in a prison.

The prospect of being caught in the anticipated house raids was more alarming than the bombing they had just survived. Farida and her children were unable to sleep even after the exhaustion of the previous day and night and the fitful sleep of the nights leading up to the artillery assault. Farida spent the early-morning hours alternately praying and fretfully trying to decide which belongings she could take as she abandoned her home. She finally realized that she could take nothing at all. Most likely they would need to walk to safety, but they had no idea where that safety would be. She put some loaves of stale flatbread into a bag with a few tomatoes, the only food she had in the house, along with a blanket. As she gathered these things together, she saw her life pass before her eyes in the way one hears about. She forced herself not to cry so that her children wouldn't witness her despair and lose hope. She felt, yet again, that she had to be strong for her family, and it occurred to her that maybe a mother's strength is the secret ingredient that gives families a fighting chance in such circumstances. She quickly checked her despair and put her faith back in God. It was four in the morning. She and her children prayed the dawn prayer in their home one last time. She left the windows open a crack to prevent them from blowing out in the next round of bombing. She shut off the main fuse even though the electricity was cut off. She wondered if she should lock the door. The soldiers would just break it down, she thought. But she locked it, anyway, putting her faith in God.

As she started down the stairs, she remembered her plants on the roof. She climbed the rough stairs to the flat roof where her carefully tended flowers lined the edge of the roof in the recycled oil and ghee tins that everyone used as planters. She watered each plant one last time and bid each of them farewell. As she made her way down the cement staircase, she noticed that an ominous crack about a centimeter wide had opened between the staircase and the wall that supported it. This was what a month of bombardment had done to her building, her house, her neighborhood, her country. She hurried out, fearing that the building would not last long but also knowing that she was still one of the lucky ones. As she left, she uttered a silent prayer that this wouldn't be the last time.

On the otherwise dark and deserted street, six or seven families were huddled in front of the building. Someone said a small bus was coming to take them to the village of Hazzeh about five kilometers away. With no other option, Farida and her children got in the van, which she remembered was full of construction debris and rubble, probably from rescue-and-recovery operations. Everyone was very quiet. They never found out whose van it was or why its driver was risking his life to help them or how so many people were able to fit inside or how it could even move under the burden and eventually get them to safety.

Checkpoint

Two weeks later, Farida was able to return to her apartment briefly for what would be the last time. Living in Salma's house in Assad Village, she had no clothes of her own, no computer. She heard rumors that the road to ʻAyn Tarma was open and that people were coming and going from the no-man's-zone she had barely escaped. She found that hard to believe, considering the conditions under which she had fled, which she likened to Judgment Day. She asked a taxi driver whether it was true that the road was open. He replied that it was neither closed nor open. There are checkpoints, he told her.[4] Some people get through, and others don't. He advised that young men stay far away, even if the road were open, but some families, he told her, were going early in the morning and leaving again by noon or early afternoon. That was what he had observed, but it was by

4. On checkpoints, see Tawil-Souri, "Qalandia Checkpoint"; Griffiths and Repo, "Women and Checkpoints in Palestine"; and Schon, "The Centrality of Checkpoints for Civilians During Conflict."

no means safe. Farida asked if he would take her back to her house, and he refused. Even though his own home was there, he didn't dare work there anymore.

Her cousin 'Abdallah called to tell her that he was going to take Iba and Hanan, who had been sheltering with their in-laws, to 'Ayn Tarma to retrieve some of their belongings. She decided to go. They planned a trip for early the next morning, despite warnings they had heard that 'Ayn Tarma and Zamalka were deserted, that the smell of death was everywhere, that there were bodies in the streets swollen with gas, and that dogs were eating the bodies. One neighbor went on and on about how they would need to kill all the stray dogs if they ever returned home because they had eaten human flesh. Farida tartly replied that there were human dogs who had been eating the people's flesh for forty years and that they should be killed first. 'Abdallah had brought his little car, and one of his in-laws drove a small pick-up truck. His passengers were tense, but the road was quite safe. There was evidence of fighting and destruction of the buildings on either side of the Mu'alaq al-Janubi highway, but they were able to navigate through as there was very little other traffic. When they got to Hanan's house, 'Abdallah dropped her off to pack what she could and told her to be down in thirty minutes. Then he dropped Farida off at her house and went with Iba to hers. There had been no real danger up until that point. There was a foul smell and an unnatural silence. Farida did not see any corpses or any dogs, canine or human. Later she was told that the FSA rebels would come at night and bury any bodies they found in the street, as religion and public hygiene required.

She had a strange feeling as she entered her building again, a feeling of alienation and a strange combination of fear, sadness, and hope. The street was completely empty, as was the building. The door to her apartment was still locked, just as she left it. She was happy that it wasn't broken and opened it with her key. Again, she was disturbed by the bad smells. She opened the windows and wiped a thick layer of dust off the table. For the second time she faced the difficult process of deciding what to take. Her brother had emphasized that she should take only the bare necessities. Half an hour to decide what to take and what to leave. She filled two suitcases with clothes and a small handbag with official papers she thought might be necessary. (She would accidentally leave one of these bags behind, she recalled.) She climbed back up to the roof to see her garden. The plants were dead. The cat and kittens that had lived up there, that her daughter had fed with eggs that they could hardly spare, were gone too. God would look after them, she hoped, as he is looking after us. She began to fill a trough with water that she could use to water her dead plants and sat on the edge of the roof.

As she tended to her dead plants, a military helicopter began to circle overhead. It passed over her several times in the pattern that meant it was about to start shelling. Farida was overcome with a strange calm. She wasn't afraid and stayed up on the roof. She repeated to herself that she was just watering her plants. The helicopter veered away and then hovered low over her neighborhood. She felt as if it were hovering directly over her head. She stared at it, looked at the sky beyond it, and prayed to God that it would go away, back to where it came from and never come back. She imagined all the people it was about to kill and the disaster it was about to wreak in their lives when they should have been safe in their homes. She murmured some verses of the Qur'an, finished up her watering, and went back downstairs. A few minutes later she heard the horrible mechanical screeching of the helicopter crashing to the ground in the next neighborhood over. "Allahu akbar!" rang out across the silent town. She and her children ran back to the roof, but all they could see was the plume of black smoke from the wreck among the residential buildings. Later she learned that no one on the ground was hurt when the helicopter fell, and boys and young men ran out to take selfies of themselves posing on the wreckage and send them to their friends. It was like a strange holiday in the middle of the hopeless asymmetrical war that was grinding them down.[5]

5. For a video of rebels downing a regime helicopter, like the scene described here, see "Fidio jadid wa ra'i' li-Isqat al-Ta'ira Hay al-Qabun."

Her son's voice cut into her thoughts to let her know that his uncle was back with the cars, and it was time to go for good. Her sisters had filled the two cars with their things already, and there was hardly room for her bags and the desktop computer she had struggled to buy, believing it would be the key to her children's future. She again left the place she had called home, feeling a strange shadow over it. 'Abdallah started slowly driving around the streets looking for the best way out of the neighborhood and back into Damascus. It was after 2:00 p.m., and he wanted to avoid the long empty highway they had driven on earlier. They saw a man standing in the street wearing a very clean and ironed white abaya. 'Abdallah asked him what the safest road back to town was, and he told them to take the Zamalka main street. 'Abdallah replied that he had been warned against that particular road many times. The man said that it had been bad in the past, but he had been there this morning, and it was fine. Farida later wondered why they weren't suspicious of a man wearing clean clothes. How did he have electricity for his washing machine and iron? In retrospect, it was clear to her that he was an informant for the government, one of the human dogs who spied on his own neighbors. But it was too late to ask those questions as they turned onto the Zamalka road.

As they turned the corner, they saw a huge checkpoint dead ahead and knew that they had been tricked. If they turned back now, it would be suicide because the soldiers would know they were scared. There were *shabbiha* thugs milling around on the ground and sniper nests in the windows of the abandoned houses. They all had rifles and machine guns. Farida felt her heart freeze with fear. As they drove ever so slowly toward the checkpoint, they heard the locking and loading of the guns. She felt the clicking of the weapons like a knife on her throat and knew that she was seeing death, but she and her sisters and children pretended that everything was fine. She wasn't sure how convincing they were but felt as if they were performing in a strange play.

'Abdallah rolled down his window and greeted the guards. One of them pushed his shoulder roughly and asked where he was coming from. ‘Abdallah smiled and said truthfully that they were just picking up some things from his cousins’ house. He laughed lightly, with just the slightest bit of nervousness, in answering the scowling officer, telling him that the kids needed so many clothes.

“Who gave you permission to enter the area?” the guard demanded.

“We just really needed our things for the family,” ‘Abdallah dodged. “It looks like you are a good man and a patriot,” he told the guard. The guard told him to open the trunk of the car. The computer caught his eye.

“What is on this computer?” he barked. ‘Abdallah said, “It’s just my cousin’s computer; she’s an accountant, and it’s just old accounting files. Go ahead and check it.”

Farida and her daughter, who had a desktop full of rebel pamphlets and songs, sweated as the guard scanned the passengers. Her feet were icy cold, and the guns stayed primed and pointed at them. It occurred to Farida that they were a good catch, fine prey for these predators, with a young girl and a young boy at their mercy. The street was completely empty except for one other taxi parked at the side of the road, whose driver, she noticed from the corner of her eye, was forced out at gunpoint. But Farida hardly registered this as the soldier took all their identity cards (*hawiyya*) and scrutinized them. He looked searchingly at them, one by one, and they looked back, struggling to keep their expressions neutral. He lingered particularly over her young son’s ID, turning it over and over for a long moment before handing it back. He gestured for the car to move on, and ‘Abdallah drove slowly away. Farida braced herself to be shot from behind. The car moved on, and they kept their faces frozen, their eyes fixed ahead. She whispered to her cousin to speed up, and he refused, sure that the soldiers would shoot if the family showed any sign of fear. As they reached the fork in the road where the pavement dipped downhill near the lumber yards and out of sight of the checkpoint, he raced west toward his home as fast as the little car would go. Farida felt as if she were born anew.

By early 2013, Damascus had effectively become two different cities. The central city and its more prosperous northern and western suburbs were held by the regime, while the Eastern Ghuta was a hellish no-man's-land. MiG fighter aircraft supplied by Russia began to supplement attack helicopters before the year was over. The various Islamist factions had entrenched their positions in the Ghuta, and the secular Local Coordinating Committees were fading in importance as nonviolent protest was pushed aside by armed conflict. Salma and her family had been hosting first Iba and Hisham and then also Farida and her children in their house in the suburbs of Assad Village. When Iba left for Lebanon in September 2012, Salma moved in with her in-laws in Rukn al-Din, a neighborhood closer to the city center, and Farida and her kids lived in Salma's house in Assad Village. For Salma, the long road between Assad Village and Damascus proper had become a gauntlet that she and her family could not bear to run every day multiple times on the way to and from work and school. But for Farida, who did not have regular work, the quiet and isolation of Assad Village was a huge improvement from life under fire. Iba, Maryam, and Hanan headed away from Syria to Lebanon, Egypt, and Jordan, respectively. Salma still had a semblance of a normal life, with a job, a car, sons in school. Getting away from the highway allowed her to live comfortably a little longer.

Farida had had very little and had lost it all and was beginning a pattern that would continue for the next five years. Every move she made after leaving her home in 'Ayn Tarma was more expensive than she could afford and took her farther away from her fragile routines of self-sufficiency. Unlike her sisters, who had the buffers of more financial security, functioning marriages, connections with in-laws invested in their survival, Farida felt every blow. More distant relatives were ready to help her with transportation, temporary accommodation, and loans, but no one was always there for her. Her cousin 'Abdallah, living outside the city to the north, working in Damascus, and making ends meet with a salary and construction contracts, regularly offered to relocate the sisters to apartments near his own, but with little success. Farida always refused these offers. She was wary of being indebted to any family member, no matter how well intentioned. 'Abdallah's own experiences of the war include a harrowing tale of being the last family to stick it out in a neighborhood that seemed safe until it was surrounded by government checkpoints during the siege of Barzeh and other towns in the Qalamun foothills.[6] Suddenly unable to leave the building for more than a week because of snipers and checkpoints, he and his family were reduced to raiding their neighbors' hastily abandoned kitchens for food and water. A week into their ordeal, government troops swept through the building, looting, and locked him, his wife, and their three children in a bedroom while they stripped the house of furniture and appliances. The family reported their greatest fear was that when the regular troops released them hours later and left, the next wave of looters would be the far more feared *shabbiha*. They eventually were able to bluff their way through a government checkpoint by claiming to be regime supporters enthusiastically on their way to clean antiregime graffiti from the buildings in town. In a later incident, local thugs seized 'Abdallah and his car on the highway into town and held him for ransom, releasing him only after he had paid the equivalent of US$6,000, a sum he could not even know how his uncles and friends raised.

It was a good thing that Iba and Farida left the 'Ayn Tarma suburbs when they did. The more the rebels pushed out of the Ghuta into the area inside of the Damascus ring road, the more the government pushed back—not with the army, which had been decimated by officer defections to the rebel FSA and was suffering from shortages of manpower and morale, but with an arsenal of escalatory technologies: mortars, helicopters, airplanes, and, finally, chemical weapons. There were two chemical attacks early in the year before the well-publicized one in August. In March 2013, the Aleppo province

6. In October 2012, the government razed 5.3 hectares of residences and commercial and industrial buildings around its military Tishreen Hospital as a counterinsurgency measure. Yazigi, *The Story of a Place*, 59.

township of Khan al-Assal came under an alleged sarin attack, and in April there seemed to be an attack in Jobar. For this reason, on the night of August 21 United Nations (UN) inspectors were not twelve miles from the chemical attack on the Eastern Ghuta towns of Zamalka and 'Ayn Tarma. Iba knew then, without a doubt, that she had made the right decision to flee. One of the missiles carrying the nerve gas sarin landed two hundred meters from her building. She wept for her neighbors, the shopkeepers, the family that had been staying in her apartment while hers was gone.[7] As her husband, Hisham, said, "We learned later that the chemical attacks had been very close to our area and that many people had died. And yet all contact had stopped, and we only heard about it on the news like everybody else. It was very difficult for so many people to see everything that we had built in our lives taken away like that. I didn't dream about it or have nightmares, but it was a horrifying reality, and I've noticed how much it affected me. I've also noticed that it affected other people even if they don't realize it."

7. On the chemical attacks, see Rodriguez-Llanes et al., "Epidemiological Findings of Major Chemical Attacks in the Syrian War"; "U.N. Report on the Alleged Use of Chemical Weapons in the Ghouta Area of Damascus on 21 August 2013"; Warrick, *Red Line*; and Higgins, *We Are Bellingcat.*

7

An Organic Architecture

Syrian memoirs, poetry, fiction, music, and everyday identity reach for a horticultural phenomenon, the metaphor of the jasmine flower, to evoke a sense of place. Although the flower's range extends from South Asia to the western Mediterranean and beyond, Damascus makes a special claim to it.[1] The materiality of the vine in the city's domestic architecture and its sense of place are noteworthy. As Faedah Totah describes the significance of the courtyard garden to the Damascene house and its poetic codification of the idea of Damascus, "The garden courtyard is an important feature of the traditional home, where the trees, flowers, and fountain beautify the lifestyle in the *bayt* (house). . . . No internal garden could be complete without the ubiquitous white fragrant jasmine, the flower of Damascus. Nizar Qabbani . . . the consummate poet, averred that he could not write about Damascus without jasmine 'trellised' on his fingers."[2]

Although the famous scent of jasmine evokes the memory and literature, Totah highlights the spatial and architectural element of Damascus, which is often taken for granted. Climbing jasmine plants adorn (or used to adorn) hundreds of thousands of structures, especially residential ones, from the grandest palaces and villas to the humblest courtyards and apartment balconies. Trained on ropes and supports, they form important shade elements within the courtyard and balcony vernacular of arid-land architecture. The flowers and

1. Green and Miller, *The Genus Jasminum in Cultivation.*

2. Totah, *Preserving the Old City of Damascus*, 111.

the scent distract from the key structural element—namely, the vine's branches that intertwine with, accent, and animate built structures, often forming a corner of shade extending up and growing out to expand cooling coverage. As the shoots harden into woody vines, they shape the space. The branches, wild or pruned and trained, become architectural elements. Nadia Khost relates the garden and house to a sense of authenticity, taste, and identity, juxtaposing the jasmine vine and its scent: "If you spend your childhood in such a house, you develop *dhawq* (taste), a feeling, a feeling for the decorations, the light, the shade. . . . You have a feeling for trees; you do not cut a tree because you know you planted it. You have a feeling for the jasmine, for the scents, the perfumes that are made from them. Not like the imported European scents of today. So that is why I say that the *ʿamara* (architecture) is very important for the education, taste and morals of people."[3]

What Khost calls *dhawq* (taste) is very like the concept of habitus, the structuring and structured environment in which a person is formed and imprinted with the practical "rules" of life.[4] The worldviews baked into the urban and domestic environments envelope any single inhabitant and create a sense of the normalcy of home. This normalcy of home is encoded in the Arabic expression for one's birthplace or hometown, *masqat ra'si*, meaning literally "the place where my head fell to earth." For all born into more or less stable structured systems—which includes most people—the dynamic and changing system around them seems rigid and nonnegotiable. Hometown and home to a small child represent one end of the assemblage spectrum, the hard side, the side that hardwires the psyche. The architecture of the house, the neighborhood, and the hometown form a shared system of cultural transcription within which children grow up and personalities and agency develop.

3. Nadia Khost quoted in Totah, *Preserving the Old City of Damascus*, 115. See also Totah, "The Memory Keeper."

4. On habitus, see Bourdieu, *Outline of a Theory of Practice*, 80–86.

The term *terroir* comes from the world of wine, far removed from the Araj sisters' world. Terroir is defined traditionally as the complete natural environment—the terrain, soil, and climate—that gives a grape and its wine its distinctive *goût de terroir*, or taste of the land and environment. The distinctive taste of a wine, like the *dhawq*/habitus, is the imprimatur of the place of origin. It serves as a suggestive metaphor for the way in which one's hometown terroir assemblage is reflected in all the people who come up in it. At the risk of using a problematic biologistic concept, we can say that the hometown assemblage is the phenotypic manifestation not of a genome but of a place and its culture. Terroir is a metaphor for a distinct local identity forged in a common environment of streets, institutions, language, and culture—in a richly layered urban assemblage with its multiplicities of cultural, social, institutional, economic axes. As so much of ethnography has shown, agency is an inherent human quality. But the terroir of a stratified and sedimented assemblage (structure) constrains much agency within its segmenting lines of division and its material features. A city changes, and identity within it is varied and variable, changeable and malleable. People themselves are unique assemblages, and they quiver and vibrate with potential energy, but their lines of sight and aspirations are framed through the gridlines of a highly crystallized formation. The Araj sisters carried with them the terroir of Damascus to new grounds, and it was one of their key resources. It would not, however, serve them as cleanly in Tripoli or Alexandria as it did in their hometown.

A city is an assemblage of heterogeneous elements and potentials that looks and feels, in its teeming but predictable animation and traffic, very much like a solid structure. In its age, layering, stratification, and political economy, the city of Damascus looked and felt permanent and natural. Although its inhabitants had latitude for agency within it, their positions on the grid were compacted by intersectionality in a way that felt unchangeable. In hindsight, the rigid cultural and urban structures can be perceived as brittle and fragile. Collapse through popular revolt and warfare in 2011 was foreshadowed by the *infitah*, or economic opening of the country to the world economy, in the 1990s. At that time, it felt as if all the wealth stored in real estate for decades and centuries with no other outlet was being released in a great flood of liquidity for reinvestment in imported cars, telecommunications ventures, and television production.

In the narratives told in the preceding chapters, each sister's recollection of how she left her city paints a graphic picture—enhanced by emotional intensity—of the home she lost, the home she remembered in essence, the home she was formed in. Each depicts the heightening dread of her realization that the familiar template for her very identity was being transformed by war into a lethal trap. The sisters and their families felt the war encroaching into their city neighborhood by neighborhood as popular uprisings that they supported and participated in, government and paramilitary blockades and reprisals, and eventually aerial bombardments upended their lives. Until 2011 and 2012, their roles seemed if not fixed and unchangeable, then routine, predictable, dignified, and comfortable. As the streets, buildings, institutions around them morphed from thoroughfares and access points into deadly lines of demarcation and targets, they feared not so much for their own lives as for their children's futures. They responded to this fear from 2011 to 2012, ultimately by fleeing to wait out the war elsewhere. They were shaken loose from a well-sedimented system that seemed unchangeable. In doing so, they unleashed reserves of resilience and agency they did not know they had.

Focusing on the mobility of refugee flight illustrates the intensity of desire for settlement, rest, stasis, centralization, and even unfair but navigable social stratification.[5] Refugee migrations foreground movement and feature the permanence of home and settlement not as a static norm but as a real and material deprivation, a precious and unique loss, as well as a memory, a goal, a dream, a prize to be rebuilt through hard work, never again taken for granted.[6]

5. Cresswell, "Towards a Politics of Mobility"; Adey, *Mobility*.

6. Brun and Fábos, "Making Homes in Limbo?"

In the next set of narratives, the sisters and their families move from the comparatively stable, structured, and stratified city of their birth (for some) and their youth (for others) to the unstable terrain of refuge in nearby countries as they try to restore their households. There they embody more clearly another side of assemblage: not the illusion of structure but the practice of assemblage (*agencement*). As each sister tries to reassemble her household and her livelihood, she gathers, hoards, repurposes the material and intangible affordances carried with her and discovered in the new place to try to compose a new life resembling and continuing the old one.[7]

7. *Agencement*, with its active connotations of human activity and intentionality, is the French back translation of the concept of assemblage popularized by Deleuze and Guattari. The French term preserves the sense of process that is lost by the anglophone translation "assemblage," which makes the concept of an assemblage sound like a static object and perfect abstraction of heterogeneity. *Agencement* retains within it the root concepts of agency, action, and intentionality, which the term *assemblage* does not. In French, *agencement* means "arrangement" (as of a display for commercial purposes). See Wise, "Assemblage"; Kennedy et al., "All Those Little Machines"; and Puar, "'I Would Rather Be a Cyborg Than a Goddess.'"

PART TWO

Unsettled Homemaking

A Damascus moon swims in my blood
Alongside songbirds, sheaves of grain, and domed vaults
Jasmine's brightness radiates from Damascus
Its scent perfumes the fragrant ether
And water flows out from Damascus
Wherever you lay your head, a babbling current runs through it

—Nizar Qabbani, "My Friend I Am Tired . . . ," translated by Leila Hudson

Jasmine plants are propagated not through fruiting seeds but by cutting and rooting.[1] Although in their cultivated Damascene form, the vines are trained to grow on trellises and shade structures, in the wild they put down roots when new tendrils and shoots droop down and contact the soil that nurtured the mother plant. But intentional cultivation of the underground root by human hand takes skill and knowledge and an appropriate soil substrate.[2] As all the Araj sisters

1. Green and Miller, *The Genus Jasminum in Cultivation.* Also see Morris et al., "Shaping 3D Root System Architecture."

2. "The rhizome has no pre-determined or fixed configurations of relations. Like crabgrass it has no centre, hierarchy or teleology, no plan or intention. Everything can be related to anything else, making connections across multiple heterogeneous chains, registers, dimensions, states of being. It is not a multiplicity of . . . anything, whether subject or object, nor is it ever constituted by or subjugated to any signification. It cannot be described or explained in terms of any deep structure or generative/genetic model. A rhizome is never a tracing of something 'that comes ready-made,' but is always a map, a creative and complex orientation 'toward an

knew and practiced when propagating their plants, a green shoot with few leaves is carefully buried into the soil for part of its length to encourage root development. Over a period of several weeks, roots will emerge from the vine, and the new plant can be cut from its mother, repotted, or planted in a new location. This is how the Araj sisters reproduced the trees from Um 'Abdallah's mother tree in the small courtyard of the house where they grew up in Masaken Barzeh when they married and moved to their own modest homes in the Damascus suburbs, none with a courtyard, but each with a small balcony and carefully tended pots of flowering plants.

Traditional rooting practices note that the shade of the mother plant and the local soil is the best place for the daughter cutting to be located while it develops its root system. For a new root system to thrive, its environment needs to be close to that of its mother to replicate. Training new plants from the rhizome is asexual reproduction or, effectively, cloning. The genetic code of the mother plant is inherited intact. The code that allowed the mother plant to thrive is demonstrably well suited to the environment. Soil, light and shade, water—the ecology that was good enough for the mother will be good enough for the identical offshoot daughter plants. In the different soils and climates of exile, however, propagation is far more challenging.[3] The code to be cloned and transplanted in a different new terrain is not assured of success. In fact, when cuttings are made, end leaves on the shoot, necessary for future photosynthetic development of the daughter plant, should be trimmed to half size so that the plant's developed above-ground structures do not rot or decay while the subterranean rhizome that will provide them with water and minerals is slowly developing.

---

experimentation in contact with the real.'" Deleuze and Guattari, *A Thousand Plateaus*, 12.

3. Tima Kurdi, the Canadian immigrant aunt of the tiny boy Alan Kurdi, whose body was photographed on the Turkish coast, shocking the world, opens her memoir with the struggle to get a jasmine plant to grow roots in Canadian soil. Kurdi, *The Boy on the Beach*, chap. 1.

The challenges of transplanted rhizomatic propagation in a new environment foreshadows the troubles that the sisters would encounter in near exile. Taking root in new soil, expecting to sustain themselves and their families in the way they always had thrived, almost as cultural clones of their mother, would take negotiation of an inhospitable new environment, skill, knowledge, and painful pruning. Habits internalized from and naturalized in the Damascene environment would not work as well as they hoped and expected even in the closest metropolises of the Arab world.

The Araj sisters and their families would very much have liked to stay and be a part of the Syrian revolution sparked by the Arab Spring of 2011, but the regime's imposition of pain and fear for one's family proved to be a winning strategy of ethnic cleansing, especially when bolstered by external allies, Iran and Russia. The families sought refuge in the neighboring Arab countries in which new urban and political neoliberal environments challenged them, and their inherited cultural codes of kinship, hospitality, and religion were severely tested. In part two, each sister recounts temporarily resettling in nearby countries—Cairo and Alexandria, Egypt; Tripoli, Lebanon; Amman, Jordan; Istanbul and Yalova, Turkey. Their attempts to clone their old households exposed the differences between Damascus and their new environments and showed the unexpected limitations of the inherited and unquestioned cultures of kinship, religion, and reciprocity that they had always taken for granted.[4] In Tripoli, Amman, Alexandria, and, later, Istanbul, the sisters and their families struggled to re-create the world they knew through the practices and bonds that they took for granted in Syria. Treasuring family, working together, sharing strong values would be their salvation, they thought. The virtues they had cultivated, the solidarity and mutuality they shared, would see them through the catastrophe all around them, they assumed. In fact, trying to support one another with drastically limited means would prove a more complicated challenge.

4. Keane, "Perspectives on Affordances"; Ingold, *The Perception of the Environment.*

The first move away from their home city, their tentative extension of roots in new grounds, involved securing the basic affordances of life. The idea of affordances as "ways to carry on your life" helps shape our understanding of the accommodations and ultimately the transformations involved in forced mobility.[5] Affordance framing helps us focus on the "reciprocity between the environment and the organism" that is critical to the economic side of displacement.[6]

In addition to navigating the local affordances of Egyptian, Jordanian, Lebanese, and later Turkish urban refuges, the sisters brought with them the affordance of kinship. Family solidarity and connection were portable resources, forming a supportive infrastructure of mutual obligation that should apply in any geography. Home is not just a place but also the people moving and intertwining in and around that place. In displacement, family connections and mutual obligations take on even more important roles as crucial affordances, relied on to compensate for the challenges of new, less familiar, and less hospitable environments.

Suad Joseph foregrounds the dynamic she calls "patriarchal connectivity." In this connectivity, the emphasis is not just on the relations of dominance implied by patriarchy but on the relational interfaces through which a family's shared power resources circulate. This connectivity takes the form of a deep enmeshment between members of the group, wherein family members speak for, feel with, act for each other in a way that Western sociology has ethnocentrically derided as pathological but that works differently in a society where family

5. Keane, "Perspectives on Affordances," 31–32. As framed by the psychologist James J. Gibson, "The affordance of anything is a specific combination of [its] properties in light of what it offers, provides, or furnishes for the animal that perceives it." According to Webb Keane, in addition to being the properties of physical objects, affordances are "anything at all that people can experience, such as emotions, bodily movements, habitual practices, linguistic forms, laws, etiquette, or narratives, [and] possess[]an indefinite number of combinations of properties" useful to the subject who perceives them. Keane, "Perspectives on Affordances," 31 (quoting Gibson), 32.

6. Macnaughten and Urry, "Bodies in the Woods," 169.

is one of the key affordances and forms of cultural capital. As Joseph writes about Arab families in Lebanon, "Persons expected intimate others to read each other's minds, answer for each other, anticipate each other's needs, shape their likes and dislikes in accordance with each other's. They saw intimate others as extensions of each other. Connectivity . . . was mainly reciprocal, with women and men, juniors and elders, equally engaged and interwoven in webs of relationality. In general, they neither expected, valued, nor supported autonomy, separateness, boundedness. They signaled maturity partly by the successful engagement in a multiplicity of connective relationships across gender and age groups, with kin and nonkin."[7]

This infrastructure of relationality is not only intricate and intimate but also scalable to larger social assemblages. Joseph's work emphasizes that these networks, dynamics, and dependencies are not static; like other assemblages, they adapt and change over time, influenced by social, political, and economic conditions. In their new conditions, relations between the sisters as well as those between each sister and her accompanying dependents distended and challenged the inherited assumptions of how family members should and could support and sustain one another.[8]

Catherine Brun and Anita Fábos conceptualize home and homemaking for the displaced that happens not only in camps and shelters but also in urban areas and in transit. They grapple with the wide array of temporalities around refugee homemaking that result in the liminalities of various periods of temporariness and protraction. With unfailing attention to the agency of the displaced in this dynamic matrix of placemaking through mobility, they present the notion of "constellations of home," which includes the work of homemaking in limbo, nostalgia for the lost homes of origin, aspirations toward new imagined homes, and the geopolitics of citizenship, rights, and

7. Joseph, "Gender and Relationality Among Arab Families in Lebanon," 467.

8. See Joseph, "Gender and Relationality Among Arab Families in Lebanon"; Joseph, "Connectivity and Patriarchy Among Urban Working-Class Arab Families in Lebanon"; and Joseph, "Brother/Sister Relationships."

belonging.[9] This work builds on a critical geography foundation that place is open and dynamic, that refugees are not constituted primarily by displacement but by the transformational work of remaking home, reimagining, reinvesting, recombining spatial imaginaries with the exigencies of new sites and circumstances that Brun has called "reterritorializing."[10] Movement, mobility, displacement, and the extension of the notion of home over space and time make "home" not the opposite of movement but a particularly significant kind of place and spatial imaginary with which and within which we experience strong attachments.[11]

Over the chapters in part two, the sisters will bring their codes of kinship, hospitality, and obligation along their quests to secure the basic affordances of life in a series of different places—small apartments and rooms providing tenuous shelter in unfamiliar cities and political economic systems that required nimble navigation and exhausting labor. The new environments challenged them to hustle, to make a living, to make homes, to procure resources and alliances that they never had to procure as Damascus housewives. Salma, Iba, and Farida moved to Tripoli, Lebanon, while older sisters Hanan and Maryam maintained their more complex households in Amman, Jordan, and Alexandria, Egypt, respectively. Through their experiences and narratives, they articulate (1) the uncanniness of cities that share history and language but are differently assembled geographically, historically, and politically than Damascus; (2) the challenge of combining households and pooling resources to make homes; and (3) the intense labor necessary to gain a foothold in a new economy as well as the growing backlash against the many Syrian refugees seeking safety. Reterritorialization involves trying to regain footing on solid earth and reorienting one's lifestyle and habits. This is where agency

9. Brun and Fábos, "Making Homes in Limbo?"

10. Brun, "Reterritorializing the Link Between People and Place in Refugee Studies."

11. Doreen Massey, Hazel Easthope, and Maja Korac cited in Brun and Fábos, "Making Homes in Limbo?," 6–8.

or arrangement comes in—trying to organize, assemble, build a home or a business, a machine for sustainable living, by using the affordances available. City, state, economy, and even religion offered the sisters precious few familiar grips and footholds. The sisters set about assembling their own livelihoods and in doing so grew away from each other rather than together. Part two is about trying to regrow connections with people and places that were uprooted in Damascus and the Ghuta.

8

Matriarchal Connectivity

Maryam in Alexandria, 2012–2014

After the murder of two neighbors on the doorstep of her apartment building, Maryam was frantic to get her son, Jamil, out of Syria. She sold some of her gold jewelry (which was part of every traditional woman's personal savings account) for his ticket to Egypt, where he had a cousin on his father's side who she felt could help him get settled. The family justified Jamil's departure to themselves that he was only going temporarily for about four months to get away from the fighting and then perhaps seek a visa to Germany or some other part of Europe to finish his studies in business if the war in Syria continued. None of the family intended for Jamil to stay more than a few months in Egypt.[1]

At that point in 2011 and 2012, going to Egypt did not require a visa; it was, as Jamil said later, just "as if you were going to a different province within Syria," so an airline ticket was all it took. Maryam's decision to send Jamil to Egypt was based on conversations with various relatives already living abroad. She and her children consulted with family already in Jordan and Lebanon, who recommended that they stay away from those places. Amman was expensive, and Lebanon was even more inflationary as well as increasingly xenophobic, so Syrians were being treated very badly there. Then after the coup in Egypt in July 2013, when General Abdel Fattah el-Sisi overthrew the

1. Ayoub, "The Situation of Syrian Refugees in Egypt."

Muslim Brotherhood government, very serious persecution of Syrian refugees as presumed partners of the criminalized Muslim Brotherhood made it impossible to get any Syrians into Egypt.

Jamil first tried to gain a foothold in the coastal city of Alexandria, working fitfully at odd menial jobs arranged by his paternal cousin. He had never lived on his own and soon fell out with his cousin, whom he felt was trying to control him and exploit him by garnishing his wages. His cousin set him up in a series of dishwashing jobs in restaurants working with his business associates and seemed to expect a cut of Jamil's meager wages and the right to give unsolicited advice about every aspect of his life. Maryam had raised her children in an atmosphere of resentment and suspicion of their father's family, so whether Jamil's unhappiness in his new situation was well grounded or not, it was real. It was exacerbated by the shock of a "mama's boy" suddenly living a typical migrant bachelor's life in close quarters with an assortment of male roommates who came and went.

Hundreds of thousands of youths would leave Syria on their own in the coming months, but for Maryam's family the idea of Jamil on his own was so unthinkable that Maryam and her two unmarried daughters soon followed him to Egypt, although her husband chose to stay in Syria. The situation at home was not nearly as dangerous for women and girls as it was for men of military age, but the fighting and economic insecurity were encroaching on their lives as well, and there was a strong emotional and material case that the family, working together, was a much more stable unit than a single individual. Cosseted by his mother and sisters, who had monitored his well-being closely since babyhood, Jamil was considered particularly soft by many of his male relatives. Other members of the family chuckled about how even as a young man Jamil would refuse to drink ice water because his "*mama* would never let him since it could give him a sore throat."

But he wasn't qualitatively different from other men in his family and in the wider society in that they all tended to rely heavily first on their mothers and sisters and then on their wives, daughters, and daughters-in-law for many of life's basic needs. Many men were more adventurous and independent in their personas than Jamil, but very few didn't return to feminized domesticity at the end of their workdays and other adventures and take their female relatives and the women's labor for granted. Food preparation, laundry, and house cleaning were often perceived as challenges that men could not handle on their own except under extreme duress. For many men, obligatory army service was their experiment in solo living, and since Jamil was a *wahid*, or only son, and thus exempted from military service, he lacked that toughening experience as well. This exemption was based on the equally gendered expectation that a family should have at least one son left to support his parents in old age should one of his brothers be killed in battle. For Maryam and her children, family separation felt like a trauma on top of the war. It felt entirely natural that Jamil's mother and unmarried sisters should follow him to refuge in Egypt. They settled in Cairo once the household reassembled. They were able to reconstruct something like their life in Damascus, especially after Jamil's older sister Amira, her husband, Mustafa, the tailor, and their two little sons joined them after fleeing their own home in the Ghuta town of Harasta.

There was no shame in mobilizing the whole family of parents and sisters to support a son, and the strong ongoing presence of a mother, a matriarch, imported one of the key structures of home.[2] Maryam comforted, cooked, adjudicated in a way that allowed her children to function independently in the urban environment but then come home to pool resources, as they had done while growing up. Family support and connections provided material and emotional infrastructure in resettlement. In Cairo, the tidy, sparely furnished apartment that Maryam rarely left felt like a familiar haven to Jamil and his sisters when they navigated the huge, teeming, polluted city of 10 million that made Damascus with its population of 3 million feel nostalgically like an easily navigated rural town.

2. Suad Joseph's work pushes back at the ethnocentricity of pathologizing family connection in Salvador Minuchin's classic of psychotherapy. See Minuchin et al., "A Conceptual Model of Psychosomatic Illness."

Maryam kept house in the small apartment in Nasr City, Cairo, while Jamil and his two unmarried sisters worked. He worked in restaurants; his sisters worked in a variety of low-paying retail jobs.[3] Each sister was energetic and sociable and took well to the retail work but saw no future in it, just a way of generating cash that allowed the family to scrape by from month to month. Maryam made sure that her children knocked at the door of every single Arab embassy, European embassy, and North American embassy to inquire about legal immigration as asylum seekers, students, or economic migrants.[4] Every one of the embassies rerouted them to overloaded internet websites that functioned as very effective filters and made it impossible to get a face-to-face interview. The family did not have personal computers or internet service, just maintained their Chinese Huawei telephones, stocking up on minutes purchased from local stores when they could afford to. An internet café would charge by the hour, something they could ill afford on a regular basis. Their optimistic view of Egypt as a steppingstone to Europe or a temporary refuge from increasingly violent Damascus began to fade.

Egypt under the newly elected Muslim Brotherhood government of Mohammad Morsi had seemed in 2012 like the most hopeful Arab refugee destination for Syrians. Morsi was openly welcoming, and the outcome of the Egyptian revolution looked at the time like a model that many Syrians appreciated.[5] In Morsi's Egypt in 2012 and the first half of 2013, international organizations provided food aid and cash assistance. When Maryam's family first arrived, each member was eligible for a nutrition voucher of 200 Egyptian pounds per person (about US$25), which they could pool together to supplement the young adults' earnings. The amount, however,

3. On Syrians working in Egypt, see "Syrian Refugees Contribute $800M Economy to Egypt's [*sic*]"; and Gozdziak and Walter, *Urban Refugees in Cairo.*

4. Refugees' legal options are discussed in M. Jones, "Legal Empowerment and Refugees on the Nile."

5. For more on the Egyptian context, see Abdelrahman, *Egypt's Long Revolution.*

was a pittance and was quickly diminished over the time they were there as international grants and pledges dwindled away in the face of increased need, especially as the welcome that Syrians had initially received quickly evaporated after the Sisi coup on July 3, 2013. Right before the coup, the UN World Food Program instituted a voucher system for about 4,000 of the poorest Syrian refugees living on the outskirts of Cairo, with plans to expand to about 30,000, which was still less than a third of the estimated population of Syrians in the city.[6] It was not enough to live off. Syrians had to depend on themselves. Thus, the more of Maryam's family that made it to Egypt, although there were more mouths to feed, the more the social climate seemed hospitable. Their household was dominated by Maryam's gentle maternal presence, and her children returned each day from Cairo's overwhelming, unsleeping vitality to their mother, an impeccably clean home, a hot meal, music, paper flowers, and a sense of normalcy.[7]

Egypt's economy was much bigger than Syria's, and work in the apparel industry would eventually attract Amira and her husband, Mustafa, to joined the household by early 2013 as things in Damascus went from bad to worse.[8] Syrians' position in Egypt had become more uncomfortable even before the Sisi takeover, and Amira and her family noticed it as soon as they arrived and moved into the apartment in Cairo where Maryam, Jamil, and his sisters lived. Amira decided to go to Cairo after it became clear she had no other safe place in Damascus for her two young sons: her home in Harasta was destroyed and part of a no-man's-zone, and her parents' home in Qabun was on the front line between rebels and the government.

6. T. Miles, "WFP Suspends Food Aid for 1.7 Million Syrian Refugees"; "WFP Restarts Food Aid for Syrian Refugees"; Hauslohner, "Syrian Refugees Find Hostility in Egypt."

7. On the importance of the mother figure in migration, see Reynolds et al., "Migrant Mothers"; and Baldassar et al., "Transnational Families."

8. For specifics on entry requirements for Egypt, see Kortam, "New Requirements for Entry of Syrians."

The toddlers had spent too many days huddled inside a wardrobe, screaming, she recalled, crying at the memory.

Life in Egypt had its own perils, though. For Amira, venturing outside the house to shop was marked by the constant danger of sexual harassment.[9] The sexualization of Syrian refugees was well underway even in 2011, and Maryam and Mustafa feared for Amira and Amani's safety. The sisters experienced it as well, but they had developed thicker skins and the ability to aggressively repel unwanted harassment with clever retorts in Egyptian and Syrian dialects. For them, working in Egypt in 2012 provided opportunities to show their skills and independence in ways they hadn't been able to do in Syria. But Amira was delicate and had married early, and she embodied the sweet, passive, and helpless wife and tender mother. As Amira put it,

> They were afraid for me every time we left the house. Every time we went into the street, Egyptians ate us up with their eyes. They think we're here as beggars and are just here to get married. Everyone loves the Syrian-style manteaus and hijabs that Abdullah manufactured in his workshops back in Damascus. Even that modest dress is very popular and highly sexualized in Egypt. Whatever you say or do, they think you're flirting with them. We tried hard to look and act differently, to try not to be attractive. We tried to speak Egyptian, but they always found us out or even thought we might be Turkish. If you speak in the Syrian accent, they think you're flirting! If I say, "How much are the tomatoes?" in the Damascus dialect, it's like saying, "Come on over here, handsome!" I always just blurted out Egyptian dialect, but they could still tell; they can distinguish us from a mile away, and they love Syrian women.

Amira's husband, Mustafa, having lost everything he had built in Damascus when his newly established tailoring workshop was

9. On refugees and sexual harassment, see "Lebanon"; Ouyang, "Syrian Refugees and Sexual Violence"; Sami et al., "Responding to the Syrian Crisis"; Anani, "Dimensions of Gender-Based Violence"; Lewis et al., "Rhythms, Sociabilities and Transience of Sexual Harassment in Transport."

destroyed and looted, saw a future for an experienced textile craftsman like himself in populous Egypt. When he first arrived in Cairo, he contributed to the three-generation household by working in a clothing-production workshop that was known to be full of Muslim Brothers. Although a pious Sunni Muslim, he always strongly denied being a member of the Muslim Brotherhood and was painfully aware of the association between Syrian refugees and the increasingly stigmatized Muslim Brotherhood, but he had to go to this shop for work. Depression began to set in when he realized that to make a living, he was associating perilously with an Egyptian element of society that he was very likely to be condemned alongside. Since the early 1980s, Syrian Muslims accused of association with the Brotherhood had been on a fast track to prison or worse.[10] In Egypt, people's workplaces were politicizing, with fingers pointing at and dangerous accusations being made about some workers being members of or sympathetic to the Muslim Brotherhood. The workflow at the shop where Mustafa was employed was often disrupted, and his contributions to the family's income, which everyone expected to sustain the household, were not increasing—indeed, were decreasing.

Life in Cairo changed abruptly when the coup of mid-2013 took place.[11] Maryam and her children once again could see evidence of a massacre from their windows: Rabia Square was just blocks from their apartment. They could see the fire and smoke from what could be the single greatest massacre in Egyptian history.[12] Hundreds of Egyptians sympathetic to the government of Mohammad Morsi lost their lives that day, and the government of Defense Minister al-Sisi would declare outright war on them and the Syrian refugees assumed to be their allies. Listening to the unfolding street battle just blocks

10. Ramírez Díaz, *The Muslim Brotherhood in Syria*; Lefèvre, *Ashes of Hama*.

11. On the coup, see Fabian, "The Second Egyptian Uprising." Also see P. Sanyal, "Egypt: Presidential Elections, 2014."

12. On the Rabia Square massacre, see al-Anani, "Upended Path"; Ardovini, "The Politicisation of Sectarianism in Egypt"; and Schielke, "There Will Be Blood."

away, smelling the smoke and tear gas, Maryam was jerked back to the violence she had fled in Damascus. Once again, they were in the thick of things, barely holding on.

Provocateurs made it seem as if all Syrians were Muslim Brothers and behind the Rabia revolution.[13] After the massacre of Brotherhood members at Rabia and the purge of the Brotherhood, the family's situation took a nosedive. On one occasion after the coup, one of Maryam's daughters was riding in the bus when she was publicly attacked by an Egyptian woman screaming at her, calling her a "dirty Syrian who was destroying Egypt."[14] There were now checkpoints all around the city—which reminded the family members of Damascus—and the UN-issued yellow card (*mufawadiyya*) granting permission to reside in Egypt was increasingly necessary to get around. The family began to hear of cases of Syrians being deported if they couldn't prove UN-sanctioned refugee status.

In another incident in Cairo in the fall of 2013, Amira was almost kidnapped. In post-Rabia Egypt, Syrians seemed to be fair game for Egyptians egged on by their new government. One day Mustafa loaded her and the children protectively as usual into a minivan service and directed the driver to take them to their destination. Other passengers shared the van, and Egyptian women in the back seat grabbed Amira's purse and tried to rob her. When Amira appealed to the Egyptian driver for help, he sided with the Egyptian women harassing her. Amira, understanding that no one would help a Syrian in that situation, desperately pulled out her yellow UN refugee identification card. Shaking, she waved it furiously in the faces of her attackers, screaming falsely but effectively, "This is from the United Nations! I am protected by the United Nations! Let me out of this car immediately, or I'll have you arrested by the United Nations." She and the boys quickly exited the van, her knees

13. On blaming Syrians, see Kouddous, "Egypt's Syrian Scapegoats."

14. On treatment of Syrians in Egypt after the coup, see Ismail, "Authoritarian Government, Neoliberalism and Everyday Civilities in Egypt."

feeling like jelly.[15] Maryam and her daughters also came to fear for Jamil and Mustafa, who as Syrian men faced a different flavor of danger in postrevolutionary Egypt.

Shortly after the massacre at Rabia Square, Mustafa's Brotherhood-dominated workshop was forced to close as his Brotherhood-linked coworkers went into hiding or were arrested. The family decided to move to Alexandria, where Jamil had first tried to settle near his paternal cousin. Before the move, they were living close to Nasr City, very near the Egyptian foreign minister's house, when there was an attack and an explosion. Maryam felt that troubles seemed to follow her family wherever they went. After July 2013, the borders were closed, the assistance was gone, and work opportunities were foreclosed by Egypt's political turmoil. The six adults and two children of the family used Jamil's connections in Alexandria to rent a fairly spacious seventh-floor apartment in the Miami district, packed up their meager belongings, and embarked on the long, tiring train journey to Egypt's second city on the Mediterranean coast.

In contrast to the exhausting crowding in and immediate threats of Cairo, the sea to their north promised new horizons and freedom. Abdullah saw opportunities to make a living by opening up his own sewing shop in Alexandria, but as a Syrian (one possibly tainted with Brotherhood associations) he could not find an Egyptian partner to invest with him. He went to the international Catholic charity Caritas, although he was tormented by the need to appeal for charity and hurt deeply by having to "beg," as he saw the complicated application process. Caritas was finally able to help him with a small grant of seed money, 2,000 Egyptian pounds (around US$285), only a quarter of the amount that he would need for a single sewing machine. In comparison to the workshop he had built up in the Harasta neighborhood of Damascus—a functioning workshop with

15. For more on the environment in Egypt at this time, see Abdelrahman, "Policing Neoliberalism in Egypt."

ten active sewing machines that were stolen in the war—the Caritas grant felt not like relief but like adding insult to injury.

In Alexandria, Amira and Mustafa's young sons were growing into school age. Maryam's grandsons had a very difficult time beginning their education. Barriers were effectively placed to try and keep Syrian children out of the already overcrowded Egyptian public schools. Teachers and students were ruthless in their bullying of the new Syrian pupils; even at the level of kindergarten and first grade, small Syrian children were taunted by both students and teachers, accused of being Muslim Brothers. Many Syrian families in Alexandria registered their children just so the kids could take the end-of-year exams, but they did not send their children out to the schools.

Maryam ended up teaching her grandchildren at home, and she especially shared with them her love of plants, gardening, and the animals they adopted to make their home feel like home. They kept two parakeets in a cage on the balcony and a cat in their little seventh-story walk-up apartment, from which they could just glimpse the Mediterranean. Maryam's daily routine focused on her two little grandsons. She taught them to water and prune vegetables and flowers, including tomato plants that supplemented their diet. The whole family, though never having had pets before, grew to love a succession of kittens that they took into their home. Every day the little boys watched and sang to the two parakeets kept in a cage on the balcony out of the cats' reach. The little comforts and connections of home made up for the harsh world beyond their walls. In the evenings, they could venture out for a walk along Alexandria's waterfront promenade, focusing on the unseen world beyond the northern horizon rather than on the crowded and hostile city behind them.

Although their home life was stable and happy, Egypt in general was less and less welcoming. Jamil worked late-night shifts in one of the many new Syrian restaurants in the seaside city, but Mustafa was despondent. The siblings became involved in humanitarian work for one of the local agencies to help refugees worse off than their family. During this time, Amani was courted by her sister's brother-in-law, who was also a friend of Mustafa, had immigrated to Germany a decade earlier, and was looking for a wife to take back there with him. This set of circumstances made Maryam feel as if the family couldn't stay in Egypt forever. Amani might well end up in Germany. Jamil had left Syria to continue his studies, not to work all night in a fast-food restaurant. In early 2014, nobody in the family was considering illegal immigration to Europe, but they also felt that the embassy route was as closed off to them as Cairo was, even though the kids often took the hours-long, dusty, exhausting train ride back to the capital to have their legal papers renewed or notarized by the UN or the Egyptian authorities. Moving to Alexandria had alleviated some of the intense pressures put on them by the capital city, but their official dealings with the UN and visits to embassies for paperwork were still extremely difficult.

When Jamil and Amani arrived home after what would often be a three-day trip and trudged up the seven flights of stairs, a home-cooked meal of *mujaddara* (lentils, rice, and onions) or *fasooliya* (beans stewed in tomato sauce, with a little meat for flavor) and the salads and desserts that Maryam was famous for gave them the renewed energy to return to work the next day. The apartment was decorated with paper cutouts and lanterns that Maryam taught the little boys to make. There was always music playing, a TV, the routine of the five daily prayers that Maryam and whoever else was in the house never missed—washing of the hands, head, and feet, spreading of the prayer rug or rugs to face toward Mecca, the women donning the prayer skirt and hood that covered their clothes as they prostrated themselves in the ritually prescribed way. The household work and play anchored the family in an unvarying routine that was exactly the same as it was back in Syria, as it always had been. Maryam was particularly naive and sheltered and didn't even know that the possibility of illegally crossing the Mediterranean to Europe existed, but Jamil's Syrian friends gradually started talking about it and then leaving, and acquaintances asked him whether he had considered going to Europe by sea. True to his image as a delicate young man, Jamil, like his mother, refused to think about illegally crossing to Italy or Greece. The family didn't think of themselves as "illegal immigrants."

Maryam's married and grown children provided a measure of security, flexibility, and support that her younger sisters' families lacked. The young adults explored, navigated, and worked in a city at least three times the size of Damascus. Their household, even as it moved in stages from Damascus to Alexandria to Cairo and back to Alexandria, felt like home because Maryam, a mother and a grandmother, was there, helping take care of her little grandsons, teaching them and entertaining them with balcony gardening. Later, in 2017, when the boys finally arrived in the United States, they charmed their hosts at the refugee resettlement agency by enthusiastically planning and tending a tiny garden in the courtyard of their new apartment complex. Maryam's legacy was one that they had deeply internalized.

From 2012 to 2014, when Jamil's older sister Amani accepted her suitor's proposal and traveled to Germany on a family visa to join him, the household had several young-adult siblings exploring the job market independently of one another and working in restaurants, retail, and the humanitarian sector. In addition, Mustafa, in his late thirties, variously worked in others' clothing-production factories or tried to start his own business. Individual and family aid allowances and the wages earned allowed the family to pay the rent on two apartments in Egypt.

When Amani left them to join her new husband in Germany, it was a dispiriting loss to the family's household and daily life, but it was a move in the right direction for a daughter who was considered to be getting a little too "old" to be single, in her late twenties. Her husband had been thoroughly vetted by Mustafa and the brother of an older sister's husband, and he had some very precious assets to contribute to Maryam's family—German residency for Amani, steady work there, enough money to provide travel expenses, wedding celebration expenses, gifts of jewelry and dresses, and a future for her and her future children in Europe. A video of the wedding party in the Alexandria apartment shows a festive scene, the walls even more colorful with more paper decorations than usual. Amani was resplendent, made up in the latest style, elegantly coiffed, wearing an evening dress that Maryam had made, dancing with her sister, mother, and nephews, eating sweets. Jamil and Mustafa brought the groom to the festivities later. The celebration was more bittersweet than engagements and marriages usually are. There is always the sense of sadness of the new bride leaving her family's home that tugs at the party atmosphere, but in this case, with all the war and refugee marriages, there was the sense of sadness at the missing aunts, cousins, and friends who normally would have been there to celebrate (usually so many that even families of modest means would have to rent an event space). Plus, Amani would be flying off to Europe, not knowing when or whether she would see her family again.

Amani's marriage consolidated very important ties to the outside world and provided the family with contacts who could help them out financially or socially. The normal business of the family could go on, although with difficulty, and success was measured not just in wages brought in and rent paid but in new beginnings, new connections, new loyalties. Maryam, the matriarch of a three-generation family in exile, was more easily able than her sisters to reconstitute outside of Damascus their mature and growing families with in-laws, more streams of income, role complementarity, and a plethora of connections, still governed by a well-established and shared code of patriarchy—or in this case matriarchy. Maryam's family had brought with them in exile most of the very important affordances that we might call social and cultural capital, and, unlike her younger sisters and their families, they did not have to establish them on the fly.

Yet even for Maryam's household, all these affordances were not enough.

9

Mothering-in-Law

Hanan in Jordan, 2012–2014

When someone fortuitously walks in on a family meal in progress in Syria, they are invariably welcomed to the meal with the expression "Hamatak bit'hubak," literally meaning "Your mother-in-law loves you." The putative delight of a mother-in-law receiving her son-in-law to a meal already prepared by the family has become a watchword for ultrareliable hospitality, that of a doting mother-in-law for the man who ideally carries her daughter and daughter's children forward, the sustaining linkage between households and families. The colloquial Arabic words for father-in-law, *hama*, and mother-in-law, *hamayeh*, convey the notion of protection—the spouse's father and mother, rather than the spouse, are designated as those who take in, provide protection for, and guard the honor of a stranger or bride. The expansion of the web of kin through marriage stabilizes and establishes the family and can be a lifeline in difficult times.

This concept of in-laws and the connections of marriage as an asset is illustrated by Maryam's daughters' marriages in and into Germany. In contrast to their aunts and cousins, these young women who received marriage proposals from established migrants to Europe or successful asylum seekers had a fast track to a new life.

Family as a valuable affordance is illustrated by Maryam's daughter Amani, who married her way to Germany. Jamil and Amira's tall and lanky sister was great with children, was the consummate fun aunt, had devoted herself to English-language study, and was not in a hurry to follow her older sisters into marriage. In her late twenties in 2013, she was definitely old enough (in her mother's and aunts' views, anyway) to be worried about finding a husband. But she was also pretty, smart, and charming enough to know that she could hold out. With a dense network of married sisters and cousins, she had access not only to their experience and hard-won knowledge about the ups and downs of marriage but also the benefits of their connections to their husbands' male relatives and friends as well as of the strong relationships and reputations for virtue, modesty, and fun that her female relations had developed among their husbands' families.

Amani's sister Rose, back in Damascus, was married to a hardworking man with good financial grounding in the garment industry, where most of Maryam's sons-in-law worked. Rose's husband had a much older brother who had long ago immigrated to Germany and gained German citizenship through a previous marriage with a German woman. Hailing from a world of relative prosperity and travel rights, he came courting to Egypt. In 2013, with the Sisi coup promising an ever-declining quality of life for Syrians in Egypt, Maryam, Jamil, Amira, and Amira's husband, Mustafa, supervised respectable visits for Rose's brother-in-law from Germany. He came and was introduced to Amani in the company of her family, and the two began their formal courtship. Within a few months, the couple was legally married, formally engaged (pledged to each other), but not yet living together, and so, with full papers as the wife of a German citizen, Amani traveled to Germany to live with her new husband, who had formerly dealt in used cars. Installed in a small apartment in a northern German city, she took German classes, kept house, and started a family.

Amani's husband had spent years in Germany, working to build up a used-car business. In a twist of fate, though, he sold his German property to buy a house and business in the suburbs of Damascus just in time for the devastation of the war. He thus couldn't settle down in Syria; he had lost everything and now worked as a mechanic in a Turkish-owned car-repair business in northern Germany, where once he had been his own boss. Instead of enjoying a big villa in

Damascus, he and his wife and baby occupied a modest apartment in Germany.

Amani and her husband were sister and brother, respectively, to Rose and her husband. Two sisters married to two brothers granted them no special legal status, of course, but it made the two families doubly close, enhancing the bonds of connectivity. Under the law of family reunification and medical asylum, Amani and her husband sponsored Rose and her husband to come to their German city. Rose's son had been born with a congenital blood disorder, which required monthly blood transfusions. The boy's medical situation in war-torn Damascus became precarious. Was blood available this month? Next month? Could he safely be transported to the clinic on the other side of town? If the blood supply was there, was it pure and sterile or subject to the new conditions favoring corruption and profiteering? Amani and her husband were able in 2015 to sponsor their sister and brother's family of four to join them, and the family did this with full visa authorization as well.

Similarly, Hanan's daughter Warda had received a proposal of marriage from a classmate and friend, Yahya, who had already gained asylum in Germany. Among the first wave of Syrians to cross the Aegean, he had sought to bring his mother and father to Germany but by 2014 was deemed too old to sponsor his natal family and so instead proposed to bring a wife. He did not have a wife yet but set about to acquire one—Hanan's daughter Warda. This surprising possibility was one of the rare affordances of joy and advancement for Hanan's branch of the family. Investing in a marriage was a gamble worth making under the circumstances.

When Hanan finally decided to leave Damascus in the summer of 2012, her exit was not like her older sister Maryam's impulsive flight into the unknown. Hanan, her husband, and Warda (not yet married) went to Amman, Jordan, for an extended visit with her married older daughter Sara, who had already been living there with her husband for several years. Compared with their younger sisters who had school-age children, Hanan's and Maryam's families experienced an easier relocation; rent was easier to manage with several separate streams of income provided by working adult sons and daughters. However, Hanan was also able to join an existing household rather than having to establish one, as Maryam and her unmarried son and daughters did in Cairo. For Hanan, the first phase of displacement was a familiar and welcoming shelter, not an existential challenge.[1] But both Maryam and Hanan brought with them the most important affordances of home in the form of their mature, multigenerational families. They brought the resources of maternal authority, domestic support, and actively nurtured kinship into their exile households. At their life stage, that of mothers-in-law and grandmothers, family was sustaining and multigenerational and thus allowed them to make more rooted homes as soon as they set foot in exile.[2]

When Hanan arrived in Jordan in 2012, that country was hosting many of the first wave of Syrians fleeing the war from the southern part of Syria near Dar'a, where the conflict began. In Jordan, many of the refugees, such as Hanan and her family, had preexisting family or business ties in Jordan, reflecting the economic, agricultural, and mercantile connections that linked southern Syria to the lands that had once been its hinterland but now constituted the separate state of Jordan.[3] For many refugees, it was a natural move to head south to the Jordanian capital. The majority of the more than 600,000 Syrians who sought refuge in Jordan before 2015 crossed into the neighboring country with just a passport and set about integrating themselves into the Jordanian economy. Until the Syrian-Jordanian border was effectively closed in the summer of 2014, most Syrian arrivals in Jordan registered for aid with the UN High Commission

1. On the challenges of displacement, see Sieverding and Calderón-Mejía, "Demographic Profile of Syrians in Jordan and Lebanon"; Hanmer et al., "How Does Poverty Differ Among Refugees?"; and Alshoubaki and Harris, "The Impact of Syrian Refugees on Jordan."

2. For more on family transitions, see Hiitola et al., *Family Life in Transition.*

3. On connections between Syria and Jordan, see Stevens, "The Collapse of Social Networks"; and Achilli, "Syrian Refugees in Jordan."

for Refugees even though Jordan is not a signatory to the Geneva statute on refugees.[4] It is estimated that 70 to 80 percent of those Syrians dispersed throughout Jordan, especially its cities, but about 20 percent were consigned to refugee camps, such as the Za'atari camp, which by 2015 famously became Jordan's fourth-largest city with a population of 80,000 warehoused refugees in the desert.[5]

Refugees with kin, friends, or business ties—such as Hanan and her family—considered themselves and were considered "guests," whereas the destitute, the dispossessed, and the wounded from the Syrian war's southern battle fronts were more likely to find themselves relying solely on UN assistance and consigned to the large refugee camps in the desert.[6] In addition to the pressure that the Syrian influx placed on Jordan's rental, labor, and even capital markets, the influx echoed the Palestinian refugees to Jordan after 1948 and 1967, who had been central to Jordanian demographics and politics, and the more recent waves of Iraqi refugees in the 1990s and early 2000s, all leading to increasing encampment and then finally the de facto closing of the border in July 2014.[7]

Hanan was the second Araj sister in birth order. She was also a grandmother, like her older sister, Maryam. Also like her older sister,

4. According to Luigi Achilli, "It must be remembered that the Kingdom [of Jordan] is not a signatory state to the UN 1951 Geneva Convention on Refugees. Jordan receives Syrian refugees within the framework of its Law of Residency and Foreigners' Affairs (according to which Syrians are allowed to enter Jordan with their passport only, whereas visa and residency permit are not required) and it is subject to the principle of non-refoulement under customary law. Refugees can receive temporary protection from the UNHCR [High Commission for Refugees] under the framework of a Memorandum of Understanding (MoU) signed in 1998 with the Jordanian Ministry of Interior." Achilli, "Syrian Refugees in Jordan," 3.

5. On the distribution of Syrians in Jordan, see Gatter, "Restoring Childhood," 89.

6. On camps, see Turner, "Explaining the (Non-)Encampment of Syrian Refugees"; and Lenner and Turner, "Making Refugees Work?"

7. Sweis, "No Syrians Are Allowed into Jordan."

Hanan was able to bring home and family to her refuge in Jordan in the form of her multigenerational household and in-law connections. The members of her household could count on her and on each other for mutuality and sympathy in their forced exile.

With three adult daughters and two adult sons, Hanan's family better illustrated the gendered dynamics of marriage arrangement in Syrian society. One of the most important forms of work that Syrian matriarchs do is to manage family and kinship through strategic matchmaking and arranged marriages.[8] It presented a challenging but familiar form of work for which Maryam and Hanan were well equipped, having watched and analyzed dozens of matchmaking episodes in their immediate and extended families and friend groups over the decades. The work they undertook to make the best matches for their sons and daughters might be called "arranging marriages," a kind of active and agentive process of assemblage at the scale of households rather than cities.[9] Like Maryam, Hanan had "married off" her older daughters and viewed the making of good matches for her sons and still unmarried daughter not only as a prime directive in life but also as a goal that gave her life in exile a set of new challenges and new opportunities.

In the conservative Sunni Muslim circles of Damascus that the Araj family inhabited, daughters wed early in marriages that were very often arranged and supervised by their parents. Usually in their late teens or early twenties, they were married to older men who could support them in the style to which they were accustomed. This was not a hard-and-fast rule, of course. The young women's educational goals, work and professional success, strong personalities, and

8. On domestic arrangements at the household level, see the classic work by Homa Hoodfar, *Between Marriage and the Market.*

9. Matchmaking may well be called a form of "matrimonial *agencement.*" I use *agencement*, the original French term behind Deleuzian assemblage, to refer to the process of arranging or assembling the elements of an emergent entity—in this case a family.

philosophies were common reasons to deviate from the script of an early marriage arranged by the family. But in those cases, the matchmakers, rather than backing off, generally accepted the challenge to find a husband progressive enough to accommodate and appreciate such self-directed women. If a young woman did not have a strongly expressed view to the contrary, the marriage game and its promise of a new life and love were compelling.

Sons, in contrast, needed to save and scrounge money, sometimes for decades, to afford the bridal gifts and household costs that burdened a groom. The financial burdens of starting a new household fell on the groom by default, powerful Islamic tradition, and law. The negotiation of a successful union seemed to require the active intervention of family matchmakers because it was an investment partnership. Once the mothers, sisters, aunts, and neighborhood experts identified a likely match and brought the two parties together, the negotiation began. The bride's family would set a *mahr*, or bridewealth level, that a groom would pay to his wife in the form of a bridal gift, half of which was made available in cash (usually) at the engagement or marriage and half was reserved as security to be paid upon dissolution of the marriage by death or divorce. In addition, the new husband was responsible for securing a home (preferably owned free and clear), buying its furnishings, and paying for the wedding celebration. The bride might contribute a kind of trousseau by purchasing or making her wedding dress, but this detail was often negotiated as part of what the husband might contribute in advance or split with the bride. This framework allowed the relatives of the new couple to ensure that financial questions would be settled in advance and that expectations about the couple's future lifestyle and compatibility were vetted, thus creating the most felicitous environment for love, gendered duty, sexuality, and fertility to flourish to everyone's advantage. This pattern of marriage resulted in an age difference between wives, ideally and often married early, and their husbands, much older, that perpetuated the necessity of arranged marriage in conservative circles where gender segregation and the husbands' dominance over their younger and financially dependent wives were the norm.[10]

Hanan, like Maryam, had been preoccupied for much of the decade preceding the war with the very serious and high-stakes business of making successful matches for her adult children, especially her daughters.[11] This "matrimonial *agencement*"—supervising, indeed managing, the marital prospects and selection of spouses for one's children—involved a complex calculus of maximizing financial security, social standing, and compatibility that might blossom into romantic love. Following their mother's path, and unlike many mothers-in-law, both Maryam and Hanan refrained from meddling in their daughters' married lives once they were settled, but receiving, evaluating, filtering, and selecting appropriate suitors for their daughters constituted one of their primary missions in life. Selecting the perfect husband for a daughter was good practice for the very different and arguably even more challenging and adversarial task of recruiting a wife for a son.

Finding partners for their children who could meet their exacting standards, build a stable and loving household for their grandchildren, and provide financial support and social connections was a tall order that fell to the older generation of women. It was especially important because Maryam and Hanan's own marriages had been so challenging. Becoming a mother-in-law and grandmother was one of the few forms of power accumulation and social mobility for pious women without education or professional opportunities. Hanan and her sisters, like most of the women of their friend and extended family circle, had been married in arranged marriages, carefully but not always successfully engineered by their parent. The sisters were

10. On this pattern of arranged marriages, see Abdulrahim et al., "Estimates of Early Marriage Among Syrian Refugees in Lebanon," 3; and al-Krenawi and Kanat-Maymon, "Psychological Symptomatology."

11. On the importance of matchmaking, see Nasser et al., "From Strangers to Spouses."

no strangers to divorce and estrangement, each of them except the youngest, Iba, having suffered abandonment or divorce for at least part of their married lives.[12] A Syrian proverb captured the inevitable risks: "Marriage is like a watermelon—you never know if it will be pink (and sweet) or white (and bitter) until you commit to it."

Because two of Hanan's three daughters were married, she, like her elder sister, Maryam, enjoyed some of the basic advantages of a mature family that had links, connections, and support through in-laws. Her life in the years before the war had not been easy. Her household was one of the poorest of all the five sisters, but her two older daughters' marriages to financially stable men and their new households provided ties that were helpful in forging connections with new relations and in new places, providing resources and pathways when the Eastern Ghuta of Damascus became a war zone. Having relatives-in-law whose families had different residences and different sources of livelihood was very helpful in facilitating the incremental movement of home from Damascus to other places.

Hanan had married her eldest daughter, Sara, into another branch of her own family. Sara's husband was a distant cousin of the five Araj sisters, so Sara married into a familiar and comfortable household rather than one that needed to be impressed. At the time that she married into that branch of the family, though, it was as the second wife for this older cousin. Accepting the stigmatized role of a second wife was a sign of limited means and limited marriage prospects. Hanan's husband had, after all, been far from home for the better part of a decade, abandoning his family and developing the reputation of someone who misled investors in his business ventures. (He did accompany her everywhere in exile, though.)

Yet Sara's marriage within her mother's family turned out to be a very useful thing for the movement of her mother's household into

12. On divorce in such marriages, see Bromfield et al., "Divorce from Arranged Marriages."

exile. Having followed her husband to Amman when he began to work there years before the start of the war, Sara could now provide her parents and her youngest unmarried sister, Warda, with a bridge to the first stage of refuge. Sara's in-laws were also Hanan's cousins, so household friction was lessened by a lifetime of friendship across the families. Sara's mother-in-law was Um 'Abdallah's younger sister, a dear and familiar *khala*, maternal aunt, so when there were tensions between Sara and her increasingly absent and difficult husband (who had yet another family on the side), family loyalties and bonds created support for her among the older women of her household.

Hanan's next child, her son Ramzi, provided another benefit of a mature family of grown children who took their filial responsibilities seriously. Ramzi was still unmarried in his mid-thirties. In the decade prior to the war, it had been impossible to think about marriage for him or his brother. The way marriage was practiced in their milieu in Damascus, it was easy for a daughter to be "married off." An acceptable groom came from a respectable family, was known to have good Islamic morals, and provided a mostly symbolic dowry to his bride as well as a home, preferably but not always independent from the parents-in-law. The marriage package was negotiated for weeks among the families, but in the end, as Hanan ruefully quoted the neighborhood ladies, "Al-banat mithl al-fijl": "Girls are like radishes," abundant and plentiful. For men, in contrast, marriage was likely to be one of the most formidable financial undertakings of their lifetime. Gathering the money for a modest upfront bridal gift, anywhere from hundreds of thousands to millions of prewar Syrian pounds, was a Sisyphean feat, whose difficulty was compounded by having to provide the *thalath mafatih*, or "three keys," that upwardly mobile Syrian women were likely to demand from their new husbands—the keys to a house, a car, and a store.

Ramzi had been a studious boy, and he had studied religion at the University of Damascus. Before the war, he sported a respectable Islamic beard and was rapidly becoming one of the most pious members of the family. He left Syria to look for work in the Gulf right before the war started and spent its first years hard up in Dubai.[13] Living in this cosmopolitan center opened his eyes and transformed him completely. The only thing about the Ramzi of Dubai that was still recognizable from the pious adolescent of Damascus was his passion for astronomy, which still survived in his new home. By 2014, after two and a half years of existing hand to mouth, he finally found work and was able to start sending money back to his parents and his last sister at home. The sister who was closest to him had been married for ten years and had two children in school. But for him, in his thirties, his first responsibility, before getting married, was to provide for his parents in their time of need. Much to Hanan's enduring chagrin, her eldest son supported her and his siblings for years and so had no savings with which to get married. She could and did lobby tirelessly with potential brides' families on behalf of her son, who was kind, handsome, educated in religion, deeply ethical, and hardworking but who had none of the financial resources sought by any young woman's family—a house of his own, a business, a car. Ramzi followed in the path of so many Syrian men and rather than marrying spent most of his late twenties and early thirties working in the United Arab Emirates. Because he could not get married and support a wife and children in Damascus (as his murdered cousin Sa'd had been able to do because he had his father's support in going into business), he went to seek work abroad. Living in precarious circumstances in the global city Dubai and working on and off as an accountant, he occupied the middle levels of labor precarity, far above the exploited South Asians who built the Emirates and far below the Western expatriates who exploited the Gulf's technocratic needs. Rather than building up a fund with which to buy a house or set up a business and make a good match for himself, Hanan's eldest son could manage only spotty earnings—barely enough for his rent with a series of roommates in a tiny Dubai flat—and sent home anything

13. For more on immigrants in the Gulf countries, see Khalaf et al., *Transit States*; Vora and Kanna, "De-Exceptionalizing the Field"; and Connell and Burgess, "The Labour Market, Immigration, and the Building of Dubai."

extra to help his mother and father. He thus provided the supplementary funds they could rustle up for a move or other emergency.

The way in which Hanan's two eldest children navigated their circumstances and progressed in their lives before the war meant that one, the married eldest daughter, was able to provide a home that her parents could join fairly seamlessly in Amman and the other, the older unmarried son, was able to provide a small cash flow for his family when they needed it. Hanan's situation and outlook and even her mood were positive compared to those of all her sisters, who not only were negotiating poverty and exile but were also challenged with difficult in-laws or, worse, lacked the connections and opportunities that in-laws provided. Uprooting younger children and trying to keep their education on track were not issues for Hanan. She had a diversified kinship network that dispersed her challenges across a wider range.

Hanan's two middle children, a son and a daughter, stayed behind in Damascus. It was intensely painful for her to leave them, but her older children abroad were able to persuade her. She reluctantly fled Damascus without her second married daughter, Fatin, whose baby had been born in the hospital raided by regime troops, and her second son, Sayf, who had been moved to join the FSA after witnessing and getting caught up in the Great Friday massacres at the Zablatani roundabout in 2011. Each of these grown children was rooted in the city in a way that their parents in their old age were not.

Fatin had married well and was living in a relatively safe area of Damascus. Her husband's family were reasonably well off and thus able to ensure a slightly more beneficial living situation in the center of Damascus, away from most of the fighting. Some young wives and mothers like Fatin might have followed their natal family, or their husbands and in-laws might have sent them away along with their children, but Fatin's circumstances encouraged her to stay. The decision about whether one would flee or stay in Damascus had much to do with the affordances proffered or destroyed in the war. For women like Fatin, marital family connections, the greater security of downtown Damascus, and a dense network of relations tipped the balance toward staying. Fatin's children were too young to go to school, so she was not pressured by the factor of adolescent boys growing into young men, as her aunts and cousins who went to Tripoli were.

Sayf stayed in Damascus to fight. By 2013, he was a key member of one of the FSA branches.[14] Unlike those male relatives who were exempt—his older brother because of his university study of religion; many of his male cousins, including Sa'd, who were Palestinian; some, such as Jamil, because they were only sons; and some, such as 'Adel and Yusuf, who were too young—Hanan's second son had no alternative in the mid-2000s but to complete his compulsory military service in the Syrian army. He had very few prospects for work; his family was deep in poverty at the time, and he was not academically inclined. Even more than his older brother, Ramzi, he could scarcely conceive of marrying. He had nothing to offer a bride from a family of their circles. When the war started, he was unemployed but was also a skilled and tested soldier.[15] Unlike his brother Ramzi, who was a religious student before his life in the Gulf, Sayf had never been particularly pious or concerned with religion. But out of all his family members, he was the one best suited and most easily motivated to take up arms and fight against the regime. Even as so many of his family members fled, he stayed at what had become ground zero of the fighting, the eastern suburbs of Damascus. He had little difficulty joining the FSA, then rose quickly through the ranks, and devoted his life to the struggle against the hated Assad regime. Sayf's contacts among the network of resistance fighters on the ground in the northeastern suburbs of the city made life marginally easier in terms of procuring goods and information that helped him navigate the war's shifting fronts and the city's checkpoints. His choice to join the resistance also made his life so precarious and exponentially

14. For more on recruitment to resistance forces, see Spyer, "Defying a Dictator"; and Huet, "When the 'Desperates' Become 'Enraged.'"

15. For more on the dynamics of the Syrian military, see Kostrounova, "Ideological Tensions in the Ranks of Syrian Officers."

more dangerous, though, that he may have encouraged his parents to leave so that his resistance and status as a wanted rebel would not imperil them, and so his family would not distract him or be leveraged against him.

Ironically, risking his life every day, hunkering down in the frontline positions in the northeastern suburbs, had one very unexpected and happy outcome. Sayf had in peacetime been the least likely member of the family to get married—he was the second and uneducated son of an impecunious family of humble reputation. Much to Hanan's delight and concern, though, he married a girl living in the war-torn neighborhoods of the Eastern Ghuta that were in even worse condition than his own frontline neighborhood—without any of the usual matchmaking labor and ritual by his mother. His new bride, from an extremely conservative background and family, was a fiery young woman whose family swore they would never leave their ancestral home. She was proud and outspoken about wanting to marry only a *mujahid*, a rebel fighter, a man worthy of her. They married without fanfare, without all the social spectacle that upwardly mobile, working-class, and middle-class families expected, and the groom's sacrosanct status as a *mujahid* was the only bridal gift necessary, other than a symbolic sum. The stakes of life were suddenly higher; everyone and anyone could die at any time. Under these circumstances, expeditious marriage and quick childbearing seemed like the natural, if fatalistic, things to do.

Hanan was secure enough in her exile in Amman that she could begin to help others. She helped Sara run her household and care for her two children but also found time to volunteer in a Jordanian charity that provided health care for Syrian refugees from war-torn southern Syria. After months living in her daughter's household in Jordan, though, and despairing of returning to Damascus, where her house now served as an outpost for her son's rebel brigade in the middle of an active front, Hanan, her elderly husband, and unmarried daughter Warda were convinced by Ramzi to move to Turkey. From his position working in financial accounting in the Gulf, Ramzi had made a friend whose family were part of a trend of Arab real estate investors in Turkey. His friend's family had bought new apartment buildings in a town an hour from Istanbul and offered to rent an apartment to Ramzi's family at an advantageous rate. Rather than risk the return to Syria or continue to be guests in the daughter's household, Hanan, her husband, and Warda moved to Turkey in 2014, where Syrians still had open access to the Turkish economy, although not with the protection of refugee status. Ramzi, exercising his obligation to his parents authoritatively, surprised them with airline reservations and a destination address, and on short notice they left for Turkey, where more and more Syrian refugees were headed.

10

Disoriented

Iba in Tripoli, 2012–2015

Having just arrived in Tripoli in September 2012, Iba and her family were confronted with a foreign city that held none of the promised delights of Beirut that her children had glimpsed from the bus passing by the highway billboards.[1] She described her arrival in the city as a series of mild shocks.[2] She found herself in a place that was visually familiar; the port city of Lebanon's North, linked by a long history to the Syrian interior, looked as if it could have been part of Damascus. Her Arabic was perfectly understandable and understood, but she still did not fit in; her Syrian accent marked her clearly as a stranger and a refugee from a place with a long, uncomfortable history with Lebanon. She found herself in an awkwardly different position vis-à-vis her new surroundings. Everything was slightly different; she was acutely aware of standing out, and none of what looked like the affordances of home—currency, transport, houses, even mosques—worked as she expected them to.[3]

One of Iba's first shocks upon arriving in Tripoli's main square by bus in September 2012 was a reminder that Lebanon was a market-based society with a weak state, very unlike the strong state

1. On Tripoli as the refugees' destination, see Khodr, "Lebanon's Tripoli"; and Rice, "The Road from Damascus."

2. Sanders, "Politics of Care and Reverberations of Trauma."

3. On the disorientation Iba experienced, see Ahmed, "Orientations Matter."

and weak economy of Syria.[4] Syria's economy was tightly controlled by the government, and changing currency was strictly illegal and harshly punished to maintain the Syrian pound's value. In contrast, the Lebanese currency fluctuated on regional markets and held very little value. On her first day in Tripoli, Iba was astonished that their driver immediately suggested a money changer he knew. "They spoke freely of such things here that had been strictly illegal in Syria. There were shops for money changing? All my life I'd known with my limited experience that you didn't talk about such things openly. OK then." When she suspected that she might be dreaming, hearing familiar Arabic pop songs on the radio reminded her that she was just a two-hour drive away from home. Her husband, Hisham, who had lived and worked in Lebanon went off with the driver to change Syrian into Lebanese pounds, and she sat on a sidewalk with her children, waiting for their return.

Iba remembered standing with her luggage and her children on a sidewalk in downtown Tripoli, feeling more exposed and vulnerable in the visual and auditory unfamiliarity of her surroundings than she ever had before: "I arrived in a town where all the signs and surfaces were strange to me. I have nobody there; I am a stranger. . . . I had nothing in common with a tourist who delights in everything that is new and strange to him. For a tourist, everything is enchanting, but for a refugee it is hardship and pain and constraints and bitterness. I have to borrow the tourists' feelings. Because I love my family. I need to do this for my family, to save their feelings, just like I saved their lives when I decided on leaving [Syria] immediately."

Iba and her family were part of a wave of an estimated 11,000 refugees from Damascus whose exodus across the open border to Lebanon was triggered by the spread of fighting to the Damascus suburbs in the summer of 2012.[5] That number would balloon to well more than a million in the coming years. From that moment on,

4. On the configuration of the Lebanese state and economy, see Mouawad and Bauman, "In Search of the Lebanese State," 60.

5. Weejses, "Timeline Refugee Crisis."

the small neighboring country that Assad's Syria had dominated militarily and politically in the aftermath of Lebanon's devastating civil wars from the 1970s to the 2000s would struggle to accommodate the Syrian refugees. By 2014, one in four residents of Lebanon would be a Syrian refugee.[6] Layers of resentment dating to Syria's military intervention and control of Lebanon's complicated multisectarian state and to Syrians laboring in Lebanon's postwar reconstruction economy made the Lebanese welcome to fleeing Syrians very short-lived.[7] By the time Iba and her family would leave in despair for Turkey and Europe, Lebanon was notorious as the most hostile and discriminatory way station for Syrians outside their own war-torn country.[8]

Iba was and is fiercely independent and decisive. The mother of three is all business. She doesn't make a move until she has thought it out, but once she makes the decision, she is determined and focused. Her dark eyes have a piercing intensity, and her once chubby cheeks are now a series of chiseled planes—straight, aquiline. The youngest of the sisters has a kind of focused energy about her, an intensity, a quickness that translates into a look of competence and determination. This contrasts sharply with her oldest sisters, whose personalities radiate a gentle warmness and stereotypical maternal softness. Of all the sisters, she had the most energy and inclination to master her situation in war through sheer determination and hard work.

Upon entering Tripoli, hoping to stay in a hotel while they got their bearings, the family immediately learned from a taxi driver that there was not a room to be found in the city. She felt so exposed to the curious and pitying gaze of this stranger. "While he was talking

6. Refaat and Kamel, "Syrian Refugees in Lebanon."

7. On Syria's involvement in Lebanon's civil war and postwar reconstruction, see Chalcraft, *The Invisible Cage*. On the short-lived welcome of Syrian refugees in Lebanon, see Makdisi, "Laying Claim to Beirut," 661; Denoeux and Springborg, "Hariri's Lebanon"; Becherer, "A Matter of Life and Debt"; Krijnen and Fawaz, "Exception as the Rule"; and Sakr-Tierney, "Real Estate, Banking and War."

8. Thorleifsson, "The Limits of Hospitality."

to us, his eyes were roaming over us and our things and suitcases." He summoned another driver and "just started loading our baggage in the car. I had question marks flying around my head, like in a cartoon. I felt embarrassed when the shopkeepers and passers-by began to look at me curiously and wanted to know our story. I tried to wipe away my tears and hide my face. And the car, with our baggage on top, was a clear indicator of our situation."

Then they were driven deep into the city's poorer neighborhoods.

> The longer we drove, the poorer and dirtier the streets became, until we reached a place that darkened my heart it was so miserable. The streets were dirty, and the buildings had once been pretty but were now black with soot and pockmarked from bullets and mortars. The houses were interspersed with mechanics and car-parts stores. The shopkeepers were sitting on the sidewalks outside their stores, and I didn't see a single woman anywhere. All men and boys. When the car stopped, and the kids got out of the car, and it was clear that this was the place we'd be staying, they begged me, "Please let us go back to Damascus." God, that was hard to hear.

The driver handed off Iba and her family to a friend of his, and this stranger led them to his unoccupied house in the one neighborhood that they had determined to avoid—the gang-ruled Sunni neighborhood of Tabbaneh, whose bullet-pocked buildings symbolized the chronic state of war with the Jabal neighborhood that loomed over it on a ridge and was home to Tripoli's Shiʿite/Alawite gangs. Only a month before the family's arrival in Tripoli, Sunni and Alawi gangs seemed to have reenacted the Syrian conflict in this very neighborhood—as if they had stepped out of one war zone marked by accelerating sectarianism between Sunnis and Alawites into a smaller but older chronic sectarian conflict that had a different undergirding of power but had been smoldering for much longer.[9] Grateful,

9. On the extension of the Syrian conflict into Lebanon, see Khashan, "Will Syria's Strife Rip Lebanon Apart?," 75; and Prothero, "Tripoli Turned into a War Zone."

however, to have a place to sleep, they were dropped off by their benefactor, who mentioned to them that the electricity would be off from now (evening) until late into the night.[10] He noticed their shock—even in embattled Syria, the electric service was more reliable than that—and made sure that they had some candles before leaving.

Alone and surveying their quarters in the gathering dusk, the family could see that the apartment was quite dirty. With only a candle to light the darkness, Iba opened the bathroom door to find a stinking and clogged toilet.[11] Most traditional Syrian households in working-class neighborhoods, like Iba's, had the default squatting toilet, and those families who did not install the Western-style flush toilet (and many who did) were horrified by the idea of sitting on a commode and cleaning with paper rather than running water. Slamming the door, she took her candle to the bedroom to try and clean the floor of an apartment that hadn't been cleaned for months. The rag that she found was filthy and made the floor dirtier; suppressing a scream, she noticed that she had disturbed the room's population of small cockroaches, which proceeded to crawl over her hands. These horrors were bad enough for her, but she had to put on a good face for her children. Despairing of what to do and badly in need of a toilet, they decided to camp out in a nearby park. There were no restrooms there, either, though. Next, they headed for the neighborhood mosque, which to their surprise was also shuttered for the evening, but fortunately the caretaker in a shop across the street noticed them and grudgingly allowed them to go in long enough to use the bathrooms. The mosque provided a moment of relief, and Iba had Hisham implore the caretaker to let them spend the night there. The caretaker was sympathetic but refused, saying that he was accountable for the mosque and that he shouldn't even have let them use the bathroom. In Damascus, where religious charity had intertwined with socialism over the decades, the mosque was a refuge for the

10. On utility service, see Shamir, *Current Flow*; Alam et al., "Neither Sensibly Homed nor Homeless."

11. On Lebanon's sewage system, see Naja and Volesky, "Sewage of Tripoli."

needy. Lebanon, with its privatized, market economy and sectarian volatility, was differently composed.[12]

For Iba, who had never been to Tripoli before, her first days as a refugee were haunted by the feeling that so many aspects of life there that looked familiar were configured just differently enough to keep her reeling; she was struck over and over with the realization that the values and environment she had been raised in were only one possible way of being. In Damascus, a mosque was always read as a place of shelter, refuge, and hygiene for the needy; here only a stroke of luck had helped them to use its restroom. She and her family were fleeing from a conflict that had an increasingly sectarian aspect—Sunni rebels versus the Alawite regime; here Sunnis and Shiʿites fought sporadically with a different rhythm and scale that made her fear the Tabbaneh neighborhood. Indeed, the very things that looked familiar were the most treacherously difficult to read accurately.

Resigned to returning to their grim quarters after their disappointment at the neighborhood mosque, they stepped back into the street, only to find themselves completely disoriented, with no idea where the nondescript apartment building was. Iba expressed surprise that Hisham, who usually had no problem with such things as directions and was familiar with Tripoli, couldn't remember where their temporary shelter was. They walked the streets of the neighborhood in vain confusion, now plagued by hunger and fatigue, not to mention embarrassment at having lost their way. When a group of the neighborhood men who sat on their sidewalks noticed their situation and asked what they were looking for, they realized they didn't even know their benefactor's name. Determined to help them, the men asked where they had encountered him, and Hisham rode off on the back of a motorbike to try and track him down in the place where they had made contact with him. He and Iba realized how vulnerable they all were as he sped off for the second time. What if the men in the street simply made off with the wife and children he

12. Allès, "The Private Sector and Local Elites."

had left standing there? Unused to loitering in the street, a street with no women at all at this hour, Iba huddled on a stool on the sidewalk, waiting for her husband. He returned with the house's owner after what seemed to be an eternity. The house owner chided them for leaving the house, and they were too mortified to mention their need to use the toilet or the condition of the toilet in his house.

Safely ensconced once more and reminded gently not to wander away again, Iba considered her situation. Exhausted and having forgotten to get food while on their odyssey, the family bunked down in the disgusting flat—Hisham laid a pallet on the tiny balcony to share with his son Bilal, and Iba and the girls fashioned a makeshift bed out of four chairs that were the living room's only furniture. The ground was too dirty to pray, so she said her de facto prayers on the chair platform. After a restless night's sleep, their chagrin was compounded when the door opened the next morning, and the mistress of the house, returning from travel, was shocked to see Iba and her daughters waking up in her living room. Iba apologized and ran to wake her husband and son so that the woman would realize that they were a family of strangers, not a girlfriend of the woman's husband. When the confusion was sorted out, Iba helped the woman clean the house but was quietly mortified at the woman's casual coarseness and the way she screamed at and hit her children.

As quickly as possible, Hisham set out to find a better place to live. Simultaneously grateful for the hospitality they had received in Tabbaneh and profoundly disturbed by the shock to their routines of hygiene and autonomy, they were happy to hear of a room for rent in a business in the upscale neighborhood of Abu Samra.

For $150 a month, well under market rents, they lived for three months in a day-care center run by a chic young woman completely unsuited to the job. The deal offered to them was that in return for helping out with the day school as caretakers/cleaners, they would have a place to sleep. Once again, Iba was shocked by the lack of cleanliness and did her best to rectify it. Their benefactor, too, was perhaps a little taken aback to find that the woman she had taken in as a cleaner/caretaker was a more qualified teacher than herself, and so she, too, promptly set about cleaning up. The two women moved a large cupboard, and Iba nearly vomited at the sight of a dozen large flying cockroaches, each as long as her finger, nesting on the filthy floor. Her new friend laughed at her as she smashed the insects with her hands, while Iba and her daughters looked on, mesmerized, in horror. All the Araj sisters, especially the older ones, were notoriously squeamish, and the sight of a single roach in their scrupulously clean homes in Damascus had invariably set them shrieking and hopping frantically around the room; Iba was a bit tougher than that but could not indulge her disgust these days. Learning to live with insects endemic to her new living spaces toughened her.

Hisham and his son would leave the center early to look for work, and Iba and her daughters would help out with ten or so children at the center. The proprietress, who was grateful for their help, cheerful, and always ready to have coffee and tea with the family, ran a poor program, yelling at the children and failing to provide food on a regular schedule, which their working parents expected. Again, Iba was shocked at what the Lebanese parents were paying so exorbitantly for but not getting. Her two daughters were popular with the little kids and would play with them and brush the girls' hair—resulting, predictably, in the two of them repeatedly getting infested with lice during this period. "Oh, the insecticide shampoo we went through in that period," Iba sighed. They hardly had the money for special shampoo.

During the day, they hardly ate, sensitive about using the school's facilities. They existed on *za'atar* and cooking oil. Using cheap vegetable cooking oil rather than traditional but more expensive olive oil to dip their bread in before dusting it in the common spice mix was the very definition of poverty. Iba had heard from her older sisters that *za'atar* with cooking oil, olives "eaten in two bites rather than one to make them last longer," and overripe cut-rate fruit scavenged from the market were how Abu 'Abdallah and Um 'Abdallah had existed as refugees before her birth, when her family was forced from the Golan Heights to Damascus in the late 1960s. Every other day Hisham would walk to a charity soup kitchen several kilometers away to get free ingredients for a hot cooked meal that they could prepare when the school closed down in the evening. His willingness not only to shop but also to cook meant that Iba could use her skills and time to secure the family in other ways.

Finding Work

The next phase in Iba and her family's life in Tripoli began when Iba was able to secure work and refugee assistance through the UN. Within weeks, she felt the familiar ease and reassurance of managing her life again. The hustling required to make a home and eke out a living in a new environment involved frugally arranging her available resources and skills while masking her vulnerability. Iba now found herself in encounter after encounter to be effective and even entrepreneurial, parlaying her skills and energies into the optimal management of her material resources. She was also doing well at the management of people—her family and soon her students. Iba's renewed sense of being able to effect change and make progress, and not simply react to overwhelming circumstances, developed from the negotiation, hustling, and placemaking activity that allows survival. As one Syrian proverb in the sisters' reservoir of pithy oral wisdom called to mind, "Al-ghazzaleh al-shatra tighizil 'ala danab al-kalb"—literally, "A clever spinner (feminine) can even spin on a dog's tail," emphasizing that the affordances at hand are not merely objectively limiting material conditions but are available for use with creativity. In less colorful language, Iba thought of her new hustle as *tadbir*, "adaptation" or "getting things done." Her older sisters Maryam and Hanan were somewhat cushioned from the new environments they found themselves in. Ensconced as they were in familiar domestic roles of homemaking, their *tadbir* involved managing family and kinship—the same affordances that accompanied them from Syria. For Iba and Hisham, with only minor children to take care of, their *tadbir* had to do with skillfully managing and arranging the limited affordances of their new environment.

Determined to have her daughters at least continue their education, Iba volunteered at a Syrian Opposition Coalition school and soon made herself indispensable there. The alternative to schooling for the girls was visible everywhere around them and a terrifying prospect: early marriage.[13] Fortunately for Iba and her preteen daughters, donors, some of a Sunni sectarian political inclination, formed educational collectives, rented Lebanese schools in the afternoon, and opened them for Syrian children.[14] Estimates of the number of Syrian students who were forgoing education are hard to come by, but it was not uncommon even for middle-class refugee children and youth to go a year or two without school. These Coalition schools adapted and taught the Syrian national curriculum in the hope that pupils would be able to go back to Syria to complete their education.[15]

On a typical day, Iba faced off against the throng of little girls. She described the scene in vivid detail.

"Line up, shortest to tallest; that's right." The words reverberated around the cinder-block courtyard in the evening light. Her voice was tired from shouting above the din of high-pitched shrieks and giggles.

"There will be no games until you line up and stand quietly. No pushing." Slowly, fitfully the girls mustered themselves into a crooked series of lines. The gym period was well underway, but the girls had come to understand that the new teacher with the Damascus accent meant business and would take as much of their favorite period as needed to get them to stand in lines. Iba peered out in the dusk over the class of forty girls with dusty braids, unruly curls, and rumpled hijabs, finally attentive and focused on her. It took all

13. On options for Syrian refugee girls, see Hattar-Pollara, "Barriers to Education of Syrian Refugee Girls in Jordan"; El Arab and Sagbakken, "Child Marriage of Female Syrian Refugees"; Mourtada et al., "A Qualitative Study Exploring Child Marriage Practices"; and Sieverding et al., "Persistence and Change in Marriage Practices Among Syrian Refugees in Jordan."

14. Schmelter, "Gulf States' Humanitarian Assistance for Syrian Refugees"; Facon, "Depoliticization and (Re)Politicization Tactics in Refugee Governance in Lebanon."

15. See Maadad and Matthews, "Schooling Syrian Refugees in Lebanon."

the energy she had to deal with her pupils. Every day since she had started work at this Syrian Coalition school in Tripoli, she had spent most of her time trying to get her students to stand in straight lines. It had become something of an obsession, and she was well aware of the other teachers' looks and whispers. Imposing a semblance of order on the chaos of her refugee life was empowering, though.

"How will we ever put our country back together again if you can't stand in a simple line?" she asked the girls again, as she did every day. Their bright eyes blinked back at her. Did they understand what was at stake? Like her, they were Sunni refugees from Syria, but many of them came from small villages and towns where, she surmised, schools had not been up to the standard of Damascus primary schools. By the end of each period, she felt that she had accomplished something. It was small but significant. The girls were responsive and eager to please. The Lebanese school officials who hosted the Coalition school also noticed Iba's no-nonsense way and effectiveness and offered her a paid job proctoring exams.

The school where Iba worked was one of a number of Syrian Opposition Coalition schools set up in Lebanese school buildings in the afternoon and evening. They were financed by wealthy donors from the Gulf countries, but students still had to pay fees, which put the schools out of most refugees' reach. Free public education was one of the things that Syrians had come to take for granted in Ba'athist Syria, but the fees charged in Lebanon weren't an option for so many families who were struggling to pay rent and put food on the table. Girls' education in particular was not usually a priority for struggling families, but many of their brothers also had to drop out to supplement the family income. A shocking number of Syrian refugee children were their family breadwinners in Tripoli.[16]

Iba, her husband, and her three children, like her pupils' families, were dependent on UN food assistance. During their first weeks in Lebanon, they registered with the UN High Commission for

16. See Habib et al., "Displacement, Deprivation and Hard Work Among Syrian Refugee Children in Lebanon."

Refugees to collect a monthly ration of basic supplies.[17] It felt like a huge accomplishment to see her charges standing quietly in rows when she remembered the ugliness of the UN camp food-distribution line. When the adults went to get their bread rations, there wasn't just jostling in line but also outright fighting to get to the front of the throng. Who could blame the children for being unable to stand in line if their parents acted like that? she wondered. But it was her job to bring order, and order was her only hope for her own and Syria's future. It gave her a concrete goal in the shapelessness of her life as a refugee.

Iba's conviction that education was the key to changing a pervasive culture of selfishness that had intensified Syria's destruction drove her on day after day, even when she wasn't receiving a salary. She had gotten her job at the school by volunteering without pay as the de facto gym teacher, working at the school to get her two daughters enrolled there. Her campaign for order on the playground and rare ability to calm and organize the boisterous girls had attracted the attention of the Lebanese director of the school that hosted the Syrian school, and he recommended her for promotion to a test-supervisor position. Her new job framed another personal challenge—fighting the pervasive culture of cheating on state exams. She was effective there as well, and in three or four months she made about $2,000, more money than she had ever earned in her life and enough for her to imagine making a life in Lebanon.

Iba's rapid advancement through the ranks of the school attracted the envy of her fellow teachers, however, especially that of the school's Syrian director. Most of the staff had come from the Syrian city of Hama, just across the Lebanese mountains from Tripoli, and they began to gossip that she had *wasta*, or political connections, as a Damascene from the capital.[18] She, in turn, was not impressed

17. On UN assistance for Syrian refugees, see Abu Hamad et al., *A Promise of Tomorrow*.

18. On *wasta*, see Huxley, *Wasiṭa in a Lebanese Context*; Tlaiss and Kauser, "The Importance of *Wasta* in the Career Success of Middle Eastern Managers."

with their work or their work ethic and suspected that keeping the school in a constant state of crisis was the strategy to extract more funds from concerned but distant wealthy patrons in the Gulf states. One day her Lebanese mentor let Iba know that the Syrian director, a woman she had had little actual contact with, was unhappy. In her forthright way, Iba immediately contacted the boss to talk through the problem. In the course of the meeting, she realized that the director's position was not just a job; it was a power base that gave the director not only a salary but also influence and revenue from favors and bribes. The director carefully marshaled her power to hire and fire. *Wasta* connections were not something one brought over from an old status in Syria, Iba realized, but were built on controlling access to salaries and wages. The pedagogical and civic goals that Iba was working on were a direct threat to her director's sinecure. She was unceremoniously fired. Her family plunged into a new phase of their struggle to survive in Lebanon.

During this period of a steady paycheck, Iba and Hisham had moved into a fairly spacious apartment in Abu Samra, leveraged with the salary she began to receive from the school. Hisham was working from home, and his primary responsibility was to cook a decent dinner for his wife and children when they came home—a chore he did cheerfully. He also collected materials and began to make shoes in one of the apartment's rooms. Using scrap material, he hand-stretched flats and lace shoes for as little as a dollar a pair and sold them wholesale for five dollars a pair to local stores.[19] But being completely dependent on the retail merchants, who were also struggling in a harsh and volatile economic climate, he had no recourse to bargain. With increasing frequency, his retailers would simply refuse to pay. If he tried to lower the price to be more competitive, his local rivals could report him to the police. He resorted to selling the shoes on street corners with his son, Bilal, while his daughters marketed

19. On refugees' use of the opportunities at hand to earn money, see Turner, "'Refugees Can Be Entrepreneurs Too!'"; and Saleh and Zakar, "The Joke Is on Us."

them to their middle-school classmates. A local university student also marketed the custom-made shoes to her classmates using WhatsApp. But this shoe business was a lot of work, and the rewards were minimal, not enough for the family to live on.

Salma Joins Iba in Tripoli

From the time Iba had left Damascus, she had been urging her sister Salma to join her. Iba and Salma had always been close, the family's two youngest sisters, the pair who had broader horizons and higher expectations than their older sisters. Iba's strong sense that Damascus was becoming uninhabitable had come earlier than her uptown sister's realization, and Iba reasoned that the joining of the two households (as they had periodically done in Damascus for very short periods) would be a good arrangement, allowing them to pool resources and support one another. She hoped that when Salma and their middle sister, Farida, came to Lebanon, as she felt certain they eventually would, they all could live together under one roof and for a single rent per month. After all, family was mutuality and connection. Family was support. But the two sisters' families did not come together as easily as Maryam and Hanan's intergenerational households had consolidated under the unifying force of a matriarch. Sibling rivalry between the younger sisters and their families, with no mother-matriarch to adjudicate, meant that the combining of their households would not be so successful.

Salma's family came first to visit and then eventually joined Iba's in the apartment in Abu Samra, and the pattern of life was one of visiting and normalcy. Traveling in Salma's Matiz or her mother-in-law's larger Kia, the new arrivals seemed to complement Iba's situation. Salma brought mobility and some possessions that were part of her middle-class lifestyle back home—an inventory of books from her husband's shop that he hoped to sell and a washing machine.

In spite of this promising arrangement, the sisters and their families found that they could not get along. The problem came down to the sharing of space. Iba and Hisham needed room in the apartment for their shoe manufacture and supplies, while Salma contributed financial assistance but needed privacy for her family. Iba had two daughters and a son, and Salma had three sons. The close connection that the two sisters had as young girls and that had developed into daily or weekly visits to each other's homes after they had married in Damascus proved difficult to translate into their new life with the sisters, their two husbands, and six children sharing an apartment. Iba, even after she lost her job at the school, had demonstrated a track record of resilience and creativity and hard work, bolstered by an intense faith. Her husband supported her unquestioningly, cooking and keeping house when she was the breadwinner, picking up the slack by manufacturing shoes in one room of the Abu Samra apartment. Iba's daughters, meanwhile, were thriving and excelling in the Coalition school, not having reached the difficult questions around graduation that Salma's sons faced. Salma, by contrast, was supported by her husband's relatives and did not have to hustle like her younger sister. She urged her husband and sons to work as hard as Iba's family did, but the chemistry was wrong.

Ultimately, the months that the two households were conjoined left them bitter and resentful. Iba and Salma fought about the house and the space they shared. Although the sisters were reluctant to speak ill about one another in the months after they parted ways, it seems that many words had been spoken between them that they wished they could take back. Sullen silence, closed doors, and ultimately distance were preferable. Each sister later confessed that she could not understand how the relationship between two best friends had devolved into smoldering resentment when each had just wanted to secure and recover success and happiness in Lebanon. Salma later said cryptically, "We had to leave because the two families were always sitting together. It was three months we were always together, and nothing was changing."

Iba and the two older sisters who followed her to Tripoli in the fall of 2012 and winter of 2013 had the task of negotiating a new urban environment to make it their home. Like Maryam and Hanan, they found themselves in a new city, but unlike them they lacked the structured networks—the extended safety net—of a mature family with multiple working adults and the mission of marrying off children. Iba, Salma, and Farida struggled with how to care for adolescent and young children for whom education was a priority and labor was a troubling and distracting option. In general, the difference between the two oldest sisters' families, who brought home with them into exile, and the three younger sisters' families, who would struggle to feel at home anywhere, was not the number of mouths to feed or the number of employable young adults, but rather the maintenance of stable and familiar patterns of kinship.

When Salma and Mazen left Iba and Hisham's house, it was with tension and hard feelings. The extra room of the apartment could be used either for work or for a second family's privacy, but not both. It became abundantly clear that each family had its own "business model" of making a living. The two ways were incompatible. Worse, neither one was sustainable. Throwing the two husbands together accelerated the breakdown. The two brothers-in-law had always gotten along well. They did not fight, as their wives did—in fact, just the opposite. Mazen distracted Hisham from his work, and Hisham was a constant reminder to Mazen that he had no viable skills. The men were able to translate that discomfort into sociability and jokes, but their wives processed all the tension into their sisterly resentment.

After the two families split up, Iba and Hisham's situation deteriorated. Hisham suffered a surprising and frightening series of cardiac events. He had been very adaptable in Tripoli—cooking and keeping house, making shoes and slippers in his home workshop for his daughters to sell to their schoolmates and online—but after Iba lost her job at the Coalition school in Tripoli, even their most enterprising attempts at making and marketing shoes could not be sustained, so that Iba and Hisham's inability to control their fates took a dramatic toll on the family's health.

Soon after the onset of Hisham's heart ailment, his eldest daughter and then Iba began to experience frightening illnesses and malaises, which only reminded them that they could never afford the specialized health care they needed and probably could never get even basic health care through humanitarian charitable organizations, which were poorly resourced and mostly unable to provide basic services to the many thousands of refugees. When their teenage daughter's face began to droop in what a Lebanese doctor thought may or may not be a stroke, Hisham and Iba agreed that their only chance was for him, even as an invalid, to set out for asylum in Europe. Hisham's heart disease and emotional collapse did not stop him from setting out for Turkey and Germany in the late summer of 2015 in a desperate bid to gain a foothold in Europe and haul his family out of Lebanon. He was keenly aware that under other circumstances he would be resting and rebuilding his strength, not embarking on a trip that would involve walking and possibly swimming to Europe in the late fall, and he was wracked with the knowledge that the cost of his trip could sustain his family for months in Lebanon. His own worsening physical state propelled him on the dangerous trip, though, as he had the clear sense that if he did not get treatment for himself, he would be unable to help his family anytime in the future. Despite this reasoning, he openly wept when his family saw him off at the port in Tripoli. He would have run back to them at the last moment, he confided, forfeiting the money he had borrowed from his brothers, had the gate not closed behind him as he was boarding the cargo ship to Turkey. Although Iba deeply trusted her husband's survival skills and had an even stronger faith in God, her strength gave way to deep depression and panic attacks after he left.

11

Car Troubles

Salma in Tripoli, 2012–2014

By the cold, wet December of 2013, Salma, Mazen, and their three sons felt that they had no choice but to leave Iba and Hisham's apartment in the Abu Samra neighborhood of Tripoli. The extra room that they felt they deserved for their contribution to the rent was taken up with Hisham and Iba's still unsustainable shoemaking operation and its materials and inventory. Salma and Mazen received regular financial assistance from Mazen's sister in Saudi Arabia, and so they felt that they were contributing their share, or even more, to the joined household's expenses. Salma avoided talking about the bitter feelings and hurtful words that must have been exchanged by the two sisters and cryptically described the problem as being that "the two men of the household tended to sit around distracting and amusing each other rather than effectively working together or supporting each other's work."

Salma and Mazen had access to two automobiles, her Matiz and his mother's Kia, which they used to drive back and forth across the Lebanese-Syrian border at various times until 2014. They thus experienced their new environment differently from Iba and Farida, for whom getting around Tripoli was dependent on public transport and walking. Maintaining and managing cars were expensive and tiring: paying for fuel, finding places to park, and especially dealing with the bureaucracy of crossing the border and keeping the cars registered. Every encounter with the state required lubrication with cash bribes. Nevertheless, Salma and Mazen felt that being able to travel by car and having a valuable asset to fall back on were important. During their time in Tripoli, their lifestyle was closer to wayfaring, engaging with the environment around their path.[1] The status, freedom of movement, and security they enjoyed as car owners were empowering in ways, but the middle-class lifestyle they had left behind was based on private property and real estate, which were now elusive. Even rent was a challenge, let alone ownership and investment.

Mazen was a shopkeeper without a shop. He was a fairly well-off property owner but dispossessed and restless, unable to channel his energy and anger into any productive activity. Unlike Hisham, he did not have a craft skill.[2] He had hoped to open up a store or business of some kind in Lebanon, but the threshold financing and expenses were simply too high. The rent on a small store would have been at least $200 a month, and any project would require a startup investment until income began coming in. Salma noted,

> The locations were poor, and on top of the rent you'd need to prepare the space and renovate it. And then you'd need the capital for the inventory; . . . the costs of starting up the kind of business he knew were prohibitive. There was nothing he could do except to work for wages for someone else. And he couldn't even do that because he does not have a skill (ma fi bi idho san'a). In the end, he was even fine working as a general assistant in a store, but even that didn't work out. He's pretty old. No one was hiring older workers.

At various times, Mazen and Salma tried making cookies at home and selling them outside Lebanese schoolyards, but peddling snacks

1. On the connection between displacement and car ownership, see Butcher, "'Sir, It Was My Right of Way!'"; Jirón et al., "Relearning to Travel in Santiago"; and Kent, "Still Feeling the Car."

2. On this topic, see Kwong et al., "Entrepreneurship Through Bricolage"; Harima and Freudenberg, "Co-Creation of Social Entrepreneurial Opportunities with Refugees"; Mawson and Kasem, "Exploring the Entrepreneurial Intentions of Syrian Refugees in the UK"; Refai et al., "Contextualizing Entrepreneurial Identity Among Syrian Refugees in Jordan"; and Bizri, "Refugee-Entrepreneurship."

to small children for their pocket money was both demeaning and discouraging.[3] Salma herself was an exemplary high-achieving professional, mother, and homemaker without a job or home of her own. She had gone to great trouble to bring her washing machine with her from Damascus. It was a valuable appliance and extremely useful in the new household:

> We were a large number of people in Tripoli, and we were washing our clothes by hand. We weren't used to that, and it became difficult. We thought about buying a used one, but that was money we needed to live on. Iba and Hisham encouraged us to bring our washing machine. Even just shipping our machine from Damascus would have cost 5,000 lira, or $70 dollars, to ship it, so we drove it over the border ourselves. Mazen brought it down after taking permission from the *mukhtar* (local authority) back in Damascus to prove we weren't stealing it. And they put it in the back seat and drove.

The washing machine, which seemed in theory like a practical solution to the large number of people living in Abu Samra, may have become a source of contention, a reminder of the different resources and class backgrounds that each sister was able to bring to the combined household. Ironically, when Salma and Mazen moved out of the Abu Samra household in December, they were unable to take the washing machine with them. It became something of an albatross. Should they sell it, return it, lend it, endure the embarrassment of storing it with Iba, whose pride prevented her from using it?

Most of the Syrians in Tripoli didn't have any money to rent apartments. Instead, they pooled their resources to rent unfinished retail storefronts. These largely vacant undeveloped commercial spaces on the bottom floors of buildings had exposed cinder blocks, undivided interior spaces, and sometimes no exterior doors or windows,

3. Chaaban et al., "Poverty and Livelihoods Among UNHCR Registered Refugees in Lebanon."

plumbing, or electricity. The price of one of these exposed and unfinished storefronts was between US$200 and $250 a month, and they were little more than a physical structure of walls and ceiling to be shared by multiple families pooling the rent. For Salma and her family, the sight of one's laundry and personal belongings exposed to the street was shocking, like a half-dressed person with no place for modesty. *Tasattur*, or privacy (literally, "being covered"), was the key tenet of the Araj sisters' lives. It described not only their lifestyle centered on modesty and hijab but also the lifestyle of respectability that they had always enjoyed—quiet, with a sterling reputation for virtue that was a working family's key form of cultural capital for its women and girls. As Salma and Mazen looked for a place of their own, they did consider renting a storefront, an expensive form of squatting, but her sons were horrified by the idea of living one step above homelessness and threatened to return to Damascus and military service.

The transition from Iba's house to their own involved camping in the kitchen of middle sister Farida's tiny apartment (who had only just arrived in Tripoli using money borrowed from a relative abroad) and days of house hunting, with only high-end properties available. "We'd spend the whole day out looking for houses. It was December by then, and the whole day we'd be out looking. We'd either find very expensive apartments or nothing at all." Finding a new home, even with the more abundant resources Salma and Mazen had, was harder than they anticipated when they left Iba and Hisham's house.

> When we left Iba's place, we got in touch with a broker, and he found us a place quickly. . . . We paid a down payment and took all our stuff the same day, and then discovered we'd been cheated. We lost $200 and didn't actually have the house—he claimed to be the agent for the house but didn't actually have the right to rent the house.
>
> With great difficulty we found a little *mulhak* (attic) that we ended up taking on the roof of an apartment building. One room and a corridor with a sink and a toilet with a door. Really, it was

> one room. This attic was 500,000 Lebanese pounds, so $330, and with "stolen" electricity—we wanted to get our own meter and asked about it, but it was simply impossible—and the water, we had to beg for it from the neighbors. When we asked about the electric meter, just having it installed would be $500. There was no way we could pay that much; the room was just a rental. We moved to that room in December; it was the height of winter. The first night we froze; there wasn't a bit of heat then since the electricity wasn't coming on until the next day.

They moved into the unheated space in December, and the electric heater they bought was unusable during the frequent electricity outages. Their roof leaked as well, and water seeped down into the walls of the room. The seeping water and the sketchy electricity made a dangerous combination, and there were regular short circuits. Salma remembered an incident in which her son 'Adel "was sleeping, and he dreamed that he was swimming. He woke up and found that water was dripping on his forehead and had woken him up." She laughed bitterly in recalling their days in the expensive rental. "The power didn't even come on each day—one day on and one day off—six hours at a time on and off. We would sit in the dark when it was off. We'd get so happy when the electricity came on, and then it would go off from a short when water soaked into our walls."

During their year in Lebanon, the boys' education was the primary matter on Salma's mind after housing. The schools available to them were the Syrian Opposition Coalition schools funded by their Sunni coreligionists in the Gulf. Iba was first employed at such a school, but their obscure sources of funding, shady procedures, and bureaucratic politics of favoritism and exploitation eroded trust in them. Salma's youngest son, Kamal, was able to complete first grade in the Lebanese public schools. At the end of the year, however, Salma was told that he would have to move over to the second-rate Coalition schools. There were problems for 'Adel and Yusuf, whose completion of high school in the Coalition schools was the reason for coming to Lebanon. Aside from the question of the schools' quality, the diplomas from these schools were politicized and thus not recognized anywhere except Turkey, the seat of the Syrian resistance. Within the year, 'Adel and Yusuf graduated from a Coalition school with their diplomas in the Syrian national curriculum but faced difficulty in applying to a university. For Salma's sons, work was easier to come by. After finishing their baccalaureate studies in the Syrian Coalition schools, they found work, 'Adel in a gas station owned by a wealthy Australian Lebanese and Yusuf in clothing stores and in riding a moped to deliver *nargileh* (hookah), a job that drove his mother frantic with fear but suited his active nature. He enjoyed weaving through traffic delivering tobacco and live coals to the customers who could afford them and tip well, but it was not what Salma had left home for.

Salma, freezing in her water-permeated Tripoli attic in December 2013 and wondering where her sons would continue their postsecondary education, was the first to realize they had to leave Lebanon. The immediate cause was the end of a sustaining stream of income. "We stayed like this for a while until Mazen's sister called one day and said she would no longer be able to support us indefinitely. She was also sending money to their other sister and had just registered her own children in college. She couldn't keep sending the money. It was difficult for her, but she asked her brother if he could find another source of income, anything." They needed to make some changes. This reversal of fortune, combined with the educational dead end in Lebanon, signaled clearly the need to move on. There was no hope of enrolling 'Adel and Yusuf in Lebanese public or private universities.

Although the boys threatened to return to Syria as a way of manipulating their parents, and Salma and Mazen traveled back and forth across the border occasionally to attend to their properties in Damascus, the situation in Syria after 2013 deteriorated, so Lebanese residency was not something they thought they should give up. News of the chemical-weapons attacks on the Eastern Ghuta in August 2013, in which the regime murdered more than a thousand sleeping civilians in 'Ayn Tarma, where Iba and Farida had lived, shocked the world. Furthermore, Salma's boys were now the ideal age for Syrian army conscription and the attendant paperwork that would constrict their movements and their futures. Also in 2013, along with the economic and educational difficulties of life in Tripoli, the conflict seemed to be spreading to Lebanon. Salma said later,

> As for security, Tripoli was not great. It certainly wasn't as bad as Damascus, of course. The worst clashes [in Tripoli] were in Jabal Muhsin and Tabbaneh. The one side was Sunni, and the Alawites on the other. There would be periodic clashes, and when there were, it might spread. When it got bad, the security services would spread out in the city, and at those times we'd tell the boys to stay in, not to go out so much. They complained, of course; they said, "Really, we left Damascus just to be imprisoned here?," but sometimes we'd need to. And one time when there were clashes between Jabal Muhsin and the Tabbaneh, they closed the schools for a week, and we had no idea when they'd start up again. Really, sometimes it was dangerous in Tripoli.

Disentangling themselves from the Lebanese phase of their lives was almost as radical an uprooting as leaving Damascus because it meant accepting that their refuge was not temporary, a couple of hours' drive from home in a familiar neighboring region. Staying safe involved cutting ties, moving farther away into new languages and cultures, and making plans to weather uncertainty in a range of forms. Ironically, Turkey, with a language completely unrelated to Arabic, was the only place where the boys' Coalition diplomas would be recognized, and so with the cold and wet seeping into the walls of their attic, when their primary income stream dried up, they knew they had to leave.

Salma described the decision-making process.

> Eventually we began to wonder if we could send the [older] boys to Turkey for their studies and that perhaps we would return to Damascus or whether we should all go together to Turkey. But it was clear that for 'Adel and Yusuf there was no future in either Syria or Lebanon. For them, either way, we'd have to send them to Turkey. For us, it wasn't clear what we would do. Even for Kamal, still in grade school, I was worried about him coming and going to

> school—it wasn't safe even at his age. The situation in Syria wasn't safe at all, at all. Mazen agreed that it wouldn't be possible to have two households with two budgets—one in Syria and one in Turkey. If they were going to study, they'd need money; they couldn't work at the same time as studying. Since that would be impossible, we decided that we'd all go to Turkey together. And at the same time the family would stay together and not break up, with each person in a different place.

Having a middle-class privilege that none of Salma's sisters enjoyed, they realized that they could liquidate assets to move most of the family to Istanbul. They had already rented out their apartment and store in Damascus; there was no income to be squeezed from home, and relatives had been completely tapped out. They would sell their car and travel to Turkey together by air. But selling the car to pay for a move to Turkey revealed how entangled their family had become in the bureaucracies of the two states of Syria and Lebanon. What Tim Ingold describes as "wayfaring"—moving and actively engaging the immediate environment through walking and driving—gave way to what he calls "transport"—the passive, destination-oriented traversal of space.[4]

4. "The wayfarer has to sustain himself, both perceptually and materially, through an active engagement with the country that opens up along his path. . . . Though from time to time he must pause for rest, and may even return repeatedly to the same place to do so, each pause is a moment of tension that—like holding one's breath—becomes ever more intense and less sustainable the longer it lasts. Indeed, the wayfarer has no final destination, for wherever he is, and so long as life goes on, there is somewhere further he can go. Transport, by contrast, is essentially destination-oriented. It is not so much a development along a way of life as a carrying across, from location to location, of people and goods in such a way as to leave their basic natures unaffected. For in transport, the traveller does not himself move. Rather he is moved, becoming a passenger in his own body, if not in some vessel that can extend or replace the body's powers of propulsion. While in transit he remains encased within his vessel, drawing for sustenance on his own supplies and holding a predetermined course. Only upon reaching his destination,

Crossing Borders

Salma described the next set of calculations that were crucial to the move.[5] Selling the car would be no easy matter. Because of its Syrian registration, it would need to be sold in Syria. Retracing her thought process, she remembered,

> Buying airplane tickets to Turkey would need a big sum of money, so we decided to sell the Matiz car. But then we discovered that there was a problem with the Matiz—namely, that it had been in Lebanon longer than a year. The paperwork and registration needed to be fixed, and that cost us $500, and a cousin helped us do that. And then we fixed that and had it driven back to Damascus to wait for a buyer. Homesick and with the excuse of selling the car, we decided to leave the older boys in Lebanon with their aunts and go back to Damascus, Mazen to look for a buyer for the car, and me and Kamal, since he was little and I couldn't leave him—especially in another country with things unsettled. And then we found out that Kamal needed an exit visa since he, too, like the car, had been in Lebanon for over a year without exiting and entering the country. Before we could go to Damascus to sell the car to go to Turkey, we had to go to Beirut twice to get his situation sorted out.[6] So, finally, since it looked fine, the three of us went down to Damascus to sell the car. We went in the bus since the car had already had its papers taken care of and had been driven back to Damascus. When we approached the border, the bus driver looked at our passports and told us that if Kamal left Lebanon, he wouldn't be able to come back in. There was a new law at the time

---

and when his means of transport comes to a halt, does the traveller begin to move. But this movement, confined within a place, is concentrated on one spot. Thus the very places where the wayfaring inhabitant pauses for rest are, for the transported passenger, sites of occupation. In between sites, he barely skims the surface of the world." Ingold, "Seven Variations on the Letter A," 182–83, citation omitted.

5. Vignal, "The Changing Borders and Borderlands of Syria"; Menshawy, "Constructing State, Territory, and Sovereignty in the Syrian Conflict."

6. For more on Syrian-Lebanese relations, see Cherri et al., "The Lebanese–Syrian Crisis," 165.

> that Syrians who had overstayed their residence in Lebanon without getting the situation fixed wouldn't be let back in. And Kamal was the only one. We hadn't paid, and he hadn't gone in and out of the country. Not knowing what to do, we stayed on the border; if Kamal was stopped, we all were stopped. We wouldn't be able to go back to Lebanon. And to this day when Kamal remembers the trip, he cries, and he says, "I remember when they wouldn't let me back into Syria!"

Salma and Mazen returned ten-year-old Kamal to Tripoli to stay with his brothers and aunts while they returned to Damascus for a week. Upon their return to Lebanon, Salma was deeply shaken by the heightened securitization of the border, foreshadowing a day when Syrians would be barred from entry. It was July 2014, and a frightening new development was sending new waves of Syrians into Lebanon. ISIS had declared the northeastern Syrian city of Raqqa as the capital of its so-called caliphate.[7] Salma described the unsettling scene at the border.

> As we were coming back to Tripoli, and Kamal and his brothers were still in Lebanon, we heard rumors that the Lebanese border was closed. No Syrians were being let in. But we bought our tickets and left anyway. The bus driver told us that the day before they had turned two busloads of Syrians back—they had let the buses and drivers in, but none of the Syrian passengers. We put our hands on our hearts that they would let us back in since our children were there. It was a disaster. We got to the border, and it was full of people from Raqqa. Raqqa had just fallen to ISIS, and the border crossing it was full of people standing around waiting to get into Lebanon. The border guards were beating the young men. The Lebanese border guards were part of Hezbollah. They were beating people and tearing up their papers, the entry visa that cost 1,200 Lebanese pounds, so they'd have to go back and buy another. It got very ugly at the border that day. More than one time they were going to tear up Mazen's passport. He was waiting in

7. Rosenblatt and Kilcullen, "How Raqqa Became the Capital of ISIS."

> line, and when he saw that they were tearing up papers, he'd leave the line. I was standing in the women's line, and they let us in, no problem. When I got in, I was so relieved because I had left my children and my baby in Lebanon. It would have been a disaster if they didn't let me in. Mazen waited until a particular customs officer took a bathroom break, and in those two minutes he got to the front of the line, had his papers stamped, and got through to where I was waiting by the bus. Two times it didn't work; then finally it worked. This all took four or five hours standing under the glaring sun. Some people had children, some people were sick, and so on.

With difficulty, Salma and Mazen returned to their children in Lebanon. A few months later, in October 2014, the Lebanese border closed completely to Syrian refugees, leaving Syrian refugees with no land egress to an Arab country other than Iraq to the east.[8] Navigating the borders and the threat of being separated from their sons, in particular their baby, Kamal, were traumatizing. Although they had never really settled into their refuge in Lebanon, they found themselves entangled in its bureaucracies and borders. Barred from further movement either back to Syria or reentry to their uncomfortable limbo made Lebanon a transit zone, like Gloria Anzaldúa's borderlands—"a vague and undetermined place created by the emotional residue of an unnatural boundary. It is in a constant state of transition. The prohibited are its inhabitants."[9] Attempts to reproduce the ease with which they had crossed into Lebanon in 2012 were now hampered by borders that had hardened. Any business they had to conduct with Syrian paperwork and possessions got progressively more difficult.

After realizing how the borders were shifting and dangerous in the landscape of the war, Salma redoubled her efforts to get to Turkey. They bought plane tickets using the money from the car they had

8. Favier, "Increasing Vulnerability for the Syrian Refugees in Lebanon"; Mouawad, "Lebanon's Border Areas in Light of the Syrian War."

9. Anzaldúa, *Borderlands/La frontera*, 3. See also Topak, "Border Violence and Migrant Subjectivities."

sold. Mazen would return to Syria with some of their more portable possessions before joining his family. Rental income from his store there would be their main source of income in Turkey. Other possessions—a floor fan, the washing machine, and the generator—would be left behind with Farida in Tripoli, who seemed as determined to stay in Lebanon as she had once been to stay in her apartment in 'Ayn Tarma.

12

Xenophobia

Farida in Tripoli, 2013–2014

Farida's trek from Damascus to Turkey by way of Tripoli began in the first weeks of 2013. Her home in the 'Ayn Tarma suburb of Damascus was squarely in the middle of a ghost town, a no-man's-land in which rebel fighters occupied the bombed-out shells of buildings and were bombarded by regime forces from the air. She was forced to leave the home she had finally established on her own. She followed her little sister Iba from their stricken Ghuta neighborhood to Tripoli, Lebanon, thinking she would then move on to Jordan, where Hanan thought Farida and her daughter might find teaching jobs. Farida began by exiting into Lebanon since direct access to Jordan from Syria was now blocked. In Tripoli, while they were lodging temporarily with Iba, her oldest son was able to find work in his area of specialization—elevator repair. This unexpected turn of luck caused her to make a decision she would later come to bitterly regret—to stay in Tripoli in violation of Lebanese residency law.

Farida, with help from a relative abroad who volunteered to subsidize her rent in hopes that Farida's son would earn enough to take over the lease, rented a small apartment of her own in Tripoli. The plan to consolidate households with Salma and Iba in the larger apartment that Iba and Hisham had rented was tarnished by Salma's experience; adding four more people to the situation that could barely contain the ten members of Salma and Iba's families without exploding was not going to happen. Farida was dismayed to see relations between her two younger sisters degenerating into nasty fights. She declined to engage but sympathized somewhat with Salma.

The two older sisters did not resent Iba's success, exactly. They did bridle at her directness and determined personality. Whether the issue was her youthful energy or her steely piety that gave her an air of superiority or her effective control and coordination of her husband and children is hard to say. But for much of the early time in Tripoli, Iba's family seemed to be thriving, while both Salma and Farida felt themselves sliding backward, palpably losing whatever control and security they had enjoyed in Damascus. Another conflict was brewing. It was humiliating and painful for Farida to call for help from a relative abroad based on her status as a divorced woman and a single mother, but her family members began to complain that her three children were certainly old enough to work and take care of their mother and criticized her for what they saw as her coddling and spoiling of her two sons and daughter. Having once had aspirations of entrepreneurship and an upwardly mobile life for her family, she was particularly reluctant to terminate her children's education or to foreclose their horizons by encouraging them to work in jobs she deemed beneath them, even at the expense of her own stress and decline. In particular, her daughter had become flawlessly fluent in American English, largely from watching English-language movies on television around the clock. That skill was the envy of all her cousins and aunts, but it never seemed to translate into steady work.

When Farida had gambled everything on an upwardly mobile marriage (that she herself arranged) to the children's father back in the 1980s, it had been an expression of her bold confidence in herself and faith in a kind of enterprising neoliberal Islamic agency. Her children were raised with a sense of possibility and entitlement, but upon losing their father and his financial support to his new wife and family, their education was cut short, and they had only visions of professional careers without the means or discipline to achieve them.

Farida's little family, even more than the others, seemed to lurch from place to place only by escalating to crisis and then succumbing to the force of circumstances and the charitable intervention of others. She was the last to stubbornly stay in place in Damascus until her building was literally uninhabitable, and then the expenses and uncertain results of moving as well as the emotional cost of trying to make and execute strategies sapped her will and her confidence. Her health had also begun to decline, with aching feet and joints, kidney disease, and frequent respiratory infections. She was left only with a lot of time for thinking and analysis.

As Farida walked the streets of Tripoli in search of schools and work, she developed an insightful and critical view of the Lebanese political economy, which she confidently shared in bombastic style with anyone who would listen.

> I began to understand that the Lebanese—their charitable organizations and academic institutes and politicians—they have gotten lots of money in our name. Even ordinary people are benefitting from the Syrians by renting their properties for sums they never could have dreamed of or employing young Syrians for pennies. That is—we rent houses and stores for very high rent, and we work for them for very low wages. And they work us like serfs, because the productivity of a Syrian is much higher than that of a Lebanese. A Syrian can work for twelve hours and not complain, not like the Lebanese, who can only work for a few hours under certain conditions. Syrians will do anything and everything, but the Lebanese won't do just any work. . . .[1]
>
> Where are the million refugees? Are they a million tourists? Or a million workers moving the Lebanese economy forward? Even better, the supposed refugee has to pay $200 every six months for the privilege of living here, just like any tourist. And a refugee has to pay rent in dollars? And buy food from their grocery stores, and then they sneer and say "refugee." I never thought I'd see a five-star refuge, like a five-star hotel, paying for everything in US dollars. It should be in *The Guinness Book of World Records*.

1. On refugees working in Lebanon, see Tarraf-Najib, "Work and Denial of Work"; S. Haddad, *The Palestinian Impasse in Lebanon*; and Chabrier, "The War of the Poor in Tripoli (Lebanon)."

Farida remembers her time in Lebanon as a constant search for work and for affordable education options for her teenage children. "During most of this time in 2013, I was looking for a school or even just free courses for my younger son so that he could complete his secondary education."[2] A key feature of both searches was the lack of public services. Lebanon is a weak state dominated by market capitalism since its independence, in contrast to the Syrian strong socialist state whose experiments with neoliberal capitalism date only to the 1990s.[3] Education would be a recurring theme of each sister's challenges in Tripoli, but for Farida the lack of affordable public transportation was the first concrete obstacle that manifested itself in her aging body: "I walked for unbelievable distances on my feet. This was the only way because transport was incredibly expensive for us. Anytime you wanted to go from point A to point B within the city on the so-called public transportation, you'd have to pay the equivalent of a dollar. And if you needed to go outside the city, it would cost you two dollars. In Lebanon, without exception, there is no such thing as government public transportation or even public-transport companies. All there is private investments for profit."[4]

Not having enough work or any other money for expenses made Farida's challenges in Tripoli resemble those of less fortunate Syrians whose placement in camps left them with problems of employment, mobility, education, and health.[5] Indeed, navigating the Lebanese city and economy quickly caused her to despair. She laughed wryly, recounting, "I'd like to say that my days in Tripoli were the worst of

2. On the question of young Syrians' education in this period, see Culbertson and Constant, *Education of Syrian Refugee Children*; Buckner et al., "Between Policy and Practice"; and Maadad and Matthews, "Schooling Syrian Refugees in Lebanon."

3. Hermez, "When the State Is (N)Ever Present."

4. On the issue of migrants' ability to get around a city, see Hansen, "Gender and Mobility"; Bissell, "Passenger Mobilities"; and Bagheri, "Tehran's Subway."

5. On refugee camps, see Turner, "Explaining the (Non-)Encampment of Syrian Refugees"; and R. Sanyal, "A No-Camp Policy."

my life, but unfortunately there are many contenders for that title. And during this time my body and soul broke, my world became black, and I became filled with bitterness." The UN cash assistance that she expected to receive was not enough to live on and dried up within weeks of her arrival. As she recalled, "We registered with the UN, and for a month or two we got assistance, and then they stopped it. We started going for charity and quickly learned that it was a big fraud. Each assistance agency was just trying to sign up the largest number of people in order to steal more and profit. We started to see the difficulties before us."[6]

Farida's material analysis of Syrians' situation in Lebanon was cutting. Their difficulties were compounded by a deep-seated resentment of Syrians among the Lebanese population. Syrian military and political presence in the smaller country during and after its civil war had the lingering aftereffect of strong anti-Syrian prejudice, of which the new refugees bore the brunt. The work that her eldest son was initially able to get as an elevator technician was not steady, and in a climate of escalating anti-Syrian xenophobia Lebanese employers and contractors systematically bypassed and underpaid Syrian workers. He ended up contributing little to Farida's Tripoli household. Farida also noted ruefully that her son had inherited some of his father's selfishness, spending much needed cash on cafés and hookah with his friends.

She bitterly described a level of xenophobia above and beyond the challenges of the streets and the market.[7] Lebanon, like Syria, had sectarian differences as part of its social fabric and system of governance but was very differently configured. Its sectarian civil war in

6. On assistance for refugees, see Janmyr, "UNHCR and the Syrian Refugee Response"; and Garkisch et al., "Third Sector Organizations and Migration."

7. On Lebanese attitudes toward the Syrian refugees, see Collard, "In Lebanon, 1 Million Syrian Refugees Live on $1 a Day"; Salhani, "Flood of Syria Refugees Tries Patience of the Lebanese"; Salhani, "The Men Who Get Rich Off Syrian Refugees"; Salhani, "Syrian Refugees Add Pressure to Beirut's Already Crumbling Infrastructure"; and Salhani, "Welcome Sours for Syrian Refugees."

the 1970s also included spasms of conflict highlighting Hezbollah's emergence and Israeli hegemony as well as Syrian dominance in the ensuing decades. The sectarian divides were legible, but they dated from a different era and manifested in ways that the Syrians found hard to predict or understand based on their Syrian template. Farida recounted her attempts to find work over the course of 2014:

> Most of the employers were straightforward. "We won't hire Syrians." Just like the proverb, "We accepted the humiliation, but it didn't accept us!" I used to read all the want ads in the papers as part of my job search, and one of them would say, "We need a night cleaner for a limited salary. (Lebanese Only)." Another example—"A Plastics Factory needs a man under the age of twenty for various jobs" (this means the worst and most deadly jobs) and then "Lebanese Only." Also " A Girl Under Thirty Needed for Nursing—No Experience Necessary (Lebanese Only)." And anyone who has looked for work for a while can explain what is meant when they specify the age and the sex in that way. But anyway—as they openly say—they only want Lebanese. Imagine, if you will, night cleaning—that fine and noble profession that can make you millions that needs a diploma from the world's best universities—no Lebanese employer would dream of letting a Syrian benefit from it.
>
> One time I responded to a billboard advertising positions for nursery teachers. At first, I didn't want to respond because I was so overqualified, and then when I saw it again, I said to myself, "Don't be a snob and go apply." I went in, and the girl looked me up and down and said, "Yes?" I said, "I am unemployed and looking for work as a teacher." She said, "Have you worked in this capacity before?" I said, "Yes, and I have a great deal of experience." She said, "Well, we need someone who specializes in this field." I said, "That is my specialization." She was silent as she searched for a better excuse. "The Ministry of Health requires that only Lebanese may apply." I understood and went away, frustrated as I had been tens of times before. And the billboard stayed up for another twenty days. They needed teachers, just not Syrian teachers. And I went into a dark depression after that rejection.

The search for a school for her sixteen-year-old son was similarly frustrating:

> After I asked at all the private institutes that claimed to have space and interest in Syrian students, I discovered I was looking in the wrong place. These were merchants of knowledge. I was looking for free or nearly free education. I looked at the vocational schools. Then I went to the Directorate of Education in Tripoli and tried to ask about opportunities for Syrian students, but I was treated like an insect. They ignored me completely. And in spite of all the suffering, I'd need to go back to the directorate because in the course of my wanderings I'd received about twenty different contradictory sets of instructions, and I needed clarification from a real person who understood the situation. I went back in and asked the janitor, and he directed me to a nasty man who waved me away with his hand and wouldn't condescend to speak to me.
>
> Finally, I found a woman working in the directorate who had enough humanity to actually speak to me like a human being. I said, "I'm a Syrian, and I'd like for my son to complete his high school education. Literary, scientific, technical, arts, religious education—it doesn't matter as long as he can finish his high school diploma." And I informed her that he had broken off his schooling because of the war in Syria since students couldn't reach their schools safely in the Ghuta region. She asked me several questions, and I was happy and optimistic that she, unlike so many others, knew and cared about the situation I was describing.
>
> Then she said to me, "You need, first, a stamped and notarized copy of his record from the Syrian Ministry of Education; second, a signature from the Syrian Foreign Ministry; then third, it must be stamped and notarized by the Department of Education in Beirut; and then fourth, stamped and notarized by the Foreign Ministry in Beirut and then accompanied by a certified statement from the United Nations in Beirut that you are bona fide refugees. And, of course, sixth, we'll need records to show that he has passed every level of school with at least 60 percent from third up to ninth grade. Then you need to find a school that will accept Syrians; not all of them do. And finally, you'll need a letter from the school director affirming that they can and will place your son."

> I smiled sweetly, stifling a rising anger and disappointment, and said to her, "Excuse me, miss, I think you have misunderstood me. My son is not running for president of the United States; he just wants to complete his secondary education in Lebanon." She smiled and directed me to the website of the Lebanese Department of Education. I thanked her and left; I had gotten my hopes up because she was the first bureaucrat who had spoken to me as one human being to another. The website was actually worse than that of the Syrian Department of Education; there was nothing to be learned or gained from visiting it. And, of course, for me, getting the seven documents required was beyond reach—very expensive, not to mention dangerous.

At one point, Farida went to the Lebanese-Syrian border crossing and begged border officials to let her back into Syria to die in her home rather than in now hated Tripoli, but she lacked the several thousand dollars to pay her residency-violation fines and was turned back.[8] Finally, Farida found a place for her younger son in a Syrian Coalition school: "Eventually, I learned about a Syrian school on the outskirts of town that held school in the afternoons under the auspices of the Syrian Opposition Coalition. I went there as fast as I could and quickly registered my son there. And even though it was very far from where I lived, and he had to walk for over half an hour each way, I was happy because he was finally back to his studies. Of course, the school was hardly perfect, and our circumstances were very far from being perfect."

In the fall of 2014, after Farida's son had been attending the school for three months, the administration sent an invitation to parents to talk to educational researchers about their experience. Farida described the scene and her lecture to the researchers:

> The meeting was attended by two Lebanese academic researchers, who had asked for it to learn about the needs of the Syrian students. They were professional and polite, and it was clear that they were carrying out research about Syrian students' needs in

8. On situations like Farida's, see Janmyr, "Precarity in Exile."

the neighboring countries. Before we began, the researchers asked the school administrator and his assistants and even the photographer he had brought to take pictures that he could frame and hang on his wall to leave the room.

That was a shock to the director and his minions, who believed that they were kings in their little kingdom. Just as they would have been in Syria. And the assistant director actually left his phone on the table as if by accident so that they could record what was happening in their absence. But [one of] the researcher[s] politely reminded him to take his phone. And they all got mad and bent out of shape, but they left, perhaps for the first time having gotten schooled in freedom and democracy and openness. [One] researcher gave a concise talk about the importance of school for refugees outside their country. And [the researchers] said they had come to hear our views and take them to the authorities. She [the woman researcher] asked why the rest of the parents hadn't come, and we all chimed in with different ways of saying the same thing—that a parents' meeting, as they had known for their entire lives, was something like the meeting of the Syrian Parliament—empty speeches and obsequious demonstrations of loyalty to hypocritical authorities.

The head researcher smiled and asked why we had come then. I told her that we were desperate and in dire straits and would be happy if she could arrange free schooling for us, and everyone laughed. They asked questions, and the people told them about their poverty, their struggle to find food, the difficulties of life as a refugee. She was sympathetic but wanted to know more about the question of education and its challenges.

One of the fathers said, "This school is funded by the Gulf even if we don't know who. All the needs are supposed to be covered, so why are we paying fees? True, it's not a lot, but in our situation it is significant. And it's a breach of trust—the bus won't take anyone who can't pay, and yet we often see it driving by empty as our students walk half an hour to the school. And the school year started very late, and we don't even know if the diplomas will be accepted. All we get is vague nonanswers."

Then I raised my hand and said, "I know you need an overview of the situation in the schools. And I understand that you need to focus for academic and theoretical purposes. But you need to put it in context. Syrians are living here in Lebanon in circumstances you might not be able to imagine. Some of them are living just because death is not available at this time. You know that if a student goes to school hungry, the best technology and technique in the world will be useless. And if he walks half an hour each way in shoes that barely protect him from the cold and rain, the results will be the same. And if he leaves the house knowing that his parents need to get the rent together in three days or they'll be out in the street, again the result will be the same. And if he can't sleep because someone in his family is in pain, or if he fears that he will lose one of his parents, the result is the same, and so on and so on and so on and so on. And our children feel a great responsibility. They can read the desperation in their parents' eyes and read all the signs of what is going on around them."

After apologizing for going on too long and too passionately, I stopped, but the researcher encouraged me to finish. I said, "I and my three children are all ready to work and be productive. We've been here for two and a half years, and only one of us has found work and for a poor wage. We can't even afford to die here. Ask yourself what that means—we'd need death certificates and coffins and permission for burial, and our corpses would decompose before we could get any of those things. For that reason, I decided to go back to die in my own country, but I was surprised to learn that I can't even leave Lebanon to go back to my own country. Why? Because I've overstayed my visa and owe fines of $1,600, and the longer I stay the more I owe, and eventually I'll be considered someone not paying the state, and my children and I will go to jail. So let me be very clear. I haven't received any assistance of any kind. Everyone takes our names so that they can steal charity meant for us. I can't find work not just because of the rising unemployment rate in Lebanon but also because of the campaign 'don't employ Syrians.' We discover that we are in a large open-air prison called Lebanon. We don't have what it takes to live, and we don't have what it takes to die."

Silence. I continued, "I only want to get out of this prison." She said to me, "I promise to take your message to the people who

> can help you. We will knock on every door and make every effort. We regret that we can't do any more than that." I said, "That is an effort that we thank you for that, and at least you can say you did what you could."

Farida ended her story by invoking the prayer for the dead: "Inna lilahi wa inna ilayhi raji'un" (We are all from God and to God we will return). But not long after that encounter, she with great difficulty fled Tripoli for Turkey, following her younger sister Salma. The growing sense of panic that she could no longer stay in Lebanon was sparked by a wave of arrests of young Syrian men in Tripoli by the Lebanese government. Her worst fear was soon realized as her eldest son was caught up in a Lebanese army sweep of young Syrian men in the streets and jailed for a few days.[9] She was frantic with worry, almost incoherent. Her contacts abroad, usually reassured by her confidence and proud bearing, were shocked and agreed to finance a trip to Turkey for her and her three children, including her son, who had been questioned and released from jail. The money came overnight on the condition that she follow Salma to Turkey and not fight with her sister in the pattern that had become common over the past year in Tripoli.

For Farida, crisis had become a means of decision-making and leveraging support. She lacked the wherewithal to plan ahead, spiraled into a situation of complete despair and immobility, and depended on outside intervention to provide lifelines. Her situation was exhausting, demoralizing, depressing, and infuriating. Every disaster shifted her position without her control or flexibility of choice. Every disaster left her weaker and angrier. This particular crisis lurched her toward Turkey.

With the wired money in hand, Farida (lugging boxes of Mazen's books left in her care, which she hated to leave behind) fought her way through immigration in Lebanon, finally able to pay the exorbitant exit fee and some bribes. Enduring taunting and harassment

9. On these sweeps, see Gade, "The Syrian Conflict."

from port officials, she paid and talked her way into being allowed to leave in a cargo ship for the Turkish port of Mersin on the condition that she never return to Lebanon.[10] Surprisingly, at the last minute her older son, whose short imprisonment had been the immediate cause of her decision to leave, refused to leave Lebanon. He had work here, he insisted, so why not stay? If his situation improved, he could help his mother and siblings by sending money. He never did, and he inherited Salma's washing machine, which he later sold in Tripoli.

10. On the status of ferry service to Turkey during the refugee crisis, see "Lebanon–Turkey Ferry Service to Bypass Syria."

13

Managing Kin

The sisters' journeys have highlighted different assemblages of home. The first such formation consisted of the original quarters they inhabited and lives they led in Damascus, which were torn apart by war. The city they came from was an urban assemblage whose coded cultural templates they carried with them into exile. What the sisters did in Egypt, Lebanon, Jordan, and later Turkey was also assemblage in its more agentive form: the assemblage of homes with the emphasis on the active processes of marshalling and arranging resources as well as reassembling families and livelihoods as best they could. In part two, the relevant assemblage was for the newcomers not so much a structural setting (although the cities they fled to are, like Damascus, unique and vibrant cultures and environments) but the urgent restorative acts the sisters initiated and carried out in composing and cobbling together safe and sustainable lives for their families. They collected and managed money, vehicles, employment, shelter, and education, but they counted also on the intimate resources of social, especially family, connections. How they approached the management of these resources and affordances was interpreted through the Damascene cultural codes imprinted on them. The meanings of family, religion, reciprocity, civic life, and personal aspirations guided their activities in near refuge, but not with the effectiveness or efficiency they could have expected in their former, preflight lives. This set of cultural codes gave them the instructions and parameters to reconstruct the constellations of people, things, and relationships they had left behind. But the results were mixed at best, even in predominantly Arabic-speaking, majority-Muslim, urban settings, which nevertheless offered no easy foothold for them; their new lives were unsustainable for longer than a few months. The cultural codes of home that the sisters reasonably expected to be universally applicable in fact frayed, stretched, and gave way, leading in some cases to new displacements to be discussed in part three.

In making the decision to leave Damascus and abandon home, protecting her family was each sister's motivation. In each resettlement, family were expected to be a practical and affective support to one another. Marshall Sahlins describes kinship as "a mutuality of being; people who are intrinsic to one another's existence . . . whether by procreation, social construction, or some combination of these."[1] A daily life based on this deep mutuality produced a kind of affective atmosphere of connection in which the radical isolation of being a single individual in a strange new environment was replaced by the comforting blanket of connectivity, a state of "relationships in which," states Suad Joseph, "a person's boundaries are relatively fluid so that persons feel a part of significant others . . . to mean an activity or intention, not a state of being . . . that can take various forms under different political economy regimes."[2] Living with family and performing the roles of wife, mother, mother-in-law, and grandmother while others play their various roles as dutiful sons, daughters, siblings, and spouses cultivated a sphere in which the exchange of affection, news, information, money, humor, and hospitality was nurtured and incubated against the backdrop of a harsh new environment. The stories of intertwined family relations—exchanges, support, rivalry, and conflict—bring kinship to life.[3] But

1. Sahlins, *What Kinship Is—and Is Not*, 2.

2. Joseph, "Gender and Relationality Among Arab Families in Lebanon," 467.

3. "New kinship studies" is based on a "sense of frustration . . . that kinship studies seemed to have become quite dry and technical, removed from the lives and liveliness, the everyday happenings and the importance of women in making kinship, which are in many ways its most essential and obvious elements." Goldfarb and Carsten, "The 25th Anniversary of 'The Substance of Kinship and the Heat of the Hearth.'"

the local environment, the new terrain, challenged the ideal family structure and function encoded in the sisters.

The critical affordance of family, one of the key components of home, was transportable more or less intact in the mature families headed by the two older sisters but was severely challenged as the younger sisters failed to support each other effectively and became estranged. Eldest sister Maryam, for example, as a stay-at-home mother and grandmother in Egypt, was able to supervise, execute, and nurture her family's mutuality and to establish the infrastructure of matriarchal carework required in her family's new Egyptian household. She headed their new household in the same loving and frugal way that she had begun to do in Damascus when her husband was working abroad or limited his time with and commitment to her and her children. In Damascus, she had not had to pay monthly rent, but caring for her grandchildren in Egypt allowed her son and daughters to work outside the home. Also on the positive side, she was finally free of the interference of her parents-in-law, far away from their meddling and suspicion. She was able to cushion the harshness of the Egyptian exile for her family.

Similarly, the next oldest sister, Hanan, was sustained in Amman and later in Turkey by the care and material resources provided by her adult children in their own established and productive households. In her exile from Syria, such provision allowed her to carry on with her homemaking, her sewing enterprise, and her active matrimonial agency for her unmarried children in the same way that she might have done back home.

In contrast, Farida, Salma, and Iba, all of whom were still lodged in the heart of young, simple nuclear families when they fled, tried their best to share the burdens of life in Tripoli by living together. More than solidarity, however, tensions and rivalries emerged in the new household they scrambled to assemble in Tripoli but were unsuccessful in replicating the abundant support of complex and mature families. The old code of sibling connectivity nurtured in childhood was challenged by their individual obligations to their own children and husbands, by the scarcity of space, money, and opportunity, and by the collision of different goals and personalities. They subscribed, per their upbringing and religion, to a benign and solidarity-based view of sisterhood as the deepest and most natural of friendships. Tatiana Rabinovich elaborates on "sisterly intimacies" as "an affective formation with spiritual and material dimensions which facilitate[s] . . . abilities to shoulder the conjoined crises."[4] Small acts of care and mutual kindness as well as more substantial forms of aid are an underestimated resource for survival in challenging times. But given the challenges of life as refugees, the psychological support of sisterly friendship provided in ordinary times—relaxing over a cup of coffee, sharing household chores, protecting each other's privacy, and giving small material and symbolic gifts—was not up to the task of fulfilling their extraordinary needs. With the limited space and resources available to them in Tripoli, and with underemployed husbands and rapidly developing school-age children to support, the younger sisters struggled to work both inside and outside the home. They jostled for position, dominance, and space, which resulted in grudges that would be papered over with difficulty only by time and distance and threatened to return months and even years in the future. Each sister was frustrated and confused by their failure to live together harmoniously and traumatized by the toll that the experience took on their relationships as sisters. Without a parent or older sister to mediate disagreements and share the care burdens traditionally assigned to women, and without independent adult children to provide financial and social resources, the frustrations of working wives, struggling husbands, and growing children caused each of the younger three sisters to remember their days in Tripoli as among the worst of their lives.

The sisters' narratives of the intensities of homemaking in their new circumstances reveal that making homes in limbo was nearly impossible for structural reasons. Not only were the environments in which they found themselves overcrowded and inhospitable, but

4. Rabinovich, "Sisterly Intimacies," 842.

the change shook and challenged the "family tool kits" they carried with them. Their household-management skills and expectations did not dovetail well with the affordances available to them in their new temporary homes. Their domestic discomfort as much as changing political circumstances would accelerate the younger sisters' flight first to Turkey and then on to Europe.

PART THREE

Taking Flight

> This time my voice departs from Damascus
> It leaves the house of my mother and my father
> The geography of my body is changing
> The cells of my blood run green
> My alphabetic code becomes green
> In Damascus my mouth brings forth a new mouth
> And my voice brings forth a new voice
> And my fingers awaken
> As a digital tribe
>
> —Nizar Qabbani, "Ablutions with the Water of Love and Jasmine," translated by Leila Hudson

By 2014, the exhausting labor of survival in refugee households presented stark choices. Propelled forward again by the gendered perceptions of young men's restless energy, young women's traditional marriageability, and parents' attempts to secure their children's futures at all costs, and with an increasing tolerance for risk and debt, the sisters began to contemplate their first irregular journeys to Europe. The three older sisters, Maryam, Hanan, and Farida, would ultimately opt to refrain from the dangerous European gambit, looking back to Syria, realistic about the risks of moving forward to Europe, although members of their households did make the leap. The younger sisters who were still in their forties, Salma and Iba, found the means and strength to push their families to Europe. The all too obvious risks of striking out for Europe were mitigated by several factors; the stick pushing them forward was the unsustainability of life in the Arab countries of near refuge and the devastation of the internationalized Syrian war in which Russian air power and Iranian-sponsored ground troops intensified the carnage. The carrot attracting them was the impression, intensified by Angela Merkel's invitation and reports from the dozens of pioneers they personally knew, that Europe offered a more dignified form of asylum.

In 2015, Chancellor Angela Merkel of Germany effectively endorsed Syrian asylum claims in Germany despite the European Union's (EU) Dublin Accord, which spelled out that the first European country entered by a migrant (usually Greece) would be responsible for their asylum case.[1] Germany, with its liberal family-reunification policy, became a viable goal for those who had not yet contemplated the journey to Europe.[2] There was also by 2015 a consolidated and easily accessed market for illegal smuggling of people in pursuit of European asylum. With millions of Syrian refugees having made their way to Turkey, and with the perils of the North African smuggling route from Egypt and Libya to Italy resounding in the media, when Chancellor Merkel made her encouragement of asylum seekers in Germany, the much shorter Aegean route from the western coast of Turkey to the nearby Greek islands (part of the EU) came to replace the Mediterranean route over the course of a few months. For millions of Syrian refugees, including the sisters, the Aegean coasts beckoned as their last pathway to their children's futures. The cities of the Arab world had exhausted them. The borders between Arab countries had become hardened and impenetrable. The Mediterranean was a place of death and terror. Even Istanbul, more accommodating than other places, was a constant challenge for the

1. The Dublin Regulation charges EU member countries as well as Iceland, Norway, Switzerland, and Liechtenstein with the responsibility of processing asylum cases in the country in which the asylum seeker first arrives. For more, see Armstrong, "You Shall Not Pass!"

2. Tjaden and Heidland, "Did Merkel's 2015 Decision Attract More Migration to Germany?"; Wolff, *Migration and Refugee Governance in the Mediterranean*, 1–24.

older generation and threatened to entrap the younger generation in an unending treadmill of low-wage labor.

Between 2015 and 2017, the changing complex of European asylum laws, cultures, and politics attracted many single men scouting the route to that continent. Also, family men with obligations hoped to gain asylum, send money to their families, and eventually take advantage of family reunification. As the Russian air war and the rise of ISIS pushed more and more Syrians out of their country, and as Lebanon, Jordan, Egypt, and even larger Turkish cities grew inhospitable and unaffordable, a growing number of women and families joined the migration to Europe. Then, when the family-reunification regimes became more rigid in the EU, some—though not the Araj clan—were desperate enough to send minor children unaccompanied as the only legal way to reunite adult family members.

These journeys involved several ruptures and risks for migrants such as the Araj sisters. Their unknown destinations were both geographically and culturally farther than they had gone before, a Syrian diaspora scattering far beyond that of 2012 to 2014. These migrants would leave behind the world in which Islamic norms were dominant and where Arabic was recognized if not understood, and they would put themselves in the hands of mercenary gangs and their extralegal smuggling. During 2015 and 2016, their challenges were not so much with difficult state bureaucracies involving borders and visas but with having to engage and negotiate with gangs and to endure harsh physical struggles on sea and land. Subsequently, new European state rules and regulations offered relief from the most direct dangers but enveloped the sisters and their families in the varying political cultures of different states with their own unfamiliar logics that used refugees as political pawns and even as scapegoats.[3]

The moves into European exile involved breaking up the fragile assemblages of the households that the sisters had preserved and

3. Gowayed, *Refuge*.

clung to as a microcosm of home. The dangerous transport depended on mobilizing and paying large sums of money. The two families that left for Europe needed to break up: some members had to go ahead to prepare and provide resources—money or an asylum application to start family reunification. The linguistic code, taken for granted, provided dubious comfort and connection on the road. Looking for Arabic speakers on the road and beyond was a source of strength and comfort.

Throughout these struggles, however, the sisters were able to sustain a belief in family reconnection and reterritorialization, and electronic communications played a critical role in holding the kin networks together across ever broader vistas of space, time, and social formations. Even as the families broke up, they stayed in digital contact. They gained information and emotional sustenance through their cell phones—voice, text, image, geolocation, and information groups served as lifelines. Families were no longer living together as they had in the previous phase of their displacement, but they stayed in contact. Navigational GPS was the first ethereal form of reconnecting with a new environment, in which affordances were no longer to be scratched from the economy but more likely to be handed out by charitable organizations.

The Mediterranean and Aegean crossings of hundreds of thousands of Syrians and other migrants marked a new phase in the massive migration forced by the war. They were in a new kind of space, the no-man's-land of the sea. The well-known lines of the cities and towns they grew up in were a memory. The lines of the places where they had taken temporary refuge had entangled and entrapped them. The "smooth spaces" (wildernesses not navigable or legible through the familiar social codes) of the sea and the borderland peripheries of the European continent beyond challenged the refugees in new ways.[4] They had to calculate and navigate using cell phones. More

4. On "smooth spaces," see Deleuze and Guattari, *A Thousand Plateaus*, 474–500. According to Edward Campbell, "They [Deleuze and Guattari] contrast the vertical and horizontal striations of embroidery with the smooth amorphous

than in the earlier stages of taking refuge in neighboring countries, when flight was a family affair, they needed to figure out how to break down the family into the most efficient subgroups for travel. They needed to front larger amounts of money for passage than they had in moving to nearby countries. They depended on their cell phones not only to stay in touch with their contacts but also for navigational technology.[5] The new affordances that the sisters depended on from day to day could not have been more different from the urban assemblage of Damascus, which was made of buildings, neighbors, and streets. These affordances were not even the same as the precarious and off-kilter assemblage of new households in exile that they had been exhausted by maintaining in Arab countries. They instead looked like a digital meshwork centered on cell phones as the families entered a period of uncertain mobility across water and new European landscapes. Texts, shared contacts, Facebook groups, YouTube videos, GPS, Google Maps—in addition to traditional voice calls—were the new anchors as Syrians set out for Europe on flimsy rafts and ancient fishing boats, pinning their hopes on the kindness of Western strangers. The sisters' narratives trace their diaspora over a wider landscape and show how their new assemblage(s) formed an ethereal web of electronic communications in which the role of place, mutual obligation of kinship, language, and memory were once again revalued.

---

nature of felt. They refer to the sea as the 'smooth space par excellence' that becomes increasingly striated for navigational purposes. The sea is consequently described . . . as 'the archetype of smooth space' . . . and it is contrasted with the city, the paradigmatic striated space." Campbell, *Music After Deleuze*, 74.

5. Marino, *Mediating the Refugee Crisis*; Cheesman, "Self-Sovereignty for Refugees?"; Tazzioli, "Extract, Datafy and Disrupt"; Jensen et al., "Together and Apart"; Milner, *Pinpoint.*

14

Little Syria

Salma, 2014

Salma and her three sons arrived at Atatürk International Airport in Istanbul in December 2014, while Mazen tied up loose ends in Damascus. They were met at the airport by Mazen's brother and his wife, who were among the 350,000 Syrian refugees already in the city of Istanbul by the time Salma, 'Adel, Yusuf, and Kamal got there.[1] Throughout Turkey between 2012 and 2019, the number of Syrians fleeing the war reached 4 million, as many as the entire population of Lebanon and more than the city of Damascus. The vast majority lived in Turkey's cities, undocumented, with the status of "guests" rather than with refugee status guaranteed by the Geneva Convention and documented by the UN.

Unlike in Lebanon, the Turkish economy easily accommodated many Syrian workers and Syrian investment capital. There was a palpable relief in being in a more generous economic environment, especially one that was less cruelly xenophobic than Tripoli. Yet although the Turkish environment was more accommodating, and the Turkish political economy (unlike the Lebanese) had a place for Syrians in its low-wage sectors, allowing many refugees to breathe, work, invest, and investigate their new surroundings, the most basic affordance of all—language—could not be taken for granted. Having studied

1. "Syrian Refugees Trying to Start a New Life in Turkey's Istanbul."

some English and French, many Syrians were able to sound out many words in Turkish, but the language bore no similarity to the grammar and everyday vocabulary of Arabic.

In selling their car and leaving behind the last of their possessions, Salma and her sons had outfitted themselves for their first plane journey. Throughout her exile, Salma was always managing to take or, rather, struggling to lug stuff with her—appliances, clothes, cars—which created a certain kind of middle-class stress while it increased convenience and marked identity. Salma described what she remembered of the journey: "We had never been in a plane before, and all we knew was that one should dress up for a plane ride. I had my leather manteau and matching scarf and these beautiful high-heeled shoes. If I had only known, I had others that were still nice but not so high! They would have matched, and we put on layers and layers of clothes, so we didn't have to put them in the suitcases. And we were nervous, hot, and sweaty."

The airplane and the set of rituals taken for granted by seasoned air travelers felt deceptively quick and easy, producing a similar uncanniness as Salma's first vacation tourism visits to Tripoli. Until they had sold their car to pay for the trip to Turkey, Salma's family's perspective also was automotive. Unlike her sisters, she was a driver and a car owner.[2] Despite all the bureaucracy of car registration that had caused the family so much stress in Lebanon, she had been used to the idea of driving or riding in her own car. The ability to navigate freely in one's own vehicle had been liberating and provided a certain sense of autonomy and control. The passenger aviation experience exchanged the freedom to pile people and things into a car and drive for the limitations of being a ticketed passenger in a restrictive and formal new system in which one yielded control to unseen others. Upon landing far more quickly than she anticipated, Salma found herself in an urban geography larger and instantly very different from

2. On the affordances of car ownership, see Butcher, "'Sir, It Was My Right of Way!'"; and Bagheri, "Tehran's Subway."

anywhere she had lived before. There was now a subway system to navigate and lots of walking between stations. Getting to and from the metro stops dressed for the adventure of air travel was a huge mistake. "We walked and walked, and I was dying in my high heels. We had already stood in lines in Beirut and in the Istanbul airport for hours, and we'd ask our relatives where the house was. 'No, no, it's still nearby,' she would say. It was so far away, *ya latif*."[3] Without money to spare, the family could afford taxis only as a rare exception. It was too expensive to put all the people in taxis, so the family would take the cheaper metro, while the luggage was more efficiently transported by a single hired taxi.

Salma and her family eventually settled in one of the neighborhoods of Istanbul where Syrian newcomers congregated, known informally as "Little Syria." When Syrian newcomers arrived in Istanbul, they headed to Fatih, the traditional area on the southern European side of the Bosphorus.[4] Inside the old Byzantine city walls, high above the waterline of the Bosporus, the area is dominated by the Fatih Mosque, one of the great Ottoman monumental houses of worship. Newcomers knowing nothing of the city could easily find this enormous complex with its sprawling refuge and park. Just outside its gate was the growing collection of shops and businesses with Arabic signage and Syrian fast-food restaurants where Arabic language filled the air. A little farther on was the area known as the Carsamba, or Wednesday Market, where traffic gave way every week to shades covering kilometers of vegetables, cheese, clothing, and notions sellers. This area is one of Istanbul's most conservative, also home to at least one important Sufi lodge hosting students and worshipers from all over Turkey and Central Asia. Lined with small retail operations, many of which came to cater exclusively to Syrians and other Muslim foreigners, the area is residential and not heavily

3. Kay, "Syrians in Turkey." *Ya latif* is an invocation of the deity, expressing surprise or dismay.

4. Tumen, "The Economic Impact of Syrian Refugees on Host Countries"; Aksu Kargin, "The Syrian Refugees in Turkey."

trafficked like nearby areas. Its population is more pious and gender segregated than anywhere else in Istanbul.

Rents here were expensive but not prohibitive for families like Salma's.[5] Those who could afford it rented apartments. The increase in rent prices over the course of 2014 and 2015 was about threefold. At the beginning of this period, when Salma's sister-in-law first arrived in Istanbul, one could get a two-bedroom apartment in Fatih for 400–500 Turkish lira (about US$200). By the time Salma and her family moved out of her sister-in-law's apartment, a small cramped two-bedroom apartment was going for 1,000 Turkish lira a month.[6] In the streets of the old Greek Orthodox quarter, affected families from the tribal areas of northern and eastern Syria were living like this, their pajama-clad toddlers playing in the gutters of the hilly cobblestone streets and rummaging through garbage containers for discarded toys and extra food, while their parents sat sometimes silently despondent, sometimes talking to each other on the sidewalks in front of their basement apartments.

The urban economy into which Salma found herself transported was bigger, more confident, less politically fraught than Tripoli as well as less deceptively and surreally similar to Damascus. Unlike in Lebanon, there was plenty of manufacturing work to be done in Istanbul. Turkish garment shops, restaurants, bakeries, hotels had plenty of long hours to be worked. With the same amount of hustle as in Lebanon, where it produced no results, work and lodging could be found in Istanbul. In fact, if one was able and willing, one could find lots of work, and it came in very long shifts with very low wages. Work was exhausting and grueling. The low wages precluded study and introduced Syrians to the ravenous labor market that had no room for the accommodations of family life and leisure still taken for granted in Syria.[7]

5. On rent and migration, see Balkan et al., "Immigration, Housing Rents, and Residential Segregation."

6. Altındağ et al., "Blessing or Burden?"

7. Esen and Binatlı, "The Impact of Syrian Refugees on the Turkish Economy."

Work, homemaking, and education competed for the family members' limited energy. As Salma settled into Turkey, daily home life—cooking, shopping, internet, transport, hosting, and visiting—looked a lot like it did back in Syria. But sociability was squeezed and compressed by the energy and time needed for work and commuting. The excitement of finding employment soon gave way to the realization that difficult choices would need to be made. As soon as Salma had found an apartment, and even before she set about looking for teaching work, she looked for any kind of work that would bring in income.

> We would walk around, and I saw another sign on the road to the Fatih Mosque, and we asked if it was for work. Signs advertising work were the first words of Turkish I learned to recognize. A girl came and took us to another sewing workshop in the same area, and she asked me if I could embroider. I said, "Yes, try me," and she said to come the next day. They didn't have anything for my son, so I went the next day. The work was on wedding dresses, the corset, full of beads and glitter. I had to take out the pins and sew on the beads and glitter. Since the corset is so stiff with whale bone and wires, each time I would prick my finger. All day from eight in the morning until eight at night pricking my fingers. The first day I got back [home], my hands were numb and tingling. And then I feared I would get blood on the white wedding dresses. The second and third day, my eyes were all on the white, I would look up and feel like I couldn't see at all. But I'm no professional. I could only work there for another two weeks. That's my limit, from 8:00 a.m. in the morning until 8:00 p.m. at night, and Kamal would be taken to school by his brothers. I was never in the house. I never saw the kids. It was very difficult.

'Adel and Yusuf found work within a couple of days—grueling shifts from 6:00 a.m. to 8:00 p.m.; they were gone all day and came back so tired they couldn't stand. The boss was "a real piece of work, trying to get people to work for a couple of days and hate it so much that they would quit, and she wouldn't have to pay them." They worked for a few days and never went back. Yusuf started working in a bakery so he could get some money for college, and when 'Adel started taking a college-prep course, he could no longer work.

One of the family's next concerns was getting Kamal into school. It was necessary because the school year had already started a month or two earlier. Salma always had the intention of combining her work with Kamal's schooling,[8] which would accomplish two important objectives—synchronize her work with her youngest son's schooling and allow her older sons to focus on their own work and studies. She collected the names of schools and contacts in them from all her friends and acquaintances in Syria and Turkey and emailed and visited each school in person, but all with no results. She would have loved to teach Arabic to Turks and, indeed, had several short-term jobs teaching French, her trained profession. But even working in Fatih took her away from her family for more time than she could stand, and commuting across the metro area to the Asian side of the city was too daunting a prospect. "I was offered a job teaching Arabic for Turks. But it would be on the Asian side and an extracurricular program. They wanted me to take off my hijab, and I refused, and they backed down. But in the end, it would have been hard for me to sleep there and leave my kids alone in the house. Instead, I sat in the house, and there were problems."

She was eventually able to find the kind of work she wanted—first by volunteering in a local Syrian school where Kamal was registered. She assisted in the summer programs, then with special-needs kids in the fall. "The salary was *zift* (dirt)," she recalled with disgust. She then found a job in another allied Arab school, this time a Libyan school, which was, as she said, "one hundred and eighty degrees different, especially in terms of the salary."[9] But after a single

8. On young refugees and school, see Aydin and Kaya, "Education for Syrian Refugees."

9. On teaching in such a school, see Mohamed, "Sources of Occupational Stress Among Teachers"; and Elkhdr and Aimer, "The Effect of Personal Factors on Organizational Commitment Among Teachers Working at Libyan Schools in Turkey."

semester in which she worked in her specialty as a French teacher, the school shifted away from mandatory French classes, and she was once again out of a job.

Salma's family was in a constant state of friction. "We were all irritable and fighting," she remembered. To pay the rent, Salma was working as hard as she ever had in her life, first at sewing wedding dresses, then at teaching in the Libyan school. 'Adel and Yusuf also worked in a bakery while trying to learn Turkish and find educational opportunities. All of them were exhausted by their efforts to make enough to pay the rent and meet their basic expenses. Then Salma's husband, Mazen, was finally able to join his family in Istanbul. As in Tripoli, his aspiration was to open his own business, but the costs remained prohibitive, and there was the language problem. The question of language and literacy, which had not been an issue in Lebanon, would become a huge practical issue for the sisters and their families in Istanbul. Throughout 2015 and 2016, language barriers would replace Lebanese xenophobia as one of the greatest problems they faced. Most obviously, the children's access to education would continue to be a question of great importance. In this new environment, too, the language-learning abilities of various family members would modify relations of seniority and dependency for the first of many times. The children were quick to learn, their mother was studious and determined, and their father was frustrated. The uncomfortable role reversal of Salma working and Mazen staying home exacerbated problems.

There was no question of going back to Damascus to live. Relatives at home told them they would be insane to return to the random violence, the eroded economy, and the prospect of arrest, with Salma still on the government's list of suspected opposition members. The boys would be subject to conscription in Assad's military. Aside from the threat of violence, when Mazen had returned to Damascus to attend to his property and business the previous year, he had found that rampant inflation and corruption forced him to spend more and more of his valuable resources on bribing officials for everyday procedures, especially those involving cars and real estate.

'Adel and Yusuf, whose interests and personalities had begun to diverge, fought constantly, and their mother felt helpless to stop it. The little flat was too small to hold the two of them, their resentments, and their anger toward one another. Each of the boys threatened to go to Germany and leave the other to support the family in Istanbul. If one or both of them left, it would cripple their parents' ability to make ends meet. Compounding the situation that spring, 'Adel and Yusuf's friends from Syria would come and stay with the family for a day or two and then continue on to Germany, smuggled across the Aegean in tiny, overcrowded inflatable rafts that sank at an alarming rate. Although households like Salma's were able to sustain themselves for months, they were also the site of fraying family nerves. The tensions were only temporarily relieved by the arrival of Syrian guests, who brought news of home and grim confirmation that things were too bad to return. These guests mobilized the family's hospitality, good behavior, and sense of normalcy. With each encounter with someone who had made up their mind to go to Europe and embarked on the process, though, the family's members were exposed to the idea and contemplated it.

When their guests, mostly young men of 'Adel and Yusuf's age, later called to report that they had made it safely to Germany in an average of eight days, the boys began to plan in earnest. The oldest son, 'Adel, surprised his mother one day when he announced that he was leaving the next day and requested the money to do so. Shocked, his parents refused, and he sulked in a particularly foul mood for several days. During this painful period, a friend of Mazen's called him and advised him to go to Germany.

To silence his sons' impulsive threats of leaving, Mazen started talking about being the one to go. He was the head of the family, and in Istanbul, as in Tripoli, he was unemployable as he approached the age of sixty. He was the most handicapped member of the family in terms of both language learning and employability. Mazen thought he would go by himself and then initiate the process known as *lam shaml*, or family reunification. He borrowed money from his brother. Salma was skeptical and concerned. "I didn't think he'd do it, not one in a hundred chance," she said later. When he began to assert himself to get his unruly sons to stay and take care of their mother, something clicked in Salma. She was particularly worried about Mazen's inability to swim. She decided that she would not let him go alone.

The family's fitful bickering and ad hoc decision-making in Istanbul turned increasingly rational, calculating, and focused on how to leverage the passage to Europe. Previous efforts up until now had been like the Syrian tongue-in-cheek proverb that evokes the criticism of the blind leading the blind, "Hat idak walhaqni," "Just be quiet, take my hand, and follow me," which involves faith, trust, and a reliable knowledge of the immediate environment. After 2015, however, the family's efforts involved less faith that things would work out and more hard calculations and planning. Salma described the dilemma of getting the whole family to Europe.

> We couldn't afford to have three different sets of expenses. We'd still need money. How could we get money? So I started thinking of all of us going out. There wasn't enough money for all five of us. But since there was no money coming in if either of the boys left, we decided that Mazen and ten-year-old Kamal and I would go using the borrowed money. We would give up the apartment and the crippling rent payment. The two older boys would continue to work in Turkey until they each earned enough money for the trip. 'Adel would go live with his paternal uncle's household, while Yusuf would share a room with his Syrian friends.

The boys, more than their parents, were integrated into the Istanbul economy, with jobs where they made decent wages. They were making great strides in their language skills; their street Turkish and school English were enough for them to navigate the city's opportunities. Not paying rent and utilities for the apartment would relieve them of a huge burden and allow them to save money for their own passage to Germany. So although 'Adel and Yusuf were the most anxious to leave for Europe and had jostled to be the first to leave, their parents and little brother would use the available resources to go first.

The packing for the family breakup and departure, set for the late summer when temperatures were still warm and the sea reportedly calm, was traumatic. Having been in Istanbul for more than a year, the family had accumulated more possessions: "We went back to the same old story of packing and redistributing our stuff. Stuff—we had collected a lot. There was the meat grinder for making *kibbeh*, a couple of old desktop computers, all the photo albums, a briefcase or two full of deeds and certificates brought from Damascus, and a surprising mass of secondhand furniture, household appliances like fans, as well as bedding and clothing. Some we sold, some we gave away, some we put with Mazen's aunt, some with Hanan. She [Hanan] was there with me for the last couple of days." Hanan, herself newly arrived in Turkey, traveled to Istanbul to provide moral and organizational support, and she witnessed the pressures that Salma and her family were experiencing. The whole family was a wreck, facing their imminent split and the risk of the crossing for the least fit, the parents and the baby of the family.

> Of course, during this time of packing I was in a terrible psychological state. I didn't want to leave my kids and from displacement to displacement, and every time we settled a bit, then we had to move on. And, praise God, everyone was so sad. Mazen couldn't sleep at all. The sea was a very frightening step. 'Adel and Yusuf were so attached to Kamal, 'Adel didn't want to pack. He tried not to speak with Kamal. We looked, and he was crying, and the two of them started to cry, and we were all crying, and Hanan was crying when she came to Istanbul to see us off.

Having borrowed the money to purchase three crossings on a "good boat" suitable for little Kamal and his mother, the family set about calling the plethora of contact numbers that flowed their way from friends and acquaintances. Everybody knew someone who knew a smuggler. Given the likelihood of death on the way, no one was eager to vouch for or give assurances, only to convey that their experience or reputation was good enough to pass on but that the travelers should make their own judgment or trust their own feelings.[10] The number for someone named Abu Marwa who promised a "yacht" was one of the first that they called. As Salma described the process,

> So we started collecting names of smugglers and studying new things like the wave height and weather conditions in the Mediterranean until we agreed with a smuggler. I told my husband that we would need to go in a proper yacht, so it would be safer. After we decided that Kamal and I would go, we got money from here and there, and we got the money together, and especially with Kamal I was able to insist on enough for a proper boat, not an inflatable raft. Psychologically, I was in a terrible state and didn't want to go, but we couldn't think of any other door to go through. It was the only option left to us. 'Adel got his father a number for a fast boat that they said would get us there in half an hour. When you get to Izmir, call this guy Abu Marwa, they told us.[11]

Not surprisingly, there was no answer at the number of the smuggler contact, who almost certainly used a false name. Later that day, Salma's Samsung phone received a call back from a number associated with a teacher at one of the schools where Salma had worked. She scolded the boys, asking them why they were calling her former colleagues at the school. Then it slowly dawned on her that one of the smuggler's cell phone numbers was the number of a schoolteacher who had taught Kamal.

> Her [the teacher's] husband was the smuggler. It was such a coincidence. If we had tried, we couldn't have worked that out. He was the smuggler, and he was the husband of my old colleague! When we found this out, I was very surprised. She was very nice and respectable, so it was hard to believe that her husband worked as a smuggler. She was Kamal's teacher, so I thought I'd talk to her and find out if she really reassured us, then it seemed OK. And

10. On choosing a smuggler, see Achilli, "The 'Good' Smuggler"; and Campana and Gelsthorpe, "Choosing a Smuggler."

11. For more on the shifting dynamics of the migration, see Düvell, "The 'Great Migration' of Summer 2015."

even more astonishing, when we talked to him, she herself had answered the phone and given him the prices and was acting as the secretary. It was her—teacher by day and smuggler by night. I decided to talk to her, to get some reassurance. Mazen tried to dissuade me, but I insisted and called her and asked. "Can you reassure me that it's safe, because Kamal is coming?" At first she said yes, and then she hesitated. After a long pause, her demeanor changed, and she suddenly said, "I don't know anything about it." She denied it. And then she excused herself, claiming that she had a Turkish lesson. She sent me a text after two hours that she had no idea what I was talking about and wished us the best of luck.

But I confirmed it when I heard that there was a ten- or eleven-year-old student who had told us that he was going with a female smuggler. When she [the teacher] denied everything, Mazen freaked out that she now knows us and wouldn't answer our calls anymore. We were afraid that we'd get caught up in smuggler-gang politics. We decided to find a new smuggler without even letting them know. We decided to go to Izmir, and then we'd call someone there. We had plenty of numbers, and we wanted to go; it would be easier to just get to Izmir and see what God has in store for us. We had a second choice with another, and we just wanted to go. With Hanan's help and her sewing machine, we packed our passports and money in plastic and sewed them in our clothes.

15

The Sixth of September

Maryam, 2014

Maryam's son-in-law Mustafa had reached the end of his tether in Alexandria. The destruction of his sewing workshop in Damascus back in 2012 had been devastating. As an entrepreneur who had tasted success, he was desperate to get things going again, and he realized he could not do it in Egypt. He saw business opportunities all around him in Alexandria, where Syrian food and fashion were very hot, but he had no capital and distrusted potential partners. A lengthy and bureaucratic encounter with the Catholic charity Caritas, involving endless paperwork and interviews, had not yielded even enough money for a single sewing machine. Fitfully, as an outlet for his frustration, he began to talk about going to Europe. Syrians like him had begun to join the perilous Mediterranean smuggling routes that African migrants and refugees had braved for decades. Sudanese, Somalis, and Eritreans had used Egypt as an embarkation point for Italy and Malta, but in 2013 and 2014 the new Syrian refugees exponentially increased the number of migrants and thus changed the smuggling business: more people meant higher prices, and more money meant more smuggling and trafficking business.[1]

Mustafa's wife, Amira, and her mother, Maryam, did not encourage the idea of setting out on an illegal and dangerous sea journey,

1. Fontana, "Migration Crisis"; Achilli, "The Human Smuggling Industry"; Syed Zwick, "Narrative Analysis of Syrians."

but they had no other plan to offer and thought that letting him express his nascent strategy was better than bottling it inside himself. Watching her husband marinate in frustration just beyond the reach of the household's cheerful atmosphere was painful to Amira and concerning to her mother. Mustafa's inability to resume the traditional role of provider was gnawing away at him, and he sank into isolation, rousing himself to his usual friendliness with others only when his old friends passed through Alexandria on their way to or from Europe or Syria. Amira, whose devoted presence was a constant reminder of his failed obligations, could not get him out of his funk. The idea of making the sea journey would eventually fade away, they thought, especially since he had no money.

But Mustafa watched a steady stream of his old friends from Syria leaving from Alexandria and getting to Europe. More and more friends and acquaintances in Cairo and Alexandria were transiting out of Egypt as well, even those whose situation was not as glum as his. One of Maryam's cousins even sent her three underage children alone on a boat from Libya to Italy, and they arrived there safely. Crossing illegally, once unthinkable to upstanding middle-class people like Mustafa and Amira, was now becoming thinkable. In the summer of 2014, Mustafa heard that yet another one of his old friends from Damascus was coming to Alexandria on the way to Europe via an illegal smuggling operation. His friend, excited about his decision, dropped off belongings at Maryam's apartment and tried to convince Mustafa to go along with him. Mustafa refused, but after bidding the family farewell, their houseguest then reappeared unexpectedly a few days later when his trip was delayed. In the little window of time in which Mustafa shared his friend's plans, watched him go, and then unexpectedly got the chance to change his mind, Mustafa determined to go. He had a cousin in Kuwait whom he had been very reluctant ever to ask for a loan, but his friend persuaded him to ask, and his cousin promptly sent him the money, happy to support an initiative that could have a life-changing outcome. Mustafa contacted his friend's smuggler and began to make arrangements by phone.

As he learned, the head of the smuggling ring was an unknown personage, sitting at the center of the operations of numerous go-betweens and recruiters. Mustafa's contact was identifiable by his accent as a Syrian from the city of Homs who went by the name "Zakariya." The going fare for a single Syrian was about $3,000, but the rate was negotiable depending on the level of perks (meal service, top deck) and, importantly, eligible for a discount if one brought along more paying passengers. Mustafa had unwittingly been drawn into a Ponzi-like recruitment scheme run by the smugglers. His friend had ascertained that Syrians who recruited friends and family for the Syrian go-betweens organizing the illegal journeys would get a reduced fare, which at that time was about $2,000–$2,500. Mustafa's friend probably negotiated a discounted rate for himself for referring Mustafa, who in turn proposed to bring his brother-in-law Jamil for a two-for-one rate, which would allow the seed-money loan from the Gulf to go further. Mustafa proposed the trip to Jamil. Like Mustafa, Jamil did not have even a hundred dollars to spare, let alone the thousands it would take to book passage on a trans-Mediterranean smuggling ship. But cobbling together the loan, the discounted rates, and the possibility of two people working off the debt in Europe, they decided to make the deal with the smugglers.[2]

Amira was caught off guard when suddenly Mustafa had the money in hand, wired from the cousin in Kuwait whom he had long declined to hit up. The decision to go happened so fast. "I never thought they would go through with it, but, praise God, it was in that little window when his friend from Damascus stayed with us." The reminder of home and promise of Europe reanimated him. And then things happened quickly. Amira and Maryam recalled, "We cried. We couldn't believe he'd really go."

When Maryam realized that her son, Jamil, was serious about joining his brother-in-law, she started to pack, even though they

2. On the variables of being smuggled, see Friebel and Guriev, "Smuggling Humans."

didn't know exactly when he would be leaving. She pulled out the old suitcases they had brought from Syria more than two years earlier. She packed pajamas, warm clothes, socks, and underwear. She didn't pack the books he had been studying. Compulsively packing was a little like the feverish homemaking she sometimes indulged in—cleaning, cooking, gardening, teaching her little grandchildren to read, making decorations out of colored paper and yarn for the bare walls. It gave her a sense of control in a world that was so far out of her control. Making people happy, providing them with a cheerful environment when they came home from the big urban landscape outside, was all she could do. She had always wanted more. She had always wanted to travel and get away from the tiny boxes she lived in. Jamil, her son, would do it for her, but he was so young and inexperienced. She stuffed his bags fuller and fuller. Everything she packed was an expression of her love, a message of caring that he would, she hoped, understand. Every item she packed was a little piece of her that would travel the world while she stayed here. Her hands rolled and packed sandwiches as her head was full of prayers to be released upon the unwrapping, upon the first bite, upon the satisfaction of hunger. Jamil, of course, was preoccupied with the journey to come. He accepted her fretting and tokens absentmindedly, with the cavalier manner of a spoiled boy. Like his father but so much more in need of her. She tried to squeeze as much of home and family into those suitcases as she could, to take care of Jamil, to be with him in the form of those things.[3]

Mustafa and Jamil's Gamble

Mustafa and Jamil's decision to leave Egypt was another one of the biggest and most fateful decisions of their lives. But as we have seen in previous chapters, the moment of decisive action was built up to the tipping point by an accumulation of signs, interpretations, affect, pressures, and triggers from the environment and circumstances. In

3. On packing, see Porzucki, "The Things They Carried."

the end, it was their decision, made at the height of agency (and with a masculine bravado).[4] Through the summer of 2014, it seemed as if the two men of the household were infected with the idea of going to Europe by any means possible. Their own despair was the key driver, but the idea of going was put into their heads by their friends' examples. The elder, Mustafa, had a material reason and incentive to take his young brother-in-law.[5] For Mustafa, making his way to Europe, earning his fare, meant in effect recruiting others—in this case Maryam's beloved only son, Jamil. The extreme objectification of human smuggling thus seemed and felt like resourceful agency—using one's contacts and acquaintances as recruits to provide cargo in bulk for the smugglers. Momentum built toward a decision that just needed a tipping point. Slowly they went from doubt and skepticism to acting impulsively. They would soon find that what felt like action would lead them into a realm of objectification. Smuggling felt like friendship, business deals, action, all the components of their lost daily masculinity, when, in fact, it led to trafficking and worse.

Jamil was at work when he got the news that he was leaving that very day. As he recalled, "I told my boss, 'Sorry, I have to go, I have to quit.'" According to him, his boss understood because his announcement was totally normal; everyone was doing this. He rushed home, and his mother got to work again, packing his bags. He wrapped his passport and telephone tightly in plastic wrap. Everyone knew this is what you did. He also wrapped in plastic about 600 euros that would be sorely missed from the household budget and sewed it into a special pocket in his pants because, as everyone knew, "You don't know who you're going to meet on these trips—criminals, bandits, gangs."

He was planning for a week-long trip. The money for his trans-Mediterranean fare would be paid once Jamil arrived in Italy and notified his relatives. The sum for his and Mustafa's fares was put in escrow with an "insurance agent" (*maktab ta'min*), and a code

4. On decision-making in these circumstances, see Suerbaum, "Becoming and 'Unbecoming' Refugees."

5. Herman, "Migration as a Family Business."

number, like a PIN or a randomly generated password used for commercial money transfers, was assigned to the deposit. When the migrant reached their destination safely, their family members would be notified and share the code number with the smuggler's representatives, who could then claim the money from the third party.[6]

After dropping everything to leave, Jamil was surprised to be driven out of town and housed at a private villa in the countryside. "We stayed at their villa, and we would eat, sleep, and drink at the smuggler's expense until the trip with him." Jamil and Mustafa and their friend stayed at the smuggler's safe-house villa for the first few days of September. Jamil remembered about forty other would-be migrants were there, too. "Actually, it was quite nice," he said. "There was a pool; it was clean, and the group consisted of very respectable people—children, families, girls, old people. It was pretty clear that it was a very respectable class of people that were leaving." Jamil was young and inexperienced enough that he was distracted by the novelty and superficial pleasures of his first week as a smuggled refugee, lounging by the side of a pool, smoking *sheesha*. Then suddenly Jamil and Mustafa were called for immediate departure. After they waited some more, the smugglers loaded about thirty of the travelers into a little microbus meant to hold only about twelve or thirteen people.

They drove and drove with no sense of when they would arrive; indeed, it soon dawned on them that being crammed into this mobile waiting room was part of the hurry-and-wait strategy. The next step of the journey—seemingly endless driving up and down the Egyptian coast between Marsa Matrouh to the west and Damietta to the east—involved the dawning realization that with the decision to engage smugglers, to agree to the transaction, they, now migrants, had submitted themselves to a state of highly constrained agency. They began to feel like prisoners. Even the driver had no idea what

6. On this process, see Van Reisen and Estefanos, "Human Trafficking Connecting to Terrorism and Organ Trafficking."

their destination was or when they would arrive. It soon became clear that this was a bus they could not get off of. The situation was suddenly no longer a test of their resolve, their resourcefulness, their decision-making calculation and skill. It was no longer a challenge in which they could test and prove their masculinity. They became passengers and eventually cargo for bands of smugglers to process, compete over, and deliver for payment. In a sense, this first phase of Mustafa and Jamil's journey was like when they and their aunts and cousins paid the fare to board a plane or a cargo boat or subway or ferry. In Mustafa and Jamil's case, though, the smugglers, brokers, and agents were familiar, spoke their language, and haggled with them. The front end of smuggling was like renting a car to take one from Damascus to Beirut and negotiating with the driver over the price, a ubiquitous and familiar manifestation of small-scale capitalism that was part of the repertoire of being a man (or an authoritative and culturally competent woman) in Syria. But this easy and familiar entry to the process lured refugees and migrants into a business model based on transportation-infrastructure capitalism. It is reminiscent of how airlines fill available seats on a rolling-price model as the time for a flight approaches. For the refugees, however, it meant being treated as a commodity, an object, reluctantly releasing themselves to the care of mercenaries whose consciences and humanity were secondary to the cruel calculations of making money through illegal smuggling regimes. Being moved on the smugglers' hidden schedule was the first sign of their status.

Aside from the bus's intentional meandering to meet some unknown timetable and destination, the next big problem was the police. Avoidance of police patrols and attention caused the bus to take detours and made the passengers engage in a strange ritual. When police approached or were near the crowded bus, the passengers would be instructed to close the curtains and be quiet and of course to hide evidence of their intended trip. The cheap but bulky life jackets would have to be hidden under the seats. When it looked like police would be boarding to inspect the bus, they would take the plastic wrap from around their papers and carry the papers as if they were just going out for an ordinary trip. As soon as the police left, they would wrap the passports back in plastic wrap from industrial-size rolls, and "the whole time you would hear the sound of plastic wrapping ripped." It was a cat-and-mouse game with the police, Jamil learned from his companions, because the busload of migrants would never get let off on a beach unless the police had been bribed to look away. That meant a specific beach, a specific police patrol—ostensibly why the trip took so long and was aborted several times. "And every time we headed back to the villa, the people there would tell us, 'I hope we don't see you again!' It was a joking atmosphere with an undercurrent of rising tension."

Around September 4 or 5, a departure from the villa and the long drive brought Jamil and Mustafa close to the neighborhood where they lived in in Alexandria. Jamil had spent most of his time on the bus sleeping uncomfortably and rearranging his papers and baggage. Endless hours on the bus were punctuated with the hiding of his flimsy life vest under the seat, the unwrapping and wrapping of his important papers. Just as his mother had spent time and emotional energy packing the affordances of family and home into his suitcases, Jamil spent the hours on the bus in the indifferent care of his smugglers processing and reprocessing the provisions for the journey he was about to take. His sensitive stomach was beginning to ache when the bus stopped and was boarded by "some suspicious-looking characters." At this point, Jamil would have been happy to see the police, get arrested, and be returned home. "Please tell us you're the police," Jamil remembers the passengers pleading. Their captors laughed and agreed that they were the police and commandeered the bus, driving it to some gardens outside of town, where everyone spent the night. These thuggish characters refused to let the passengers go, especially Jamil, who was tantalizingly close to his mother's and sister's apartment.

The veneer that this was a friendly enterprise in which they had choice was falling away. The bus resumed its endless driving the next day, and the passengers begged for a stop. Jamil sent a message to Zakariya, the broker, secretly texting with him about this apparent kidnapping. When the kidnappers noticed Jamil texting, they requested his contact's information from him; then they called Zakariya and began negotiating with the person on the other end of the line. They turned out to be a rival gang of smugglers who were demanding a ransom of $300 for each of Zakariya's charges. Panicking, Jamil texted Zakariya the GPS coordinates, and soon the terrified migrants were careening down the highway in the middle of a running gun battle between the two groups of smugglers. The passengers screamed that they would gladly pay $300 to be free of this, but it was out of their hands. This was a turf war and raid because Zakariya's driver had apparently encroached upon the other gang's protected beach territory. Finally, the go-between arranged for the prisoners to be released, and Jamil and Mustafa unexpectedly returned home to Maryam and Amira for the night.

The go-between called them the next morning and told them to come back, reminding them that he had saved them from the kidnappers and that this was just a slight detour in the plan to reach Europe, which they had committed to. For future journeys, they'd simply stick to their own stretch of beach. Amira's anxiety was triggered by the chance offered after the kidnapping attempt. "When they told us that they had been kidnapped and came home after they got away, I went crazy. I told them not to leave again, but I didn't feel good about it, and they left again the next day. 'Don't take the risk,' I said, but Mustafa wouldn't be deterred. And then they left again on September 6. I felt as if my soul left with them," she remembered.

Although Jamil had hours upon hours to process his new plight while sitting squashed and trapped in the minibus, he was not prepared for the shock of the actual final departure. The passengers were herded onto a beach in pitch blackness. The smugglers barked for them to run as fast as they could down the sand to the water. Small rowboats would ferry them out to the cargo ship hundreds of meters off the beach, out of reach and perhaps sight of the authorities. The mad scramble was timed to coincide with the break in police patrols, which the smugglers might have arranged with a bribe. In any case, the smugglers unleashed the passengers' pent-up panic.

Rushing madly hundreds of yards toward the vague perception of the shoreline, Jamil was immediately overcome. Someone yelled at him to drop his suitcases, that the police were just behind them. Jamil had no intention of dropping his suitcases or his life vest. He would need all those things that his mother had packed. Breathless and overwhelmed, he stopped every few meters to rest his arms and get his bearings. Mustafa and the others they had been with in the minivan were nowhere to be seen. Men and then more women and children rushed with him in the dark, and he realized, burdened with his suitcases, he was among the stragglers. When he stumbled in the sand and felt the harsh grip of a policeman on his shoulder, he was almost relieved. Exhausted, he left his suitcases on the beach and let himself be hauled off for a night in jail.

Facebook Groups of the Lost

Maryam's middle daughter, Amira, was beautiful, girlish, and flirtatious, looking and sounding more like a cute teenager than a stressed-out mother of two. She had always been her father's favorite daughter, and her husband, at least ten years older than her, doted on her. The resulting learned helplessness and apparent passivity that she used as a default attitude worked well to get her through the first few days after Jamil returned. Her brother finally returned from his adventure, including a night in detention, relieved but deflated and depressed. His shame at having failed to get on the boat and the comforting suffocation of going nowhere blended with Amira and Maryam's growing realization that Amira's husband, Mustafa, had succeeded in leaving. For a few days more, Amira could pretend that Mustafa was just away at work, to return home eventually to take care of things, as he always had.

The whole time that Mustafa had been at the villa, making the false starts to leave, he had talked to Amira every day. Even once he got on the boat, he called to tell her that Jamil had missed the boat and to ask where he was. He also told her not to expect to hear from him for a few days while he was at sea. He described his mad rush down the beach with the police on his heels, shooting wildly. Amira was able to tell him that Jamil had made it back home, thanking God for that. The next days were quiet, almost normal. Amira and Maryam went about their household chores, and Jamil eventually emerged from his room and went back to work at the restaurant. The radio silence while Mustafa was on the boat crossing the sea was expected and normal. The smugglers had made clear that communications would be cut off because they lacked access to Thuraya satellite phones. Amira would occasionally call the go-between, who would regularly reassure her that he had been in contact with the ship via Thuraya. After a few days went by, Amira was alarmed not to hear from her husband. The contact assured her that the boat had arrived at its destination, Italy, a couple of days ago but that maybe the travelers had been arrested or were stuck in a place without coverage or had lost their phones.

As Amira recalled, "I kept calling the go-between, and he kept reassuring me and telling me not to worry: 'They're on the way, and you wouldn't hear from them yet.' I felt that he was lying; either it didn't go or something else. I kept talking to him for five days. 'Did you talk to them?' 'Yes, I talked to them, don't worry.'" The arrangement was that she'd release the money only when she heard Mustafa's voice. She credited her husband's foresight in making sure she wouldn't pay. Two days more went by, and still no call from Mustafa.

The normalcy came to an abrupt end when the smuggler's contact, the man they knew as Zakariya, began demanding the release of the money. This was alarming because payment would be made only when Amira heard Mustafa's personal confirmation by voice that he had reached Europe. This was the sum that had been put in escrow with a third party, an insurance agency (*maktab ta'min*). When voice contact was established at the journey's end, the relatives would provide the encryption code to the smugglers to release the money. If the passengers did not arrive and give permission, the smugglers would not get the money protected by the encryption number. Amira, like many other family members, waited impatiently for her husband's call from Italy. Zakariya's jarring demand for the encryption code and money was not the way this was supposed to end. Mustafa would never have left Amira to face the smugglers' demand alone. A creeping sense of foreboding leaked into the family's daily routine.

Then the news of some kind of accident off Malta trickled through the community, on Facebook, and soon via the Egyptian media. At first, Zakariya, the Syrian from Homs at the other end of her calls, told Amira it almost certainly didn't involve Mustafa's boat. Then a few hours later a call from the same number opened with the crushing words "Allah yirhamu"—God rest his soul.

Details of Mustafa's last phone calls before he embarked came rushing back to her. Mustafa had told her about how the main boats would be anchored off Damietta—out at least a kilometer from the shore. The travelers on the buses were loaded ten by ten into little rowboats from the dark beach. For the men and boys that was not a problem, but for the women and children it seemed strange. They might change rowboats several times before getting to the main boat. If you had a bag or backpack with some supplies, the smugglers might throw it in the water. Then they would row you out over the horizon to the main boat, onto which smugglers with weapons would herd you. They might steal your belongings if you hadn't lost them already. It quickly became clear that the smugglers were filling up the boat from several points along the shore, so it wasn't unusual to wait on the ship for days while it filled up.

Amira deflected the news of her husband's probable death with complete denial and numbing sedatives. The sense of being lied to by Zakariya over the past few days clicked into a refusal to believe or even hear what he was saying—that he was suddenly confirming Mustafa's death after denying it again and again. Amira had a nervous breakdown and physiological faint, which turned into something like a coma after a well-meaning doctor administered a huge dose of sedatives. She went in and out of consciousness and paralysis, while Maryam and Jamil went into action, desperately making phone calls that led them to family members of the other people who were on the same boat. There were phone calls from reporters and humanitarian agencies and phone calls from the relatives of other missing people. As the news of the accident trickled out and the scale of the tragedy dawned on the world, Amira, Maryam, and Jamil found themselves at the center of a web of incomplete information, lies, rumors, media stories. The smugglers' go-between was desperate to play on Amira's hope that Mustafa may have been rescued and made it to shore in Malta, Greece, or Italy.

Zakariya talked about what happened as an "accident." He gave them the number of an eyewitness survivor, a woman who he claimed had been transported to Greece by the tanker that rescued her. They were soon in touch with a Syrian woman called Randa who claimed to have seen Mustafa. According to her story, the boat, with up to five hundred people on it, was intentionally rammed by another boat as they approached the Italian coast. Mustafa, she said, was one of the passengers on the top deck who survived the initial impact, unlike the hundreds locked below deck. She identified Mustafa as the man who saved her life by giving her a wooden plank and telling her to escape. She then watched as he saved a couple of children before she lost sight of him. This story gave them hope that Mustafa might also have been picked up like Randa and taken to some random destination, where he might be sick or perhaps in prison. They initially clung to her every word, which fueled Amira's resistance to accepting Mustafa's loss. But after talking to other survivors and comparing accounts on Facebook, they realized that this woman whom the smuggler had put them in touch with was telling the exact same story to many victims' families, at least forty families of Syrian and Palestinian missing passengers, and they realized that she was systematically playing on these desperate people's hopes. It was, they began to believe with hardening cynicism, another attempt to scam money from them, to encourage the news they hoped to hear.

In Amira's case, the hope that Mustafa was saved and languishing in an Italian jail allowed her to talk about him as if he were alive for the next four years. At the same time, her fury was directed at the woman, Randa. "It turns out she had no credibility, that the smugglers told her what to say, that she had a script in front of her that she was reading from, and that people were paying her money to keep hearing what they wanted to hear," Amira alleged bitterly.[7] The fog of confusion thickened—there was no boat name to confirm, just an unending series of questions and quests for answers. The smugglers' contacts, the Red Cross, the Coast Guard, the Egyptian media were at most a source of new leads, not real answers. Amira felt herself being grilled as a source of information and an object of pity. New information came encased in skepticism and the fear of being exploited again. Zakariya and Randa, to whom they had clung for hope, were at best disembodied voices on a phone line, their last untrustworthy links to Mustafa. At worst, they came to fear with growing horror that they might be talking to Mustafa's killers. In the end, piecing together news reports and conversations with family members, Jamil and Maryam came to accept that Mustafa was gone. Jamil recognized a photo of a body that washed up in Malta as one of his companions from the villa and the bus rides. Another was a small girl whose grandmother was in regular contact with them.[8]

While trying to discover the fate of their missing loved one, Amira, Jamil, and Maryam entered into and formed networks of urgent exchange of both emotional and informational content. In-laws, siblings, and spouses like them who may have been held at arm's length by the lost family member were now in hourly contact with one another, weaving webs of new connections around the place that their missing loved ones had occupied. The families of people brought together by random chance were engaged in forging links based on the sudden disappearance of the people they had loved. Contacts were exchanged as everyone sought out anyone who offered information. Rumors and suspicions festered, even as helpful information gave relief. Over time, the telephone relationships naturally

7. One woman's story that echoes parts of this account was later memorialized in Melissa Fleming's book *A Hope More Powerful Than the Sea.*

8. For more on the attempts to count, archive, and identify the missing, see International Organization for Migration, "Mediterranean: Missing Migrants Project."

morphed into Facebook groups in which the bereaved and investigating relatives could share news stories, emotions, even emoticons.

One Facebook group that focused on exchanging information on the trip was called "Bus Station of the Displaced" and featured regular inquiries into costs of passage, locations of brokers, and practical advice for those underway. Another group gave those who, like Amira, had no closure on the disappearance of their loved ones, places to congregate and grieve together. Adorned with a cover photo from the American TV show *Lost*, it is called "Network of People Looking for Those Lost at Sea."[9] None of this new normal could convince Amira that her husband was dead, though. She held on for years to the hope that her husband might be alive, arrested by the Egyptian or Italian governments and held in a secret prison.

After the flurry of pain and publicity and networking, no official news ever came. The story was pieced together afterward under the names "September 6 Wreck" and the "Malta Shipwreck." Mustafa had been part of a scheme organized by a Syrian from Homs, whom Maryam, Amira, and Jamil later learned was named Abu Hamada and nicknamed "the Doctor." As Amira later put it, "There's one called Abu Hamada, the leader of the group, and he's become a millionaire. And he's the high leader, and they can't touch them. But no one is going after them." According to the *New York Times*, Abu Hamada's operation was a pyramid scheme to recruit Syrians to recruit other Syrians for the Mediterranean passage.[10] "The go-between—not the actual smuggler—we called him and asked for the names that were with you. He said don't bother, don't even try, and went on to try and flirt with us. A real loser. His name was Zakariya, but we don't think that was his real name. He wanted to come and get the money even before we knew that they [our family members] hadn't arrived [in Italy]. Then he would say, 'Don't

9. On the bereaved families' use of the internet, see Yaseen and Al Omoush, "Mobile Crowdsourcing Technology Acceptance and Engagement in Crisis Management."

10. Yardley, "Shipwreck Was Simple Murder."

bother, don't ask, God rest their souls.' We think he's still smuggling." She didn't want to consider that Mustafa himself was acting in the Ponzi scheme when he recruited Jamil as the original way of financing the trip.

Although Randa's account of a man saving her and saving children was deeply suspicious and disturbing to Amira and Jamil, the other chilling aspects of her story were corroborated by subsequent interviews with survivors, by journalism, and by Egyptian and International Organization for Migration researchers. As many as five hundred people are thought to have been on the ship, including a hundred children. The vessel came to be known to the world as the "September 6 Ship" or the "Malta Shipwreck" of 2014. Amira said, "In the reports, they have names of boats and registrations, but frankly I don't trust these accounts." Subsequent journalistic and investigative reports describe the passengers as being from Sudan, Palestine, and Egypt, so it appears that Abu Hamada's operation to recruit Syrian refugees was piggybacking on a preexisting route that channeled poor Black Africans and Arabs through Alexandria.[11]

Mustafa hadn't told Amira about certain details in his last phone calls from the boat. She learned them later from the "Network of People Looking for Those Lost at Sea" Facebook group. Mustafa, even if he had seen or heard such things, couldn't tell Amira about how they would put the African men in the hold like animals. Sometimes there might be a little food, sometimes not. People were vomiting on each other; there was nowhere to go to the bathroom. The ships were Egyptian, of course. By the time the refugees would get out to the boat, they were at the mercy of sometimes armed smugglers. Rape and the theft of money, gold, and cell phones were easy because they were already in the middle of the sea. Sometimes the smugglers would put people in the engine room, mostly Africans, and they would die before the trip even started. They had to go without

11. On this type of operation, see Kuschminder and Triandafyllidou, "Smuggling, Trafficking, and Extortion."

food for days. These were the details that Mustafa couldn't tell his wife and mother-in-law. "We didn't know any of these stories at the time," said Amira.[12]

Some of the nine survivors plucked from the Mediterranean by passing oil tankers recounted how they had come from Gaza to the Egyptian coast, where Jamil had been picked up by the police. They, like Mustafa, had been ferried out in rowboats to the larger ship anchored at least a kilometer offshore. The problem with using large, decommissioned cargo ships was that they were identifiable and traceable—hence the necessity of keeping them well away from shore at both their point of origin and their destination. As Amira eventually learned, "When they'd get to the Italian coast, they'd take the passengers out and blow up the ships. We don't know what, only God knows, what happened to the September 6 ship." During the initial days, boatloads of Palestinians from Gaza joined the Syrians, Egyptians, and Sudanese on the boat off Damietta. Midway through the journey, a smaller boat full of smugglers arrived and commanded the hundreds of passengers to transfer to a smaller, less seaworthy craft. The passengers refused. A sixteen-year-old Palestinian boy named Hamad was one of up to a hundred children on board. He survived the wreck and was saved by a Panamanian-registered merchant vessel. The international press quoted him as saying, "When they told us that we had to go on to that other boat, we refused because we'd doubtless have finished up at the bottom of the sea," he said. "At that point, the traffickers . . . rammed us, smashing the bows, and we all finished up in the sea. . . . We were asking for help and about to drown, and they were watching us as if they were in a cinema." Hamad added: "A lot of us, myself included, did not know how to swim. I'd never seen the sea before. Seven or eight of us clung to a lifebelt, but as time went by, a lot of them didn't make it, and only two of us—I and another lad, a compatriot who was wearing a

12. On the horrors experienced by smuggled refugees, see Kingsley, *The New Odyssey*.

life jacket—were left. Then he disappeared, too. Others were clinging to little bits of wood, and the current carried them away. For many hours—I don't know how many—we remained in the water in those conditions."[13]

Another Palestinian from Gaza who was also saved, Khamis, twenty-seven, corroborated the story, and a third, Shady, thirty-three, said, "After they hit our boat, they waited to make sure that it had sunk completely before leaving. They were laughing." Khamis's account added that the smugglers had already been paid and before ramming the ship threatened to return them to Egypt.[14] The migrants still refused to transfer to the new craft, saying they would rather return to Egypt. Then their boat was rammed, killing all below deck immediately and leaving those on the upper decks to drown as the smugglers watched. All the survivors, including by some accounts a two-year-old baby girl, clung to bits of wood and life preservers for days. The most detailed account in English was given by the Dogmosh and 'Awadallah brothers from Gaza, who were recruited by the Syrian Abu Hamada from Gaza and extorted along the way.[15] They reported that the boat that sank was "the third boat they [the refugees] got onto at sea . . . first the little row boats to an intermediate boat to the fated ship of 500 passengers." It was the ordered shift to a fourth smaller boat that caused the confrontation culminating in the deliberate sinking of the ship. According to this account, even the captain of the boat refused to let his passengers change boats and engaged in a heated phone call with Abu Hamada back in Egypt. At that point, the smugglers rammed the ship. These Palestinian

13. Quoted in Walker, "100 Children Among Migrants 'Deliberately Drowned' in Mediterranean."

14. Khamis and Shady quoted in Jabari, "Deadly Migrant Shipwreck off Malta Highlights Desperation." See also Walker, "Migrant Boat Was 'Deliberately Sunk'"; and Walker, "100 Children Among Migrants 'Deliberately Drowned' in Mediterranean."

15. Yardley, "Shipwreck Was Simple Murder"; Khoury, "Thousands of Gazans Fleeing to Europe"; Achilli and Abu Samra, "Beyond Legality and Illegality."

brothers were part of a circle of early survivors who linked elbows to try and stay alive but one by one slipped beneath the surface of the water over the next three days.[16]

Was Mustafa one of those who survived the initial attack only to sink and drown, as Randa's disputed account suggested? Amira and her family were too traumatized to know what to believe. Italian police and the International Organization for Migration found the survivors' accounts to be credible and worthy enough to launch a murder investigation and tribunals.[17] All of the Palestinian survivors seem to have paid between US$2,000 and $3,500 for the trip. Researchers estimated that smuggling operations at that time may have brought in a billion dollars a year. The business model collected fares from up to a million migrants secreted in safe houses on the Egyptian coast. It relied on networks of bus drivers, boat crews, and brokers to organize the trips, but the introduction of the Syrian middlemen like Abu Hamada increased the traffic from a half-dozen boats a week through 2013 to a half-dozen boats a day in 2014.

This was the first of the Araj family stories of heading for Europe. It ends in complete disaster. There is more hardship, mental and physical, in their future. This story provides a template for understanding the emotional and structural pivots so important in becoming a refugee. The new environment requires so much energy be devoted to reproducing home, but unsuccessfully. It launches the bolder family members into the unknown, into the hands of a merciless machine of vessels and smugglers, far more devastatingly impersonal and murderously cruel than a transport infrastructure with its impersonal accidents and dehumanizing commutes and passages. Mustafa's decision led to trafficking and death. The journalistic accounts show how the thin line between smuggling and trafficking was crossed.

16. Yardley, "Shipwreck Was Simple Murder."
17. Smith-Spark, "Laughing Traffickers Ram Boat."

16

Aegean Odyssey

Salma, 2015

The Araj sisters and their families were rocked by the news of Mustafa's death in the September 6 Malta shipwreck. Just as with their nephew Sa'd's death in Damascus the previous year, shocking news revealed itself slowly to them, like a creeping nausea, as hope and faith gave way to doubt, rumor, fear, and despair. Again, one of the men taking risks to protect and advance his family was caught up in a cruel new system of violence emerging from the Syrian war. Once again, they learned of the tragedy in a piecemeal and fragmentary fashion through unreliable chains of whispers and wails via Facebook posts and WhatsApp groups. There was no closure, no common mourning, just a reminder that the way forward to safety, like the way back home, was haunted by the risk of death as well as by the ghosts of their loved ones and countless others. Yet the number of family members heading for Europe only increased in 2015.

Salma, her husband, Mazen, and their ten-year-old son, Kamal, left Turkey for Germany in mid-October 2015. It was a big surprise to all who knew them that her grown sons decided to stay in Istanbul for the time being, and that the parents and their youngest son would make the perilous journey first.[1] Borrowing money from relatives of both husband and wife, they had collected about $10,000, enough

1. For the state of in-betweenness and randomness of migrant trajectories, see Crawley and Jones, "Beyond Here and There."

they thought, for the illegal crossing on a sound boat rather than an inflatable raft and for the overland trip through Greece, Macedonia, Serbia, Hungary, and Austria to Germany and asylum.[2]

Between 2014 and 2016, the Syrian refugee traffic diverted dramatically from the central Mediterranean route out of Egypt, on which Mustafa had perished, to the Aegean. The Aegean coastline provided many more opportunities for hidden launching points, and increasingly there were no captained or crewed boats, just the ubiquitous *bilim*, or inflatable raft. The journey was shorter, but the death rate would surpass that of the central Mediterranean route over the two years it was used because of the sheer number of Syrians and other migrants making the trip and the deadly business model of the smuggling sector, which made huge profits, had a callous disregard for human life, and maintained a network of expensive connections, it was clear, in the Turkish government.[3] Salma and her family were traveling in midautumn; the weather throughout eastern Europe was foul and wet, and the Aegean crossing had never been more dangerous, with high waves, yet the flimsy inflatable boats continued to leave every hour around the clock. Armed with other people's accounts of the crossing and phone numbers of contacts, Salma and her family closed up their apartment in Istanbul.[4] Salma recalls being overcome with sadness upon leaving yet another home where they had lived together. Worst of all was leaving 'Adel and Yusuf to fend for themselves.

The Basmane neighborhood of Izmir had become the new hub of the Syria refugee route. Unlike the warehousing of refugees in Egypt that Jamil experienced at the villa, Basmane in Izmir was something of

2. For the assessment of destination conditions, see Machetanz, "Public Opinion, Refugee Programs, and State Welfare in Twenty Countries."

3. For more on the Aegean smuggling route, see İçduygu, "Decentring Migrant Smuggling." For deaths, see Squire, *Europe's Migration Crisis*.

4. For more on access to and the exchange of information throughout migrants' decision-making and journeys, see Caarls et al., "Evolution of Migration Trajectories"; and Wall and Campbell, "Syrian Refugees and Information Precarity."

an open-air market for smugglers. Although there seem to have been "big bosses" involved, who hired land transport, collected batches of travelers recruited by their lieutenants, and bribed the local police, coast guards, and officials, differences from the Egyptian smuggling business emerged. Instead of hiding their "passengers" in safe houses, the refugees housed themselves in hotels. Instead of being the location of a controlled process, as in Jamil's kidnapping story, Basmane was a chaotic market of desperate recruiters competing openly with one another for each fare.[5]

By the time Salma, Mazen, and Kamal arrived there, several of their family members had passed the same way already. They had phone numbers and contacts, and there was more choice and competition among smugglers. Families and single travelers shared rooms in hotels around the Basmane train station and met with smugglers' representatives in the outdoor cafés. Streets were lined with shops prominently displaying life jackets. After the shock of having encountered one of her son's teachers while trying to contact a smuggler, Salma and Mazen now had a bewildering number of other choices for smugglers; the stakes were very high, and their information about them very low.

They booked a hotel room and set about looking for a smuggler to replace the connection they had begun to forge with the schoolteacher's smuggling ring back in Istanbul. They reached out to quite a few contacts because their greatest concern was safety, and, unlike so many, they felt they had the resources to buy a greater measure of safety—that is, if they could reliably assess such a thing. They found Izmir to be chaotic and frightening. The family felt very exposed, suddenly out of their home with the clock ticking and a limited amount of borrowed money. In the street outside their hotel, refugees who couldn't afford hotels had cloths spread out on the street and were just sitting there. Smuggler's agents, overconfident young men, circulated through the public spaces, pitching and recruiting.

5. For more accounts of the crossing, see Bauer, *Crossing the Sea*.

"People were sitting, and the smugglers were whispering to them, 'There's a boat leaving today,' and their faces were dripping with poison. Everyone just wanted to get a customer. This is all in the coffeehouses and the lobbies, and they were scouting for people to take," Salma remembered. They had an appointment with Hisham's (Iba's husband's) brother, who had been in Izmir for a while, but he failed to show up. In their attempts to find someone else, all they heard was the word *bilim*, or "inflatable raft," in repeated offers.

Until now, the operative word that had allowed them to keep moving forward had been *yacht*, which in Arabic could refer to anything from a luxury yacht to a decent speedboat, but not an ancient wooden fishing boat or a raft with a sputtering outboard motor. As they prepared to leave Istanbul and borrowed money for the journey, a "yacht" had been part of their scenario. The only way they could justify such a dangerous and expensive trip was the assurance of superior safety. When their first contact, the only one vouched for by people they trusted, failed to appear for their appointment, they started asking around the streets of Basmane for a yacht. One broker they talked to was honest enough to laugh in their faces. "If you find a yacht, I'll cut my hand off!" Another potential smuggler sent them a picture of a speedboat, which they were just naive and hopeful enough to almost believe would be the vessel they wanted.[6]

They eventually just settled on a random guy who happened to answer their increasingly anxious calls. Once they had taken his bait, he kept telling them that there was a boat leaving that very night, but then demurring. The family asked to see the insurance/escrow agent where their money would be held. He took them to an "insurance office" to reassure them about leaving their money in escrow there.[7] They found the office closed, so the broker quickly then began a hard sell for them to leave the money with him. Just as he had sensed their anxiety and weakness, they immediately realized they were being

6. Karaçay, "Shifting Human Smuggling Routes Along Turkey's Borders"; Yıldız, "Impact of the EU–Turkey Statement on Smugglers' Operations."

7. For escrow practices, see Campana, "Human Smuggling."

scammed. Making hurried excuses, they could not get away from him quickly enough. This kind of hurry-up-and-wait, bait-and-switch maneuver kept happening with the same smuggler for days, "like a kind of courtship dance." After too much of it, when they felt they couldn't leave their hotel without being stalked by him, they gathered the courage to turn him down decisively and engaged another smuggler who promised them a boat rather than a rubber inflatable raft. With their growing fear of the broker that they had barely escaped from, it became urgent to get out of the hotel at once.[8]

As Salma put it later, "In the end we did get on a boat, rather than a raft, but what a 'yacht' it was." A crowded and ancient wooden boat with a tiny wheelhouse, sitting very low in the water. But before they could even get on that boat, they needed to escape from their previously engaged smuggling gang, which had grown proprietary about them and their large cache of money. With the cooperation of their new smugglers, who had won them over by promising protection from the rival gang, the family stayed another night in the hotel and left at 4:00 a.m. the next morning to evade what they now understood to be gang patrols circling the hotel and were relieved that their first predatory contact or his partners didn't see them as they left the hotel.

They had prepared their things, including life jackets. They had bought life jackets in Istanbul, but then they forgot to bring them on the bus trip, so they bought new, low-quality ones from one of the many shops in Basmane featuring them on mannequins in the street. They were transported in a hired taxi with another family of four—a mother, father, and two children—who had been brought in at the last minute just to make some extra money, which would make the situation worse through overcrowding. They were ordered to hide their bags and life jackets and silence their phones, Salma remembered.

8. On the difficulties of choosing a smuggler, see Achilli, "The 'Good' Smuggler"; and Campana and Gelsthorpe, "Choosing a Smuggler."

> We drove through pitch darkness with no idea of where we were or where we were going. It was extra dark, the dark of the countryside and deserted beaches at night, and soon it began to rain. At first it began to drizzle, and we said, "God help us and protect us so that it won't drizzle when we are at sea." And we kept driving, maybe another hour. The driver was on the phone, and it became apparent that he didn't know where he was going, that someone was giving him directions. And we would come to a fork in the road, and there would be a car full of men who would give the driver instructions. They were gangs—formal, organized gangs. They would tell the driver to go this way, and [we'd] come to another intersection where a man would be standing and gesture for which way to go. They had flashlights and would wave them around, and I felt like I was in an action film.

Finally, they got to a place that was even darker than before, if that was possible, and they could hardly see each other. It was a field or beach, and they could hear and smell the sea, but Salma couldn't see the water. They got out of the taxi and knew this was the collection place. Little Kamal wanted to go back and get a bag of his belongings forgotten in the taxi, but one of the smugglers started yelling at him in Turkish "like a crazy person." In trying to evade one group of smugglers and jumping into the arms of another gang, they saw their illusion of choice and careful calculation collapse. As trafficked people, they had no control and felt it acutely.

On the Water

Salma recalled boarding the boat.

> After we got to the dark place, they yelled at us to shut off our phones, and everyone was too scared to speak. We followed Mazen into the boat, and the people sat on top of us. We figured there would be movement and adjustment, and we would wiggle around, and that the packing in was just temporary, but this was the way it would be, layers of people sitting on top of each other. We got a glimpse into the little pilot's room as we were boarding, and it was already stuffed with people, the interior was already crammed

> tight. Apparently, we were the last load, and they had been waiting for us. The boat [could] fit twenty-four people, and they filled it with forty-five people. Fifteen or twenty of them were children. The outside deck where we were sitting was about a meter square, with three people sitting on each side of the perimeter and with about four or five sitting squashed in the middle between them.

Some people had brought their suitcases in, Salma noticed, guessing that those who came first or paid a premium were allowed to bring their things. She had wanted to bring an inflatable life ring for each of them in addition to the life vests, but their guards told them that they couldn't, that the rings would be thrown overboard. They were able to bring only one small black rubber ring. They snuck it in quickly with Kamal, and Salma told him to "just cling to this no matter what happens." Salma had her elbow hooked through the ring, as did Kamal, and she hugged him tightly in her lap as her arms began to go numb. The boat began to move. They had climbed into the boat in total dark in such deep water "you could already drown there."

They hadn't gone ten meters when the boat began to rock back and forth as if it would capsize. Salma didn't know if it was the people moving around or the waves suddenly got high, but immediately they felt as if they could tip over. Everyone started screaming, "No one move!" Even Mazen started shouting, "Don't move, don't move!" Because of the weight and the overload, if one person moved on the right, the boat would immediately jerk to the left and vice versa. As they went, they kept looking back at the shore to see how far they had come and were praying to God that it wouldn't start to rain. They had hoped to leave on the previous day because a storm was forecast for the night they left. But the gangs' business model of filling the boat to the brim with parties of passengers coordinated by different brokers preempted their plans to beat the dangerous weather forecast.

> We were now on Wednesday night, and, thank God, the rain started to come down. We were soaked. The rain came down hard;

it was the first rain of the fall season. And they brought a tarp to put on top of the boat to prevent water from filling the boat's deck. Not for the people, mind you, [but] for the deck not to be swamped with rainwater and [the boat to] sink down even lower. The tarp was so heavy, and we were holding it up around the edges. If we had sunk, the tarp itself would have drowned people. I kept telling them to remove the tarp and let the rain flow down, but nobody listened. Even better, they were tilting it a little so the rain would flow away outside the boat, and I was holding up the low end, and the water was flowing down my sleeve onto my back. This was the first rain of the three.

Under the tarp, I started texting and sending out our location and GPS to Yusuf and 'Adel. When the rain stopped, and I turned on the phone to try to call them, other passengers—in particular a Lebanese guy—would scream like crazy, "People turn off your phones! The Turkish Coast Guard will come!" I saw this situation, and eventually I stopped caring; the water was coming down, and I was soaked, and Kamal was sitting soaked in my lap, holding his ring. And there was a big boy, as big as a donkey, holding onto our ring as well and sitting on my leg for the whole four or five hours. He also wouldn't let go of Kamal's ring. Normally I would have felt sorry for this other child who was terrified, but all I could think of was that he might steal Kamal's ring or take my child down with him.

The boat would tilt, and we would see only blackness and just feel ourselves getting farther and farther away from the shore. I was searching for the island we were heading toward that should have been just an hour away, but I couldn't see anything at all. After two hours, some people saw lights on the island, but I didn't, and Mazen started to comfort people, saying, "It won't be long now," but, for me, every time I looked, I couldn't see anything, and we never seemed to get nearer. And I started begging them, "Let me call the Turkish Coast Guard; we've gone halfway, and I don't see anything yet. Please let me call the Coast Guard!"

After two hours with everyone praying to God, "Ya rabb, ya rabb" ("Oh, Lord"), someone suddenly told me to get up. Get up, where? I discovered I was sitting on the fuel opening, and they needed to put in more diesel. There was nothing to hold on to. Where would I get up? Every time I moved, the boat would feel like it was capsizing. Another man on the other side and I had to move together to balance the boat. And everybody was on top of everyone else, so the other guy had his legs under people, and they couldn't move. He had to shift his weight to balance mine with people on top of him. I had to stand while they filled the tank, and it felt like an eternity. And we went on.

We saw the faraway light, and we weren't getting closer. I looked at my GPS and started to cry, and Kamal started to cry. Mazen later told me that he even began to think that the light we were seeing was attached to the boat because the distance stayed the same; we never got closer. Every now and then I'd look at the water, at the blackness, and I couldn't see anything but black. My phone was around my neck and in a plastic bag and the whole time I'd secretly check our location and send texts. They would yell at me, and I would ignore them and keep on sending out our coordinates. I was texting, and Mazen and the other people around us were praying. And we were going like this when the second rainstorm started. And it came down and came down, as much as God could give. And that cursed tarp, every time they raised it up, I'd imagine that it was going to push me down and drown me. They'd put it up and tilt it so the water would run off straight onto our backs. I'd try and adjust it so that the water would run into the sea, sometimes it would work and sometimes not. We only brought out the tarp when it was really pouring; the rest of the time we sat in the drizzle. Kamal was completely soaked through.

There was another little boy, about ten years old but chubby, and someone was sitting on his leg. His leg was going to break, and he just wanted to move it, but he couldn't. When he would try to move, the boat would tilt. Then after a while he didn't care anymore as his leg was going numb, so he just had to get up. And the boat would rock, and they all would scream, "Don't move!," but the boy was in pain and couldn't control himself. That's why I kept Kamal in my lap the whole time. When we first got in, he was farther away, but I made sure he sat with me. And Kamal would cry, and I'd try and keep his legs over mine, but this other kid was

> big, and Kamal couldn't move. His father yelled that his son's leg was going to break, and they stood up, and the boat rocked. And then we settled in again.
>
> Then it was time to fill up with gas again. I needed to get up because I was sitting on the mouth of the tank. I didn't have a choice, but I certainly wouldn't have sat on the tank if I had known. The same as the first time, I got up, grabbed onto a pipe or someone's arm or something, the boat swayed, and they poured the fuel in behind me. The first time the smell of the gas didn't bother me, but this time it made me sick and faint, and they took so long because it was so hard with the people all around. After what seemed like forever, I sat down again with Kamal in my lap, and the third rainstorm began.
>
> Before that, when I was nauseous, I asked Mazen for the seasick pills. He handed me the pill, and, of course, I didn't have any water since all the bags were underneath people. My throat was bone dry from fright, but I managed to choke down the pill. It got very warm from all the bodies huddled together. Kamal and I took off our coats and sat on them since we still had on the life vests. Mazen had his coat on atop [many layers of clothes] and couldn't get it off, so he used the opportunity while they were filling the tank to squeeze out of one sleeve and then later somehow the other. And a third time we needed to fill up with gas. For five hours, three times to fill. Each time I could hardly stand, and we were almost going to tip, and this time I almost vomited. Another young man had the same reaction, and his head fell back over the railing, and we thought he'd fall into the water.

Throughout the trip, Salma continued to send out coordinates and communicate with her sons all while hiding the light from her phone from her angry fellow passenger. As the dreadful night wore on, she convinced herself that they were lost because although the smugglers had assured them of an hour-long journey, it had already taken at least five hours. The boat was so slow and low from the ponderous weight of so many bodies that they could touch the water with their hands. After about four hours of this, Salma texted 'Adel and Yusuf secretly to alert the Turkish Coast Guard. 'Adel sent a text to his mother informing her that he and Yusuf, relatives back in Damascus, and Maryam's family in Egypt had contacted helplines and that the Coast Guard was coming to help them.[9] When anyone claimed to see lights in the distance, possibly a Coast Guard cutter, Salma stuck her hand outside the perimeter of the rail and the tarp and began to signal with the flashlight of the phone. The Lebanese guy started cursing her and yelling and screaming something that Salma didn't understand—now they'd be taken back to Turkey after they were more than halfway to their destination. Salma's fellow passengers had reason to be cautious about contacting the Coast Guard, above and beyond being taken back to Turkey.

But thankfully, amazingly, with a momentary sense of providence, the boat reached landfall just before dawn. The investment in the wooden fishing boat with a skipper forestalled the scenarios that so many others in the inflatables suffered.

> A little while before we arrived, as people were seeing the light (it wasn't me; I couldn't see anything), the island began to appear in the dark. The pilot said he was taking us away from the sandy beach where the rafts would beach to a rocky area, so he could let us off and go back. People kept saying, "Look, look!," but I couldn't make out anything. I began to see when we were right along the shore. I could make out the mountain and the large rock where we would get dropped off. We stopped where the water was just below our necks. And the people swarmed out in a hurry. I was uncurling myself and just looking for my coat and bag; I looked up, and there was no one in the boat except me. Mazen had picked up Kamal, but as soon as he stood up, the two of them were going to fall into the water because his legs were so weak. He called to a man, who picked the boy up, and Kamal kept his hands on his father's neck and dragged him along since Mazen's legs were completely numb, and together they were dragged off the boat through the freezing

9. For more on how migrants used digital and information technology, see Alfeo et al., "Assessing Refugees' Integration"; and Nedelcu and Soysüren, "Precarious Migrants, Migration Regimes and Digital Technologies."

> water and pulled up onto the rocks. And I stayed behind, even though I felt foolish, to look for our coats and bags. Thank God, thank God, thank God I did because of the cold we were about to feel on the next part of the journey. As soon as I got into the water, I peed my pants in the sea. And Kamal is saying he did too!

Mazen and Kamal sat dazed on the shore. Kamal whispered, "Where is Mama?," and Mazen pulled himself together and comforted his son, "Look, there she is." They were soaked and completely limp. Small acts stood out for Salma.

> We threw away the seasick pills. We just had our coats and a small bag. We couldn't find our flashlight. Some people were using their mobile phones and lighters. Finally, we found that Kamal had a little laser penlight that we had hung around his neck. We threw the life vests away. Some people were taking pictures and selfies, but these were some of the people who were inside the cabin who had had their suitcases and premium service. And the Lebanese guy started yelling at no one in particular again—"What's wrong with you? Are you here for tourism? Now they'll find us and come and get us!" As we were walking toward the airport, we saw hundreds of life vests and dozens of rafts along the beach. We thought to ourselves that we should have come to the beach. We had to walk three hours to get here. But that would have meant traveling on one of the inflatable rafts. Easy to say once you got to the destination.

Humanitarian Assistance

Salma continued the story of the next phase of their journey:

> As we were walking, we saw three cars marked with the United Nations sign parked by the side of the road, and they gave us sandwiches, bananas, and water, and they told us to wait for a bus that would take us to the camp. We waited for the bus out in the open but under a little covered roof. I was shivering and felt that I was getting sick. The first bus came, and there wasn't enough room, so we kept waiting. It felt to me like ten hours. Then the second bus came, and the driver was wearing a face mask. It was as if we were

insects or vermin. My God, that was insulting. He was afraid of us and shouting.[10]

Mazen and Kamal got on, and I was still on the ground chasing the bus as it started up, and I kept shouting, "My husband, my son!" in English until [the driver] finally let me on. Imagine me getting left behind just because of language difficulties. It was easier to see how families got separated from each other. Finally, we got to the refugee camp at Moria—like nothing you've ever seen.[11] Mud, mud everywhere, a swamp perfect for growing rice. And the rain came pouring down, down, down. They let us off here and said we needed to take numbers and get in line. And people who had arrived before us were fighting to get their number so they could start working on getting their asylum papers.[12]

Kamal was getting dizzy and sick, and we just wanted our number. Mazen pushed to the front of the line, saying, "Look at our son, he's going to faint." And they gave him his number. We just wanted to get somewhere so Kamal could rest. Everyone already assigned in a tent was acting as if they were protecting their castle. No one would let us in; everyone would say, "We're all full here." And every tent we looked into was full of mud and the smell of feet and socks. Finally, a family let us leave our things in their tent while we kept on looking. We sat for ten minutes with the excuse of handing off our things. Some food and a small bag. The passports and papers were always with us. We went to drink something hot and bought some snacks. A car was driving around announcing numbers, and we heard that we'd be here until tomorrow night. How would we sleep? Someone had told us in the port there were hotels; then they would come back and do their paperwork after sleeping in town. People told us how to get there and that

10. For analysis of images and stereotypes of migrants, see Etem, "Representations of Syrian Refugees in UNICEF's Media Projects."

11. For more on Moria camp, see Bulley, "Shame on EU."

12. On the processing of refugees, see Majcher, "The Schengen-wide Entry Ban"; Koca, "Bordering Processes Through the Use of Technology"; and Şanlıer, "Empowering Experiences of Digitally Mediated Flows of Information for Connected Migrants."

> we shouldn't pay more than five euros for a room, and we looked for a hotel, and I bought Kamal a new tracksuit. We went into a hotel by midafternoon and started drying all our clothes and shoes and sat drying them all night long. They didn't dry completely, but when we went back to the camp, it rained again, and we got soaked through again with no change of clothes except the new tracksuit I'd bought for Kamal so he could sleep.

The rest of the journey was exhausting as well, dominated by poor weather, mud, and sickness. Little Kamal had stomach problems and diarrhea, and Salma, too, was sick on the way. The next day they wanted to buy ferry tickets, but they were sold out, so they had to sleep another night in the same hotel. They were frustrated to be spending money they would surely need in the days ahead but continued to dry out and went the next day along with about eight hundred fellow migrants to the ferry that would take them from Lesbos to the mainland.

> More rain, more wet. The people—there were thousands in the ferry—all kinds and nationalities—all wet, smelly. It was disgusting.[13] The police inside were shouting and fighting. It was 12:00, and we still hadn't left. The trip would be delayed for another day due to weather—the same system [in which] we had crossed the Aegean in our tiny boat. But they locked the doors, and we were trapped on the boat. It was good we had a little food for those twenty-four hours imprisoned in the ship because the food on the ferry was very expensive. We were rotting. Let alone the toilets, clogged and spilling out onto the floors, and the people, the people. Finally, the ferry left, and after about five hours we came to Athens. But about an hour before they announced that whoever wants to go all the way to the border should get tickets for 150 euros here in

13. On the mixed group of migrants from various places, see Rexhepi, "Arab Others at European Borders"; Etem, "Representations of Syrian Refugees in UNICEF's Media Projects"; Gowayed, "Resettled and Unsettled." The description here raises the issue of the racialization of other refugees who were not Syrian. This issue connects with the whiteness question among Middle Eastern diaspora communities; see Maghbouleh, *The Limits of Whiteness*.

> the boat. We did, and we went on to the land. On the bottom floor, there were police controlling the exit, so we didn't get trampled. When it opened, all the people started cheering and whistling. Before that there were Syrians trying to get a group together so we could all travel together—some young men and women and children—and we joined them. And tens or dozens of Syrians started chanting, "Suriya hurra hurra, wa bashar byitla' li barra!" (Free, free Syria, out with Bashar!)

The ferry had comparatively few Arabs, maybe 25 percent in Salma's estimation, and the other three-quarters were Afghans.[14] Salma had already noticed on the fishing boat that her tormentor was Lebanese, not Syrian. She developed a strong sense that opportunistic migrants from Lebanon, Iran, and South Asia as well as people who may well have been refugees from previous wars in Iraq and Afghanistan were capitalizing on the Syrian migration and what she understood as a German invitation to Syrians. The experience of encountering so many non-Syrians in the unprecedented numbers of people on the road did little to enhance her perceptions of those other refugees and migrants.

> When we got to Athens, the Syrian group wanted to all get into a bus together. We forfeited the 150 euros that we had already paid in advance just so we could be with a group of Syrians that we trusted. We got on the bus and went all the way to the Macedonian border. We got there about 2:00 at night. It was so very cold, but we couldn't sleep from the cold, and people were smoking in the tents. These were cloth cots, and people were also sleeping on the ground. This was the coldest until later when we reached Croatia. Kamal and I tried to make a little fire, but there was an official going around putting out the fires as journalists took pictures. As soon as we got there, they gave us numbers, so we'd go in groups. They gave everyone a bag with food that was filling and good.

14. On Afghan refugees in this same period, see Aikins, *The Naked Don't Fear the Water.*

17

Reunions and Farewells at Yalova

Hanan, 2015

Months before Salma, Mazen, and Kamal would make their difficult journey, on a late night during Ramadan, 2015, Hanan and her husband had just hosted a festive dinner at Salma's apartment in Istanbul, breaking the fast with a meal of *tisiyeh*—a chickpea and hummus casserole caramelized on top with a glaze of sizzling ghee. Pickles, onions, salads made up the rest of the meal, and the group of more than ten people knelt around a plastic cloth set on the floor of the living room, as they had for countless meals in better times. Dinner was finished up with a fancy dessert of crepes and Nutella, prepared by Hanan's daughter Warda, who was tonight the center of attention in the room, sharing her good fortune with the special dessert. Her family—Hanan's family—had come to Istanbul from Yalova, Turkey, to secure travel authorization from the otherwise hostile Syrian consulate in Istanbul.

After iftar, the breaking of their fast, the family came to life. The men walked to the nearest mosque for the *tarawih* prayers, which they found amusingly hurried by the Turkish congregants, who, unlike them, they claimed, did not understand or savor the Arabic words of the Qur'an in the more leisurely Damascus style of the postbreakfast prayer. The women preferred to pray in the larger mosque a little farther away and after prayers would usually meet their children young and old in a large park adjacent to the Yavuz Selim Mosque. Hanan and one or another of her three younger sisters would walk and chat and sometimes engage in impromptu games of soccer or kickball with the kids, but on this night Hanan was feeling focused and purposeful.

In Istanbul for the weekend, she was determined to pursue her winning streak of marital politics. She had names of other newcomers to Istanbul that her daughter and friends in Damascus had sent her via WhatsApp, and she sat on a park bench and began cold-calling them. She also wasn't shy about approaching women strangers strolling in the park—that is, as long as they wore the familiar Syrian middle-class Sunni uniform of white headscarf and manteau. Several groups of such women were in the park tonight, and, dragging a reluctant Salma with her, Hanan practically skipped over to them to make friends and to try and find a bride for her son Ramzi, ready to introduce herself and exchange phone numbers that might lead to a prospect.

Throughout 2015, Hanan supervised departures for Germany from the calm of her small apartment at Yalova, Turkey. The most important was for her daughter Warda, who would fly to Germany as the wife of a Syrian refugee with legal asylum and the standing to reunite his family there. Hanan's home would also serve later as the staging ground for Salma and Iba and their families as they prepared to cross the Aegean illegally on a boat or raft to reach the Greek islands and European asylum.

Hanan, her elderly husband, and unmarried daughter, Warda, had moved to Turkey in 2014 when her son Ramzi, still in Dubai, strongly encouraged them to do so. Their tiny but new ground-floor apartment in the small Turkish city of Yalova had become the new center of the extended scattered family.[1] Syrian and Iraqi migrants in the Gulf countries knew Yalova and were buying real estate there.[2]

1. On the importance of a family "center," see Miles et al., "Syrian Caregivers in Perimigration."

2. On investment in Turkey by Syrian and other migrants, see "UAE-Based Developer Launches New Real Estate Project in Turkey"; and Z. Polat, "Legal, Economic, Geographical and Demographic Analysis of the Acquisition of Real Estate by Foreign Nationals in Turkey."

On the outskirts of town, a small stream meandered through agricultural fields and nearly empty tree-lined streets in a new housing development. Hanan and Warda had planted a little garden near the front door, which produced cucumbers, squash, and tomatoes. Less challenging than Turkey's larger cities, the seaside resort nestled on the southeastern shore of the Sea of Marmara was a favorite destination for middle-class Arab refugees able to pay rent without needing to generate wages from the Turkish economy.

Hanan was solidly grounded. She became the central node for news of family members scattered around the region. For Salma, whose family had also journeyed to Turkey in the summer of 2015 because of their deteriorating situation and health in Tripoli, her older sister was a lifeline of comfort. Maryam, their eldest sister who was a continent and world away in Alexandria, was consumed with the ongoing trauma of Mustafa's death and the toll it was taking on her family and her own health. Farida and Iba were locked in conflict and cut off contact with Salma in anger, so Hanan was the central pillar of the scattered family.

Hanan also convinced another branch of the family to join hers in Yalova, that of her maternal uncle Muhammad, now elderly and similarly supported by children in the Gulf. His wife and his children were a little overwhelmed by the sheer size of Istanbul and found life in this seaside resort and its much cheaper rent much less of a hassle. They rented an apartment in a building five minutes away by foot, and the presence of another familiar household allowed for daily coffee and tea visits, walks in the park or along the stream, and gossip and talk. There was work to be found for meager wages in the restaurant sector. Hanan's cousin, an energetic divorcée who looked younger than her age, worked long shifts wrapping cutlery in napkins for a seaside restaurant.

As the bird flies, Yalova is comfortably close to Istanbul. But the primary means of access to Istanbul for the family members was an hour-and-a-half-long ride on vehicle-carrying ferries with passenger seating on the upper decks and room for more than a hundred passenger cars on the lower. These ferries shuttled back and forth to

Istanbul a dozen times a day since Yalova was also a favorite day trip for all Istanbul residents. It was geographically close enough to Istanbul but felt like another world, and the ferry ride was something of an event, exciting and relaxing at the same time. It was pricey for the families' limited budgets, so paying the equivalent of US$15 for a round-trip ticket made it something that Farida, who in desperation had secured passage on a cargo ship from Lebanon to Turkey in late 2014, never could afford and that challenged Salma's budget during their visits to Istanbul in 2015 and later. The ferry crossed the small inland gulf known as the Sea of Marmara, but for at least an hour there was no sight of land. The ferries, named after Ottoman sultans, symbolize perfectly President Erdoğan's nostalgia for Ottoman glory and pursuit of economic revitalization. They are huge, solid, and seaworthy, if not state of the art. The İDO (İstanbul Deniz Otobüsleri, or Istanbul Sea Buses) complex of ferry boats serving as the main transit conduit for traffic between Istanbul and Yalova is run in partnership with other companies, such as McDonald's, Nero Caffee (which operates onboard cafés), and Tvalet private-toilet facilities, and its logo is a dolphin inside a television set. Peering from the decks and the cloudy windows, the sisters had their first taste of seafaring along the Turkish coast.

Hanan had settled in the town of Yalova because her son Ramzi financed and arranged her move to Turkey. He had a friend whose family had invested in some of the new housing being built in this beach resort town. The location was extremely popular among Arab real estate investors with capital to buy property in Turkey, and so communities of prosperous Gulf Arabs, Iraqi refugees with capital, and Syrian refugees with money and connections grew up there. The town where Hanan had settled represented the changing face of Turkey. Neoliberal Turkey was on full display. It was one of the hottest property markets in Turkey for foreign buyers. The town of about 100,000 inhabitants was full of new buildings. A bustling downtown, a seaside park, a ferry terminal with a modern new seafront and mall. Swathes of new housing were built in pleasant postmodern domestic style—three- or four-story apartment blocks with commercial properties on the main street and small, new, light-bright apartments on top. Initially for less and now for the same price as an old, dark Istanbul apartment, these living spaces were inevitably attractive, even if they meant living in a kind of dull suburban limbo.

Hanan's family's small one-bedroom apartment was owned by an acquaintance of her son, and they rented it for about 800 Turkish lira, or about US$320 a month. That made them one of about six hundred Syrian families who moved to Yalova as part of an Arab property boom. Syrians weren't actually buying the Yalova properties in great numbers; Syrians with a lot of money would buy in more prestigious locations, but Iraqis, Kuwaitis, Russians, and Bulgarians were buying the $50,000 to $80,000 flats and the commercial properties in the expanding suburbs.[3]

The Yalova that Hanan moved into was a bright, shiny new neoliberal town because the old Yalova had been destroyed in the earthquake of 1999. In fact, it sits along a major northern Anatolian fault line at a meeting point with two others. At least 18,000 people died in Yalova and the neighboring areas in 1999, and the town's seaside corniche is reclaimed land built on the rubble of the old city destroyed in the disaster.[4] Middle-class outsiders did not know or remember the old town, and most new arrivals did not even know about the disastrous earthquake. They were ideal customers for the new building boom in the town. Fleeing their own upheaval, Syrian refugees did not know and did not care to know much about their new neighborhood. For the time being, it felt a great deal more stable than any of their other options.

Warda's Wedding

Hanan's daughter Warda had received a proposal of marriage, a serious one based on a school friendship, and her family had to figure

3. On the buying of real estate in Turkey, see Betts et al., "What Difference Do Mayors Make?"

4. Fisk, "Earthquake in Turkey"; Akgiray et al., "Case Study: The 1999 Marmara Earthquakes in Turkey."

out how to make her wedding happen. Warda and Yahya had met years earlier as pupils in the Damascus School for the Deaf. Like her, her future husband was completely deaf and communicated in Arabic sign language. Like her, he was a refugee, but one who had made his way to Germany in 2014. After attaining asylum in Germany, he couldn't bring his parents because of a tightening of the family-reunification laws, but he could bring a wife, and so he asked for the hand of the girl he remembered from school. According to custom, the two could meet and court in Turkey, and if they got along well, she could join him in Germany.

The family was thoroughly delighted at Warda's good fortune. She was the youngest of her siblings and the last at home, helping her mother and taking care of her father. They would miss her terribly, but for a traditionally raised young woman whose disability and the war had prevented further education, marriage was the highest priority and safest bet for the future. The prospect of marriage and a visa to Germany, if Warda and Yahya had a promising period of engagement, was like hitting the jackpot. In Warda's case, her aunts, uncles, and cousins did not conceal the fact that they had never expected her to marry at all, given a disability that just a generation ago would have been seen as a stigma that diminished her prospects to near zero.

The preparations for Warda's departure were festive, if constrained. Hanan designed the elegant gowns and dresses of a traditional if minimal trousseau and made them on her sewing machine. Warda, in her mid-twenties, had never left her parents' home and was the light of their lives, communicating with them in the Arabic sign language they had learned when it became clear shortly after her birth that she was deaf. After her older sisters married in Jordan and Damascus, she helped her parents around the house, becoming the family social media expert as well as cooking, baking, and doing decorative crafts.

True, when Yahya took Warda to Germany, they had not yet lived together, but that was a mere technicality. Once he made it clear that his motives were honorable and straightforward, that he was a person of good moral standing—actively vetted by all members of the extended family—that he admired their daughter, and that she fancied him, Hanan and her family felt that Warda's future was secure.

Throughout 2015, Hanan and her husband made periodic visits from Yalova to Istanbul to get Warda's Syrian paperwork in good order. They also set up powers of attorney so that one of Warda's paternal uncles could meet with Yahya's father in Damascus to conduct a marriage by proxy. A small bribe would allow them to officially backdate the marriage by law to before the actual marriage ceremony of *katb ktab*, or "writing of the book." Another technicality. When Yahya's papers in Germany allowed him to travel freely in and out of Germany, he went to visit the family in Turkey. Warda and Yahya exchanged elaborate expressions of love on Facebook, sometimes raising eyebrows among their relatives. A party was held, and the stream of generic and very public expressions of love on Facebook intensified.

Hanan held an engagement party for her youngest daughter in Yalova. The two of them held back tears that not one of Warda's sisters and only two of her maternal aunts, Farida and Salma, were able to attend. For the young women of the family who had married before the war, an engagement party was one of the highlights of their social lives. Men were exiled, while the women, girls, and children of the family and their female friends celebrated in the elaborately decorated apartment for hours—singing, dancing, eating sweets. Salma had brought with her a video CD of her wedding to Mazen. It reminded her, Hanan, and Warda of the numerous parties of the past. In the safe, all-female party recorded on the CD, each of the aunts and cousins stepped forward for a dance solo, without hijab, their beautiful hair and celebratory dresses resplendent. In Yalova, the women cried as they watched as each sister, aunt, and cousin as well as their beloved late matriarch, Um 'Abdallah, each more beautiful and glowing than the last, stepped forward to dance. In an echo of the traditional practice of gender segregation, Salma would show the tape only to women and girls. Her husband had never seen the video played on the screen of the battered desktop computer, and the women laughed and wept for the days gone by. Salma noted sadly that she would have to destroy the tape because she had only sons, and as pious Muslims who observed a modest lifestyle, the sons could never see their beautiful cousins dance, even on film.

Warda's party was a subdued affair, but her mother did her best to create a special day for her youngest daughter. The two of them had been sewing a trousseau of elegant gowns to wear during the evening. The women of Uncle Muhammad's family were invited, and even Farida and her daughter, Tala, were persuaded to come in for the day from Istanbul, although the ferry was a luxury they could afford only once or twice a year. The men of the family gathered at Uncle Muhammad's apartment about a block away over Yalova's new roads, entertaining Yahya's father and the groom until they all escorted him to the women's party, which only he would be allowed to join. All the women on the bride's side put their hijab back on, leaving Yahya to see only his wedded wife for the first time without the precaution of modest dress—indeed, dressed in her dream clothes, sewn by hand. Then he flew back to Germany.

Nine months later, with the legal marriage executed and the social marriage celebrated, family reunification (*lam shaml*) could take place. Warda's paperwork, fresh from the Syrian representatives in Turkey, was sent to Germany for processing. By December 2016, her visa to Germany was processed, and Yahya went to meet her at the Frankfurt Airport, accompanied by an entourage of his friends from the deaf refugee community of his new German hometown. He waited nervously for his bride, holding a large bouquet of metallic balloons with her name printed on them and an armful of flowers. She arrived and slipped into a new life in Germany. Her domestic life was one she was well prepared for. Her married sisters and cousins had coached her well on her role and responsibilities. She and her new husband shared an effervescent love, but she would be living out that new life in a cloudy German city very far from anything she had ever known.

The next departures Hanan would facilitate were not so easy. They would be illegal smuggled journeys with desperate hope of asylum. As Salma and her family in Istanbul made the decision to set off for Europe, they consulted with Hanan and her family, who were comfortable enough in Yalova to serve as the staging point for Salma's journey. The two sisters were in close contact by phone and the occasional overnight ferry visit. Hanan periodically came to Istanbul to do paperwork for her daughter's impending marriage that would take her legally to Germany, and as Salma, suffocating in Istanbul, came to the decision that she would have to leave, she took the ferry to Yalova several times to move her possessions and papers to the most stable household of the family in the seaside resort. But it was Iba, fleeing Lebanon in a panic and desperate to get to Europe before asylum was out of reach, who depended the most on her older sister's hospitality in Yalova.

Staging Point for Aegean Smuggling—Iba's Family and Salma's Son Yusuf

Hanan and Iba were overjoyed to see each other again in early 2016. Four long years had passed since they had been separated, after living a mere ten minutes away from each other in the Ghuta towns that were currently smoldering ruins. Hanan had refrained from taking sides in any of the strife among her three younger sisters, and she and Iba, with plenty of space and privacy in two apartments in the same building, experienced a few weeks of routine that recalled their life in Damascus. The families ate their meals together, visited with Uncle Muhammad and his family a short walk away, and took long walks through the quiet streets and the suburban playgrounds of Yalova to pass the time. Iba's children circled around her—Bilal, her oldest, nearly seventeen years old, shy, newly very tall, but still very much a boy, with a head full of hair focused into a mohawk stripe; her middle daughter, Lamya, fourteen, newly wearing a hijab to conceal a cascade of long dark hair; and the youngest daughter, Aya, twelve, pretty, dark, quiet, and watchful, hovering at her mother's side. Lamya's pretty face drooped ever so slightly on one side, the left half of her mouth fixed in a horizontal line and a slight heaviness on her eyelid and cheek. This condition had emerged as part of the complex of illnesses and stresses that marked the family's transition to the hardships of life in Tripoli.

Before arriving in Yalova, while Iba was still in Tripoli, she desperately put out a call to Araj relatives abroad via WhatsApp. It was December 2015, and she needed money fast. She had never borrowed money after arriving in Tripoli back in 2012, but she felt that she had no choice now. She had been waiting since the fall for her husband, Hisham, who had traveled to Germany alone, to send for her and the children, but borders and windows of opportunity were closing all around her. Her son, Bilal, was seventeen. After he turned eighteen, he would no longer be eligible for family reunification in Germany but would instead be considered a single adult man. Also, his Syrian passport would expire, trapping him in Lebanon with no choice but to stay there or return to the war in Syria. Since it was increasingly clear with each passing day that the visa papers would not arrive from Germany before Bilal's birthday, Iba decided to take her son and his young sisters to Turkey, while the boy still had a valid passport. If the visas did not arrive in time from Germany, they would cross the Aegean illegally like so many others.

The plan had been to save money and travel to Turkey in the spring, but in December 2015 Iba learned that Syrian refugees would need a visa to enter Turkey as of New Year's Day 2016. Iba realized she couldn't wait for the formal process. The gears of the bureaucracy in Lebanon, Turkey, and Germany seemed to move inexorably to trap her family, and she felt herself flailing in trying to negotiate this giant crushing machine. Iba and the children had to get to Turkey before the open border there closed on January 1. The stress had already caused her to experience several emotional collapses that she could not afford or, of course, have treated. Money was sent in response to her uncharacteristically urgent pleas, and she and the children, leaving most of their possessions behind with neighbors in Tripoli, paid for exit visas and passage and boarded the very last ship from Lebanon to Turkey on New Year's Eve. They were the last boatload of Syrian refugees from Lebanon to Turkey whose passengers did not require an expensive Turkish visa. Upon arrival, they learned that the very next ship to dock after theirs was refused entry, and hundreds of refugees without visas were sent back to Lebanon. For the next four months, Iba had the sense that she was squeaking through doors just as they were slamming closed. If 2015 was the year of risk and open borders, 2016 would be the year in which the governments of refuge and transit countries used control of their borders to regulate and weaponize the stream of migrants for political advantage.

Upon arrival in the Turkish port of Mersin, Iba and her children boarded a bus directly for Yalova. Hanan had arranged for Iba to let an unfurnished apartment in the same building on a month-to-month lease. As soon as the frigid Turkish weather improved, Iba and her family would set off on their illegal trip across the Aegean.

In early 2016, Hanan's tidy rented apartment at Yalova would be the scene of another reunion. Salma's son Yusuf, tired of living on his own in Istanbul after his family had left, was ready to join his aunt Iba and her son and daughters on the road to Europe. He and his cousins had not seen each other since their mothers had fought and had separated on bad terms in Tripoli. But the two estranged branches of the family would come together as each tried to reunite its separated members in Germany. Yusuf was proud that he had earned and saved enough money for the trip in just three months. Not having to pay rent and utilities allowed him to contribute to a shared room, eat in cheap restaurants, and otherwise entertain himself in Istanbul, but he was in a hurry to get to Germany. Like his brother 'Adel, who had already set out separately for Germany and been caught and turned back at least once, he had abandoned thoughts of college in Turkey. Having a strong young man who spoke Turkish and had developed some street smarts would enhance Iba and her children's chances of making it to Germany.

In February 2016, Yusuf made regular journeys on the Yalova ferry to meet with Iba and get Hanan's help in preparing them for travel. He could now quite easily afford the fare, which had been prohibitive when he was providing for his family and was responsible for rent and utilities. He was slowly taking possessions that his parents had left with him back in October to Hanan for safekeeping. Briefcases, backpacks, duffel bags of kitchen equipment that he had never used, copies of the important family papers—deeds, school certificates, lease papers, car registrations, heavy evidence of prosperity and success back in Syria, which were tempting to ditch but were always dragged along for when they could recover their status. Yusuf spoke quite a bit of Turkish, unlike Iba, who was only passing through, so he served as the communicator and negotiator with the smuggling gang, a different one than his parents and little brother had used.

For several evenings a week, he would travel from Istanbul to the cozy apartment at Yalova, where Hanan's household was joined by Iba's and sometimes Uncle Muhammad's family for special meals that were almost like old times in Damascus. With so many people, Hanan and Iba would spread out a picnic cloth made of Turkish plastic grocery bags on the floor, and everyone would squeeze around, as they always had. Yusuf would regale his cousins and aunts with tales of his solo life in the big city. They would drink tea and coffee.

Lest they forget that the occasion for this coming together was not a pleasant one, after dinner the adults would sit on the floor and sew in preparation for the upcoming journey, while the kids played on their phones, using temporary hot spots. Hanan got out her sewing machine; Iba and her kids and Yusuf would present her with jeans, sweatshirts, hoodies, and she would create secret pockets in their seams and interiors for cash and papers. Meanwhile, Yusuf and Bilal would periodically pop out to the neighborhood grocery stores to buy more rolls of plastic wrap, the key waterproofing for tiny gum-size packets of cash and medicine as well as the multiple bulky packages of personal identity papers each person would layer into their outfits. They joked that the layers of papers would act as extra insulation. Iba sorted through photocopies of each of her children's and her own Syrian identity papers, the all-important "family register" (*daftar al-'a'ila*) that showed their relation to one another and to their asylum-claiming father, UN identity papers from Lebanon, passports, and cash, organizing multiple separate caches for each person to carry, some to be hidden for the entire journey and safeguarded for European asylum claims, others to be surrendered as necessary to border guards or bandits, or possibly accidentally lost at sea. Traveling back to his boardinghouse in Istanbul each night on the ferry, Yusuf looked out into the darkness of the sea, trying to gauge the wind direction and wave height from the safety and security of the ship's deck, wondering if it would prepare him in any way for the journey ahead.

The shadow of a dangerous journey at the height of winter hovered over the family gatherings in Yalova. The smuggler they had contracted with through Yusuf scheduled them for a March 5 departure. By then, the worst of the winter weather and choppy seas should be behind them. But there were rumors that eastern European countries, following the lead of Hungary, which closed its border to refugees in October, would stop the flow of migrants to Germany. And so they moved up the date of departure into the last weeks of February. As their smuggler directed, they left Yalova, returned to Istanbul, and then went to the meeting place.

18

The Camp at Idomeni

Iba, 2016

When Iba, her children—Bilal, Lamya, and Aya—and her nephew Yusuf arrived in Istanbul from Yalova, they waited in a park for a big bus. The Syrian passengers waited quietly, while a combination of local Turkish- and Arabic-speaking smugglers fought among themselves about their lucrative cargo. They eventually boarded the bus and were distressed to find themselves going back through Yalova to Izmir. When they were almost in Izmir, the escort smugglers discovered that the receiving smugglers were not ready for them, so the bus simply turned and went all the way back to Istanbul. If Iba, with her obsession with order and efficiency, had known about the twenty-hour bus trip back and forth, she might have saved some time and met the gang in Izmir, but because of the rigid smugglers' rules and the refugees' lack of control, she spent the better part of two days in nausea on the bus.

They sailed from a beach about two hours away from Izmir on February 26, 2016. Iba was prepared for the worst. Several months earlier, Iba's husband, Hisham, had set out on the journey across the Aegean despite his heart condition and worsening mental health. His departure in September 2015 occurred almost a year to the day after the sinking of Mustafa's boat off Malta. Like Mustafa before him, Hisham was determined to get to Europe to gain asylum and bring his family later in a process of family reunification known in Arabic as *lam shaml*.[1] He

1. On earlier immigrants' family reunification, see Velling, "Immigration to Germany in the Seventies and Eighties."

was well aware of the risk of death on the sea. Although his health was precarious, he felt he had no other choice.

Hisham used WhatsApp to tell Iba of his arrival in Greece as the weather turned cold in the autumn of 2015. His crossing had cost him $1,200, and the dinghy was packed with men, women, and children. When they reached the Greek shore, a family with two babies had the usual trouble getting from the unstable boat to the shore. One of the babies was handed to another man but was soaked and swallowed a lot of water before being brought to shore. The frantic parents were able to keep the baby breathing, and the group struggled in the dark up a muddy hillside to a road above. They hailed a passing motorist from Italy, who at first refused to stop but then agreed to drive the family to a hospital when he saw the limp baby. Hisham learned later in the camp at Lesbos that, despite the parents' best efforts, the baby died a few hours later at dawn. With Hisham's trauma echoing in her head, Iba steeled herself for the ordeal of putting her own children, who did not know how to swim, out to sea.

By the first weeks of 2016, a disproportionate number of the undocumented Aegean migrants from Syria were women and children, whose husbands and fathers had made the trip but were unable to sponsor their families legally and safely. In the first two months of 2016, more than 110,000 people crossed into Greece. A year earlier, that same period had seen fewer than 20,000 arrivals. They faced the perils of a winter water crossing in the flimsy inflatable *bilims*, which were launching at a rate of dozens a day because family reunification in Germany was becoming more difficult by the week. Iba's situation was better than so many others. She had a place to stay in Turkey while waiting for an uncertain departure and could afford to avoid the worst sea conditions of January and early February.

Finally, the tiring bus ride came to an end. Iba's smugglers deposited the family and the other travelers by the side of the road, and they made their way through thick underbrush down a steep dirt path to a rocky beach. There was the usual yelling and chaos, but at least it was daytime. The trip was better made in darkness to avoid patrols, but the passengers were glad to feel the sun rising behind them as they headed west. The weather was unusually warm for February, warmer than it had been for a while, and Iba reported that they were not particularly scared. One after another, the passengers stepped out just to the edges of the beach clearing and relieved themselves—men and women alike. Iba surprised herself by doing the same, as if responding to some unspoken physiological signal, and was even more surprised that her normally fastidious children quickly, quietly, and efficiently stepped aside, too, imagining that it would be far worse to need to go while on the raft. When the time came to board the clearly insufficient raft, some of their travel companions, a large party of nonswimmers from eastern Syria, especially the young men of the party, began to panic and shout, refusing to get on it. A Turkish smuggler and an Arabic-speaking smuggler were yelling and screaming at everyone to get on the boats. As Yusuf and Bilal helped the women into the boats to the accompaniment of the screaming men, the smugglers looked around and asked who would drive the boat. A stolid taxi driver from Aleppo agreed to drive based on his experience with taxis, much to the party's later amusement. The smugglers took a photograph of each passenger as they boarded, perhaps some kind of recordkeeping system if there were any disagreement about payment or, ominously, loss of life. Iba was worried when one of the smugglers assigned her son Bilal to hold the boat because he couldn't swim and had an inordinate fear of water, but he waded in and accepted his job like a man.

Once in the boat, the seating arrangement was completely random, some people sitting on top of others. They had been warned not to sit at the back end of the boat, which tended to be lowest in the water, but Yusuf found himself there as the last person aboard. Iba's teenage daughters, Lamya and Aya, were crushed by the large men sitting on top of them. The frightened men of the eastern Syrian party wailed the whole way, sitting on Iba's daughters and exhorting their fellow passengers to pray to God with such irritating regularity that the normally pious Iba found herself muttering blasphemies to herself. They were probably regular kafirs (infidels), she thought angrily, smoking, drinking, and swearing; suddenly they had gotten all religious but would probably forget their oaths the moment they got to shore. There was a pregnant woman with three small children who clearly needed assistance, and Iba regained a sense of control by helping her. One man was smoking, much to Iba's consternation, but he made up for it by self-importantly holding a GPS navigator and giving instructions to the taxi driver in charge of the outboard motor. The panicky men were not above yelling instructions to the taxi driver, who stubbornly and wisely refused to go above first gear. The smugglers still onshore were also connected to the boat by phone and conveying instructions, and the passengers listened with mixed emotions as their "guides" were apprehended by police back on shore.

But the refugees had their own problems to worry about. Once they reached international waters, they were to call the Greek Coast Guard to come and rescue them, but early on they were terrified to see what they thought was a Turkish Coast Guard plane circling overhead and a boat in the distance that might take them back to Izmir. Then a white ship began heading right for them. Some people on their boat who were on their fifth crossing attempt began to cry in relief, and within minutes everyone was crying. The rescue ship approached and started issuing orders through a megaphone. They were told in English to turn off the motor, hand up the children first, then the women. Iba bruised her leg climbing up the ladder. Yusuf stayed last, as usual, to hand up the luggage. Their rescuers punctured the boat, forbade people from using phones, and separated the men from the women. In the next twenty minutes, they waited on deck while two more dinghies were rescued—one, Iba noted, was full of Afghans, who were properly lined up and seated around the inner edges of the boat. Another was full of Syrians and other Arabs, and her first thought was of how Bashar al-Assad had forced his people to this state.

Two days after arriving in Lesbos and then taking a ferry to Athens and the northern border of Greece, by Sunday, February 28, 2016, Iba and her family were stopped at a bottleneck that would be far more challenging than their Aegean crossing. As they were getting across the sea to Lesbos in their raft and getting ferried from Lesbos to the mainland on the long but secure ferry ride, the land passage to Germany through Europe that they still had to navigate was closing down. A million refugees and migrants had passed through the overland conduit of non-EU countries (Macedonia, Serbia, Hungary, Croatia, Slovenia) that separated EU member Greece from the rest of the union to Austria and then Germany. Following the lead of Hungary's right-wing Orban government in October, the Balkan countries attempted to control the migration route by fortifying their borders.

On the day Iba, Yusuf, and her three children arrived at the Greek-Macedonian border crossing at a rural junction called Idomeni, where the train lines entered Macedonia through farmers' fields, the regional geopolitical situation was shifting. Several thousand people were already jammed at the closed crossing, the same one that Hisham first and then Salma, Mazen, and Kamal had passed through without much difficulty after a couple hours of waiting and paperwork.[2] The closure of the Macedonian border started after February 15, 2016. On that date, two things happened. The EU pledged 10 million euros to help fortify migrant management at the Macedonian crossing points, while at the same time a group consisting of Poland, Hungary, the Czech Republic, and Slovakia invited the Macedonian and Bulgarian officials to consolidate a plan to keep migrants in Greece. These steps came on the heels of an Austrian plan to drastically limit the number of asylum applications and transit visas granted daily. The new border to European asylum would effectively be in Austria, and the mobilization of the Balkan non-EU countries was intended to ensure that the backlog would occur in Greece, not in any of the countries between Greece and Austria, the two EU member states that marked different entries into the

2. On the various and shifting European countries' border regulations, see R. Jones, *Violent Borders*; Bossong and Carrapico, eds., *EU Borders and Shifting Internal Security Technology*; Cornelisse, "Territory, Procedures and Rights"; and Bendixsen, "The Refugee Crisis."

Schengen and Dublin Areas, respectively.[3] Iba and her family, after having narrowly gotten in and out of Lebanon and Turkey, were now trapped by the adjustments of the transit countries trying to keep refugees in Greece and even push them back to Turkey.

Blocked at the Macedonian Border

Of the crowd of about 7,000 people who arrived at the Macedonian border that day in mid-February, only 22 were allowed to file applications for asylum in Macedonia, and approximately 300 were allowed transit through to Serbia. Only Syrians and Iraqis with documentation had any hope of moving through to Europe.[4] Iba observed with alarm that the growing number of Afghans whom she and the others had noticed on the crossing were treated far more harshly than the Syrians. The growing number of other Arabic speakers who could fool the European authorities into believing they were Syrians fleeing from a war zone were also competing with real Syrians like herself for access to the border. She noticed that the Syrian identity papers that gave refugees the best chance of being recognized as "real refugees" were in great demand. There was a market for stolen or forged Syrian papers, and she was glad that each member of her family had several copies secreted in different layers of their clothes in case of pickpockets.

They were traveling with a group of people from Syria whom they had met on the Athens ferry and with whom they pooled resources and information. The hope was that with their Syrian documentation and with the presence of Iba's youngest daughter, Aya, who was

3. Geddes and Scholten, "Towards Common EU Migration and Asylum Policies?," 144. Also perhaps relevant, see Feischmidt, "Deployed Fears and Suspended Solidarity Along the Migratory Route in Europe"; Svensson, "Resistance or Acceptance?"; Schwiertz and Schwenken, "Mobilizing for Safe Passages and Escape Aid." The Schengen zone is a group of twenty-nine European countries that officially agreed to have no border controls between them; the Dublin regime, originally established among twelve states in 1990 but amended and expanded several times, laid out EU member states' responsibilities regarding asylum seekers.

4. Afghans were being deported back to Athens. See Dimitriadi, *Irregular Afghan Migration to Europe*.

still clearly a child, they might be processed through in the groups of 300 that would be allowed through each day. They had received one of several hundred tents provided by volunteers on the second night at the crossing, but their tent was wet and muddy despite occasional sunny weather. People were convened in groups of fifty, assigned a number, and told to stay back from the border fence until their turn was called. Iba left a voice message for Hanan. "They have opened up the borders," she reported, "and people are going through . . . but they are in numbered groups of about fifty people. Our group number is 218, and they are on 56, but the problem is that the refugees are forging their numbers and tickets and breaking into the queue. We don't dare do that . . . we just saw a man have his ID card torn up for cheating in line."

Yusuf reported cynically that the lack of organization was intentional.[5] "They are doing this on purpose," he declared, "to keep us like animals." Both Iba's and Yusuf's voices on the recorded messages they sent to family had changed and sounded congested, as if they were sick, which indeed they were from days of exposure to the cold. One of Iba's congested messages said, "Please, God, just don't make us stay here another night," she implored. "We can't sleep. It is so wet and cold; we're hungry. We don't dare leave the tent; we don't know these people around us and what their intentions are. And we are afraid that we will miss our turn to cross the border. But our number is far off and getting farther because of the people—may God curse them—who are forging their group numbers."

As it happened, their number was called in the middle of the night when people were sleeping. Iba and Yusuf did hear their number but would not think of leaving without the other members of the group they had joined for solidarity and so rushed around in the dark to find their tents and wake their traveling companions. Yusuf wanted

5. On the disorganization in processing the refugees, see Fleischmann, *Contested Solidarity*; Svensson, "Resistance or Acceptance?"; Block and Bonjour, "Fortress Europe or Europe of Rights?"; and Van Oort et al., *Baseline Study on Access to Protection, Reception and Distribution of Asylum Seekers.*

to tell them, but as a properly raised Muslim man he felt he could not just poke his head into tents with women and family in them, so he waited for Iba and her daughters to come and do it. When they did, they discovered that the group had abandoned them and were long gone, leaving the empty tents behind. Through their selfless act, Iba, Yusuf, and her children had missed their chance and so joined the crowds of people trapped with no hope of getting across.

Soon it was apparent that the several nights spent sleeping on the ground were grinding the travelers down. The weather began to turn cold, and the family was unable to sleep in their soaked tent. Aya developed a fever and fell on the ground in a seizure, and Iba thought something serious had afflicted Yusuf from the way his body was wracked with chills and shivering. Nevertheless, he and Bilal stayed outside, milling about with the restless throngs of young men, leaving the tent to the females. The girls had been trying not to eat or drink in order to minimize their need to relieve themselves. Going into the filthy mixed-gender latrines shared by thousands was something they avoided at all costs, preferring a muddy field. With a complete lack of organization in the growing camp, the family needed to balance the distance they preferred to keep between themselves and the crowds (especially the non-Syrians, whom they had come to mistrust) and the importance of keeping an eye on the border crossing in case it opened up. Once again, Iba was personally frustrated by the complete lack of orderly lines. All these factors were exacerbated by the unyielding border authorities. Then a small glimmer of hope penetrated the misery.

On March 2, Iba's husband, Hisham, sent word via WhatsApp that he had finally received his three-year asylum residency permit in Germany and with the help of his friends in the German Red Cross was applying for and would soon be sending visas to Iba and the children. Deeply traumatized by the death of the baby on his Aegean crossing, Hisham had moved on through Greece, Macedonia, Serbia, Croatia, Slovenia, and Hungary by bus, train, and taxi as well as long stretches on foot. When he arrived in Germany, he was granted temporary asylum, pending the processing of his application for a three-year asylum residency permit. He was housed in the special medical unit of one of many temporary refugee housing complexes in an old US military barracks in central Germany, where he spent his days with the injured and wounded from Syria's many battlefronts, befriending them and the Red Cross employees who fast-tracked his case. The mostly younger refugee men in his wing called him "Hajji" out of respect for his age and experience. As his physical health gradually improved, he made friends by cooking for his fellow residents and the German employees and volunteers in the communal kitchen. But none of that sped up his family-reunification paperwork to meet the timeline Iba faced. He paced back and forth through the hallways of the asylum center, taking the long walk from the center into the nearest town, and studied hard in his German classes, although he had never finished high school in Syria. His wife and children were always on his mind, and he broke down easily into tears when talking about them. He quickly befriended the volunteers and workers of the German Red Cross, and together they worked on the necessary paperwork for family reunification.

The numbers and misery at Idomeni continued to grow. Now in March, the rain, cold, and mud, the endless lines for french fries and sandwiches, the misery of the stinking latrines, the fevers and coughing, the cheating and forging had continued. Yusuf sent a message to his parents:

> There is nothing worse or shittier than this camp. There are thousands of people, crowding for everything. In line for soup there are five hundred men. They are banging and making noise behind me because they want blankets, and the blanket distribution was delayed. There are five hundred guys in line here, and that's just the men. The women have their own line of five hundred. We are staying and sleeping with a group; we've put blankets on the ground in a muddy patch of farmland and are sitting on them. The situation really cannot be described. In my life I've never seen anything like this.[6]

6. For more on the dynamics and conditions of temporary settlement camps in Greece, especially in Piraeus, see Mavrommatis, "Grasping the Meaning of Integration in an Era of (Forced) Mobility."

As Iba, Yusuf, and the children spent day by miserable day through March, they learned, along with the other inhabitants of the de facto camp at Idomeni, that a summit between the Turkish government and the EU would soon be held to strike a deal on how to deal with the migrants. They were dependent on Macedonian border guards and a parade of well-meaning volunteers, so their access to information from the outside world was unreliable, though camped refugees did their best to stay in touch with their relatives via WhatsApp and avidly consumed news via Facebook and YouTube. Everyone trapped at the border was desperate to see if the summit would open the border at last. Monday came and went, and as the European leaders went into a dinner and evening session with Prime Minister Ahmet Davutoğlu of Turkey, there was still no reliable word. Yusuf's contacts were able to provide some early rumors of the Turkish deal offered by Davutoğlu. They sent his spirits spiraling downward: Turkey would take back "irregular" migrants in return for 6 billion euros and accelerated talks on Turkish visa liberalization in the EU.[7] As Monday rolled over into Tuesday, the deal was not finalized, although the migrants realized that Turkey, until then one of the most

7. On this deal, see Reiners and Tekin, "Taking Refuge in Leadership?" For every one migrant returned to Turkey from the Greek islands, EU member states would accept one Syrian refugee from among the 250,000 who were still living in the Turkish border camps and had not made an illegal crossing. Ironically, the best chance for scuttling the terrible deal that used these campers as pawns for cynically narrow Turkish advantage was that the same eastern European states blocking the refugees' way would never acquiesce to the European visa concessions for Turks being proposed by Turkey. In addition, the Turkish government's own behavior was acting against the proposal. The AKP government had just seized the oppositional newspaper, the *Zaman*, mouthpiece of the Gülen Hizmet movement, and turned it over to trustees, who ran it as a government mouthpiece. Journalists were being jailed and detained at a frightening rate, and though the Turkish government's war against the country's Kurdish political movements was easier to ignore in the illusory war against ISIS, it was nevertheless proceeding apace. By EU rules, the AKP's human rights violations would prevent rolling over for Turkish deals.

beneficent of de facto asylum states, had sold them out and that Angela Merkel, whose invitation for asylum they were responding to, looked likely to acquiesce. After enduring the worst of the Greek camps, Iba, Yusuf, and the other migrants now understood that they were in danger of being forcibly returned to Turkey as part of a formal treaty. It was not just gangs that commodified migrants.

Over the weekend, the British Channel 4 broadcast recorded footage of demonstrating migrants being beaten with truncheons, and on Monday a group of four desperate Afghans who had snuck into Macedonia were returned in exhausted humiliation. The lack of authoritative word one way or the other was torture. "Is it possible," Iba asked in a series of WhatsApp messages, "that they would take us back to Turkey after the expense, the twelve days shivering at the godforsaken border? The children, too? Unthinkable." Surely, everyone hoped, the inhabitants of the Idomeni camp would move on through before then. But wishful thinking had not worked in any of the unthinkable predicaments of the past years, and the press headlines were ominous—"Balkan Route Closed." According to Iba, anyone with evidence in their passports of presence in Turkey for longer than a month was not to be let through to Europe. Of course, nearly everyone had been in Turkey for longer than a month—even she and her children, who had transited through as quickly as possible from Lebanon. For this reason, they resolved to hide their passports with this incriminating evidence and pass through any borders using only internal Syrian ID papers and family notebooks, claiming to have lost their passports.

The next day in Idomeni heaped insult upon injury when a drenching thunderstorm accompanied the news that not only was the Macedonian border shut, but Slovenia would also be requiring EU visas, Croatia was closed, and hundreds of refugees and migrants who had gotten through Macedonia to Serbia were being bussed back to Greece from the Macedonian-Serbian border. The flow of people had completely stopped on the Slovenian border with Austria, which marked reentry into the Schengen Area, and the previously bustling camp at Šentilj was strangely empty and silent.[8] As the Idomeni residents began digging drainage ditches to divert the puddles and streams of rainwater around their shuddering tents, they wondered whether to continue to hope for a chance to cross into Macedonia or just get on the buses that had already carried more than a hundred people back to Athens to await resettlement in the new urban camps that were supposed to be in place by mid-March. In order to get rid of the evidence that they had been in Turkey for more than a month and thus be vulnerable to deportation, Iba sent their original Syrian passports via the DHL van that visited the camp periodically to Hisham in Germany at an address written out carefully in the children's best English handwriting. The anxiety produced by this high-stakes decision was palpable. What if they needed those passports later for a new policy twist? More likely, what if their passports were lost or stolen in transit for their value to other migrants who needed the legitimacy of Syrian refugee status? How could they trust that a package sent from an ad hoc northern Greek wheatfield would arrive at one of Germany's hundreds of emergency asylum centers teeming with migrants? They had no choice.

Hisham did receive the passports and was using his contacts at the Red Cross to expedite the processing of his family and Yusuf. Then he would have to get the passports back to them so they could get their visas validated at the German embassy in Athens. Meanwhile, the rain continued to pour down as days and nights ran together in a foggy, gray, unending chill. Iba and her daughters tried not to leave the tent at all so they wouldn't have to look at the depressing scene around them. It was hard to recall that when they first arrived, they couldn't bear to think of spending a single night here. Now they had been in their waterlogged tent in the mud for

8. On the closure of European borders, see Weiher, "Borders and Boundaries on the Balkan Route"; Bird et al., "The 'Badlands' of the 'Balkan Route'"; Parzer, "Double Burden of Representation"; Murphy, "The Double Articulation of Sovereign Bordering"; and Isakjee et al., "Liberal Violence and the Racial Borders of the European Union."

weeks. The DHL truck, their lifeline to the outside world, kept arriving at Idomeni with the papers that people thought would speed up their transit appeals. The barber from Aleppo kept shaving people to make money and help people feel clean in the freezing muck and dejection. In Iba and Yusuf's tent, everyone was sick. Yusuf was coughing, Iba was sniffling, and Aya was crying with an earache.

On March 10, three days after the Turkey-EU summit in Brussels and its disheartening outcome, it became clear that the Macedonian border was not going to reopen, certainly not before March 17, the date of the EU summit to ratify the infuriating "one back, one from the Turkish camps" agreement. The rain drummed on, and the family were beyond miserable, each of them sick with a different set of symptoms. Hisham sent a message with the good news that he had procured the paperwork to get his family their needed visas to Germany from the German embassy in Greece. But they would need their passports, of course. Not trusting the DHL delivery van to get the documents back to them in the camp, he advised them to get on the buses taking people back to Athens. On that same day, March 10, international news headlines pronounced the Macedonian border completely and irrevocably closed. This pronouncement reinvigorated people smuggling, with $800 now the new standard price for the promise and risk of bypassing the Macedonian border with local smugglers. With the help of his relatives and social workers, Hisham made a booking for the family in a hotel near the German embassy in Athens, and they got on the bus that would take them back to where they had been nearly a month earlier.

Back to Athens

On Friday, March 11, 2016, Iba, her three children, and Yusuf boarded a bus for Athens. For Yusuf, the decision to get on the bus for Athens and abandon his vigil at the crossing was more difficult. Having traveled with Iba for the past few weeks, he hoped vainly that Hisham's intervention might work for him, too, but he knew that it wouldn't because he was a single adult male. His own parents, Salma and Mazen, now safely in Germany, had been frantically contacting their own camp administrators, trying to replicate the move that Hisham had apparently pulled off. But unlike Hisham, they had not yet received their temporary residence permit, and, crucially, Yusuf was no longer a minor child. After a sleepless night, Salma resigned herself: she had done all she could for her middle son. Communicating with him by WhatsApp, she urged him to go with Iba's family to Athens, if only to get out of the rain, and to leave the camp voluntarily with the possibility of disappearing into Athens rather than be formally reassigned to one of the hypothetical relocation "hot spots" to which the Idomeni refugees were to be relocated as soon as those could be built. He would always have the option of applying for asylum in Greece in the future, but better to be on his own in Athens and even to accompany his aunt to the German embassy for now.

Using the location feature on WhatsApp, the group received the coordinates of the hotel in the Syrgou main road of Athens and even directions to the German embassy three kilometers away. The eight-hour bus ride was an event to look forward to, a haven of warmth and sleep, as the family returned to Athens. The party arrived in Athens about midnight and took a taxi straight to the hotel near the German embassy that Hisham's friends had booked for them on the internet. They bathed and collapsed. The next morning, the children were rested and better and went down to the luxury of a breakfast buffet, but Iba was wracked by fever and chills and could hardly speak from coughing and the pain in her throat from her swollen lymph nodes. Yusuf was even worse and couldn't get out of bed to go down to breakfast. It was as if the sudden warmth of the bus ride had brought on the symptoms that they had suppressed out of sheer necessity while at Idomeni.

Hisham immediately put their passports in the mail to the hotel's address, and the children hovered around the reception desk until the package arrived the next day. Iba was finally able to breathe more easily when the DHL package containing her family's passports was in her hands. After a couple of days, Iba and Yusuf were able to get out of bed and keep down some food. They had almost no cash left, so relatives abroad reserved an apartment via Airbnb, which had a washing machine, and they spent the next few days washing and drying the clothes they had lived in since Yalova. The visit to the German embassy revealed that for Iba and her family, the visas might take up to three weeks, but they needed to get their papers stamped by the German embassy in Beirut and/or Istanbul—involving more costly DHL overnights, not to mention contacts within the embassies. As for Yusuf, who tagged along on the embassy visit, the consular officers just laughed sympathetically at his request that he travel with his aunt and cousins and told him that he could apply for a student visa, handing him the forms. There was nothing to be done. With this mixed news, Iba was down to her last 40 euros because when she had changed her stash of dollars in the main square in Yalova, she had received one forged 50-euro note. Yusuf was also down to his last 100 euros. Coming up on three weeks inside Greece, they had reached a dead end and had used up their money. They made plans to move into a refugee camp in Athens for the three weeks it would take for the cumbersome transfer of papers to go through.

They moved to the refugee camp in Athen's port of Piraeus. Inside the sprawling warehouse teeming with refugees, they created a little privacy by stacking cardboard boxes of provisions to form a little sitting area. Iba's daughters were once again treated for dehydration and anemia after Aya fainted unexpectedly and was rushed to a public hospital with Iba at her side. The next day Aya was released from the hospital with some rehydration salt and sugar mixture, as far as Iba could understand from the doctors. They returned to the camp at Piraeus to wait. It was Syrian Mothers' Day, and she and Salma exchanged internet greetings via WhatsApp.

Yusuf, facing isolation again in a strange new city, threw himself into the conflicts of Piraeus. At Piraeus, there were three different camps, one exclusively for Syrians, one for Afghans, and one combined. As tempers grew short, the tensions between the populations increased, the Afghans credibly complaining that the Syrians were getting better treatment from the authorities. He manned the ramparts of one of the camp's subsections when a rumor went out that a large number of Afghan men had gotten drunk and were coming to attack the Syrian camp. He stood his ground at the front of a makeshift barricade, and a large rock hit him in the neck, twisting it, and another hit his collarbone, fracturing it. He laughed when recalling that all the Syrians, with false bravado, were urging each other not to back off even as they withdrew to safety.

When Iba and Yusuf's cousins boarded a plane for Germany later in the month, Yusuf stayed alone in Athens to plot his own trip to Germany, just as he had once been left behind in Istanbul. It was not the education he had left Syria for, but it was quite an education.

19

Left Behind

Farida, 2015

"How did I find myself homeless, friendless, alone on the street in Istanbul?" Farida asked bitterly. When Farida stormed out of Salma's apartment in the Little Syria neighborhood of Istanbul in January 2015, it was cold and wet, and Farida was wracked with a terrible cough. Simply to keep out of the rain, she and her children holed up in a tiny basement room without running water or plumbing. Her pride prevented her from answering her phone, and soon her prepaid minutes ran out anyway. Salma, who had evicted her after a bitter and painful fight, was frantic with worry about her older sister. She never thought that Farida would actually leave, but each of them seemed to underestimate the other's determination.

Farida had arrived in Istanbul in December 2014 after a desperate flight from Tripoli when she feared that her oldest son would be imprisoned there. It was ironic that he stayed behind in Lebanon and sent her and her two younger children on alone. After a long and difficult journey in the cargo hold of a ship that left them seasick and disoriented, Farida and her daughter and younger son moved into Salma's tiny flat in Istanbul's Fatih neighborhood at the tail end of 2014, already home to Salma and her three sons. Farida expected a welcome as warm and unconditional from Salma in Istanbul as she had provided for them when they stayed with her in Tripoli for a cramped month during their house search. But Salma's husband, Mazen, would be joining them soon, and Farida failed to understand how her presence was stressing her younger sister, who was wrestling with the painful calculus of keeping her own family intact.

The oddly shaped apartment shared with Salma's family for a month in January 2015 had a tiny bathroom and kitchen, a living room, a dining room, and a tiny bedroom. As long as it was just the sisters and their children, the women and young Kamal slept in one room, the young men in the other. But Mazen would be joining them in the new year of 2015.

Back in Tripoli, Farida had hosted Salma and Mazen in her one-room apartment for weeks after they had left Iba's house. She had made it clear at the time that as a single woman she objected to Mazen sharing her quarters, but Salma and Mazen had not always heeded her polite hints and objections. She felt strongly that now in their time of need, she and her children should continue to live with Salma in the slightly larger Istanbul apartment. But tensions were rising. Salma was working, first spending hours hunched in a sewing workshop embroidering bling onto Turkish wedding dresses, later volunteering, and then appointed as a teacher in a Libyan school. Farida stayed home, supporting her daughter, Tala, who was looking to use her superior English skills to find a better type of work as an executive secretary. The boys were in and out of the house working, taking language classes, and spending much of their time at home sleeping or playing on their mobile phones. Farida took charge of the household but continued to coddle her children. Tala, ostensibly looking for work and occasionally working, slept late, left her bedding in the common living space, and did not help her mother with the housework. The two of them would retreat into the only room with a door to talk privately, while Salma fumed silently outside. When Salma was at work, Farida began allowing Salma's little son Kamal to stay home from school. This was the last straw for Salma, whose life philosophy was all about school and hard work.[1]

1. For more accounts of the life/lives of Syrian families in Turkey, see Causadias et al., "Trauma and Resilient Functioning Among Syrian Refugee Children"; and El-Khani et al., "Syria."

The situation exploded in January 2015. Mazen would be arriving in a week or so, and the two sisters celebrated the new year by drinking coffee together, friendlier and more upbeat than they had been in weeks. But one night Tala was dropped off in the early hours of the morning by a colleague at her new job and immediately retreated to the room where she and her mother spent hours with the door closed. Salma's irritation about their monopoly of a room in the apartment that she and her sons were working so hard to pay for had been quietly growing. What were they talking about? Why did they shut the door? Why did they take a whole room of the apartment as if it were theirs? Her resentment was probably exacerbated by the fact that Tala was the only girl in the whole extended family who had shed the hijab. Salma exploded in anger and announced that under her roof girls would not be coming and going at all hours, dropped off by unknown persons. All the frustrations of the past weeks came flooding out, and Salma impulsively stated that if this was Tala's new lifestyle, she could move to an apartment of her own.

Farida chose to take this pronouncement as an expulsion of her whole family from the apartment. She interpreted it as revealing her sister's true nature, and the next morning she took her children, her things, and the money in her pocket and left. A single phone call to her relative abroad to appeal for money also ended in disaster when he angrily revealed that he blamed her for the fight, ever the headstrong and stubborn sister known for spoiling her children. In a fury, she disappeared into the streets of Istanbul with her children. Were it not for one of her daughter's work friends, who located a tiny cellar room for them in February 2015, they would have been homeless.[2]

Farida ghosted Salma and the rest of her family for months. Hanan and her children, also in Turkey, and even Maryam and her children in Egypt and Germany tried calling and posting appeals on Facebook—although they were struggling with their own loss as well

2. For more on the migrant neighborhood of Kumkapi, see Özservet, "'You Know, We Live in Fear'"; K. Biehl, "Spatializing Diversities, Diversifying Spaces."

as with Maryam's and Amira's poor physical and mental health—but to no avail. Only Iba, ostracized by Salma and Farida back in Tripoli for their expulsions from her apartment and watching her own early success fade into ill health and despair, declined to join in the search. Relatives abroad, sobered by the prospect of a single mother and her children living on the streets of Turkey's largest city, finally were able to contact Farida and arrange for regular transfers of rent money via Western Union.

Farida declined to talk in detail about the weeks she spent on the streets, except to note that she "considered everything." She recounted how back in Damascus when the bombs were falling around her, she used to pray and even fantasize that she and her children would be swiftly and simultaneously killed by a single missile or volley of precisely aimed snipers' bullets. In Istanbul, the environment was less directly lethal. As a pious Muslim, she felt she could not contemplate suicide, but she did admit to rolling the idea around in her mind, thinking about methods. Illness was the most likely way out, and she often had no choice but to huddle in blankets, coughing and feverish, while her children hovered helplessly around her.[3] She was not embarrassed to admit that she briefly considered marriage to nearly anyone "who would have her" as a way out of her problems but noted that although many, many men still found her attractive in her late fifties, "they only wanted a girlfriend, not a wife." She even fleetingly considered that unthinkable option, she said, laughing bitterly, only to dismiss it with the broken self-deprecation that she was "too old" and would require appropriate attire that she could not afford. She said it as a joke, but it was a very sad joke. As long as a trickle of aid flowed in from her faraway relatives, she avoided that extreme fate, and she was the mother of a daughter whom she needed to protect and advance at all costs.

3. For more on the violence experienced by other Syrian women, see Wringe et al., "Altered Social Trajectories and Risks of Violence Among Young Syrian Women."

In this way, Farida's situation looked like that of many of the new Syrian residents of the Fatih district of Istanbul. Most of the Syrian migrants integrated themselves into Turkish life, seeking work and educational opportunities. Never having registered formally or having any work permits, they were wary of announcing themselves to the Turkish government for fear they would be put in camps on the border or deported back to Syria. The vast majority received no government or humanitarian agency assistance. In the camps on the Turkish-Syrian border, it was different, but with shrinking budgets even the UN and the World Food Project made only a small dent in filling their needs. Nongovernmental organizations, governments, and the UN could meet only a fraction of the complex needs of the displaced. Once their emergency needs were met, people set their sights on moving into the Turkish economy. There was a good deal of cynicism that some aid agencies were merely corrupt for-profit schemes using Syrians to advance their own aims.

By the summer of 2015, Farida found herself living in a room the size of a large prison cell. One of Tala's acquaintances from an office job she had briefly held directed her to a boardinghouse where groups of migrants and students from Asia and Africa lived, moving in and out in a never-ending stream of strangers. It was not cheap, and the rent again was subsidized by relatives abroad, who were able to provide just enough to keep Farida and her two children off the street. She paid 1,000 Turkish lira (around US$400) a month for a room that was furnished with three single beds, which took up nearly all the floor space. The tiny fourth-floor room cost as much as her sister Salma's three-room apartment. But because the boardinghouse catered to transient students and workers, the utilities were paid for, and there was just enough room between the three beds for a small box to store that day's food. There was no refrigerator; they had only a tiny bathroom for water and a shelf for a small gas burner. There was a wall-mounted television, and there was a window. When Farida had been there for some time, she planted a tiny windowsill garden, and, much later, when her sisters were vainly looking for her, they claimed they would have recognized her from the tiny plants on the window had they only known about them.

All the sisters were shocked to find themselves in 2015 forced apart by deep divisions more than by the geography of their flight. Salma, Iba, and Farida refused to speak to each other at various times in Tripoli and Istanbul, and Maryam and Hanan felt powerless to mediate between them from a distance. Growing up, this flock of beautiful, smart, happy girls had been the envy of their neighborhood. Maybe, Farida thought, that was the problem, the evil eye. Everything in her upbringing, her piety, her considerable self-taught philosophy worked against that kind of superstition—the idea that an envious gaze could hurt you—but circumstances had led her to consider that possibility because of how bad things had gotten for her. Estranged from her family, refusing to make contact with Salma, she found it easy to lose herself in the immigrant neighborhood of Kumkapi.[4] Always obsessed with the costs and risks of moving, she found herself finally stuck in Istanbul with neither the means nor the motivation to move.

Farida was a very strong woman, but Istanbul was beating her down, and she was already reduced from her time in Tripoli. Her life was about to enter a holding pattern; she was stuck as a pawn in Turkish politics. Like her sister Salma, she found that Istanbul provided more material opportunities and affordances than Tripoli, but language was a barrier that had not existed in Tripoli. There she had been fluent and eloquent, and here she was unable to express herself in anything but basic utilitarian phrases. Even if it was easier to find a job, daily life was also much more expensive. She preferred to stay in Istanbul because of the many job opportunities, but finding and getting to them meant spending valuable time, money, and energy navigating the enormous urban system. In comparison to Lebanon,

4. On Syrians' survival tactics in Istanbul, see Özaşçılar et al., "Crime Reporting Behavior Among Syrian Immigrants in Istanbul"; Putz, "Syrian Refugees Sell Organs to Survive"; and Sahin et al., "Vulnerabilities of Syrian Refugee Children in Turkey."

there was much more to hustle for, much more possibility of negotiation, more long-term staying power, but less flexibility, especially in language and rights of belonging. What Farida, like Salma, was discovering was that settling in Turkey could easily lead to sedimentation in Turkey.

One year later, in February 2016, Farida and her children were still living in their room, looking for work. Her sisters still could not locate her in the dense urban fabric of Istanbul because she would not answer her phone, and they had resigned themselves to having lost track of her. She had cultivated the tiny windowsill garden in her tiny expensive room but lacked the facilities to do any serious cooking or the money to buy any meat. Her children continued to look for work, although their maternal cousins, when briefed later about their situation, could not understand why they were unsuccessful in their quest. There was plenty of work available in Istanbul for energetic young people, the cousins emphasized. Farida began to look for childcare work in Istanbul. She answered ads posted on Facebook and had gotten a couple of nibbles.

Finally, Farida got a call back for a babysitting job offered by a fellow Syrian in Istanbul. The request was exactly what she had hoped for and similar to a job she briefly had in Tripoli, caring for two small children while their mother, a fellow Syrian schoolteacher, was working. When Farida asked about the salary, the woman on the line balked, saying it might be a little low. When the woman finally named a sum, Farida could not believe that she was being offered only 350 Turkish lira (US$130) a month. Reverting to her usual didactic persona, she paused dramatically before asking the woman if she loved her children. "Yes, of course," the woman said. If so, asked Farida, "would you really leave them with someone desperate enough to accept that salary—not even enough to cover public transportation?"

"I thought I might find someone in the same neighborhood," the woman faltered.

"Aren't you afraid they might kidnap your children and sell their organs?" she countered, shocking the woman on the other end of the line into stunned silence before hanging up in disgust. When Farida's sisters learned of this conversation much later, they thought mournfully that she must have lost her mind from stress or illness to speak in such a way.

Farida didn't have friends in Istanbul. She saw other Syrians in the market, and one had even invited her over, but because she was living in a single room, she couldn't reciprocate. She and her children were unable to hold up their end of the hospitality exchange and were sliding into self-imposed isolation. It was easier for her son, who could have met his friends, if he had any, in the street. Her daughter was always at her mother's side, mentioning unexpectedly that she had quite a few potential suitors, but under the circumstances these courtships would be conducted in a Western style, and of course that was out of the question. Such suitors always wanted more, Farida said darkly. Her family's new world was full of lurking dangers.

After effectively being imprisoned in her tiny room, Farida became an avid reader on the internet. One of the results was her strong support for the Turkish president Recep Erdoğan and the basic philosophy of the AKP.[5] Erdoğan appealed to Farida both for his adherence to a kind of activist Islamism and for his openness to the Syrian refugees. At the height of her depression, Farida used to say sarcastically, "There are three people who love me—Iba, Salma, and Bashar al-Assad," so she appreciated the hospitality she believed to be extended by Erdoğan and the Turkish state in her early years in Turkey. Over time, that gratitude would sour as she experienced the host state's growing hostility. Inflation meant that in a few years she could no longer afford to live in Istanbul and would move to Yalova and then to a small village in its hinterland, all she could afford on her limited stipend.

As always, Farida's little family were guarded and defensive. The children were loyal to their mother to a fault. Their ambitions were

5. On the AKP's discourse regarding Syrian refugees, see Polat, "Religious Solidarity, Historical Mission and Moral Superiority."

bigger than their abilities—looking only for "worthy" work, speaking perfect Turkish, using computers. They read more than anyone else in the family—Farida was particularly fond of Noam Chomsky and frequently referred to him in her speeches. But their fortress lifestyle with its abstract philosophy, codependency, fatalistic religiosity, snobbish view of labor, and obstinate refusal to engage with family kept them treading water.

20

Reterritorializing

Syria, Turkey, and Germany, 2016–2024

Maryam's Return to Syria

Throughout 2015, Maryam's household in Alexandria struggled to recover from the disaster of September 6, 2014, and the loss of Mustafa. His distraught wife, Amira, became addicted to sedatives and refused to give up hope for his return. Her family, now in disarray, treated her like an invalid, haunted and isolated by her loss. On top of everything, Maryam was increasingly bothered by digestive problems. Egyptian doctors she consulted ascribed her health concerns to stress, and she was not encouraged to pursue more expensive scans and tests. When she was finally sick enough for scans to be taken, she was diagnosed with stage-four colon cancer. Her last wish was to return to Damascus to die, and relatives contributed money for airfare for her to go back home in the spring of 2016. Reunited with her husband and other relatives after four years in exile, she passed away peacefully in June 2016. Her children in Germany and Egypt never saw her again and would continue their refugee journeys without her. Rose and Amani flourished in Germany, excelling in their language studies. Amani had two babies in quick succession, and Rose arranged for a life-saving medical procedure for her younger son, all the while working as a popular preschool teacher. Jamil, Amira, and Maryam's two grandsons in Egypt endured a lengthy vetting process by the UN and the International Organization for Migration, and based on Amira's high-profile widowed status, they were eventually approved for asylum and residency in the United States. They flew to the United States in 2017, having procured their travel papers in time to avoid the Trump administration's "Muslim ban" executive order. They learned English, learned to drive, bought cars, and worked in the health-care and hospitality sectors before getting their US citizenship four years later. As soon as they did, they traveled regularly to Germany to be with their sisters, aunts, and cousins there.

Hanan and Farida Settle in Turkey Indefinitely

Hanan and Farida monitored Maryam's decline and demise from Turkey via WhatsApp, shared photographs, and old-fashioned prayer. Hanan's daughter Warda lived in central Germany, not too far from her cousins Rose and Amani in the country's northernmost city. Warda also quickly had two babies, whom Hanan reported with delighted bemusement to be fully endowed with hearing, raising questions about how they would learn spoken Arabic and not just Arabic sign language from their two deaf parents. Her eldest daughter, Sara, followed her husband to asylum in Britain, got a divorce and a master's degree in translation and interpretation from a British university, and opened a small Arabic/Islamic school for refugees. Son Ramzi, for whom Hanan had scoured the refugees of Turkey for a bride, eventually married a Ukrainian woman in the Gulf without any assistance from his family, also to his mother's bemusement. He and his wife, established in the United Arab Emirates, could visit Turkey regularly. And as if to fill the emptiness left by Warda, Hanan's son Sayf, who had been a resistance fighter in Syria, paid onerous bribes to have himself, his wife, and baby smuggled across the Turkish border. He had been grievously wounded in a battle—ironically against rival rebel forces. Although he had gained a certain notoriety, his escape from Syria was bought by greasing the palms of senior officers in the Syrian army proper. By 2016, corruption was even more central to the Syrian wartime economy than ever. According to Salma's husband, Mazen, who traveled back and forth between Syria and Turkey in 2015, "everything was for sale." Cash was king, and the fierce principles of resistance and loyalism that had ripped the country apart in 2011 and 2012 were compromised by deep corruption. In any case, Sayf, his fiery young wife, and soon their three baby daughters enlivened Hanan and her husband's routine in Yalova.

Farida had the opportunity to make the Aegean crossing to Greece in 2016 but found herself locked into Turkey when that window closed in March as Turkey cracked down on the smuggling route in its bid to negotiate with the EU. The relations who had helped to finance Salma's trip in 2015 and Iba's trip in early 2016 provided Farida with about 4,000 euros as well, the amount estimated for her and her two children to engage the smugglers. Understandably, Farida, in poor health and worse spirits, was reluctant to make the strenuous journey that her younger sisters had made. As Iba squeaked through into Europe just as the Turkish-EU negotiations were closing the borders of Macedonia and Greece to refugees, Farida chose to wait until the calmer waters of April or May. By then, however, it was too late. Illegal crossings and the smuggling business declined drastically. Farida used the money instead to travel to Yalova and rent a house near Hanan. But even then she isolated herself and her children from her sister and her sister's family. By the time of the COVID-19 pandemic, they rarely talked or visited. Farida and her two children eventually moved to a small town an hour from the regional center of Yalova. Rents were cheaper, but the lack of work and contact with outsiders were suffocating. Farida's sisters eventually stopped trying to reach her, and she chose to keep her phone and internet off both to cut costs and to avoid contact.

Salma's Family Reunited and Apart

After the grueling journey from Greece to Germany, with little Kamal sick for much of the way, Salma, Mazen, and Kamal crossed into southern Germany in late 2016. The family settled into a routine of camplike dormitories that challenged their family norms. Their first stop was a repurposed high-school gymnasium, where each family was assigned to an area defined by a bunkbed and its immediate perimeter. The families lived and slept in immediate proximity to complete strangers and erected cardboard walls with scavenged resources to mark off their areas.

After several weeks, they were moved to a dormitory-style *Asylantenhaus* in an idyllic Bavarian Alpine village. The building housed about twenty families, with mothers and children assigned family rooms on the ground floor, and men doubling up in the rooms on the second floor. Mazen was assigned an Iraqi roommate, a single man, who felt he had won the jackpot because Mazen would effectively live downstairs with his wife and son, leaving his bunkmate in peace. Indeed, Mazen moved into Salma and Kamal's assigned room, a tiny oblong with two single beds pushed together under the window at the far end to form a kind of sleeping platform. The room was furnished with a table and some chairs from a shed full of recycled secondhand furniture. There was a lot of storage space in the form of shelves and built-in closets along the long wall, which quickly filled up with donated toys. Kamal had become the recipient of so many toys that the room resembled a shop. Kitchen, bathroom, and laundry facilities were shared with the other residents of the *Asylantenhaus*.

Tensions were quick to erupt in the dormitory, where Salma and her family were the only Syrians. They shared facilities with Iraqi Kurds, Afghans, and refugees from various parts of Africa. Salma and her family, new arrivals with a linguistic disadvantage, felt overwhelmed less at the surrounding German infrastructure than at being lumped together with migrants from various countries. The other migrants—earlier arrivals from previous wars and other hardships—resented the attention and perceived privilege of the Syrians in the de facto racist hierarchy of immigrants. It didn't help that Salma and her Kamal were conspicuously fair and blond, resembling Germans more than their fellow asylum seekers.

Frictions inevitably arose over the shared facilities. Washing-machine cycles in the shared laundry room were interrupted, wet wash was dumped from dryers—acts committed not by indifferent college students but by house-proud homemakers who had proved their resilience by surviving exponentially more difficult trials than the sharing of a laundry room. Tempers flared. Salma began to feel that Kamal was not safe from the malicious glances of the non-Arabic-speaking refugee women and insisted that she or Mazen always be with him when he left the tiny room, especially to use the bathroom at night. In the shared kitchen, where the women spent a lot of time cooking, especially during Ramadan, Salma locked horns with a Nigerian woman. This longtime resident of the home spoke good German and had an entourage of friends and acquaintances, including the German *Hausmeister*, the ostensible authority in the residence. Salma felt the woman was trying to intimidate her and especially little Kamal. In one of their altercations, Mazen intervened on behalf of his wife, and the woman notified the *Hausmeister* that an unauthorized male was harassing her on the women's and family floor. More than once, the local police were called by one side or the other.

The building management, volunteers, and residents eventually came up with a clumsy, racist, and inequitable solution to the chronic distrust among the residents. One washing machine was designated for "Syrians," one for "Afghans," and one for "Africans." Labels were posted over the machines designating them as such. Similarly, when local German volunteers built a garden for the house (at Salma's suggestion), they were careful to replicate the segregated structure of a section for "the Syrians," a section for "the Afghans," and a section for "the Africans." Complaints by the Nigerian and Ghanaian residents about this unfair, illogical, and disproportionate categorization fell on deaf ears, and it crystallized the perception of Syrians as a privileged class of refugees. This alarming attempt at segregated equity, which foreshadowed the eventual rise of racist and anti-immigrant far-right parties in Germany, seemed at the time like the best that the assorted traumatized newcomers and Bavarian elderly volunteers could come up with. New patterns and dividing lines that combined old and new prejudices were emerging.

Salma's older sons, 'Adel and Yusuf, separately made their own overland journeys from Greece to Germany and sought asylum. Considered adults, they went through their own asylum processes as single young men in different localities. The immigration and asylum system of their new refuge prevented the immediate reunification of the family because each son needed to stay and begin integration and language study in the locality where his application was filed. As they gained fluency in German and familiarity with the modes of public transport, Salma's sons rejoined the family periodically for weekend excursions but learned to live in Germany as single young men. When their asylum was granted, and they could move around the country more freely, they moved closer to their parents but continued to live alone and, at long last, pursue their post-secondary education.

Iba and Hisham, "Model Refugees"

Iba's husband, Hisham, living a few hours away from Salma's family, was distressed when he heard about the tensions in their temporary home. On his own for nine months in communal refugee housing in Germany while waiting for Iba and the children, he had made a point of making friends with all the people he found around him. He had developed a reputation as a mediator, a solver of problems, just like Iba had described him in Damascus. He cultivated a large circle of friends, and because in his forties he was among the oldest of the travelers in his group, the younger men called him "Hajji," a title of respect. He took pains to cultivate good relations with the non-Syrians—Iraqi Arabs, Kurds, Afghans, Sudanis, Somalis, and Nigerians—he met along the way. Sharing, offering, and making food, a particular interest of his since his youth, made it easier to form connections and develop trust and friendships. When he went to collect Iba and the children from the airport upon their arrival from Greece, he had a driver and an entourage of his friends there to receive the family he had waited so long for.

In the first year after Iba arrived, she outpaced her husband in language studies and was eagerly competing with a Syrian engineer and a visual artist to be the top student in her language class. She was determined to finish the intermediate-level national German curriculum and then proceed into her *Ausbildung* (vocational training) to complete certification as a lab technician. In the meantime, she had two part-time jobs. She worked in the kitchen of a local village restaurant, helping with food prep in the kitchen. She made it clear from the start that she could not work with pork or alcohol, and her German boss, after trying to reassure her that she could simply wash her hands afterward, was happy to respect her wishes when she laughingly explained why the issue was one of religious principle, not just a question of hand hygiene. She was also hired as a basketball coach at her daughters' middle school, running the girls through drills. The school even asked her to drill the boys, and she made it clear that her refusal had more to do with her lack of time and linguistic skills rather than with Islamic gender norms or modesty. Hisham was indispensable in his work at a small orthopedic shoe factory that made world-class, quality, custom-fit footwear for clients all over the country and the world.

Iba, Hisham, and their children were well known in their southern German village, with a population of not more than a couple of thousand people. Most Syrians avoided such German country towns at all costs, finding them far too quiet and isolated from the larger immigrant community and most potential jobs. But Iba and Hisham found it the perfect place to learn the language and culture. After first purchasing bicycles for each member of the family, they soon bought a car. They moved from cramped shared housing to a rented single-family house, which they renovated with the help of their landlord. The walls were adorned in the early days with Arabic-German vocabulary lists.

Iba and Hisham were practically local celebrities and had "a hundred German language partners and people to help them when their papers arrived in the mail," Iba remembered proudly. Iba drew modest crowds with illustrated lectures about Syria in the local civic center. One afternoon as they parked their new car after picking up a visitor, they were stopped in the street by one of their German neighbors, who called them over to show them pictures of his newest grandchild. Other cars stopped on the street, and Iba and her husband cheerfully congratulated the man and conveyed his news to the other villagers who were caught in the minor traffic jam. "And they say that Germans aren't friendly!" Hisham commented later. "You just have to get to know them." They participated good naturedly in the local Christmas celebrations, in which a schoolteacher dressed as St. Nicholas discussed their wishes and goals in front of a giggling audience of local folk. The locals loved this family—their family—of Syrian refugees. To many of the inhabitants, they appeared to be a kind of "model refugee" family, a problematic category to be sure, but one that eased their integration experience. As Syrians who eschewed welfare and contributed to their community through work and civic life, they were not merely tolerated but respected.

As Iba charged ahead, setting and meeting goals that would eventually secure her a permanent position as a research laboratory supervisor at a German university, Hisham mastered his new vocation of orthopedic shoemaking, planned for his own enterprise in the future, and was intensely interested in paying forward his good fortune. His new German neighbors could scarcely believe that he took regular trips to the local senior-care home to sit with elderly Germans, listen to their stories, speak to them in his broken German, and even bring them Syrian food. He had a passion for feeding people, and his new neighbors were charmed by his habit of cooking great feasts of Syrian foods and demonstrating Middle Eastern hospitality.

Passing the daunting German driver's license course with its twelve hundred questions was another milestone for Hisham, who was among the first to take the test in Arabic. Owning his own car again was also a huge step, as he and his wife and children could now drive easily all around the country. It meant freedom and power, a sign of how he had succeeded. He thanked God every day. As the only Syrian in the area with a car, he was often asked to transport other refugees in the region to get medical care and have job interviews. He rarely turned down a request despite his full-time job and continuing language classes. This was part of his personal approach to Germany: giving back. It had not failed him yet. Iba and Hisham's children excelled at German and were soon fluent. Their older daughter received medical treatment for the facial paralysis that had struck her in Lebanon when the family was at its lowest point. She also manifested a new talent that impressed the local people; her voice, she discovered, was a beautiful vehicle for English- and German-language pop music, and she was not afraid to use it. At local village gatherings, a Syrian girl in hijab who belted out American pop covers unselfconsciously shattered stereotypes that the locals had about girls and women in the *Kopftuch*, or headscarf. She would enter university and pursue information and media studies, while her younger sister excelled at high school, and her brother, Bilal, like his cousins, grew to adulthood as an independent young man, training in a gym, working in security, studying mechanical electronics, and roaming the German landscape in his own newly purchased sports car.

The Fall of the Assad Regime

By 2024, Um 'Abdallah's daughters, grandchildren, and great-grandchildren had sojourned in more than six countries on four continents since their initial flight from Damascus in 2012. They spoke Turkish, English, and German as well as Arabic—the youngest generation doing so with perfect fluency. Drivers' licenses and automobiles were integral to their lifestyles. They worked in retail, hospitality, health care, skilled crafts, and technical professions. University degrees and vocational certificates were now the norm and the expectation for the young adults in the family. With more and more members of the extended family obtaining European and US citizenship and Turkish residency, international air and car travel had become part of their lives. For all but Farida and her children, the cold, hunger, and precarity the sisters and their families had suffered receded to the realm of memory, replaced by the cadence of jobs and school that seemed normal to the youngsters and exhausting to their parents. Although the grandchildren and great-grandchildren spoke Arabic well enough, many of them had no real recollection of their life in Syria and were growing up bicultural; some of the young men openly challenged their Islamic patrimony with European secularism, which concerned their sisters and parents. Their elders complained about the coldness of the weather, the stiffness of their new linguistic and cultural milieus, and the impenetrability of the societies that regarded them with suspicion. They longed for the easy and generous sociability of Syria and the immersion in familiar language, custom, and culture. But even they had resigned themselves to a lifetime of exile. As Hanan put it, "We lived a long, long period that we thought would last until the ends of our lives and those of our children. From the depth of the tyranny and oppression, we really could not imagine it would ever end."

Iba walked into her research lab office early on December 4, 2024, a cold German winter day, to see her Romanian coworker scrolling through her laptop. This woman, who had initially regarded her new Syrian colleague with suspicion but had been won over by Iba's persistent civility, asked her what was going on in Syria because headlines of a rebel advance into Aleppo were dominating the news. Since the beginning of the rebel advance in late November, Iba had been determined to manage her expectations. She reported feeling almost schizophrenic, marshalling her strong self-control to counter her growing excitement about the possibility of liberation. They had dared to hope before but had been bitterly disappointed. She answered her colleague's questions with studied nonchalance, explaining the geography of Syria and the history of the war before making up an excuse to leave the room. Surprised at her own ability to repress her emotions, she wondered briefly if she had lost her love of Syria. No, she decided, she was as devoted as ever and was still an ambassador for her country; she simply could not afford to get her hopes up and did not want her officemates to watch her rollercoaster of feelings.

At home, however, she couldn't tear herself away from her phone. Every member of the family was glued to their phone, and every development was shared by WhatsApp group messages. As it happened, Hanan's son Ramzi and his wife came to Germany for a visit on December 6, and Iba had taken two days' vacation to receive them. The rebels had advanced to Hama. Iba and Hisham were stunned that the advance felt more like a tourist itinerary through Syria than the series of bloody battles they expected. The next day, after taking Ramzi and his wife to visit a local *Christkindlmarkt* (traditional Christmas market), they drove to Salma's house and watched events unfold on television, laptops, and phones. (Iba and Salma had reconciled through periodic visits while living a few hours apart in southern Germany over the previous years.) As Homs fell to the rebels, relatives in other parts of Europe and the United States started sending congratulatory messages full of happy emojis to the group chat. Iba commanded everyone to stop the dangerous and premature celebratory messages and had them erased. Great joy competed with terrible dread about the battle that everyone expected to unfold in Damascus the next day.

On the night of December 7, 2024, Salma fell asleep at 2:00 a.m. German time with her cell phone clutched tightly in her hand. She and her family had spent the past ten days following every step in the progress of the HTS rebel militia advancing through the country. As she recounted in a WhatsApp voice recording, "We all were excited from the start, but we hardly dared to hope. At each stage of the rebel advance, we were watching, and the hope would grow and fade. We started assessing the distances between Aleppo and Hama and Homs and Damascus by comparing them to distances between the cities we travel to by car in Germany. At that point, when the rebels were going from Homs to Damascus, we hardly dared to breathe because we had had our hopes dashed before during the war."

Trying to express the feeling of waxing and waning hope, alternating excitement and fear, she laughingly grasped at the metaphor of a laboring mother's contractions: "It was like giving birth. From the beginning [in late November], it felt like cycles of increasingly intense contractions, rising and falling. Each city they took, each stage of the campaign, was like a new contraction, with rising hope and then fear and then fading away as we waited for the next one. The stages were like that until finally it was liberated, until finally they reached Damascus, and freedom was born." The last nights of the campaign swept together all the assemblages of home the sisters had lived. One of the boys posted about his feelings of joy and anticipation as the rebel offensive moved from Hama to Homs, and Salma reflexively liked the posting with a thumbs up. Neither of them would have dared to openly express themselves this way even a week earlier. Relatives in Damascus who saw the post called her and obliquely let her know that it was still too early to reveal one's position on the rebel offensive. There might still be a regime pushback, particularly in Damascus. If the regime prevailed, such posts would be as dangerous as they were before—for everyone concerned, especially those in Syria. Salma wrote,

> Of course, I immediately went back and erased my like and had my son erase the whole post. I was so worried for our family still in Damascus, and they were worried too as the rebels approached the city, not knowing whom to trust, what to believe. There's a group chat for all the family outside and inside the country, and we were all on it all the time. I wanted to ask how they were in Damascus, and they were all watching and waiting in their homes, but I didn't dare ask anything directly in case there were clashes or the phone lines or WhatsApp were being watched by the government. I didn't dare ask—until we saw that they were finally able to talk, and then they started telling us what was going on, and we asked and talked freely for the first time ever.

Salma, her husband, and two of her sons sat all night long watching the satellite news channels, continuously texting with the other son and with her nieces about every new report from the Damascus front. The combination of her long workdays studying computer drafting and the emotional roller coaster of the situation in Syria got the best of her early in the morning of December 8. She remembered, "I got so sleepy I fell asleep in the middle of texting. At two I fell asleep. Rose and 'Adel were texting me minute by minute. I woke to a text from Rose trying to wake me up. She said, "Wake up, wake up, it happened! Turn on the news!" The feelings were incredible. I jumped up and ran into the next room, and I found Yusuf watching the news and shouting. We started hugging and kissing each other, and I felt in love with the whole world."

Iba finally let herself relax and rejoice the next day when she heard that Bashar had fled Damascus.

> Against all our fears, it was announced that the cowardly traitor Bashar had left by plane for an unknown destination, and the rebels had entered Damascus without any bloodshed. At that point, the fear and caution were giving way—and may God curse the Assad family forever for never giving us even a moment of joy unadulterated by fear up to that point—and I felt a surge of irrepressible joy. I wanted to call or write to the group chat or to Damascus but still did not dare. I started sending out streams of emojis of beating hearts, praying hands, and smiles. Fifty minutes later, a relative in Damascus sent a message that the family there were safe and the regime had fallen, and I immediately performed a prayer of thanksgiving.

As Hanan put it, watching from Turkey, "Thank God, thank God. There are no words to describe the joy we are feeling. It is indescribable. Praise God, we woke up to texts from everyone to a reality we couldn't believe, that couldn't be described. As everyone says, we were afraid we'd wake to find it was only a dream, and Bashar did not fall."

But the texts, calls, WhatsApp groups, Instagram and Facebook posts continued circulating and confirmed that the dream was indeed a reality. The digital communications fired up and joined together the scattered family members in northern and southern Germany, Turkey, the United States, and finally Syria as people shared memes, news stories, flags, and words, filling and erasing the space between them with vibrating signals of information and joy.

21

Phase Changes

Damascus, the city of jasmine, was one of many premodern centers producing jasmine-based essential oils and airborne perfumes.[1] But the delicate petals of the *Jasminum grandiflorum* are not tough enough for the steam distillation used on other blossoms first documented by the medieval philosopher and scientist Ibn Sina.[2] Traditional methods for jasmine perfumerie involve the principle that oil dissolves oily volatile scent compounds. Soaking generation after generation of fresh fragrant petals of jasmine in oil transfers the odor to the new fatty, rich form.[3] The French called this process *enfleurage*, the imprinting of the bloom's essence on a lipid substrate.[4] Permeating the oil in intensity and then gradually diffused into the ether, the jasmine-impregnated volatile molecules of airborne scent escape both solid and liquid bonds and spread outward in a concentration not produced in nature. The transformed and intensified essence of the flowers is translated into new media—oil and air. In those new

1. Mitra, "Enzymatic Production and Emission of Floral Scent Volatiles in *Jasminum sambac.*"

2. Aftel, *Fragrant*; see also al-Kindi, *Kitab kimiya' al-'itr wat-tas'idat.*

3. The affective atmospherics of gases and vapors have also begun to generate social science literature, even as they trigger intense nostalgia. See Howes, "Multisensory Anthropology."

4. The art, science, and even therapy of perfume were known to the ancients and medieval scientists of the cosmopolitan Islamic world, and even as the perfume industry migrated to its modern industrial center in France, the jasmine that came from the Mediterranean was considered the base of all bouquets. See Barbe, *The French Perfumer*; and Cristiani, *Perfumery and Kindred Arts.*

forms, like the Proustian sense of taste, the concentrated distillations provoke a synesthesia that often defies words and seems almost to instantaneously transport one through space and time to the point of origin.[5] But it exists in a different realm, in a different medium. The jasmine's new form is intensive, extractive, and transportable—free of its original plant form and bonds.[6]

The phase change from fresh flowers to lipid base and volatile essence—the physically rough and even traumatic harvesting, extraction, translation, concentration, and essentializing process—resonates with the final leg of Salma and Iba's journeys, which pushed them out into new dimensions, new lines of flight. The grid of their home city and the temporary households that they had desperately assembled after leaving that city were replaced by a pressure-filled and violent trafficking in which they were objectified, commodified, and pushed beyond their past experiences. When they reached Europe, joining the nieces who had already married there in the brave new world of European coldness, language learning, and asylum and immigration bureaucracy, the family network reconnected digitally rather than physically, sharing electronic links that flickered ephemerally but reliably. The family assemblage spread across continents and time zones, switching in and out and on and off with point-to-point signals, carrying love, longing, and information. It was nothing

5. For more Proustian effects, including specifically the smell of jasmine, see Drobnick, "Eating Nothing," 342; Aftel, *Fragrant*; and Ameri, *The Scent of Jasmine*.

6. The renowned thirteenth-century philosopher Ya'qub ibn Ishak al-Kindi described the medieval Islamic process and equipment for extracting the scent from flowers into a sesame-oil base, which produces essential oil of jasmine. Using variations on the cucurbit, the *karka*, and alembic *al-anbiq*, the blossoms were exposed to sesame-seed oil, which then absorbed their fragrance over a period of weeks or months, and the old flowers were replaced with fresh ones several times a week. The oil would be heated into vapor and then separated into the essence. See al-Kindi, *Kitab kimiya' al-'itr wat-tas'idat*. Also see al-Qasimi et al., *Qamus al-Sina'at al-shamiyah*; Inoue, "Al-Kindi's Attack on Alchemy"; and Ryding, "Alchemy in Islam."

like the urban assemblage of houses, visits, and streets in Damascus they had fled nor like the uncomfortable, overcrowded, stressed, and cramped households they had arranged in Tripoli. But the family bonds now maintained primarily through cell phones and WhatsApp groups still carried the essence of their shared code and intensified it in a world characterized by new forms of physical danger and by loneliness, isolation, and individuation.

The diasporic scattering across new continental vistas that took place in 2016 after some of the sisters fled the shelters in near refuge is also an assemblage of home, one in which digital technology, cell phones, and social media are key integuments. For more than a decade up through and until the sisters' diaspora, their *mobiles* were an ever more important accessory and part of their lives, but the phones complemented rather than replaced proximal relations of connectivity within the family. In digitalized diaspora, new forms of connection that had previously complemented or enhanced physical proximity took on ever more important roles as the very means of connection that facilitated the geographic separations that had become a feature rather than a bug as sibling rivalry intensified. Technology in near exile had in addition become a mediator between the old homes and the new refuge homes, buffering the trauma of war while serving as a conduit of news and affect. In the farthest flight, technology developed a new vitality as the only way to communicate with those left behind, the spidery lifeline to former habitats, the navigator, the archive of the journey. The *mobile* had previously been an optional tool; it was now increasingly necessary because it was where kinship resided.

Linked by technology and Wi-Fi, meeting ever more frequently in the intense centers of Facebook and WhatsApp group texts, meeting the hardships of being smuggled through navigational software and video documentation, the flighted assemblages that reconfigured kinship across landscapes of smooth new spaces are tempting to view teleologically, as some sort of "happily ever after," the fulfillment of Western liberal feminist subjecthood's narrative arc. They are not that but rather something richer, more ambiguous, and not for outsiders to analyze. Jasbir Puar, referring to Donna Haraway, invokes the technobody of the cyborg as the expression of reterritorialization and recoding after extreme deterritorialization.[7] Whether in the form of the technobody or the form of the technodiaspora, the end of this retracing of parts of the sisters' journeys is not the end of anything important. Their lives proceed, full of potential; the sisters continue to adapt, engage—innovating, processing, and integrating new cultural codes and languages alongside old ones.

The most dramatic line of flight, the successful arrival in European asylum, is only the beginning of an open-ended set of new narratives. Europe did not happen for all the sisters, only those most endowed with energy, desperation, resilience, adaptability, cultural capital, and luck. Many of the protagonists could not muster the launch energy; some even died in the process. For the few that reached European shores and the chance for asylum, the energy previously devoted to the microfashioning of kin and work into precarious assemblages in near exile was violently "cashed in" to provide passage fare. Families that made the transition to Europe did not fuse and grow but painfully fissioned and split into smaller groups and individual missions. The perilous and desperate continental crossings were dramatic in comparison to the quietly exhausting survival strategies and tactics of the near refuge.

The conventional codes of origin—language, kin, religion, reciprocity, and political modesty—were carried forward from Damascus to near refuge, where they did not quite fit in the new environment. The sisters' language, although intelligible, was accented and marked them as resented strangers. Family was more intensely than before mobilized for survival and sustenance in a new urban environment. The sisters' selves were less supported by the environment in passive acceptance and were more activated to work very hard to arrange all the affordances to sustain livelihoods. The cultural codes employed

7. Haraway, *Simians, Cyborgs and Women*; Puar, "'I Would Rather Be a Cyborg.'"

began to change away from the easy assumptions of the culture of origin as the sisters grasped for purchase in new, very differently sedimented soils.

For the final phase of flight, huge energy and collected resources were required. Fusion of families brought friction, not strength, so the hard-working mothers began the painful, fraught, and risky process of breaking down their families into smaller traveling groups. They also began to sell off assets and borrow large sums of money to mortgage and invest in passage. The small correspondences of reciprocity, the daily attempts to micromanage survival, gave way to major and fateful transactions. Quiet, inherited religious habit gave way to desperate trust in untrustworthy strangers and loudly vocal pleas to the deity invoked on flimsy rafts on the open sea at night.

Ultimately, the way feminist philosophy should frame the lives of women like the Araj sisters, who try to live enveloped in dignified modesty (along with a demonstrated resilience and power) is not only or even primarily by expressing, for them or through them, the imbalances of the embedded patriarchy within which they live. The sisters live, know, and analyze their patriarchy and the critical situations emergent from it. They do not, on the whole, benefit by presenting it to the world, though, because sustainable private family, in any of its forms, is at the heart of their lives and goals. One of their primary values is modest privacy, *tassatur*, so they are not served by being represented with the lingering odor of orientalism and privileged white feminism of outside scholarship. The articulation of the insults, injuries, and grudges they bear at the hands of their menfolk has been backgrounded here because their transformative becoming is not based there. Their reticence to collaborate with the feminist project of amplifying their voices, conjuring their agency, or airing their patriarchal dirty laundry has opened up space for other transformations to be observed and learned from. Their power and modesty preclude the traps of saviorism or exhibitionism. The actual contribution made by feminism here may come in the form of posthumanist materialism, an openness to how the self and the family are assembled, deterritorialized, and reassembled in new environments with changing codes. The nonhuman elements of the assemblages do not share or diminish the hard-won agency and intentionality of humans. Rather, the agency of the Araj sisters and others like them builds and rebuilds ways of living that leave no part of what they consider God's creation off-limits in the crafting of new moral selves and better worlds.

Acknowledgments

Glossary

Bibliography

Index

Acknowledgments

The research for this book was conducted between 2015 and 2017 in Turkey and Germany, supported by a University of Arizona College of Social and Behavioral Science Research Fellowship and a Center for Middle Eastern Studies Research Travel Fellowship. Interviews with the Araj sisters, their husbands, and children took place in person in July 2015, July and August 2016, and August 2017 in Turkey and Germany, with follow-up interviews done through WhatsApp after that. The sisters and their families also shared some family photographs and videos and oriented me to videos publicly available on YouTube.

I have kept myself out of the text to provide more clarity about the sisters' various trajectories, although I occasionally lent a hand with the transportation of their possessions (for example, when Salma and Yusuf moved from Istanbul to Yalova), assisted with financial transfers (Iba's loan from a relative in February 2016), and provided modest aid (purchasing a mini refrigerator for Farida's room). Also, I assisted Iba and Yusuf in finding temporary accommodations in Athens, using Airbnb and a credit card because Syrian refugees had difficulty accessing these online services.

I thank my colleagues Ricardo Laremont, Fatma Müge Göçek, Emmanuela Del Re, and Anton Escher for helping me frame the study early in the process. Julie Ellison Speight, Danielle Van Dobben Schoon, Akram Khater, and Gary Nabhan helped me sharpen aspects of the work through workshops and presentations. I thank my mentors Julia Clancy Smith and Linda Darling for their patience and wisdom. I thank my doctoral students, who worked alongside me on their own projects, for their inspiration and engagement—Tatiana Rabinovich, Mija Sanders, Abbass Braham, Feras Klenk, Miriam Wolfley, Alainna Liloia, Rose Hattab, Saffo Papantonopoulou, and Brittany Power especially. My late father, Michael C. Hudson, provided a natal family assemblage during COVID and an anchor in the study of the politics of the Arab world and region. My own sister, Aida Hudson, was an unwitting interlocutor throughout. Genie Joseph guided me through the practicalities of the project's early drafts. Carine Bourget and Ewa Elsbiei prompted me with academic and architectural examples, respectively. Aditya Adiredja and Celeste González de Bustamante provided writing companionship and discipline during the pandemic. Annika Hudson-Laursen was invaluable as a bibliographer and formatter. Mona Hymel, Ted Downing, Wolfgang Fink, and Katie Zeiders were wonderful comrades who shouldered extra burdens in faculty representation and governance at the University of Arizona, which allowed this project to proceed. Joseph Stoll created quick, clear maps for the project, and Laura Fish provided critical guidance and encouragement as an editor. The Syracuse University series editors, copy editor Annie Barva, and my anonymous reviewers improved the manuscript with their constructive comments. I am grateful to all, but I alone am responsible for any factual or interpretive errors.

From start to finish, my children, Zayna and Zayd, provided a filmmaker's and an artist's eyes as well as accompanying me in early fieldwork, an inquisitive engagement with the project's narrative and emotional complexity. My husband, Riad, was my incredibly patient emotional support and my most important affordance in this undertaking.

To the Araj sisters and their families, I am eternally thankful for their honesty, deep friendship, intelligence, humor, and vulnerability and for all that they taught me. I hope that the new political circumstances will allow them to return freely and safely to their Damascus homes to contribute to the new Syria all that they have become and to write their own stories as only they can.

Glossary

A note on Arabic transliteration: many of the words or expressions transliterated in the text are from the Syrian dialect and are rendered phonetically rather than formally.

abaya, عباية: a long robe.

"Allahu akbar," الله اكبر: "God is great," expression of enthusiasm for Muslims.

"Allah yirhamu," الله يرحمه: "May God have mercy on his soul," traditional expression of condolence.

***'amara*, عمارة:** building.

***'ammo*, عم / عمه:** paternal uncle, "my uncle," form of address between men and children.

Ba'ath Party, Ba'athist, بعث / بعثي / حزب البعث: A Pan-Arabist political party first founded in 1943 in Syria, advocating for a single Arab socialist nation; the ruling party in Syria from 1963 to 2024 and in Iraq from 1968 to 2003.

"Al banat mithl al-fijl," البنات مثل الفجل: "Girls are like radishes," folk expression meaning that there are plenty of available marriageable young women.

"Bashar byitla' li barra," بشار بيطلع لبرا: literally "Bashar, leave the country," a popular chant.

***bayt*, بيت:** house.

***bilim*, بلم:** inflatable raft used in Aegean crossings.

Da'esh/ISIS (Islamic State of Iraq and Syria), داعش: an Islamist extremist organization that emerged from al-Qaeda in 2014 and took advantage of the instability in Iraq and Syria, bolstering its population there and taking over territory.

***daftar al-'a'ileh*, دفتر العائلة:** traditional family ID, "family notebook."

dhawq, **ذوق:** taste or habit, habitus.

fasooliya, **فاصولية:** green beans or green bean stew.

Free Syrian Army (FSA), الجيش السوري الحر: a rebel group formed by defectors from the Syrian military in 2011.

ghada, **غداء:** main cooked meal served in the afternoon.

"Al-ghazzaleh al-shatra tighzil 'ala danab al-kalb," الغزالة الشاطرة تغزل على دنب الكلب: "A clever spinner can spin on a dog's tail," traditional expression meaning that talent will manifest in spite of difficult circumstances.

Ghuta, الغوطة: the agricultural belt around Damascus.

hajji, حجي: pilgrim, elder.

hama, hamayeh, **حماه / حماية:** father-in-law and mother-in-law, but literally "protector."

"Hamatak bit'hubak," حماتك بتحبك: literally "Your mother-in-law loves you," traditional expression used when someone walks into a meal in progress just in time to eat.

"Hat idak walhaqni," هات يدك وألحقني: literally "Take my hand and follow me," traditional expression used to refer to randomness, lack of a plan, blind trust.

hawiyya, **هوية:** identity card.

Hay'at Tahrir al-Sham (HTS), هيئة تحرير الشام: Entity for the Liberation of Syria, the rebel organization that was formed in 2017 and liberated Damascus in 2024.

hijab, حجاب: Islamic modest dress for women, especially the headscarf.

ibni, binti, **ابني / بنتي:** my son, my daughter.

'Id, عيد: one of the two Islamic holy days after the lunar months of Ramadan and Dhu al-Hijja.

iftar, إفطار: the breaking of the fast during Ramadan.

Ikhwan, اخوان مسلمون: the Muslim Brotherhood, outlawed under the Assad regime.

infitah, **انفتاح:** economic liberalization in the early days of Bashar al-Assad's regime.

"Inna lilahi wa inna ilayhi raji'un," إنا لله وإنا إليه راجعون: Islamic expression of condolence, literally "We are from God and to God we return."

Jabhat al-Nusra, جبهة النصرة: the al-Nusra/Victory Front, a Syrian jihadist group fighting against Bashar al-Assad's regime that split from al-Qaeda and later produced the HTS offshoot, which toppled the regime.

kafir, كافر: unbeliever.

karama, كرامة: dignity.

kashar 'an anyabih, كشر عن انيابه: snarled, revealing canine teeth like a predator.

katb ktab, كتب الكاتب: "writing of the book," the act of formalizing a legal marriage.

khala, خالة / خالتي: maternal aunt or general mode of address between a woman and a child.

khattabat, خطابات: women engaged in traditional matchmaking or arrangement of marriages.

kibbeh, كبة: traditional Levantine fancy food, usually consisting of a spiced meat enclosed in a meat-and-wheat shell.

laji', pl. *laji'un*, لاجىء / لاجئون: refugee, refugees; asylum seekers.

lam shaml, لم شمل: family reunification in asylum.

madhalliyyat, مضليات: the "parachute girls" deployed by the regime in the 1980s to strip women of hijab head coverings.

"Ma fi bi idho san'a," ما في بيده صنعة: literally "He doesn't have a trade or skills."

mahr, مهر: bridal gift paid by a groom to the bride.

maktab ta'min, مكتب تأمين: literally "insurance agency," a third-party escrow holder for smuggling payments.

manteau, مانطو: trench coat worn as part of hijab in Syria.

masqat ra'si, مسقط رأسي: literally "the place where my head fell to earth," place of birth, hometown.

mikro, pl. *mikroyat*, مكرو: shared taxi.

mithl 'ayn al-dik, مثل عين الديك: literally "like a rooster's eye," the perfect color of brewed tea.

mufawadiyya, مُفَوَّضية: UN-issued yellow card granting permission to reside in a country.

muhajjabat, محجبات: Muslim women who observe modest hijab discipline in public.

mujaddara, مجدرة: traditional meal of lentils, rice or wheat, and fried onions.

mujahid, مجاهد: a fighter of jihad, جهاد, or holy war, member of the Islamist resistance.

mukhabarat, مخابرات: feared secret police or intelligence operatives of the regime.

mukhtar, مختار: local official.

mulhak, **ملحق:** attic apartment.
narghile, ارغيلة / نارجيلة: water pipe for smoking tobacco.
nasiha, **نصيحة:** advice.
nazih, **pl.** ***nazihun***, **نازحون / نازح:** internally displaced person, people.
niqab, نقاب: a style of modest dress that covers most or all of a woman's face.
Qubaysiyyat, قبيسيات: women's Islamic movement tolerated in Assad's Syria.
"As-salamu 'aleikum," السلام عليكم: traditional Islamic greeting literally meaning "Peace be upon you."
"Sallu 'anabi," صلوا عالنبي: literally "Pray for the Prophet," traditional expression used to urge patience or to stall for time.
shabbiha, **شبيحة:** literally "ghosts," paramilitary regime thugs.
sha'bet al-tajnid, **شعبة التجنيد:** military draft board, formally the Office of Military Records and Conscription.
shahada, **شهادة:** an Islamic oath and creed, one of the Five Pillars.
shahid, **pl.** ***shuhada***, **شهداء / شهيد:** martyr, used for all persons killed in a war perceived to be righteous or defensive.
Sham, الشام: Damascus or Syria.
sheesha, **شيشة:** waterpipe for smoking tobacco.
"Suriya hurra," سوريا حرة: "Free Syria."
Syrian lira, ليرة سورية: the Syrian currency valued at 50 to the US dollar prior to the Syrian Civil War and then a massively inflated 25,000 to the dollar by 2024.
tadbir, **تدبير:** adapting, arranging, making ends meet.
tamsheet, **تمشيط:** literally "combing," or performing house-to-house searches by the regime.
tarawih, **ترويح:** special evening prayers after breaking the Ramadan fast.
tassatur, **تسطر:** modesty and concealment from the common gaze.
thalath mafatih, **ثلاث مفاتيح:** literally "three keys" that a groom should provide—keys to a house, car, and store.
tisiyeh, **تسقية:** a popular Syrian dish of chickpeas, stale bread, hummus, and ghee or olive oil.
wahid, **وحيد:** a single son exempt from military service to support elderly parents.
wasta, **واسطة:** social connections useful for bypassing bureaucracy or obtaining privilege.

***wudu*, وضوء:** ablutions.

"Ya hayf," يا حيف: the song "What a Shame" by Samih Choukeir that became the anthem of the uprising in Syria.

***ya latif*, يا لطيف:** invocation of the deity, expressing surprise or dismay.

***ya rabb*, يا رب:** invocation of the deity, literally "Oh, Lord."

***za'atar*, زعتر:** mixture of thyme, sumac, and sesame eaten with olive oil and bread.

***zift*, زفت:** dirt or tar.

Bibliography

Ababsa, Myriam, Baudouin Dupret, and Eric Denis, eds. *Popular Housing and Urban Land Tenure in the Middle East: Case Studies from Egypt, Syria, Jordan, Lebanon, and Turkey*. American University in Cairo Press, 2013.

Abdelrahman, Maha. *Egypt's Long Revolution: Protest Movements and Uprisings*. Routledge Studies in Middle Eastern Democratization and Government, vol. 4. Routledge, 2015.

———. "Policing Neoliberalism in Egypt: The Continuing Rise of the 'Securocratic' State." *Third World Quarterly* 38, no. 1 (2017): 185–202.

Abdulrahim, S., J. DeJong, R. Mourtada, and H. Zurayk. "Estimates of Early Marriage Among Syrian Refugees in Lebanon in 2016 Compared to Syria Pre-2011." *European Journal of Public Health* 27 (supp.), no. 13 (2017): art. ckx189.049. https://doi.org/10.1093/eurpub/ckx189.049.

Abouzeid, Rania. "The Jihad Next Door: The Syrian Roots of Iraq's Newest Civil War." *Politico*, June 23, 2014. https://www.politico.com/magazine/story/2014/06/al-qaeda-iraq-syria-108214/.

Abu Hamad, Bassam, Nicola Jones, Fiona Samuels, Ingrid Gercama, Elizabeth Presler-Marshall, and Georgia Plank. *A Promise of Tomorrow: The Effects of UNHCR and UNICEF Cash Assistance on Syrian Refugees in Jordan*. Overseas Development Institute, 2017. https://reliefweb.int/attachments/c5927321-e13a-3e1b-ad0b-1ea1f7a6feae/ODIUNICEFUNHCRCTreportfinalHR71117.pdf.

Abu Hamed, A. *Syria's Local Coordination Committees: The Dynamo of a Hijacked Revolution*. Polity Press, 2016.

Achilli, Luigi. "The 'Good' Smuggler: The Ethics and Morals of Human Smuggling Among Syrians." *Annals of the American Academy of Political and Social Science* 676, no. 1 (2018): 77–96.

———. "The Human Smuggling Industry: Nuances and Complexities." DHS Symposium Series no. 14, June 13, 2018. Center for Law and Human Behavior, University of Texas at El Paso.

———. "Syrian Refugees in Jordan—a Reality Check." Migration Policy Centre Policy Brief, 2015.

———. "Tariq al-Euroba: Displacement Trends of Syrian Asylum Seekers to the EU." Migration Policy Centre Research Report, 2016. https://hdl.handle.net/1814/38969.

Achilli, Luigi, and Mjriam Abu Samra. "Beyond Legality and Illegality: Palestinian Informal Networks and the Ethno-Political Facilitation of Irregular Migration from Syria." *Journal of Ethnic and Migration Studies* 47, no. 15 (2021): 3345–66.

Aciksoz, Salih Can. "Medical Humanitarianism Under Atmospheric Violence: Health Professionals in the 2013 Gezi Protests in Turkey." *Culture, Medicine, and Psychiatry* 40, no. 2 (2016): 198–222.

Adey, Peter. *Mobility*. 2nd ed. Routledge, 2017.

Aftel, Mandy. *Fragrant: The Secret Life of Scent*. Riverhead, 2014.

Agha, Albert Nasser. "Intonations of Grief: Samih Choukeir's 'Ya Haif' and the 2011 Syrian Revolution." PhD diss., Northern Illinois University, 2013. ProQuest 1552338.

Ahmed, Sarah. "Orientations Matter." In *New Materialisms: Ontology, Agency, and Politics*, edited by Diana Coole and Samantha Frost, 234–57. Duke University Press, 2010.

Aikins, Matthieu. *The Naked Don't Fear the Water: An Underground Journey with Afghan Refugees*. Fitzcarraldo, 2022.

Akgiray, Veda, Gulay Barbarosoglu, and Mustafa Erdik. "Case Study: The 1999 Marmara Earthquakes in Turkey." In *Large-Scale Disasters: Lessons Learned*, 77–92. OECD, 2004. https://www.oecd.org/content/dam/oecd/en/publications/reports/2004/04/large-scale-disasters_g1gh3f46/9789264020207-en.pdf.

Aksu Kargin, İnci. "The Syrian Refugees in Turkey: Their Living Conditions and the Ways in Which Their Presence Has Affected Turkish Society." PhD diss., Indiana University, 2016. ProQuest 10196169.

Alam, Ashraful, Andrew McGregor, and Donna Houston. "Neither Sensibly Homed nor Homeless: Re-Imagining Migrant Homes Through More-Than-Human Relations." *Social & Cultural Geography* 21, no. 8 (Oct. 2020): 1122–45.

Albertsen, Niels, and Bülent Diken. "Society With/out Organs." In *Deleuze and the Social*, edited by Martin Fuglsang and Bent Meier Sørensen, 231–50. Edinburgh University Press, 2006.

Alfeo, Antonio Luca, Mario G. C. A. Cimino, Bruno Lepri, Alexander Sandy Pentland, and Gigliola Vaglini. "Assessing Refugees' Integration via Spatio-Temporal Similarities of Mobility and Calling Behaviors." *IEEE Transactions on Computational Social Systems* 6, no. 4 (2019): 726–38.

Al-Ali, Nadje, and Nicola Pratt. *Women and War in the Middle East Transnational Perspectives*. Zed, 2009.

Allan, Diana. *Refugees of the Revolution: Experiences of Palestinian Exile*. Stanford Univ. Press, 2016.

Allès, Christèle. "The Private Sector and Local Elites: The Experience of Public–Private Partnership in the Water Sector in Tripoli, Lebanon." *Mediterranean Politics* 17, no. 3 (2012): 394–409.

Alshoubaki, Wa'ed, and Michael Harris. "The Impact of Syrian Refugees on Jordan: A Framework for Analysis." *Journal of International Studies* 11, no. 2 (2017): 154–79.

Altındağ, Onur, Ozan Bakis, and Sandra Rozo. "Blessing or Burden? Impacts of Refugees on Businesses and the Informal Economy." *Journal of Development Economics* 146 (2020): art. 102490. https://doi.org/10.1016/j.jdeveco.2020.102490.

Ameri, Anan. *The Scent of Jasmine: Coming of Age in Jerusalem and Damascus*. Interlink, 2017.

Amnesty International. *Amnesty International Annual Report 1982*. Amnesty International, 1982.

Anani, Ghida. "Dimensions of Gender-Based Violence Against Syrian Refugees in Lebanon." *Forced Migration Review* 44 (2013): 75–78.

Al-Anani, Khalil. "Upended Path: The Rise and Fall of Egypt's Muslim Brotherhood." *Middle East Journal* 69, no. 4 (2015): 527–43.

Anderson, Paul. "'Order' and 'Civility': Middle-Class Imaginaries of Citizenship Before the Syrian Uprising." *Anthropological Theory* 18, nos. 2–3 (2018): 248–70.

Anzaldúa, Gloria. *Borderlands/La frontera: The New Mestiza*. Aunt Lute, 1987.

Anzalone, Christopher. "Zaynab's Guardians: The Emergence of Shi'a Militias in Syria." *CTC Sentinel* 6, no. 7 (2013): 16.

El Arab, R., and M. Sagbakken. "Child Marriage of Female Syrian Refugees in Jordan and Lebanon: A Literature Review." *Global Health Action* 12, no. 1 (2019): art. 1585709. https://doi.org/10.1080/16549716.2019.1585709.

Ardovini, Lucia. "The Politicisation of Sectarianism in Egypt: 'Creating an Enemy,' the State vs. the Ikhwan." *Global Discourse* 6, no. 4 (2016): 579–600.

Arendt, Hannah. "We Refugees." *Menorah Journal* 31, no. 1 (Jan. 1943): 69.

Armstrong, Ashley Binetti. "You Shall Not Pass! How the Dublin System Fueled Fortress Europe." *Chicago Journal of International Law* 20, no. 2 (2020): 332–83.

Atasü-Topcuoğlu, Reyhan. "Syrian Refugee Entrepreneurship in Turkey: Integration and the Use of Immigrant Capital in the Informal Economy." *Social Inclusion* 7, no. 4 (2019): 200–210.

Aydin, Hasan, and Yeliz Kaya. "Education for Syrian Refugees: The New Global Issue Facing Teachers and Principals in Turkey." *Educational Studies* 55, no. 1 (2019): 46–71.

Ayoub, Maysa. "The Situation of Syrian Refugees in Egypt." *Orient* 57, no. 1 (2016): 32–39.

Azmeh, Shamel, and LSE Middle East Centre. "The Uprising of the Marginalised: A Socio-Economic Perspective of the Syrian Uprising." LSE Middle East Centre Paper Series, no. 06, 2014. https://eprints.lse.ac.uk/60243/1/__lse.ac.uk_storage_LIBRARY_Secondary_libfile_shared_repository_Content_LSE%20Middle%20East%20Centre%20Papers_Uprising%20of%20marginalised_2014.pdf.

Baczko, Adam, Gilles Dorronsoro, and Arthur Quesnay. *Civil War in Syria: Mobilization and Competing Social Orders*. Cambridge Univ. Press, 2018.

Bagheri, Nazgol. "Tehran's Subway: Gender, Mobility and the Adaptation of the 'Proper' Muslim Woman." *Social & Cultural Geography* 23, no. 3 (2017): 304–22.

Bakkour, Samer. "Daraa and the Altered Trajectory of the Syrian Crisis." *Asian Journal of Middle Eastern and Islamic Studies* 16, no. 2 (2022): 225–42.

Baldassar, Loretta, Majella Kilkey, and Laura Merla. "Transnational Families." In *The Wiley-Blackwell Companion to the Sociology of Families*, edited by Judith Treas, Jacqueline Scott, and Martin Richards, 155–75. Wiley, 2014.

Balkan, Binnur, Elif Ozcan Tok, Huzeyfe Torun, and Semih Tumen. "Immigration, Housing Rents, and Residential Segregation: Evidence from Syrian Refugees in Turkey." IZA Institute of Labor Economics, Discussion Paper Series, June 2018. https://docs.iza.org/dp11611.pdf.

Barbe, Simon. *The French Perfumer Teaching the Several Ways of Extracting the Odours of Drugs and Flowers and Making All the Compositions of Perfumes for Powder, Wash-Balls, Essences, Oyls, Wax, Pomatum, Paste, Queen of Hungary's Rosa Solis, and Other Sweet Waters . . . : Also How to Colour and Scent Gloves and Fans, Together with the Secret of Cleansing Tobacco and Perfuming It for All Sorts Of Snuff, Spanish, Roman, &c. / Done into English from the Original Printed at Paris* (1697). Early English Books Online, University of Michigan Library Digital Collections. https://name.umdl.umich.edu/A30869.0001.001. Accessed January 22, 2025.

Batatu, Hanna. *Syria's Peasantry, the Descendants of Its Lesser Rural Notables, and Their Politics.* Princeton Univ. Press, 1999.

Bauer, Wolfgang. *Crossing the Sea: With Syrians on the Exodus to Europe.* And Other Stories, 2016.

Bayat, Asef. *Revolution Without Revolutionaries: Making Sense of the Arab Spring.* Stanford Univ. Press, 2017.

Becherer, Richard. "A Matter of Life and Debt: The Untold Costs of Rafiq Hariri's New Beirut." *Journal of Architecture* 10, no. 1 (2005): 1–42.

Bendixsen, Synnøve K. N. "The Refugee Crisis: Destabilizing and Restabilizing European Borders." *History and Anthropology* 27, no. 5 (2016): 536–54.

Betts, Alexander, Fulya Memişoğlu, and Ali Ali. "What Difference Do Mayors Make? The Role of Municipal Authorities in Turkey and Lebanon's Response to Syrian Refugees." *Journal of Refugee Studies* 34, no. 1 (2020): 491–519.

Biehl, João, and Peter Locke. "Deleuze and the Anthropology of Becoming." *Current Anthropology* 51, no. 3 (2010): 317–51.

———. *Unfinished: The Anthropology of Becoming.* Duke Univ. Press, 2017.

Biehl, Kristen Sarah. "Spatializing Diversities, Diversifying Spaces: Housing Experiences and Home Space Perceptions in a Migrant Hub of Istanbul." *Ethnic and Racial Studies* 38, no. 4 (2015): 596–607.

Bird, Gemma, Jelena Obradović-Wochnik, Amanda Russell Beattie, and Patrycja Rozbicka. "The 'Badlands' of the 'Balkan Route': Policy and Spatial Effects on Urban Refugee Housing." *Global Policy* 12, no. S2 (2021): 28–40.

Bissell, David. "Gender and Mobility: New Approaches for Informing Sustainability." *Gender, Place & Culture* 17, no. 1 (2010): 5–23.

———. "Passenger Mobilities: Affective Atmospheres and the Sociality of Public Transport." *Environment and Planning D: Society and Space* 28, no. 2 (2010): 270–89.

Bizri, Rima. "Refugee-Entrepreneurship: A Social Capital Perspective." *Entrepreneurship & Regional Development* 29, nos. 9–10 (2017): 847–68.

Block, Laura, and Saskia Bonjour. "Fortress Europe or Europe of Rights? The Europeanisation of Family Migration Policies in France, Germany and the Netherlands." *European Journal of Migration and Law* 15, no. 2 (2013): 203–24.

Bogard, William. "Sense and Segmentarity: Some Markers of a Deleuzian-Guattarian Sociology." *Sociological Theory* 16, no. 1 (1998): 52–74.

Bossong, Raphael, and Helena Carrapico, eds. *EU Borders and Shifting Internal Security Technology, Externalization and Accountability.* Springer, 2016.

Bourdieu, Pierre. *Outline of a Theory of Practice.* Cambridge Univ. Press, 1977.

Bromfield, Nicole F., Sanaa Ashour, and Kennon Rider. "Divorce from Arranged Marriages: An Exploration of Lived Experiences." *Journal of Divorce & Remarriage* 57, no. 4 (2016): 280–97.

Brownlee, Billie Jeane. "Mediating the Syrian Revolt: How New Media Technologies Change the Development of Social Movements and Conflicts." In *The Syrian Uprising: Domestic Factors and Early Trajectory,* edited by Raymond Hinnebusch and Omar Imady, 188–206. Syrian Studies. Routledge/St. Andrews, 2018.

Brun, Cathrin. "Reterritorializing the Link Between People and Place in Refugee Studies." *Geografiska Annaler* 83B, no. 1 (2001): 15–25.

Brun, Cathrin, and Anita Fábos. "Making Homes in Limbo? A Conceptual Framework." *Refuge: Canada's Journal on Refugees / Revue canadienne sur les réfugiés* 31, no. 1 (2015): 5–17.

Buckner, Elizabeth, Dominique Spencer, and Jihae Cha. "Between Policy and Practice: The Education of Syrian Refugees in Lebanon." *Journal of Refugee Studies* 31, no. 4 (2018): 444–65.

Bulley, Dan. "Shame on EU: Europe, RtoP, and the Politics of Refugee Protection." *Ethics & International Affairs* 31, no. 1 (2017): 51–70.

Butcher, Melissa. "'Sir, It Was My Right of Way!' Examining Cultural Change and the Contested Entitlements of Automobility." *Mobilities* 14, no. 6 (2019): 795–808.

Caarls, Kim, Özge Bilgili, and Sonja Fransen. "Evolution of Migration Trajectories and Transnational Social Networks over Time: A Study Among Sub-Saharan African Migrants in Europe." *Journal of Ethnic and Migration Studies* 47, no. 14 (2020): 3310–28.

Cabot, Heath. "The Business of Anthropology and the European Refugee Regime." *American Ethnologist* 46, no. 3 (2019): 261–75.

Campana, Paolo. "Human Smuggling: Structure and Mechanisms." *Crime and Justice* 49, no. 1 (2020): 471–519.

Campana, Paolo, and Loraine Gelsthorpe. "Choosing a Smuggler: Decision-Making Amongst Migrants Smuggled to Europe." *European Journal on Criminal Policy and Research* 27, no. 1 (2021): 5–21.

Campbell, Edward. *Music After Deleuze*. Bloomsbury, 2013.

Carlisle, Jessica. "From Behind the Door: A Damascus Court Copes with an Alleged Out of Court Marriage." In *Les métamorphoses du mariage au Proche-Orient*, edited by Barbara Drieskens, 59–74. Presses de l'Ifpo, 2008.

Carpi, Estella. "Against Ontologies of Hospitality: About Syrian Refugeehood in Northern Lebanon." Middle East Institute, October 27, 2016. https://www.mei.edu/publications/against-ontologies-hospitality-about-syrian-refugeehood-northern-lebanon.

———. "The Everyday Experience of Humanitarianism in Akkar Villages." Civil Society Knowledge Center, Lebanon Support, March 2014. https://civilsociety-centre.org/paper/everyday-experience-humanitarianism-akkar-villages.

———. "The Political and the Humanitarian in Lebanon: Social Responsiveness to the Emergency Crisis from the 2006 War to the Syrian Refugee Influx." *Oriente moderno* 94, no. 2 (2014): 402–27.

———. "Towards a Neo-Cosmetic Humanitarianism: Refugee Self-Reliance as a Social-Cohesion Regime in Lebanon's Halba." *Journal of Refugee Studies* 33, no. 1 (2020): 224–44.

Carpi, Estella, and H. Pınar Şenoğuz. "Refugee Hospitality in Lebanon and Turkey: On Making 'the Other.'" *International Migration* 57, no. 2 (2019): 126–42.

Causadias, José M., Dante Cicchetti, and Fatima Tuba Yaylaci. "Trauma and Resilient Functioning Among Syrian Refugee Children." *Development and Psychopathology* 30, no. 5 (2018): 1923–36.

Chaaban, Jad M., Karin Seyfert, Nisreen I. Salti, and Gheed S. El Makkaoui. "Poverty and Livelihoods Among UNHCR Registered Refugees in Lebanon." *Refugee Survey Quarterly* 32, no. 1 (2013): 24–49.

Chabrier, Pierre-André. "The War of the Poor in Tripoli (Lebanon)." *Confluences en Méditerranée* 85, no. 2 (2013): 87–102.

Chalcraft, John. *The Invisible Cage: Syrian Migrant Workers in Lebanon.* Stanford Univ. Press, 2008.

Chatty, Dawn. *Displacement and Dispossession in the Modern Middle East.* The Contemporary Middle East, vol. 5. Cambridge Univ. Press, 2010.

Cheesman, Margie. "Self-Sovereignty for Refugees? The Contested Horizons of Digital Identity." *Geopolitics* 27, no. 1 (2022): 134–59.

Cherri, Zeinab, Pedro González, and Rafael Castro Delgado. "The Lebanese–Syrian Crisis: Impact of Influx of Syrian Refugees to an Already Weak State." *Risk Management and Healthcare Policy* 9 (2016): 165–72.

Christmann, Andreas. "Islamic Scholar and Religious Leader: A Portrait of Shaykh Issam Sa'id Ramadan al-Buti." *Islam and Christian–Muslim Relations* 9, no. 2 (1998): 149–69.

Clark-Kazak, Christina. "Ethical Considerations: Research with People in Situations of Forced Migration." *Refuge: Canada's Journal on Refugees / Refuge: Revue canadienne sur les réfugiés* 33, no. 2 (2017): 11–17.

Collard, Rebecca. "In Lebanon, 1 Million Syrian Refugees Live on $1 a Day." *Christian Science Monitor*, April 3, 2014. https://www.csmonitor.com/World/Middle-East/2014/0403/In-Lebanon-1-million-Syrian-refugees-live-on-1-a-day.

Conduit, Dara. "The Syrian Muslim Brotherhood and the Spectacle of Hama." *Middle East Journal* 70, no. 2 (2016): 211–26.

Connell, Julia, and John Burgess. "The Labour Market, Immigration and the Building of Dubai." *International Employment Relations Review* 17, no. 2 (2011): 21–36.

Cornelisse, Galina. "Territory, Procedures and Rights." *Refugee Survey Quarterly* 35, no. 1 (2016): 74–90.

Crawley, Heaven, and Katharine Jones. "Beyond Here and There: (Re)Conceptualising Migrant Journeys and the 'In-between.'" *Journal of Ethnic and Migration Studies* 47, no. 14 (2021): 3226–42.

Crawley, Heaven, and Dimitris Skleparis. "Refugees, Migrants, Neither, Both: Categorical Fetishism and the Politics of Bounding in Europe's 'Migration Crisis.'" *Journal of Ethnic and Migration Studies* 44, no. 1 (2018): 48–64.

Cresswell, Tim. "Towards a Politics of Mobility." *Environment and Planning D: Society and Space* 28, no. 1 (2010): 17–31.

Cristiani, Richard S. *Perfumery and Kindred Arts: A Comprehensive Treatise on Perfumery.* H. C. Baird, 1877.

Culbertson, Shelly, and Louay Constant. *Education of Syrian Refugee Children: Managing the Crisis in Turkey, Lebanon, and Jordan.* RAND, 2015.

Culcasi, Karen. "'We Are Women and Men Now': Intimate Spaces and Coping Labour for Syrian Women Refugees in Jordan." *Transactions of the Institute of British Geographers* 44, no. 3 (2019): 463–78.

Cumming-Bruce, Nick. "U.N. Reports Syria Uses Hospital Attacks as a 'Weapon of War.'" *New York Times*, September 13, 2013. https://www.nytimes.com/2013/09/14/world/middleeast/un-panel-accuses-syria-of-attacking-hospitals.html.

Davies, Rodger. "Syrian Arabic Kinship Terms." *Southwestern Journal of Anthropology* 5, no. 3 (1949): 244–52.

DeLanda, Manuel. *Assemblage Theory.* Edinburgh Univ. Press, 2016.

———. *A New Philosophy of Society: Assemblage Theory and Social Complexities.* Continuum, 2006.

Deleuze, Gilles, and Felix Guattari. *A Thousand Plateaus: Capitalism and Schizophrenia.* Translated by Brian Massumi. 1987. Reprint. Continuum, 2008.

Denoeux, Guilain, and Robert Springborg. "Hariri's Lebanon: Singapore of the Middle East or Sanaa of the Levant?" *Middle East Policy* 6, no. 2 (1998): 158–73.

Al-Dewachi, Omar. *Ungovernable Life: Mandatory Medicine and Statecraft in Iraq*. Stanford Univ. Press, 2017.

Di Giovanni, Janine. *The Morning They Came for Us: Dispatches from Syria*. Norton, 2016.

Dimitriadi, Angeliki. *Irregular Afghan Migration to Europe: At the Margins, Looking In*. Palgrave Macmillan, 2017.

Drobnick, Jim. "Eating Nothing: Cooking Aromas in Art and Culture." In *The Smell Culture Reader*, edited by Jim Drobnick, 342–56. Berg, 2006.

Düvell, Franck. "The 'Great Migration' of Summer 2015: Analysing the Assemblage of Key Drivers in Turkey." *Journal of Ethnic and Migration Studies* 45, no. 12 (2019): 2227–40.

Elden, Stuart. "Secure the Volume: Vertical Geopolitics and the Depth of Power." *Political Geography* 34 (2013): 35–55.

Elkhdr, Hassan, and Nagmi Mofta Aimer. "The Effect of Personal Factors on Organizational Commitment Among Teachers Working at Libyan Schools in Turkey." *European Journal of Business and Management Research* 5, no. 1 (2020): 1–8.

Emre Cetin, Kumru Berfin. "The 'Politicization' of Turkish Television Dramas." *International Journal of Communication* 8 (2014): 2462–83.

Esen, Oğuz O., and Ayla Oğuş Binatlı. "The Impact of Syrian Refugees on the Turkish Economy: Regional Labour Market Effects." *Social Sciences* 6, no. 4 (2017): 129–41.

Etem, Jülide. "Representations of Syrian Refugees in UNICEF's Media Projects: New Vulnerabilities in Digital Humanitarian Communication." *Global Perspectives* 1, no. 1 (2020): art. 12787. https://doi.org/10.1525/gp.2020.12787.

Fabian, K. P. "The Second Egyptian Uprising: The Beginning of the End?" *Indian Foreign Affairs Journal* 8, no. 2 (2013): 178–84.

Fabos, Anita. *"Brothers" or Others? Propriety and Gender for Muslim Arab Sudanese in Egypt*. Studies in Forced Migration, vol. 22. Berghahn. 2008.

Facon, Clothilde. "Depoliticization and (Re)Politicization Tactics in Refugee Governance in Lebanon: Comparing Western and Gulf Donors' Interventions." *Territory, Politics, Governance* 11, no. 4 (2022): 712–29.

Farías, Ignacio. "The Politics of Urban Assemblages." *City* 15, nos. 3–4 (2011): 365–74.

Fassihi, Farnaz, and Jay Solomon. "Syria Regime Rocked by Protests." *Wall Street Journal*, March 25, 2011. https://www.wsj.com/articles/SB10001424052748704517404576222350109783770.

Favier, Agnès. "Increasing Vulnerability for the Syrian Refugees in Lebanon: What's Next." Middle East Directions (MED) Policy Brief, March 2016. https://doi.org/10.2870/388671.

Feischmidt, Margit. "Deployed Fears and Suspended Solidarity Along the Migratory Route in Europe." *Citizenship Studies* 24, no. 4 (2020): 441–56.

Fisk, Robert. "Earthquake in Turkey: Sounds of Fury Rise from Wreckage of a Town That Became a Charnel House." *The Independent*, August 20, 1999.

Fleischmann, Larissa. *Contested Solidarity: Practices of Refugee Support Between Humanitarian Help and Political Activism.* Transcript, 2020.

Fleming, Melissa. *A Hope More Powerful Than the Sea: The Journey of Doaa Al Zamel.* Fleet, 2018.

Fontana, Iole. "Migration Crisis, Organised Crime and Domestic Politics in Italy: Unfolding the Interplay." *South European Society and Politics* 25, no. 1 (2020): 49–74.

Freedman, Jane. "Women's Experience of Forced Migration: Gender-Based Forms of Insecurity and the Uses of 'Vulnerability.'" In *A Gendered Approach to the Syrian Refugee Crisis*, edited by Jane Freedman and Zeyneb Kivilcim, 125–41. Routledge, 2017.

Friebel, Guido, and Sergei Guriev. "Smuggling Humans: A Theory of Debt-Financed Migration." *Journal of the European Economic Association* 4, no. 6 (2006): 1085–111.

Gade, Tine. "The Syrian Conflict and the Dynamics of Civil War in Tripoli, Lebanon." *Maghreb-machrek* 218 (2013): 61–84.

Gallagher, Sally. *Making Do in Damascus: Navigating a Generation of Change in Family and Work.* Syracuse University Press, 2012.

Garkisch, Michael, Jens Heidingsfelder, and Markus Beckmann. "Third Sector Organizations and Migration: A Systematic Literature Review on the Contribution of Third Sector Organizations in View of Flight, Migration and Refugee Crises." *VOLUNTAS: International Journal of Voluntary and Nonprofit Organizations* 28 (2017): 1839–80.

Gatter, Melissa. "Camps Revisited: Multifaceted Spatialities of a Modern Political Technology." *Journal of Refugee Studies* 32, no. 3: 530–32.

———. "The Digital Is Political in 'Mediated Lives': A Review of Mirjam Twigt's 'Mediated Lives: Waiting and Hope Among Iraqi Refugees in Jordan.'" *Journal of Refugee Studies* 35, no. 3 (2022): 1426–30.

———. "Preserving Order: Narrating Resilience as Threat in Jordan's Azraq Refugee Camp." *Territory Politics Governance* 11, no. 2 (2021): 1–17.

———. "Restoring Childhood: Humanitarianism and Growing Up Syrian in Za'tari Refugee Camp." *Contemporary Levant* 2, no. 2 (2017): 89–102.

———. *Time and Power in Azraq Refugee Camp: A Nine-to-Five Emergency.* American Univ. in Cairo Press, 2023.

———. "Who Labels the Camp? Claiming Ownership Through Visibility in Jordan." In *Branding the Middle East: Communication Strategies and Image Building from Qom to Casablanca*, edited by Steffen Wippel, 567–84. De Gruyter, 2023.

"Gaza Is 'Running out of Time' UN Experts Warn, Demanding Ceasefire to Prevent Genocide." Question of Palestine, United Nations, November 2, 2023. https://www.un.org/unispal/document/gaza-is-running-out-of-time-un-experts-warn-demanding-a-ceasefire-to-prevent-genocide/.

"Gaza: UN Experts Call on International Community to Prevent Genocide Against Palestinian People." Office of the High Commissioner of Human Rights (OHCHR), United Nations, November 16, 2023. https://www.ohchr.org/en/press-releases/2023/11/gaza-un-experts-call-international-community-prevent-genocide-against.

Geddes, Andrew, and Peter Scholten. "Towards Common EU Migration and Asylum Policies?" In *The Politics of Migration and Immigration in Europe*, 2nd ed., 144–72. Sage, 2016.

Goldfarb, Kathryn E., and Janet Carsten. "The 25th Anniversary of 'The Substance of Kinship and the Heat of the Hearth': Feeding, Personhood, and Relatedness Among Malays in Pulau Langkawi." *American Ethnologist*, October 4, 2020. https://americanethnologist.org/online-content/interviews/the-25th-anniversary-of-the-substance-of-kinship-and-the-heat-of-the-hearth/.

Goodman, Amy, and Ghassan Abu Sitta. "Systematic Destruction of the Healthcare System in Gaza." *Democracy Now!*, December 30, 2024. https://x.com/democracynow/status/1873722012675269008?s=43&t=Fsl36dlg87jYCs30_Py6yQ.

Goodman, David. "Syrian Protesters Clash with Security Forces." *New York Times*, April 1, 2011. https://www.nytimes.com/2011/04/02/world/middleeast/02syria.html?ref=world.

Goulden, Robert. "Housing, Inequality, and Economic Change in Syria." *British Journal of Middle Eastern Studies* 38, no. 2 (2011): 187–202.

Gowayed, Heba. *Refuge: How the State Shapes Human Potential*. Princeton Univ. Press, 2022.

———. "Resettled and Unsettled: Syrian Refugees and the Intersection of Race and Legal Status in the United States." *Ethnic and Racial Studies* 43, no. 2 (2020): 275–93.

Gozdziak, Elzbieta, and Alissa Walter. *Urban Refugees in Cairo*. Institute for the Study of International Migration, 2013.

Green, Peter, and Diana Miller. *The Genus Jasminum in Cultivation*. Royal Botanic Gardens, 2009.

Gregory, Derek. "The Everywhere War." *Geographical Journal* 177, no. 3 (2011): 238–50.

———. "Tahrir: Politics, Publics and Performances of Space." *Middle East Critique* 22, no. 3 (2013): 235–46.

Grehan, James. *Twilight of the Saints: Everyday Religion in Ottoman Syria and Palestine*. Oxford University Press, 2014.

Griffiths, Mark, and Jemima Repo. "Women and Checkpoints in Palestine." *Security Dialogue* 52, no. 3 (2021): 249–65.

Grjasnowa, Olga. *City of Jasmine*. Oneworld, 2017.

Gualtieri, Sarah. *Arab Routes: Pathways to Syrian California*. Stanford Univ. Press, 2019.

Habib, Rima, Micheline Ziadee, Elio Abi Younes, Houda Harastani, Layal Hamdar, Mohammed Jawad, et al. "Displacement, Deprivation and Hard Work Among Syrian Refugee Children in Lebanon." *BMJ Global Health* 4, no. 1 (2019): 1122–34.

Haddad, Bassam. *Business Networks in Syria: The Political Economy of Authoritarian Resilience*. Stanford Univ. Press, 2011.

Haddad, Simon. *The Palestinian Impasse in Lebanon: The Politics of Refugee Integration*. Studies in Peace Politics in the Middle East. Academic Press, 2003.

Hamidi, Ibrahim. "Revealed: The Inside Story of Assad's Flight and Sharaa's Arrival." *Al Majalla*, December 11, 2024. https://en.majalla

.com/node/323549/politics/revealed-insider-story-assad%E2%80%99s-flight-and-sharaa%E2%80%99s-arrival.

Hamilton, Jennifer A., and Aimee Placas. "Anthropology Becoming . . . ? The 2010 Sociocultural Anthropology Year in Review." *American Anthropologist* 113, no. 2 (2011): 246–61.

Hanmer, Lucia, Diana Jimena Arango, Eliana Rubiano, Julieth Santamaria, and Mariana Viollaz. "How Does Poverty Differ Among Refugees? Taking a Gender Lens to the Data on Syrian Refugees in Jordan." Policy Research Working Paper no. 8616, World Bank, October 17, 2018. https://hdl.handle.net/10986/30586.

Hansen, Susan. "Gender and Mobility: New Approaches for Informing Sustainability." *Gender, Place & Culture* 17, no. 1 (2010): 5–23.

Haraway, Donna. *Simians, Cyborgs and Women: The Reinvention of Nature*. Free Association, 1991.

Harima, Aki, and Julia Freudenberg. "Co-Creation of Social Entrepreneurial Opportunities with Refugees." *Journal of Social Entrepreneurship* 11, no. 1 (2020): 40–64.

Harkin, James. "Good Media, Bad Politics? New Media and the Syrian Conflict." Reuters Institute, 2013. https://reutersinstitute.politics.ox.ac.uk/our-research/good-media-bad-politics-new-media-and-syrian-conflict.

Hartocollis, Anemona. "Traveling in Europe's River of Migrants." *New York Times*, August 30, 2015. https://www.nytimes.com/interactive/projects/cp/reporters-notebook/migrants#:~:text=River%20of%20Migrants,-By%20Anemona%20Hartocollis&text=Tens%20of%20thousands%20of%20migrants,other%20countries%20in%20northern%20Europe.

Harvey, David. *Rebel Cities: From the Right to the City to the Urban Revolution*. Verso, 2012.

Hass, Mark, and David Lesch. *The Arab Spring: The Hope and Reality of the Uprisings*. Routledge, 2016.

Hattar-Pollara, Marianne. "Barriers to Education of Syrian Refugee Girls in Jordan: Gender-Based Threats and Challenges." *Journal of Nursing Scholarship* 51, no. 3 (2019): 241–51.

Hauslohner, Abigail. "Syrian Refugees Find Hostility in Egypt." *Washington Post*, September 7, 2013. https://www.washingtonpost.com/world/middle_east/syrian-refugees-find-hostility-in-egypt/2013/09/07/fc54b832-17cc-11e3-961c-f22d3aaf19ab_story.html.

Hearst, David. "Revealed: How Israel's Plan to Carve Up Syria Was Thwarted by Assad's Downfall." *Middle East Eye*, December 20, 2024. https://www.middleeasteye.net/news/revealed-how-assads-downfall-thwarted-israels-plan-carve-syria.

Herman, Emma. "Migration as a Family Business: The Role of Personal Networks in the Mobility Phase of Migration." *International Migration* 44, no. 4 (2006): 191–230.

Hermez, Sami. "When the State Is (N)Ever Present: On Cynicism and Political Mobilization in Lebanon." *Journal of the Royal Anthropological Institute* 21, no. 3 (2015): 507–23.

Higgins, Eliot. *We Are Bellingcat: Global Crime, Online Sleuths, and the Bold Future of News*. Bloomsbury, 2021.

Hiitola, Johanna, Kati Turtiainen, Sabine Gruber, and Marja Tiilikainen. *Family Life in Transition: Borders, Transnational Mobility, and Welfare Society in Nordic Countries*. Routledge, 2020.

Hinnebusch, Raymond A., and Omar Imady. *The Syrian Uprising: Domestic Factors and Early Trajectory*. Syrian Studies. Routledge/St. Andrews, 2018.

Holmes, Seth, and Heide Castañeda. "Representing the 'European Refugee Crisis' in Germany and Beyond: Deservingness and Difference, Life and Death." *American Ethnologist* 43, no. 1 (2016): 12–24.

Hoodfar, Homa. *Between Marriage and the Market: Intimate Politics and Survival in Cairo*. University of California Press, 1997.

hooks, bell. "Remembered Rapture: Dancing with Words." *JAC* 20, no. 1 (2000): 1–8.

Hopfinger, Hans, and Raslan Khadour. "The Development of the Transportation Sector in Syria and the Actual Investment Policy." *Middle Eastern Studies* 35, no. 3 (1999): 64–71.

Howes, David. "Multisensory Anthropology." *Annual Review of Anthropology* 48 (2019): 17–28.

Hudson, Leila. "Neopatriarchy in Syrian and Turkish Television Drama: Between the Culture Industry and the Dialect Imagination." In *Media Evolution on the Eve of the Arab Spring*, edited by Leila Hudson, Adel Iskander, and Mimi Kirk, 127–38. Palgrave Macmillan, 2014.

Huet, Romain. "When the 'Desperates' Become 'Enraged': An Ethnographic Study of Syrian Mudjahidin (2012–2014)." *Cultures et conflits* 97 (2015): 31–75.

Huxley, Frederick Charles. *Wasiṭa in a Lebanese Context: Social Exchange Among Villagers and Outsiders*. Univ. of Michigan Press, 1978.

İçduygu, Ahmed. "Decentring Migrant Smuggling: Reflections on the Eastern Mediterranean Route to Europe." *Journal of Ethnic and Migration Studies* 47, no. 14 (2020): 3293–309.

Imady, Omar. "Organizationally Secular Damascene Islamist Movements and the Syrian Uprising." In *The Syrian Uprising: Domestic Origins and Early Trajectory*, edited by Raymond A. Hinnebusch and Omar Imady, 106–27. Syrian Studies. Routledge, 2018.

Ingold, Tim. "Against Space: Place, Movement, Knowledge." In *Being Alive: Essays on Movement, Knowledge and Description*, 145–55. Routledge, 2011.

———. "Back to the Future with the Theory of Affordances." *HAU: Journal of Ethnographic Theory* 8, nos. 1–2 (2018): 39–44.

———. "On Human Correspondence." *Journal of the Royal Anthropological Institute* 23, no. 1 (2017): 9–27.

———. *The Perception of the Environment: Essays on Livelihood, Dwelling and Skill*. Routledge, 2000.

———. "Point, Line, Counterpoint: From Environment to Fluid Space." In *Being Alive: Essays on Movement, Knowledge and Description*, 76–88. Routledge, 2011.

———. "Seven Variations on the Letter A." In *Being Alive: Essays on Movement, Knowledge and Description*, 181–95. Routledge, 2011.

Inoue, Takatomo. "Al-Kindi's Attack on Alchemy and His Perfume Making." *Orient* 52 (2017): 72–92.

International Organization for Migration. "Mediterranean: Missing Migrants Project." 2014. https://missingmigrants.iom.int/region/mediterranean?migrant_route%5B%5D=1377.

Isakjee, Arshad, Thom Davies, Jelena Obradović-Wochnik, and Karolina Augustová. "Liberal Violence and the Racial Borders of the European Union." *Antipode* 52, no. 6 (2020): 1751–73.

Ismail, Salwa. "Authoritarian Government, Neoliberalism and Everyday Civilities in Egypt." *Third World Quarterly* 32, no. 5 (2011): 845–62.

Ismat, Riad. "Nizar Qabbani: Jasmine Never Dies." In *Artists, Writers and the Arab Spring*, 39–44. Palgrave Macmillan, 2019.

"Israel Warned Assad About Iran Weapon Smuggling, Documents Show—Report." *Jerusalem Post*, December 11, 2024. https://www.jpost.com/middle-east/article-832979.

Jabari, Lawahez. "Deadly Migrant Shipwreck off Malta Highlights Desperation." *NBC News*, September 17, 2014. https://www.nbcnews.com/storyline/europes-border-crisis/deadly-migrant-shipwreck-malta-highlights-desperation-n205441.

Janmyr, Maja. "Precarity in Exile: The Legal Status of Syrian Refugees in Lebanon." *Refugee Survey Quarterly* 35, no. 4 (2016): 58–78.

———. "UNHCR and the Syrian Refugee Response: Negotiating Status and Registration in Lebanon." *International Journal of Human Rights* 22, no. 3 (2018): 393–419.

Jarrah, Nouri. *A Boat to Lesbos, and Other Poems*. Banipal, 2018.

Jensen, Ole, Mimi Sheller, and S. Wind. "Together and Apart: Affective Ambiences and Negotiation in Families' Everyday Life and Mobility." *Mobilities* 10, no. 3 (2015): 363–82.

Jirón, Paola A., Walter Alejandro Imilan, and Luis Iturra. "Relearning to Travel in Santiago: The Importance of Mobile Place-Making and Travelling Know-How." *Cultural Geographies* 23, no. 4 (2016): 599–614.

Jones, Martin. "Legal Empowerment and Refugees on the Nile: The Very Short History of Legal Empowerment and Refugee Legal Aid in Egypt." *International Journal of Human Rights* 19, no. 3 (2015): 308–18.

Jones, Reece. *Violent Borders: Refugees and the Right to Move*. Verso, 2016.

Joseph, Suad. "Brother/Sister Relationships: Connectivity, Love, and Power in the Reproduction of Patriarchy in Lebanon." *American Ethnologist* 21, no. 1 (1994): 50–73.

———. "Connectivity and Patriarchy Among Urban Working-Class Arab Families in Lebanon." *Ethos* 21, no. 4 (1993): 452–84.

———. "Gender and Relationality Among Arab Families in Lebanon." *Feminist Studies* 19, no. 3 (1993): 465–86.

———, ed. *Intimate Selving in Arab Families: Gender, Self, and Identity*. Syracuse University Press, 1999.

Joubin, Rebecca. *Mediating the Uprising: Narratives of Gender and Marriage in Syrian Television Drama*. Rutgers Univ. Press, 2020.

———. *The Politics of Love: Sexuality, Gender, and Marriage in Syrian Television Drama*. Lexington, 2013.

Juhasz, Alexandra, and Alisa Lebow. "Beyond Story: An Online, Community-Based Manifesto." *World Records* 2 (2018): art. 3. https://worldrecordsjournal.org/beyond-story-an-online-community-based-manifesto/.

Kadkoy, Omar. "Syrian Entrepreneurs in Turkey: Emerging Economic Actors and Agents of Social Cohesion." In *Turkey's Political Economy in the 21st Century*, edited by Emel Parlar Dal, 115–29. Palgrave Macmillan, 2020.

Kahf, Mohja. "The Syrian Revolution, Then and Now." *Peace Review* 26, no. 4 (2014): 556–63.

Kanna, Ahmed. "Urban Praxis and the Arab Spring." *City* 16, no. 3 (2012): 360–68.

Karaçay, Aysam Biraz. "Shifting Human Smuggling Routes Along Turkey's Borders." *Turkish Policy Quarterly* 15, no. 4 (2017): 97–108.

Kay, Shannon. "Syrians in Turkey: A Grassroots Perspective." *Turkish Policy Quarterly* 15, no. 3 (2016). http://turkishpolicy.com/article/834/syrians-in-turkey-a-grassroots-perspective.

Kaymaz, Timur, and Omar Kadkoy. "Syrians in Turkey: The Economics of Integration." Al Sharq Forum Expert Brief, September 2016.

Keane, Webb. "Perspectives on Affordances, or the Anthropologically Real: The 2018 Daryll Forde Lecture." *Journal of Ethnographic Theory* 8, nos. 1–2 (2018): 27–38.

Kennedy, Rosanne, Jonathon Zapasnik, Hannah McCann, and Miranda Bruce. "All Those Little Machines: Assemblage as Transformative Theory." *Australian Humanities Review*, no. 55 (2013): 45–66. https://australianhumanitiesreview.org/wp-content/uploads/2015/09/AHR55_3_Kennedy_etal_FINAL.pdf.

Kent, Jennifer L. "Still Feeling the Car—the Role of Comfort in Sustaining Private Car Use." *Mobilities* 10, no. 5 (2015): 726–74.

Khalaf, Abdulhadi, Omar AlShehabi, and Adam Hanieh, eds. *Transit States: Labour, Migration and Citizenship in the Gulf*. Pluto Press, 2015.

Khalil, Mustafa. *Suquṭ al-Julan*. Al-Ṭab'ah 2. Dar al-I'tisam, 1980.

El-Khani, Aala, Fiona Ulph, Sarah Peters, and Rachel Calam. "Syria: Coping Mechanisms Utilised by Displaced Refugee Parents Caring for Their Children in Pre-Resettlement Contexts." *Intervention* 15, no. 1 (2017): 34–50.

Khashan, Hilal. "Will Syria's Strife Rip Lebanon Apart?" *Middle East Quarterly* 20, no. 1 (2013): 75–80.

Khayr, S. *Ghuṭat Dimashq: Dirasah fi al-jughrafyah al-zira'iyah*. Wizarat al-Thaqafah wa-al-Irshad al-Qawmi, Mudiriyat al-Tarjamah wa-al-Ta'lif wa-al-Nashr, 1966.

Khodr, Zeina. "Lebanon's Tripoli: The Transit Hub for Syrian Refugees." Al Jazeera America, November 6, 2015. https://www.aljazeera.com/news/2015/11/6/lebanons-tripoli-the-transit-hub-for-syrian-refugees.

Khoury, Jack. "Thousands of Gazans Fleeing to Europe via Tunnels, Traffickers and Boats." *Haaretz*, September 17, 2014. https://www.haaretz.com/2014-09-17/ty-article/.premium/thousands-of-gazans-fleeing-via-tunnels/0000017f-e624-df5f-a17f-fffe5fb60000.

Al-Kindi, Ya'qub ibn Ishak. *Kitab kimiya' al-'itr wat-tas'idat*. Vol. 30. Translated by Karl Garbers. Kraus Reprint, 1966.

Kingsley, Patrick. *The New Odyssey: The Story of Europe's Refugee Crisis*. Guardian Faber, 2016.

Koca, Burcu Torgral. "Bordering Processes Through the Use of Technology: The Turkish Case." *Journal of Ethnic and Migration Studies* 48, no. 8 (2020): 1909–26.

Kortam, Hend. "New Requirements for Entry of Syrians." *Daily News Egypt*, July 10, 2013.

Kostrounova, Jana. "Ideological Tensions in the Ranks of Syrian Officers: The Trigger of Military Circles Transformation in the Country?" *Obrana a strategie* 12, no. 1 (2012): 73–78.

Kouddous, Sharif Abdel. "Egypt's Syrian Scapegoats." *The Nation*, Sept. 30, 2013. https://www.thenation.com/article/archive/egypts-syrian-scapegoats/.

Kraidy, Marwin, and Omar Al-Ghazzi. "Neo-Ottoman Cool: Turkish Popular Culture in the Arab Public Sphere." *Popular Communication* 11, no. 1 (2013): 17–29.

Al-Krenawi, Alean, and Yaniv Kanat-Maymon. "Psychological Symptomatology, Self-Esteem and Life Satisfactions of Women from Polygamous and Monogamous Marriages in Syria." *International Social Work* 60, no. 1 (2017): 196–207.

Krijnen, Marieke, and Mona Fawaz. "Exception as the Rule: High-End Developments in Neoliberal Beirut." *Built Environment (1978–)* 36, no. 2 (2010): 245–59.

Kurd 'Ali, Muhammad. *Ghuṭat Dimashq*. 3rd ed. Dar al-Fikr, 1984.

Kurdi, Tima. *The Boy on the Beach: My Family's Escape from Syria and Our Hope for a New Home*. Simon and Schuster, 2018.

Kuschminder, Katie, and Anna Triandafyllidou. "Smuggling, Trafficking, and Extortion: New Conceptual and Policy Challenges on the Libyan Route to Europe." *Antipode* 52, no. 1 (2020): 206–26.

Kusters, Annelies. "Autogestion and Competing Hierarchies: Deaf and Other Perspectives on Diversity and the Right to Occupy Space in the Mumbai Suburban Trains." *Social & Cultural Geography* 18, no. 2 (2016): 201–23.

———. "When Transport Becomes a Destination: Deaf Spaces and Networks on the Mumbai Suburban Trains." *Journal of Cultural Geography* 34, no. 2 (2017): 170–93.

Kwong, Caleb Cy, Cherry Wm Cheung, Humera Manzoor, and Mehboob Ur Rashid. "Entrepreneurship Through Bricolage: A Study of Displaced Entrepreneurs at Times of War and Conflict." *Entrepreneurship & Regional Development* 31, nos. 5–6 (2019): 435–55.

Larson, Mary. "Steering Clear of the Rocks: A Look at the Current State of Oral History Ethics in the Digital Age." *Oral History Review* 40, no. 1 (2013): 36–49.

Lavrov, Anton. "The Russian Air Campaign in Syria: A Preliminary Analysis." Center for Naval Analyses, June 2018. https://www.cna.org/archive/CNA_Files/pdf/cop-2018-u-017903-final.pdf.

"Lebanon: Syrian Refugees Face Sexual Harassment, Abuse." *Al-Akhbar English*, January 24, 2014.

"Lebanon–Turkey Ferry Service to Bypass Syria, Boost Tourism." *Al-Monitor*, June 12, 2012.

Leenders, Reinoud. "Collective Action and Mobilization in Dar'a: An Anatomy of the Onset of Syria's Popular Uprising." *Mobilization: An International Quarterly* 17, no. 4 (2012): 419–34.

Lefèvre, Raphaël. *Ashes of Hama: The Muslim Brotherhood in Syria*. Oxford Univ. Press, 2013.

Lenner, Katharina, and Lewis Turner. "The Jordan Compact, Refugee Labour and the Limits of Indicator-Oriented Formalization." *Development and Change Journal* 55, no. 2 (2024): 302–30.

———. "Making Refugees Work? The Politics of Integrating Syrian Refugees into the Labor Market in Jordan." *Middle East Critique* 28, no. 1 (2019): 65–95.

Lesch, David. "Bashar's Fateful Decision." In *The Syrian Uprising: Domestic Factors and Early Trajectory*, edited by Raymond Hinnebusch and Omar Imady, 128–40. Syrian Studies. Routledge/St. Andrews, 2018.

Lewis, Sian, Paula Saukko, and Karen Lumsden. "Rhythms, Sociabilities and Transience of Sexual Harassment in Transport: Mobilities Perspectives of the London Underground." *Gender, Place & Culture* 28, no. 2 (2020): 277–98.

Lister, Charles R. *The Syrian Jihad: Al-Qaeda, the Islamic State and the Evolution of an Insurgency*. Oxford Univ. Press, 2016.

Lund, Aron. *Syria's Salafi Insurgents: The Rise of the Syrian Islamic Front*. UI Occasional Papers no. 17. Swedish Institute for International Affairs, March 2013.

Lysen, Flora, and Patricia Pisters. "Introduction: The Smooth and the Striated." In "The Smooth and the Striated," edited by Flora Lysen and Patricia Pisters. Special issue, *Deleuze Studies* 6, no. 1 (2012): 1–5.

Maadad, Nina, and Julie Matthews. "Schooling Syrian Refugees in Lebanon: Building Hopeful Futures." *Educational Review* 72, no. 4 (2018): 459–74.

Machetanz, Alexandra. "Public Opinion, Refugee Programs, and State Welfare in Twenty Countries." PhD diss., Georgetown University, 2020.

Macnaughten, Phil, and John Urry. "Bodies in the Woods." *Body and Society* 6, nos. 3–4 (2000): 166–82.

Maghbouleh, Neda. *The Limits of Whiteness: Iranian Americans and the Everyday Politics of Race*. Stanford Univ. Press, 2017.

Majcher, Izabella. "The Schengen-wide Entry Ban: How Are Non-Citizens' Personal Data Protected?" *Journal of Ethnic and Migration Studies* 48, no. 8 (2020): 1944–60.

Makdisi, Saree. "Laying Claim to Beirut: Urban Narrative and Spatial Identity in the Age of Solidere." *Critical Inquiry* 23, no. 3 (1997): 660–705.

Malkki, Liisa. "Refugees and Exile: From 'Refugee Studies' to the National Order of Things." *Annual Review of Anthropology* 24, no. 1 (1995): 495–523.

Marcus, George, and Erkan Saka. "Assemblage." *Theory of Culture and Society* 23, nos. 2–3 (2006): 101–6.

Marder, Michael. "In (Philosophical) Defense of Trees." March 4, 2015. http://teoretisketirsdage.net/files/gimgs/In%20Philosophical%20Defense%20of%20Trees.pdf.

Marino, Sara. *Mediating the Refugee Crisis: Digital Solidarity, Humanitarian Technologies and Border Regimes*. Springer International, 2020.

Masoud, Tarek, Jason Brownlee, and Andrew Reynolds. *The Arab Spring: Pathways of Repression and Reform*. Oxford Univ. Press, 2015.

Mavrommatis, George. "Grasping the Meaning of Integration in an Era of (Forced) Mobility: Ethnographic Insights from an Informal Refugee Camp." *Mobilities* 13, no. 6 (2018): 861–75.

Al-Mawed, Hamad Said. *The Palestinian Refugees in Syria: Their Past, Present and Future*. International Development Research Centre, 1999. https://prrn.mcgill.ca/prrn/al-mawed.pdf.

Mawson, Suzanne, and Laila Kasem. "Exploring the Entrepreneurial Intentions of Syrian Refugees in the UK." *International Journal of Entrepreneurial Behavior & Research* 25, no. 5 (2019): 1128–46.

McFarlane, Colin. "Assemblage and Critical Urbanism." *City* 15, no. 2 (2011): 204–24.

Menshawy, Mustafa. "Constructing State, Territory, and Sovereignty in the Syrian Conflict." *Politics* 39, no. 3 (2019): 332–46.

Middle East Watch. *Syria Unmasked: The Suppression of Human Rights by the Asad Regime*. Yale Univ. Press, 1991.

Mikati, Massarah. "Women and the Syrian Conflict." *Washington Report on Middle East Affairs* 35, no. 5 (2016): 62–63.

Miles, Elly, Angela Narayan, and Sarah Watamura. "Syrian Caregivers in Perimigration: A Systematic Review from an Ecological Systems Perspective." *Translational Issues in Psychological Science* 5, no. 1 (2019): 78–90.

Miles, Tom. "WFP Suspends Food Aid for 1.7 Million Syrian Refugees." Reuters, December 1, 2014. https://www.reuters.com/article/world/wfp-suspends-food-aid-for-17-million-syrian-refugees-idUSKCN0JF20G/.

Mills, Amy. "Cultures of Assemblage, Resituating Urban Theory: A Response to the Papers on 'Assembling Istanbul.'" *City* 18, no. 6 (2014): 691–97.

Milner, Greg. *Pinpoint: How GPS Is Changing Our World*. Granta, 2016.

Minuchin, Salvador, Lester Baker, and Bernice Rosman. "A Conceptual Model of Psychosomatic Illness in Children: Family Organization and Family Therapy." *Archives of General Psychiatry* 32, no. 8 (1975): 1031–38.

Mitra, Adinpunya. "Enzymatic Production and Emission of Floral Scent Volatiles in *Jasminum sambac*." *Plant Science* 256 (2017): 25–38.

Mohamed, Taher. "Sources of Occupational Stress Among Teachers: A Field of Study for Teachers Working in Libyan Schools in Turkey." *International Journal of Academic Research in Economics and Management Sciences* 7, no. 1 (2018): 1–15.

Morris, Emily, Marcus Griffiths, and Agatha Golebiowska. "Shaping 3D Root System Architecture." *Current Biology* 27, no. 17 (2017): R919–R930.

Mouawad, Jamil. "Lebanon's Border Areas in Light of the Syrian War: New Actors, Old Marginalization." Middle East Directions (MED), March 20, 2018. https://middleeastdirections.eu/new-publication-lebanons-border-areas-light-syrian-war-new-actors-old-marginalisation/.

Mouawad, Jamil, and Hannes Bauman. "In Search of the Lebanese State." *Arab Studies Journal* 25, no. 1 (2017): 60–65.

Mourtada, Rima, Jennifer Schlecht, and Jocelyn DeJong. "A Qualitative Study Exploring Child Marriage Practices Among Syrian Conflict-Affected Populations in Lebanon." *Conflict and Health* 11, no. 1 (2017): 53–65.

Mueller, Martin. "Assemblages and Actor-Networks: Rethinking Socio-Material Power, Politics and Space." *Geography Compass* 9, no. 1 (2015): 27–41. https://doi.org/10.1111/gec3.12192.

Muhanna, Aitemad. *Agency and Gender in Gaza: Masculinity, Femininity and Family During the Second Intifada*. Routledge, 2013.

Murphy, Michael. "The Double Articulation of Sovereign Bordering: Spaces of Exception, Sovereign Vulnerability, and Agamben's Schmitt/Foucault Synthesis." *Journal of Borderlands Studies* 36, no. 4 (2019): 599–615.

Naja, Ghinwa, and Bohumil Volesky. "Sewage of Tripoli: A Review of the Current Situation and of the Future Planning." *International Journal of Environmental Technology and Management* 16, no. 4 (2013): 312–25.

Nasser, Khaled, Yasmine Dabbous, and Dima Baba. "From Strangers to Spouses: Early Relational Dialectics in Arranged Marriages Among Muslim Families in Lebanon." *Journal of Comparative Family Studies* 44, no. 3 (2013): 387–406.

Nedelcu, Mihaela, and Ibrahim Soysüren. "Precarious Migrants, Migration Regimes and Digital Technologies: The Empowerment–Control Nexus." *Journal of Ethnic and Migration Studies* 48, no. 2 (2020): 1821–37.

Ngo, C. *Crossroads in a Crisis: The Syrian Refugee Response in Lebanon.* American Univ. of Paris, 2014.

O'Bagy, Elizabeth. *The Free Syrian Army.* Middle East Security Report no. 9. Institute for the Study of War, 2013.

Ouyang, Helen. "Syrian Refugees and Sexual Violence." *The Lancet* 381, no. 9884 (2013): 2165–66.

Özaşçılar, Mine, Nilüfer Narli, and Osman Öztürk. "Crime Reporting Behavior Among Syrian Immigrants in Istanbul." *Crime & Delinquency* 65, no. 14 (2019): 1997–2018.

Özservet, Yasemin Çakırer. "'You Know, We Live in Fear': Transit Migrants with Their Neglected Disabilities in Istanbul Kumkapı." *Iconarp International Journal of Architecture and Planning* 2, no. 1 (2014): 20–36.

Parzer, Michael. "Double Burden of Representation: How Ethnic and Refugee Categorisation Shapes Syrian Migrants' Artistic Practices in Austria." *Journal of Ethnic and Migration Studies* 47, no. 11 (2021): 2459–76.

Patton, Paul. *Deleuze and the Political.* Routledge, 2000.

Pearlman, Wendy. *We Crossed a Bridge and It Trembled: Voices from Syria.* Mariner, 2017.

Peteet, Julie. *Landscape of Hope and Despair: Palestinian Refugee Camps.* Univ. of Pennsylvania Press, 2009.

Phillips, Christopher. "Sectarianism and Conflict in Syria." *Third World Quarterly* 36, no. 2 (2015): 357–76.

Pictet, Jean S. "The Geneva Conventions of 12 August 1949 Commentary—IV Geneva Convention Relative to the Protection of Civilian Persons in Time of War." Red Cross, 1952. https://www.un.org/en/genocideprevention/documents/atrocity-crimes/Doc.33_GC-IV-EN.pdf.

Pierret, Thomas. *Religion and State in Syria: The Sunni Ulama from Coup to Revolution.* Cambridge Univ. Press, 2013.

Polat, Rabia Karakaya. "Religious Solidarity, Historical Mission and Moral Superiority: Construction of External and Internal 'Others' in

AKP's Discourses on Syrian Refugees in Turkey." *Critical Discourse Studies* 15, no. 5 (2018): 500–516.

Polat, Zeynel Abidin. "Legal, Economic, Geographical and Demographic Analysis of the Acquisition of Real Estate by Foreign Nationals in Turkey." *Land Use Policy* 85 (2019): 207–17.

Porzucki, Nina. "The Things They Carried: What Refugees Take on Their Journey." *The World*, September 4, 2015. https://theworld.org/stories/2015/09/04/things-theyre-carrying.

Prothero, Mitchell. "Tripoli Turned into a War Zone as Rivals Fight Street Duels with Grenades." *The Guardian*, August 16, 2012. https://www.theguardian.com/world/2012/aug/25/lebanon-tripoli-turned-into-war-zone.

Puar, Jasbir. "'I Would Rather Be a Cyborg Than a Goddess': Becoming-Intersectional in Assemblage Theory." In *Feminist Theory Reader: Local and Global Perspectives*, edited by Carole McCann, Seung-kyung Kim, and Emek Ergun, 405–15. Routledge, 2021.

"Public Statement: Scholars Warn of Potential Genocide in Gaza." *Third World Approaches to International Law Review*, October 15, 2023. https://twailr.com/public-statement-scholars-warn-of-potential-genocide-in-gaza/.

Putz, Von Ulrike. "Syrian Refugees Sell Organs to Survive." *Spiegel Online*, November 12, 2013. https://www.spiegel.de/international/world/organ-trade-thrives-among-desperate-syrian-refugees-in-lebanon-a-933228.html.

Qabbani, Nizar. "Ana ya sadiqi mut'ib bi 'Urubti." https://nizarq.com/ar/poem299.html. Translated as "My Friend I Am Tired . . ." by Leila Hudson, 2024.

———. "Damascus, What Are You Doing to Me?" Translated by Shareah Taleghani. Words Without Borders, June 1, 2005. https://wordswithoutborders.org/read/article/2005-06/damascus-what-are-you-doing-to-me/.

———. "Al-wudu' bi ma' al-'ishq wal-yasmin." https://nizarq.com/ar/poem829.html. Translated as "Ablutions in the Water of Love and Jasmine" by Leila Hudson, 2024.

Al-Qasimi, Muhammad Sa'id, Jamal al-Din al-Qasimi, and Khalil al-'Azm. *Qamus al-Sina'at al-shamiyah*. Mouton, 1960.

Rabil, Robert. "The Syrian Muslim Brotherhood." In *The Muslim Brotherhood: The Organization and Policies of a Global Islamist Movement*, edited by Barry Rubin, 73–88. The Middle East in Focus. Palgrave Macmillan, 2010.

Rabinovich, Tatiana. "Sisterly Intimacies: Islam, Gift Giving and Women's Relations of Care in Russia." *American Anthropologist* 125, no. 4 (2023): 840–52.

Ramadan, Adam. "From Tahrir to the World: The Camp as a Political Public Space." *European Urban and Regional Studies* 20 (2013): 145–49.

Ramírez Díaz, Naomi. *The Muslim Brotherhood in Syria: The Democratic Option of Islamism*. Routledge, 2017.

Refaat, Marwan M., and Mohanna Kamel. "Syrian Refugees in Lebanon: Facts and Solutions." *The Lancet* 382, no. 9894 (2013): 763–64.

Refai, Deema, Radi Haloub, and John Lever. "Contextualizing Entrepreneurial Identity Among Syrian Refugees in Jordan: The Emergence of a Destabilized Habitus?" *International Journal of Entrepreneurship and Innovation* 19, no. 4 (2018): 250–60.

Reiners, Wulf, and Funda Tekin. "Taking Refuge in Leadership? Facilitators and Constraints of Germany's Influence in EU Migration Policy and EU–Turkey Affairs During the Refugee Crisis (2015–2016)." *German Politics* 29, no. 1 (2020): 115–30.

Rexhepi, Piro. "Arab Others at European Borders: Racializing Religion and Refugees Along the Balkan Route." *Ethnic and Racial Studies* 41, no. 12 (2018): 2215–34.

Reynolds, Tracey, Umut Erel, and Erene Kaptani. "Migrant Mothers: Performing Kin Work and Belonging Across Private and Public Boundaries." *Families, Relationships and Societies* 7, no. 3 (2018): 365–82.

Rice, Xan. "The Road from Damascus." *The New Statesman*, December 26, 2015. https://www.newstatesman.com/world/middle-east/2015/12/road-damascus.

Rodriguez-Llanes, Jose, Debarati Guha-Sapir, and Benjamin-Samuel Schlüter. "Epidemiological Findings of Major Chemical Attacks in the Syrian War Are Consistent with Civilian Targeting: A Short Report." *Conflict and Health* 12, no. 1 (2018): 1–6.

Rogers, Paul, and Richard Reeves. "Russia's Intervention in Syria: Implications for Western Engagement." Oxford Research Group, Global

Security Briefing, October 2015. https://www.files.ethz.ch/isn/194291/PR%20briefing%20October%202015.pdf.

Rollins, Tom. "Smugglers Threw Asylum Seekers into Mediterranean." *Al-Monitor*, September 18, 2014. https://www.al-monitor.com/originals/2014/09/smugglers-sink-migrant-boat-syrian-survivor.html.

Rosenblatt, Nate, and David Kilcullen. "How Raqqa Became the Capital of ISIS: A Proxy Warfare Case Study." New America Foundation, July 25, 2019. https://www.newamerica.org/future-security/reports/how-raqqa-became-capital-isis/.

Rothwell, James. "Migrants Attempt to Hang Themselves in the Centre of Athens." *Telegraph*, February 26, 2016. https://www.telegraph.co.uk/news/worldnews/europe/greece/12174453/Migrants-attempt-to-hang-themselves-in-the-centre-of-Athens.html.

Ryding, K. "Alchemy in Islam." In *Encyclopaedia of the History of Science, Technology, and Medicine in Non-Western Cultures*, edited by Helaine Selin, 180–83. Springer, 2016.

Safi, Lubna. "Jasmine Fingers." *Guernica Magazine*, August 22, 2019. https://www.guernicamag.com/jasmine-fingers/.

Sahin, Ecem, Tolga E. Dagli, Ceren Acarturk, and Figen Sahin Dagli. "Vulnerabilities of Syrian Refugee Children in Turkey and Actions Taken for Prevention and Management in Terms of Health and Wellbeing." *Child Abuse & Neglect* 119, pt. 1 (2020): art. 104628. https://doi.org/10.1016/j.chiabu.2020.104628.

Sahlins, Marshall. *What Kinship Is—and Is Not*. Univ. of Chicago Press, 2013.

Sakr-Tierney, Julia. "Real Estate, Banking and War: The Construction and Reconstructions of Beirut." *Cities* 69 (2017): 73–78.

Saleh, Elizabeth, and Adrien Zakar. "The Joke Is on Us: Irony and Community in a Beirut Scrapyard." *Anthropology Today* 34, no. 3 (2018): 3–6.

Saleh, Zainab. *Return to Ruin: Iraqi Narratives of Exile and Nostalgia*. Stanford Univ. Press, 2021.

Salhani, Justin. "The End of Fear in Syria." Al Jazeera, December 30, 2024. https://www.aljazeera.com/features/2024/12/30/syria-end-of-fear-assad-damascus-aleppo.

———. "Flood of Syria Refugees Tries Patience of the Lebanese." *Los Angeles Times*, Mar. 18, 2013. https://www.latimes.com/world/middleeast

/la-xpm-2013-mar-18-la-fg-lebanon-syria-refugees-20130318-story .html.

———. "The Men Who Get Rich Off Syrian Refugees." *The Atlantic*, June 25, 2013. https://www.theatlantic.com/international/archive/2013/06 /the-men-who-get-rich-off-syrian-refugees/277171/.

———. "Syrian Refugees Add Pressure to Beirut's Already Crumbling Infrastructure." *Next City*, Nov. 7, 2013. https://nextcity.org/urbanist -news/syrian-refugees-pouring-into-beirut-add-pressure-to-an-already -crumbling-in.

———. "Welcome Sours for Syrian Refugees." *Seattle Globalist*, May 30, 2013. https://seattleglobalist.com/2013/05/30/welcome-sours-syrian -refugees/13505.

Sami, Samira, Holly A. Williams, Sandra Krause, Monica A. Onyango, Ann Burton, and Barbara Tomczyk. "Responding to the Syrian Crisis: The Needs of Women and Girls." *The Lancet* 383, no. 9923 (2014): 1179–81.

Al-Samman, Ghada. *Farewell Damascus*. Darf, 2018.

Sanders, Mija A. "Politics of Care and Reverberations of Trauma: Syrian Refugees in Izmir, Turkey." PhD diss., Univ. of Arizona, 2020. ProQuest 28152100.

Sands, Phil, Justin Vela, and Suha Maayeh. "Assad Regime Abetted Extremists to Subvert Peaceful Uprising, Says Former Intelligence Official." *National News*, January 21, 2014. https://www.thenationalnews.com /world/assad-regime-abetted-extremists-to-subvert-peaceful-uprising -says-former-intelligence-official-1.319620.

Şanlıer, Ilke. "Empowering Experiences of Digitally Mediated Flows of Information for Connected Migrants on the Move." *Journal of Ethnic and Migration Studies* 48, no. 8 (2020): 1838–55.

Sanyal, Paulami. "Egypt: Presidential Elections, 2014." *Contemporary Review of the Middle East* 2, no. 3 (2015): 289–307.

Sanyal, Romola. "A No-Camp Policy: Interrogating Informal Settlements in Lebanon." *Geoforum* 8 (2017): 117–25.

Schielke, Samuli. "There Will Be Blood: Expectation and Ethics of Violence During Egypt's Stormy Season." *Middle East Critique* 26, no. 3 (2017): 205–20.

Schmelter, Susanne. "Gulf States' Humanitarian Assistance for Syrian Refugees in Lebanon." *Civil Society Review* 3 (2019): 16–47.

Schon, Justin. "The Centrality of Checkpoints for Civilians During Conflict." *Civil Wars* 18, no. 3 (2016): 281–310.

Schwiertz, Helge, and Helen Schwenken. "Mobilizing for Safe Passages and Escape Aid: Challenging the 'Asylum Paradox' Between Active and Activist Citizenship, Humanitarianism and Solidarity." *Citizenship Studies* 24, no. 4 (2020): 493–511.

Segal, Raz. "A Textbook Case of Genocide." *Jewish Currents*, October 13, 2023. https://jewishcurrents.org/a-textbook-case-of-genocide.

Shally-Jensen, Michael, ed. *Defining Documents in American History: The Legacy of 9/11*. Salem Press, 2018.

Al Shami, Leila. "Syria: The Struggle Continues: Syria's Grass-roots Civil Opposition." Tahrir-ICN, September 16, 2013. https://tahriricn.wordpress.com/2013/09/16/syria-the-struggle-continues-syrias-grass-roots-civil-opposition/.

Shamir, Ronen. *Current Flow: The Electrification of Palestine*. Stanford Univ. Press, 2013.

Shopes, Linda. "Oral History, Human Subjects, and Institutional Review Boards." Oral History Association, Baylor University, 2018.

Shuster, Simon. "Inside the Tiny Greek Village on the Front Lines of Migrant Crisis." *Time*, April 28, 2016. Reprinted in *Yahoo! News*. https://www.yahoo.com/news/inside-tiny-greek-village-front-080055390.html.

Sieverding, Maia, and Valentina Calderón-Mejía. "Demographic Profile of Syrians in Jordan and Lebanon." In *Comparative Demography of the Syrian Diaspora: European and Middle Eastern Destinations*, edited by Elwood D. Carlson and Nathalie E. Williams, 109–35. Springer, 2020.

Sieverding, Maia, Caroline Krafft, Nasma Berri, and Caitlyn Keo. "Persistence and Change in Marriage Practices Among Syrian Refugees in Jordan." *Studies in Family Planning* 51, no. 3 (2020): 225–49. https://doi.org/10.1111/sifp.12134.

Simmel, Georg. "The Metropolis and Mental Life." In *The Blackwell City Reader*, edited by Gary Bridge and Sophie Watson, 11–19. Wiley-Blackwell, 2002.

Sissons, Jeffrey. "Reterritorializing Kinship: The Maori 'Hapu.'" *Journal of the Polynesian Society* 122, no. 4 (2013): 373–91.

Slackman, Michael. "Syria's Cabinet Resigns: Concessions Expected." *New York Times*, March 29, 2011. http://www.nytimes.com/2011/03/30/world/middleeast/30syria.html.

Smit, Rik, Heinrich Ansgard, and Marcel Broersma. "Witnessing in the New Memory Ecology: Memory Construction of the Syrian Conflict on YouTube." *New Media & Society* 19, no. 2 (2017): 289–307.

Smith-Spark, Laura. "'Laughing' Traffickers Ram Boat Full [of] Migrants and Kill 500, Survivors Say." CNN, September 16, 2014. https://www.cnn.com/2014/09/16/world/europe/europe-migrant-deaths/.

Spyer, Jonathan. "Defying a Dictator: Meet the Free Syrian Army." *World Affairs* 175, no. 1 (2012): 45–52.

Squire, Vicki. *Europe's Migration Crisis: Border Deaths and Human Dignity.* Cambridge Univ. Press, 2020.

Stack, Liam, and J. David Goodman. "Syrian Protesters Clash with Security Forces." *New York Times*, April 1, 2011. https://www.nytimes.com/2011/04/02/world/middleeast/02syria.html?ref=world.

Stepan, Alfred, and Juan J. Linz. "Democratization Theory and the 'Arab Spring.'" *Journal of Democracy* 24, no. 2 (2013): 15–30.

Stevens, Matthew. "The Collapse of Social Networks Among Syrian Refugees in Urban Jordan." *Contemporary Levant* 1, no. 1 (2016): 51–63.

Strathern, Marilyn. *The Gender of the Gift: Problems with Women and Problems with Society in Melanesia.* Univ. of California Press, 1988.

Suerbaum, Magdelena. "Becoming and 'Unbecoming' Refugees: Making Sense of Masculinity and Refugeness Among Syrian Refugee Men in Egypt." *Men and Masculinities* 21, no. 3 (2018): 363–82.

Svensson, Sara. "Resistance or Acceptance? The Voice of Local Cross-Border Organizations in Times of Re-Bordering." *Journal of Borderlands Studies* 37, no. 3 (2020): 493–512.

Sweis, Rana. "No Syrians Are Allowed into Jordan." *New York Times*, October 8, 2014. http://www.nytimes.com/2014/10/09/world/middleeast/syrian-refugees-jordan-border-unitednations.html?_r=0.

Syed Zwick, Hélène. "Narrative Analysis of Syrians, South Sudanese and Libyans Transiting in Egypt: A Motivation-Opportunity-Ability Approach." *Journal of Ethnic and Migration Studies* 48, no. 9 (2022): 2223–44.

Syrian Local Coordinating Committees. "We Are All Syrians and Syria Is for All Against the Inflammatory Sectarian Speech That the Regime Is Spreading." *LCC Statements*, June 16, 2011. https://web.archive.org/web/20120806173224/http://www.lccsyria.org/923.

"Syrian Refugees Contribute $800M Economy to Egypt's [*sic*]." *Egypt Today*, May 18, 2017. https://www.egypttoday.com/Article/3/5297/Syrian-refugees-contribute-800M-economy-to-Egypt%E2%80%99s.

"Syrian Refugees Trying to Start a New Life in Turkey's Istanbul." Xinhua News Agency, December 28, 2015.

Tamboukou, Maria. "Mobility Assemblages and Lines of Flight in Women's Narratives of Forced Displacement." *European Journal of Women's Studies* 27, no. 3 (2020): 235–49.

Tarraf-Najib, Souha. "Work and Denial of Work: Palestinians in Tripoli and in Northern Lebanon Refugee Camps." *Revue du monde musulman et de la Méditerranée* 105–6 (2005): 283–305.

Tawil-Souri, H. "Qalandia Checkpoint as Space and Nonplace." *Space and Culture* 14, no. 1 (2011): 4–26.

Taylor, Alan. "Stranded on the Macedonian Border." *The Atlantic*, March 2, 2016. https://www.theatlantic.com/photo/2016/03/stranded-on-the-macedonian-border/471933/.

Tazzioli, Martina. "Extract, Datafy and Disrupt: Refugees' Subjectivities Between Data Abundance and Data Disregard." *Geopolitics* 27, no. 1 (2020): 70–88.

Tergeman, Siham, *Daughter of Damascus: A Memoir.* Univ. of Texas Press, 1994.

Thomas, Timothy L. "The Battle of Grozny: Deadly Classroom for Urban Combat." *US Army War College Quarterly: Parameters* 29, no. 2 (1999): 87–102.

———. "The Caucasus Conflict and Russian Security: The Russian Armed Forces Confront Chechnya. III. The Battle for Grozny, 1–26 January 1995." *Journal of Slavic Military Studies* 10, no. 1 (1997): 50–108.

Thorleifsson, Cathrine. "The Limits of Hospitality: Coping Strategies Among Displaced Syrians in Lebanon." *Third World Quarterly* 37, no. 6 (2016): 1071–82.

Thornton, Edward. "On Lines of Flight: The Theory of Political Transformation in *A Thousand Plateaus*." *Deleuze and Guattari Studies* 14, no. 3 (2020): 433–56.

"Through My Eyes: From Douma to Damascus." *Syria Stories*, April 20, 2011. https://syriastories.net/through-my-eyes-from-douma-to-damascus/.

Tjaden, Jasper, and Tobias Heidland. "Did Merkel's 2015 Decision Attract More Migration to Germany?" *European Journal of Political Research* 64 (2025): 389–405.

Tlaiss, Hayfaa, and Saleema Kauser. "The Importance of *Wasta* in the Career Success of Middle Eastern Managers." *Journal of European Industrial Training* 35, no. 5 (2011): 467–86.

Topak, Özgan. "Border Violence and Migrant Subjectivities." *Geopolitics* 26, no. 3 (2021): 791–816.

Totah, Faedah M. "The Memory Keeper: Gender, Nation, and Remembering in Syria." *Journal of Middle East Women's Studies* 9, no. 1 (2013): 1–29.

———. "'Nothing Has Changed': Social Continuity and the Gentrification of the Old City of Damascus." *Anthropological Quarterly* 87, no. 4 (2014): 1201–27.

———. "Palestinian Refugees Between the City and the Camp." *International Journal of Middle East Studies* 52, no. 4 (2020): 607–21.

———. *Preserving the Old City of Damascus*. Syracuse Univ. Press, 2014.

Tsing, Anne Lowenhaupt. *The Mushroom at the End of the World: On the Possibility of Life in Capitalist Ruins*. Princeton Univ. Press, 2015.

Tumen, Semih. "The Economic Impact of Syrian Refugees on Host Countries: Quasi-Experimental Evidence from Turkey." *American Economic Review* 106, no. 5 (2016): 456–60.

Turner, Lewis. "Defining, Operationalising and Translating 'Vulnerability' in Humanitarian Work in Jordan." *Journal of Ethnic and Migration Studies* 51, no. 7 (2025): 1647–66.

———. "Explaining the (Non-)Encampment of Syrian Refugees: Security, Class and the Labour Market in Lebanon and Jordan." *Mediterranean Politics* 20, no. 3 (2015): 386–404.

———. "Give Refugees Access to the Agreements That Govern Them." *Border Criminologies Blog*, University of Oxford Faculty of Law, April 13, 2023. https://blogs.law.ox.ac.uk/border-criminologies-blog/blog-post/2023/04/give-refugees-access-agreements-govern-them.

———. "'Refugees Can Be Entrepreneurs Too!': Humanitarianism, Race, and the Marketing of Syrian Refugees." *Review of International Studies* 46, no. 1 (2020): 137–55.

———. "Syrian Refugee Men as Objects of Humanitarian Care." *International Feminist Journal of Politics* 21, no. 4 (2019): 595–616.

———. “Who Is a Refugee in Jordan? Hierarchies and Exclusions in the Refugee Recognition Regime.” *Journal of Refugee Studies* 36, no. 4 (2023): 877–96.

“UAE-Based Developer Launches New Real Estate Project in Turkey.” News from Türkiye, February 17, 2014, Presidency of the Republic of Türkiye, Investment Office. https://www.invest.gov.tr/en/news/news-from-turkey/pages/180214-uae-developer-launches-new-turkey-project.aspx.

“U.N. Report on the Alleged Use of Chemical Weapons in the Ghouta Area of Damascus on 21 August 2013.” In *Defining Documents in American History: The Legacy of 9/11*, edited by Michael Shally-Jensen, 259–66. Salem Press, 2018.

Van Dam, Nikolaos. *Destroying a Nation: The Civil War in Syria*. Bloomsbury, 2017.

———. *The Struggle for Power in Syria: Politics and Society Under Asad and the Ba‘th Party*. Rev. 4th ed. I. B. Tauris, 2014.

Van Oort, Hans, Hemme Battjes, and Evelien Brouwer. *Baseline Study on Access to Protection, Reception and Distribution of Asylum Seekers and the Determination of Asylum Claims in the EU*. CEASEVAL Research on the Common European Asylum System no. 1, May 2018. https://www.tu-chemnitz.de/phil/iesg/professuren/geographie/Publikationen/CEASEVAL/01_vanOort_Baselinestudy.pdf.

Van Reisen, Mirjam, and Meron Estefanos. “Human Trafficking Connecting to Terrorism and Organ Trafficking: Libya and Egypt.” In *Human Trafficking and Trauma in the Digital Era: The Ongoing Tragedy of the Trade in Refugees from Eritrea*, edited by Mirjam van Reisen, 159–92. Langaa RPCIG, 2017.

Velling, Johannes. “Immigration to Germany in the Seventies and Eighties: The Role of Family Reunification.” ZEW–Leibniz Centre for European Economic Research Discussion Papers no. 93–18, 1993.

Venn, Couze. “A Note on Assemblage.” *Theory, Culture & Society* 23, nos. 2–3 (2006): 107–8.

Vignal, Leïla. “The Changing Borders and Borderlands of Syria in a Time of Conflict.” *International Affairs* 93, no. 4 (2017): 809–27.

Vora, Neha, and Ahmed Kanna. “De-Exceptionalizing the Field: Anthropological Reflections on Migration, Labor, and Identity in Dubai.” *Arab Studies Journal* 26, no. 2 (2018): 75–101.

Walker, Peter. "100 Children Among Migrants 'Deliberately Drowned' in Mediterranean." *The Guardian,* September 16, 2014. https://www.theguardian.com/world/2014/sep/16/migrants-children-drowned-boat-mediterranean.

———. "Migrant Boat Was 'Deliberately Sunk' in Mediterranean Sea, Killing 500." *The Guardian,* September 15, 2014. https://www.theguardian.com/world/2014/sep/15/migrant-boat-capsizes-egypt-malta-traffickers.

Wall, Melissa, and Madeline Campbell. "Syrian Refugees and Information Precarity." *New Media & Society* 19, no. 2 (2017): 240–54.

Wall, Melissa, and Sahar el Zahed. "Syrian Citizen Journalism: A Pop-Up News Ecology in an Authoritarian Space." *Digital Journalism* 3, no. 5 (2015): 720–36.

"War Reaches Assad; 'Damascus Volcano' Erupts as Rebel Bomb Kills Hardliners, Including President's Brother-in-Law." *The Times*, July 19, 2012.

Warrick, Joby. *Red Line: The Unraveling of Syria and America's Race to Destroy the Most Dangerous Arsenal in the World.* Doubleday, 2021.

Wedeen, Lisa. *Ambiguities of Domination: Politics, Rhetoric, and Symbols in Contemporary Syria.* Univ. of Chicago Press, 1999.

Weejses, Elke Sabella. "Timeline Refugee Crisis—from May 2011–February 2016." Natural Hazards Center, February 15, 2016. https://hazards.colorado.edu/article/timeline-refugee-crisis-from-may-2011-february-2016.

Weiher, Leona. "Borders and Boundaries on the Balkan Route." Master's thesis, Univ. of Aalborg, 2018.

"WFP Restarts Food Aid for Syrian Refugees After Campaign." Reuters, December 9, 2014. https://www.reuters.com/article/world/wfp-restarts-food-aid-for-syrian-refugees-after-campaign-idUSKBN0JN15F/.

Windsor, Joshua. "Desire Lines: Deleuze and Guattari on Molar Lines, Molecular Lines, and Lines of Flight." *New Zealand Sociology* 30, no. 1 (2015): 156–71.

Wise, John. "Assemblage." In *Gilles Deleuze: Key Concepts*, edited by Charles J. Stivale, 91–102. Acumen, 2013.

Wolff, Sarah. *Migration and Refugee Governance in the Mediterranean: Europe and International Organisations at a Crossroads*. Instituto Affari Internazionali, 2015.

Wringe, Alison, Ekua Yankah, and Tania Parks. "Altered Social Trajectories and Risks of Violence Among Young Syrian Women Seeking Refuge in Turkey: A Qualitative Study." *BMC Women's Health* 19, no. 1 (2019): 1–8.

Yardley, Jim. "Shipwreck Was Simple Murder, Migrants Recall." *New York Times*, October 20, 2014. https://www.nytimes.com/2014/10/21/world/europe/shipwreck-survivors-recount-a-deadly-journey-from-middle-east-to-europe.html.

Yaseen, Saad, and Khaled Saleh Al Omoush. "Mobile Crowdsourcing Technology Acceptance and Engagement in Crisis Management: The Case of Syrian Refugees." *International Journal of Technology and Human Interaction* 16, no. 3 (2020): 1–23.

Yassin-Kassab, Robin, and Leila al-Shami. *Burning Country: Syrians in Revolution and War*. Pluto Press, 2016.

Yaylacı, Feliz, and Mina Karakuş. "Perceptions and Newspaper Coverage of Syrian Refugees in Turkey." *Migration Letters* 12, no. 3 (2015): 238–50.

Yazigi, Sana. *The Story of a Place, the Story of a People: The Beginnings of the Syrian Revolution 2011–2015*. Creative Memory of the Syrian Revolution and Friedrich Ebert Stiftung, 2017.

Yıldız, Ayselin. "Impact of the EU–Turkey Statement on Smugglers' Operations in the Aegean and Migrants' Decisions to Engage with Smugglers." *International Migration* 59, no. 4 (2021): 141–57.

Zuntz, Ann-Christin. "Displacing Female Labor: A Gendered Perspective on Transnational Families During the Syrian Conflict." In *Migrations in Jordan: Reception Policies and Settlement Strategies*, edited by Jalal Al Husseini, Valentina Napolitano, and Norig Neveu, 195–214. I. B. Tauris, 2024.

———. "Human Routers: How Syrian Refugee Brokers Build the Infrastructure of Displacement." *Cultural Anthropology* 38, no. 4 (2023): 517–40.

———. "Refugees' Transnational Livelihoods and Remittances: Syrian Mobilities in the Middle East Before and After 2011." *Journal of Refugee Studies* 34, no. 2 (2021): 1400–1422.

Zuntz, Ann-Christin, Mackenzie Klema, Shaher Abdullateef, and Stella Mazeri. "Syrian Refugee Labour and Food Insecurity in Middle

Eastern Agriculture During the Early COVID-19 Pandemic." *International Labour Review* 161, no. 2 (2021): 245–66.

Zuntz, Ann-Christin, George Palattiyil, Abla Amawi, Ruba Akash, Ayat Nashwan, Areej Al Majali, et al. "Early Marriage and Displacement—a Conversation: How Syrian Daughters, Mothers and Mothers-in-Law in Jordan Understand Marital Decision-Making." *Journal of the British Academy* 9 (2021): 179–212.

Videos

Adichie, C. N. "The Danger of a Single Story." *TED Talk*, July 2009, video, 18 mins. https://www.ted.com/talks/chimamanda_ngozi_adichie_the_danger_of_a_single_story?language=en.

Albayan. "Mudhaharat Jum'at Isra al-Huriyya Hay al-Qabun" [البيان - مظاهرات جمعة أسرى الحرية حي القابون]. YouTube video, 1:00, July 15, 2011. https://www.youtube.com/watch?v=EoR57iluirI.

"Barmu wa li Shuhada' Hay al-Qabun al-Dimashqi" [برمو ولسهداء حي القابون الدمشقي]. YouTube video, 7:45, October 17, 2013. https://www.youtube.com/watch?v=Sy6O4001E2I.

"Fidio jadid wa ra'i' li-Isqat al-Ta'ira Hay al-Qabun" [فيديو جديد و رائع لإسقاط الطائرة حي القابون]. YouTube video, 0:31, August 27, 2012. https://www.youtube.com/watch?v=4kqmLuOmZwk.

Firas, Abdullah. "Awal Mudhahara fi Duma (Salat al-'Asr fi Sahat al-Baladiya)" [أول مظاهرة في دوما (صلاة العصر في ساحة البلدية)]. YouTube video, 2:39, November 24, 2012. https://www.youtube.com/watch?v=Z3hx7vzI3ZQ.

Freeqabon. "Dababa tuhadim al-Mahalat fi Hay al-Qabun" [دبابة تهدم المحلات في حي القابون]. YouTube video, 1:04, September 23, 2012. https://www.youtube.com/watch?v=e3j9Lh9Fm08.

———. "Dimashq, haaaam al-Tahsinat hawl Fir' al-Mukhabarat al-Jawiya wa Nasb lil-Mudhadat al-Tayran 'ala Suth al-Fir'" [دمشق, هاااااام التحصينات حول فرع المخابرات الجوية و نصب لمضادات الطيران على سطح الفرع]. YouTube video, 0:50, August 16, 2012. https://www.youtube.com/watch?v=T0phpmXp8vc.

FreeShamSon. "Iqtiham al-Amn wal-Shabiha Hay al-Qabun fi Dimashq" [اقتحام الأمن والشبيحة حي القابون في دمشق]. YouTube video, 0:39, December 30, 2011. https://www.youtube.com/watch?v=PCucAyOp9fs.

Al Jazeera English. "Violence Continues Across Syria." YouTube video, 2:11, April 14, 2011. https://www.youtube.com/watch?v=Gwle0-pP7r4.

Qisetna: Talking Syria. "Seeking the Jasmine Breeze." YouTube video, 3:12, December 6, 2015. https://www.qisetna.com/seeking-the-jasmine-breeze/.

Redmarch 1. "Zufaf Shuhada' al-Qabun" [زفاف شهداء القابون 23 4 a]. YouTube video, April 23, 2011. https://www.youtube.com/watch?v=xdURRsUSM-M.

"Sham – Dimashq – al-Qabun bi Mudhaharat al-Jum'a al-'Adhima 4/22" [شام - دمشق - القابون بمظاهرة الجمعة العظيمة 22-4 ج1]. ShaamNetwork SNN, YouTube video, 1:11, April 22, 2011. https://www.youtube.com/watch?v=wRAFFSeej04.

"Taqrir kamil 'an al-Qasf wal-Damar wa Harq Mashfa al-Fatih Kafr Batna" [تنسيقية كفربطنا]. YouTube video, 9:47, September 8, 2012. https://www.youtube.com/watch?v=HZ6aumkny3w&feature=youtu.be or https://www.facebook.com/Syrian.Revolution/videos/107018706046981/.

Index

Leila Hudson is associate professor of Middle Eastern studies at the University of Arizona. An anthropologist and historian, she studies culture and political economy in the modern and contemporary Arab world. She is the author of *Transforming Damascus: Space and Modernity in an Islamic City* (2008) and coeditor of *Media Evolution on the Eve of the Arab Spring* (2014).

www.ingramcontent.com/pod-product-compliance
Lightning Source LLC
Chambersburg PA
CBHW031842130925
32295CB00002B/3

* 9 7 8 0 8 1 5 6 1 1 9 5 0 *